Articles on

Witchcraft, Magic and Demonology

A Twelve Volume Anthology
of Scholarly Articles

Edited with introductions by

Brian P. Levack
University of Texas

A Garland Series

Contents of Series

Volume 8

Witchcraft in Colonial America

edited with introductions by
Brian P. Levack

Garland Publishing, Inc.
New York & London 1992

Introductions copyright © 1992 by Brian P. Levack
All rights reserved.

Library of Congress Cataloging-in-publication Data

Witchcraft in colonial America / edited by Brian P. Levack
     p.   cm. — (Articles on witchcraft, magic and demonology ; v. 8)
Reprint of works originally published 1869–1985.
Includes bibliographical references.
ISBN 0-8153-1030-7 (alk. paper)
    1. Witchcraft—Massachussetts—Salem—History. 2. Trials (Witchcraft)—
Massachussetts—Salem—History.   3. Persecution—Massachussetts—
Salem—History. 4. Demonology—United States—History. 5. Witchcraft—
United States—History. I. Series.
BF1563.A77   1992 vol. 8
133.4'09 s—dc20
[133.4'3'097309032]   92-22874
                                           CIP

Printed on acid-free, 250-year-life paper
Manufactured in the United States of America

Contents

Series Introduction

The main purpose of this collection is to bring together a large number of scholarly articles on the subject of witchcraft, magic and demonology. These articles are drawn from a broad selection of journals in many different disciplines. They reflect the sustained interest of historians, anthropologists, legal scholars, psychologists, sociologists, art historians, and literary scholars on the subject. In one way or another they all deal with man's belief in and fear of supernatural evil.

In early modern Europe a witch was believed to be a person who not only practiced harmful magic but who also made a pact with the Devil and sometimes worshipped him in nocturnal assemblies. The magical powers of the witch were generally the concern of her neighbors, who accused her of causing physical harm or bringing about some kind of misfortune. The witch's commerce with the Devil, however, remained the main concern of the clergy and the 'educated elite, who believed that she was a heretic and apostate involved in a vast conspiracy to undermine Christianity and destroy the moral order. As a scholarly subject, witchcraft involves an investigation of both aspects of the witch's alleged crime. On the one hand it studies magic, which is the human exercise of some preternatural, supernatural, or occult power to produce empirical effects, and on the other hand it is concerned with demonology, the study of evil spirits and its alleged activities. Most of the articles in this collection are concerned with witchcraft in the full early modern European sense of the word, but some focus exclusively on magic, while others are concerned mainly with demonic spirits and their relations with humans.

The majority of the articles in this collection deal with the historical process of witch-hunting in Europe and America between 1450 and 1750. During these years the prosecution of more than 100,000 persons, mostly women, has led scholars to investigate the development of learned and popular beliefs regarding witchcraft, the social and religious tensions which resulted in accusations, the legal processes that were used to bring witches to trial, and the ultimate end of witchcraft prosecutions. Six of the twelve volumes deal with different aspects of this massive judicial assault on witchcraft. Volume 3 includes a variety of interpretations of the entire process of witch-hunting in Europe, while volumes 5, 6, 7, and 8 deal successively with local and regional witchcraft prosecutions in continental Europe, England, Scotland, and Colonial America. Volume 4 explores the large body of printed treatises on witchcraft that helped to spread learned witch beliefs throughout Europe and thus inspired and reinforced the prosecutions.

Three volumes treat themes that are closely related to the great European witch-hunt. Volume 2 studies the various beliefs regarding magic and the Devil that originated in the classical and medieval periods and eventually came together in the cumulative concept of witchcraft in the fifteenth and sixteenth centuries. Volume 9 is devoted to the subject of demonic possession and exorcism. Possession did not always involve the agency of a witch, but a number of witchcraft trials in the sixteenth and seventeenth centuries resulted from allegations that witches had commanded demons to take physical possession of other persons. Volume 10 addresses the question: why do witches, both in Europe during the early modern period and in other cultures at other periods of time, tend to be women? A further objective of that volume is to examine the social and economic context in which witchcraft accusations and prosecutions arose.

The remaining three volumes deal with topics that are only indirectly related to the witchcraft prosecutions of the early modern period. Volume 1 is devoted to anthropological studies of witchcraft and magic among non-literate peoples. This literature has had a strong influence on historical scholarship during the past twenty-five years, and it has contributed to a deeper understanding of the nature of witchcraft, magic and religion. Because of the theoretical value of this literature, the volume serves as an introduction to the entire collection. Volume 11 discusses the learned magic that was practiced during the Renaissance. Although this magic is not directly connected to witchcraft, it possesses enormous importance to the intellectual history of the early modern period and even made a contribution to the development of modern science. The final volume explores the ways in which witchcraft and demonology have served as themes in both art and literature.

The articles reproduced in these volumes were selected on the basis of many different criteria. Some were chosen because of the wealth of information they provide regarding particular witch-hunts or witch beliefs, while others were included because of the cogency of their arguments or the importance of their approaches to the problem of witchcraft. The great majority of the articles were written in the past thirty years, during which time the most valuable scholarship in the field has been done. A few articles, however, date from the late nineteenth and early twentieth centuries, when some of the pioneering work in this field was undertaken.

Introduction

When English, French and Spanish settlers established colonies in the New World they brought with them their witch beliefs and fears of witchcraft. Generally, however, they engaged in far less witch-hunting than they had in Europe. With the exception of New England, where 234 persons were indicted for witchcraft in the seventeenth century, the New World did not appear to have much of a witchcraft problem. In the southern English colonies there were only occasional prosecutions and hardly any executions. The same was true for New France, while in the Spanish colonies the Inquisition developed a most remarkable record of leniency in dealing with this crime. Even in New England, the intensity of witchcraft prosecutions was not particularly high. The number of prosecutions in relationship to the population was only marginally higher than in Essex County, England, which by Continental or Scottish standards was a relatively low ratio. Indeed, if it were not for the Salem episode, in which 141 persons were charged and 30 were convicted, New England would appear to have had a relatively mild or restrained witch-hunt. Of the 36 executions for witchcraft in seventeenth-century New England, 19 occurred as a result of the Salem trials.

It would be misleading to simply explain New England witchcraft in terms of Puritanism. We know from work on witchcraft prosecutions in England that there is no simple correlation between intense witch-hunting and Puritanism. Puritan communities in England did not necessarily prosecute more witches than Anglican or conformist ones, nor did Puritan magistrates or judges necessarily treat witches more harshly in court. There is, moreover, no causal connection between Puritan or Calvinist theology and hostility to witchcraft. Nevertheless, it is impossible to explain witch-hunting in New England without recognizing the importance of the Puritan ideas held by members of the ruling elite and without understanding the challenges that New England Puritanism faced in the 1690s.

Most of the pressure for witchcraft prosecutions in New England, as in England, came from below, from villagers who feared that their neighbors were causing them harm by magical means. These villagers had little knowledge of witchcraft as a spiritual crime of diabolism, heresy or apostasy; their only concern was the magic used against them. Members of the clerical and ruling elite, however, defined witchcraft almost exclusively in religious terms, basing their witchcraft laws on biblical injunctions against witches. For them, witchcraft was essentially a crime of commerce with demons, one that involved making a pact with the Devil. In adjudicating witchcraft trials, moreover, New England magistrates used standards of proof developed by English clerical writers, such as Richard Bernard and William Perkins, who emphasized the spiritual nature of the witch's crime. These rules of evidence required proof of a pact with the Devil for conviction. The difficulty of adducing such proof, especially from villagers who would testify only to the effects of magical harm, resulted in the acquittal of most of the New England witches before 1692.

This trend toward acquittal was reversed at the beginning of the Salem episode, although ultimately most of the witches accused in that witch-hunt were also set free. The hunt began with authorities attempting to explain the fits and other forms of unusual behavior of some young girls in the household of minister Samuel Parris. After the suspicion grew that the affliction was demonic in nature, the girls named a number of witches as the cause of their maladies. In this regard the episode resembled other cases of demonic possession in England and Europe, in which the victims named a witch as the human agent of their demonic possession. In the Salem trials, the judges accepted the girls' identification of the persons they claimed to have seen tormenting them in spectral form. They also encouraged confessions, both by using physical and psychological pressures and by taking the unprecedented step of offering clemency to all who confessed. Most of the convictions obtained during the witch-hunt of 1692, which spread to Andover and other areas of the colony of Massachusetts, were based on either spectral evidence or confessions.

The witch-hunt at Salem has been the subject of an enormous and highly controversial literature; only a small portion of which is reproduced in this and other volumes of this anthology. In trying to explain the Salem episode, scholars have focused on political and religious factionalism, the economic status of the accused women, the novel political context of the trials, the prevalent fears of Indian attacks, and the role of the clergy. It is difficult, however, to ignore the anxiety that the members of Salem village experienced about the imminent collapse of their ideal Puritan community and the preoccupation of the Massachusetts ruling elite with the heretical dangers facing Puritanism in the late seventeenth century. The founders of Massachusetts had as their goal the establishment of a godly state, a New Jerusalem, and the prosecution of witches cannot be divorced from the efforts made to sustain that mission.

The majority of the articles reproduced in this volume deal with witchcraft in Massachusetts. They discuss such matters as the social status of the accused, the actual guilt of the witches, and the literature produced during the Salem crisis by men like Cotton Mather. In order to present a broader view of colonial witchcraft, however, the volume also includes articles on witchcraft in Maryland, Virginia, New York, and Connecticut, as well as one article on New France.

Further Reading

Boyer, Paul and Nissenbaum, Stephen. *Salem Possessed: The Social Origins of Witchcraft*. Cambridge, Mass., 1974.

Burr, George. "New England's Place in the History of Witchcraft," in *Proceedings of the American Antiquarian Society*, new series, 21 (1911), 185–217.

Butler, Jon. *Awash in a Sea of Faith*. Cambridge, Mass., 1990.

Demos, John P. *Entertaining Satan: Witchcraft and the Culture of Early New England*. New York, 1982.

Erikson, Kai. *Wayward Puritans: A Study in the Sociology of Deviance*. New York, 1966.

Fox, Sanford. *Science and Justice: The Massachusetts Witchcraft Trials*. Baltimore, 1968.

Godbeer, Richard. *The Devil's Dominion: Magic and Religion in Early New England*. Cambridge, 1992.

Greenleaf, R. E. *Zumarraga and the Mexican Inquisition, 1536–1543*. Washington, D.C., 1962.

Hall, David, ed. *Witch-Hunting in Seventeenth-Century New England: A Documentary History, 1638–1692*. Boston, 1991.

Heyrman, Christine L. "Specters of Subversion, Societies of Friends: Dissent and the Devil in Provincial Essex County, Massachusetts" in *Saints and Revolutionaries*, ed. D. Hall. New York, 1984, pp. 38–74.

Hansen, Chadwick. *Witchcraft at Salem*. New York, 1969.

Karlsen, Carol F. *The Devil in the Shape of a Woman: Witchcraft in Colonial New England*. New York, 1987.

Kittredge, George L. *Witchcraft in Old and New England.* Cambridge, Mass., 1929.

Konig, David. *Law and Society in Puritan Massachusetts.* Chapel Hill, 1980.

Matossian, Mary. "Ergot and the Salem Witchcraft Trials," in *Poisons of the Past.* New Haven, 1989.

Owen, Dennis E. "Spectral Evidence: The Village Witchcraft Cosmology of Salem Village in 1692," in *Essays in the Sociology of Perception*, ed. Mary Douglas. London, 1982, pp. 275–301.

Silverblatt, Laura. *Moon, Sun, and Witches: Gender Ideologies and Class in Inca and Colonial Peru.* Princeton, 1987.

Starkey, Marion L. *The Devil in Massachusetts: A Modern Inquiry into the Salem Witch Trials.* New York 1949.

Taylor, John Metcalf. *The Witchcraft Delusion in Colonial Connecticut.* New York, 1908.

Wiseman, Richard. *Witchcraft, Magic and Religion in 17th-Century Massachusetts.* Amherst, 1984.

NEW ENGLAND'S PLACE IN THE HISTORY OF WITCHCRAFT

BY GEORGE LINCOLN BURR

It is now more than twenty years since I reached the threshold of this theme. Happily it was to learn in time its perils. I was about to read before the American Historical Association a paper on "The Literature of Witchcraft" and my friend Mr. Justin Winsor naturally guessed that it must touch upon New England's share. "Don't be afraid," he encouraged me, "to say just what you please. If Poole pitches into you, I'll come to your support."

But what I had then to say about New England could give offense not even to Mr. Poole. The Salem panic was dismissed with a single sentence as "but the last bright flicker of the ghastly glare which had so long made hideous the European night," and in apology for ignoring the literature of American witchcraft I pleaded that in such a presence it would be a work of supererogation, if not an impertinence, to treat that literature with the brevity its place in the history of the delusion would demand. Perhaps these words satisfied even Mr. Poole that thus far I was no partisan. At any rate, though more than once it was my privilege to discuss with him New England witchcraft, he remained, like Mr. Winsor, till death my friend.

Till now I have been too wise to skirt the theme again. But age has brought temerity. Much as has been written, and well written, on the New England episode, no student has yet devoted a paper to its place in the history of witchcraft as a whole. Yet perhaps I should

1

not even now attempt it, had not two studies, both by members of our society and read before its meetings, done much to pave the way. In 1895 Professor Justin Winsor himself, in a paper on "The Literature of Witchcraft in New England,"[1] not only much more than made good what my own essay had lacked, but brought to light many a channel through which the thought of the old England told upon the new; and in 1906 a younger colleague of his and ours, Professor George Lyman Kittredge, in a paper bearing the modest title of "Notes on Witchcraft,"[2] went much further. Alleging the antiquity and the universality of belief in witchcraft, he pointed out more fully than had hitherto been done the relations of New England thought to English, the intelligibility of the superstition, the complexity of the problem on both sides of the sea, the inadequacy of its explanation by Puritanism or by pedantry, the relative slightness and transiency of the Salem episode; and, with the keen eye of the practised critic, he swept away a host of misstatements and exaggerations which have distorted the story. It is a service for which every lover of New England must be grateful; and, though there is much more to say and some things which I could have wished said otherwise, I could hardly, had he stopped with this, have cared to add a word. But when, in the generous zeal of his apology, he proceeded to lay down a body of theses which declare the belief in witchcraft "practically universal in the seventeenth century, even among the educated," and "no more discreditable to a man's head or heart than it was to believe in spontaneous generation or to be ignorant of the germ theory of disease," and which pronounce "the position of the seventeenth-century believers in witchcraft" . . . "logically and theologically stronger" than that of their opponents, and "the impulse to put a witch to death" "no more cruel or otherwise blameworthy, in itself, than the impulse to put a murderer to death,"

[1] Proceedings, N. S., Vol. X, pp. 351-373.
[2] Proceedings, N. S., Vol. XVIII, pp. 148-212.

he reached results so startlingly new, so contradictory of what my own lifelong study in this field has seemed to teach, so unconfirmed by the further research to which his words have stirred, and withal so much more generous to our ancestors than I can find it in my conscience to deem fair, that I should be less than honest did I not seize this earliest opportunity to share with you the reasons for my doubts—aye and to suggest a reading of history which, without undue harshness to the past, may leave it more intelligible how the present could honestly come to be.

If such a protest be anywhere in place, it is surely here. And if even here it seem too frankly polemic, let me plead that to take another's work so seriously is the best tribute to its weight, and to offer one's own in return the best gratitude for its help. In any case I could hardly diverge more widely from my predecessor than did he from his; and, so sweeping are his conclusions, any later study must choose between the disrespect of silence and the frankness of debate.[3]

And if to any here it seem treason to those who made New England to dissent from aught that can be urged in their praise, bear with me while I plead that, despite my birth and home in the wilds beyond the Hudson, there flows in my own veins none but New England blood; that that blood is almost wholly Puritan; that the English county which I believe the home of those who bore my name was that most deeply stained by this superstition; that the first who brought that name across the sea must at Springfield have had some part (though I trust it is only Dr. Holland's imagination that in *The Bay Path* gives him so large part) in the earliest New England witch-trial known to us in its details; that a few years later, at Fairfield, his son John Burr, my forebear, with Abigail his wife, had part unquestion-

---

[3] Perhaps I should not fail to add that the debate indeed has been opened by himself; for it is to questions involved in what his paper (else over-generous to my own) calls "the error into which Professor Burr has fallen" that the present study is chiefly devoted.

able in such proceedings; and that my other traditions are mainly of like ancestry and of a like ancestral faith.

Yet, to me, to urge in defense of those who in the seventeenth century—in New England or elsewhere—hung women as witches that the belief in witchcraft is universal seems a juggling with words. That belief which in the seventeenth century caused women to be done to death was never universal—in place or time. Let us define our terms. To assert or to deny anything whatever of witchcraft without a definition is to talk in the air: the word has had widely different meanings. When we affirm the universality of witchcraft or of the belief in it, it is in a sense which neither the etymology nor the history of that word suffices to explain. Only by analogy has its meaning gained so wide an application; and, unless I err as to what the anthropologists teach us, it is only in a sense that would make it inclusive of both religion and magic that witchcraft can be demonstrated universal. If, however, we discriminate between religion and magic, understanding by magic the art of winning supernatural aid, not by submission or persuasion, but by human cleverness or lore, and if then witchcraft be identified with magic, as is often done, we shall still, I fear, have fallen short of an excuse for its repression. But if, as is most common of all, we make witchcraft to mean "black magic" alone— and this is clearly what Professor Kittredge does, since he counts *maleficium*, harm to others, its essence—we come up against a difficulty not less grave. For to the devotees of a religion not only the users of black magic, nay not only all the users of magic, be it black or white, seem to employ illicit aid against their fellows; but, so fierce is the struggle for existence, the users of a rival religion are almost sure to be confused with these. And if the religion be monotheistic and claim monopoly, then *presto* all other gods and all other worships are branded with the stigma. Now, from almost or quite the first, this was precisely the attitude of Christianity, both toward all magic and toward all pagan faiths.

4

She did not deny the existence of gods other than her God. She did not deny them power. She denied them only goodness. They were "fiends," and those who sought their aid, for whatever end, by whatever means, were alike guilty of witchcraft. For now it is that we first meet that word. It belonged alone to our English forefathers, and before they were Christians they seem to have meant by it nothing evil. The word "witch," if scholars are right, is but a worn form of the word "witega," by which the Christian translators of that earliest day rendered into their own English the sacred name of "prophet." It can at first have implied in those who were known by it no graver fault than wisdom. Christianity it was that degraded it to a meaning wholly bad, the awful shadow of her awesome light, including within it not only all she learned to know of English heathendom, but darkening yet more the notion with all she remembered of Hebrew or Greek or Roman superstitions—for to her the Devil, like God, was one.

Yet all this was but the germ of her full-grown idea of witchcraft. A change more fundamental was in store. Thus far there was reality in the things she fought. However she might confuse them or exaggerate, the old superstitions were not dead. But a mass of them she had from the first despised or laughed away; and under her stern teaching their survivals fell ever more and more into neglect. As the danger lessened, her own bearing wisely grew less stern. The growing Canon Law punished now a practice, now the belief in it, and presently forgot to punish at all. However now and then superstition might well up in violence from the masses, it looked for a time as if under the enlighten-ing care of Church and State its most cruel terrors might be outgrown.

Alas, what was swept out at the door crept in at the key-hole. The old ideas had found an anchorage in theology. The old names still lived on. As our fathers brought with them over the sea memories of robin or partridge, and their children, grown familiar with the

word, must somehow find a thing to wear the name, so
then the teachers of that docile age worked into the
patchwork of their school theology these tatters of the
past. The superstitions of the lowly may be met by
education; but who shall save us from the superstitions
of the learned? The long and complex history through
which witchcraft came to mean what it meant to Christian Europe from the fourteenth century to the seventeenth, I must not here rehearse. Suffice it that that
meaning had grown definite and fixed—formulated and
prescribed by school and court and pulpit—and that
none were so strenuous in insisting on that definition,
so hot in denying the identity of this their witchcraft
with any other, as were the witch-haters themselves.
Nor were they wrong; for to write of robin or of partridge
and ignore the change which has made the words mean
one thing in Old England and another in New would
be less misleading than to ignore the change which had
come in the meaning of witchcraft—a change from objective to subjective—from the deed of a culprit to the
dream of an inquisitor.

I do not mean, of course, that there was no intelligible
chain of thought between the older meanings and the
new. I do not mean that there were not, then as now,
those who confused the two. I do not mean that men
and women were not sometimes brought into suspicion
of witchcraft in the new sense by some dealing with
witchcraft in the old. I mean only that the witchcraft
for which during these centuries men and women were
punished by church and state was a theological fantasy,
and that for any sort of witchcraft known before the
advent of this theological conception men and women
would no more have been done to death in seventeenth-
century Salem than in Salem of to-day. This is what
I meant when in that old paper I wrote: "Magic . . .
is actual and universal; . . . but witchcraft never
was. It was but a shadow, a nightmare: the nightmare
of a religion, the shadow of a dogma. Less than five
centuries saw its birth, its vigor, its decay."

6

Later research, at least, has but confirmed these words. Joseph Hansen, the eminent German scholar who has since given the world the most careful book on the rise of this conception,[4] would narrow its period yet more closely than I. And Mr. Lea, from whom, after a lifetime's study of this subject, we hoped the most learned of all books upon it, wrote in 1907 in one of those chapters of his great histories of the Inquisition which may remain our only substitute for that unfinished work: "The culmination of sorcery was witchcraft and yet it was not the same. . . . The witch has abandoned Christianity, has renounced her baptism, has worshipped Satan as her God, has surrendered herself to him, body and soul, and exists only to be his instrument. . . . There are no pages of European history more filled with horror than those which record the witch-madness of three centuries, from the fifteenth to the eighteenth; . . . [and] this witch-madness was essentially a disease of the imagination, created and stimulated by the persecution of witchcraft."[5]

Professor Kittredge, too, counts sound and necessary the distinction between witchcraft and magic; but he thinks it less vital than do I in the history of witchcraft, and less true for England than for the Continent. To this point, therefore, and especially to England I have first addressed my study.[6]   I am far yet from being ready to pronounce a final opinion; but I must confess that thus far I have found no reason to adopt his view.[7]

---

[4] *Zauberwahn, Inquisition und Hexenprozess im Mittelalter* (Munich and Leipzig, 1900).

[5] *The Inquisition of Spain* (New York, 1906-1907), IV, p. 206. Mr. Lea once wrote me that all his study of the Inquisition grew out of his study of the history of witchcraft.

[6] This has been the more tempting because during these last months there has fallen upon me, as the chairman of a committee of the American Historical Association, the pleasant task of aiding to prepare for the press a prize essay by a young American scholar on the history of English witchcraft (Wallace Notestein, *A History of Witchcraft in England from 1558 to 1718*, Washington, 1911). Alas, though I owe to this a stimulating companionship and many additions to my knowledge, and for both am glad here to express my warm thanks to the author, it has needed from me more time than I foresaw; and to the inopportune demands during these last days of the page proofs of that volume I must ask you to impute in part the crudeness and the incompleteness of the present paper.

[7] He cites (note 2) Hansen as also recognizing "the difference between England and the Continent in the development of the witchcraft idea and in the history of prosecution."

Instead of finding in England popular superstition more
continuous than on the Continent I seem to find it less
so. Nor does this seem hard to explain. The English
were a migrant people, and superstitions do not migrate
easily. Germanic beliefs were peculiarly local, and the
students of Germanic origins have often pointed out
how largely, even on the Continent, they failed to survive the wandering. But the English migrated over sea,
lost touch almost wholly with the home land, were long
cut off by speech and faith from the superstitions of
the land to which they came. For long the migrants
were men—less prone than women 'to the practice or
the fear of sorcery. And scarcely were they well settled
in the new home when a new faith, Christianity, made
them its converts,—and more swiftly and thoroughly
than any other Germanic folk till their kinsmen the
Normans should under circumstances very similar
repeat the story.

How much of superstition that new faith brushed
away, how sternly, though so credulously, it fought
the remainder, we have already noted. It is in the
Penitentials, not the laws, that we first find mention of
witchcraft; and what the English Penitentials find to
punish is slight compared with what is found by Continental ones—nay, much of even this little seems only
borrowed from Continental canons.[8] And while the
pre-Christian Germanic laws of the Continent punish
witchcraft only when harm to person or to goods is
charged, and only later, under church influence, make
it penal as a dealing with evil powers,[9] Alfred's law, the
earliest English one, is but an echo of the Mosaic "Thou

I am unable to read so much, however, out of the passage he names (*Zauberwahn*, p. 24,
note 1). What Hansen seems to me to say is only that his own book does not deal with
England, which "though it shared indeed largely in the witch-trials, reflects only the
general course of the development."

[8] It is to be noted that much of what is published by Spelman and by Thorpe as belonging to the Penitential of Theodore, in the seventh century, or to Egbert's, in the eighth,
is now known to be later interpolation from Continental sources. See Wasserschleben,
Bussordnungen, pp. 13-32, 162-219, 251-348; Haddan and Stubbs, *Councils*, iii, pp.
173-186, 179-190, 413-416, 424; Lea, *Auricular Confession and Indulgence*, iii, p. 103-104.

[9] See Hansen, *Zauberwahn*, pp. 61 ff. and authorities cited by him; and especially
Brunner, *Deutsche Rechtsgeschichte*, ii, pp. 678-691.

shalt not suffer a witch to live."[10] The laws of Ethelred and Cnut are scarcely less redolent of Scriptural suggestion;[11] and when, with the Norman Conquest, the influence of the Continent and of Rome grows more direct, the English theologians and chroniclers reek with precisely the same witch and devil lore that was popular beyond the Channel.

But in England, as on the Continent, the attitude of Church and State toward what they deemed witchcraft seems for a time to grow milder, not sterner. In England, as on the Continent, it was only in the train of the newly organized repression of heresy that sternness came back. "Indeed," say the historians of English law, "it is probable that but for the persecution of heretics there would have been no persecution of sorcerers."[12] Everybody knows how, when Bishop Stubbs had taught us that even in England the authority of the Canon Law was greater than we had dreamed, Mr. Maitland, layman and skeptic, went much further and showed it greater than Bishop Stubbs had dreamed. Especially did he prove this as to heresy, showing beyond question that heretics were burned, and by the civil authorities at the instance of the Church, before the statute *de haeretico comburendo*.[13] By the Canon Law witchcraft had now been brought into the closest connection with heresy —it was only a higher treason against Heaven—and the Church's pressure for its punishment was not less urgent.[14] As in 1401 the Canon Law was reinforced, as to heresy, by the statute, so in 1406 there was won from the same churchly king, and doubtless by the prelate to whom our extant copy of it is addressed—Philip Repington, Bishop of Lincoln, late the king's chaplain

---

[10] See Liebermann, Die Gesetze der Angelsachen (Halle, 1906), i, pp. 38-39.

[11] Same, pp. 248-249, 310-311.

[12] Pollock and Maitland, *History of English Law* (2d ed., Cambridge, 1898), ii, p. 552.

[13] Maitland, *Canon Law in the Church of England* (London, 1898), especially pp. 79-80, 158-179; and the *History of English Law*, ii, pp. 544-552.

[14] See as to this Mr. Lea's chapters on "Sorcery" and "Witchcraft" in his *The Inquisition of the Middle Ages* and Hansen, *Zauberwahn*, ch. iv. Not all the decretals as to witchcraft were to find a place in the authorized *Corpus* of the Canon Law; but this was then only in the making.

and confessor and still his bosom friend, an ex-Lollard now with the zeal of a renegade hunting down his ancient brethren and soon to be rewarded with the cardinal's hat—a royal letter calling for the ferreting out of witches.[15] Nor can I find that in England the theory of witchcraft differed then in any point from that of the rest of Latin Christendom. That, however, there followed in England no such epidemic of witch-persecution[16] as on the Continent I readily admit; but it seems to me more easily explained than by any difference in the development of the witchcraft idea. There was in England no Holy Inquisition; and on the Continent it was, as is well known, to the Holy Inquisition, now left at leisure by its success in the extirpation of heresy, that the new quest of witches was almost wholly due. There was in England no use of torture; and the torture, as is not less well known, was the fruitful source of nearly all witch-epidemics. When in the seventeenth century English procedure, in spite of English law, learned to use torture, England too had her witch-epidemic. I gladly admit, too, that both these causes must have retarded in England the diffusion of the witch-idea. That England had no Holy Inquisition may have been, as has been said, only because she had no need of one; but in its absence she lacked those from whom came all the treatises expounding the new dogma, and whose prestige must have done much to give it vogue. The torture, too, not only wrested, from the innocent, confessions of guilt and the names of accomplices to be tortured into like confession, but through the wild tales it forced from their delirious fancy or enabled the leading questions of bookish in-

---

[15] The Bishop of Lincoln it was, not the Bishop of Norwich, as say Pollock and Maitland (*History of English Law*, ii. p. 555). The error is borrowed from Thomas Wright (introduction to *Proceedings against Dame Alice Kyteler*, Camden Society, London, 1843), who, however, prints the document in full and with the correct name. It may be found also in Rymer; and see the *Calendar of Patent Rolls, Henry IV, 1405-1408*, p. 112. Mr. Lea assumes (*Inquisition of the Middle Ages*, iii, p. 467), and I think reasonably, that the same letter was sent to all the English bishops.

[16] I am sorry that I must use this word "persecution," so scrupulously avoided by Professor Kittredge. "Prosecution," which he uses instead, does not mean the same thing; and, if it did, I fear it would lose no time in falling under the same stigma.

quisitors to put into their mouths—tales published through the reading of these confessions to the crowds which gathered at sentence and execution or diffused through the no less effective medium of common gossip —was a most potent popularizer of the delusion. And, though from both these sources, through written book and word of mouth, there filtered slowly into England all this teaching, it was not till after the middle of the sixteenth century that it began to tell on public polity.[17] Till that time, as I too believe, the idea of *maleficium*, or actual harm, played a larger part in English action toward witchcraft than on the Continent was now accorded it.

But with the accession of Elizabeth there found entrance into England a Continental influence which was to change all this. The Marian exiles, who so largely manned her bishoprics, were fresh from lands and towns where witch-burning was in full career, and at Geneva, Zurich, Basel, Strasburg, had had ample opportunity to learn its theory; and the law which was now to embody this differing attitude they from the very outset of the new queen's reign demanded at her hands. That law was introduced in her first Parliament, though to be passed only by its successor; and in the interval one of these exiles, Bishop Jewel, who had already reported to his Continental mentor, Peter Martyr, the enormous number of witches his trained eyes now found in England,[18] burst forth, in a sermon before the queen, into an appeal to her for action against them.[19] It is true that he finds a ground for this appeal in the "horrible using" of her poor subjects, whom his eyes have seen to "pine away even unto the death." Nay, he even insinuates some such danger from the witches to the queen herself: "I pray God," he said, "they never prac-

---

[17] Of the transient statute under Henry VIII or of its disappearance under Edward, I must not pause to speak. As was long ago pointed out, there is reason to doubt whether it was honestly meant or seriously enforced.

[18] Jewel, *Works* (Parker Soc., 1845-1850), iv, pp. 1216-1217; or (translation only) *Zurich Letters* (Parker Soc., 1842), 44.

[19] As to the date of this sermon see Notestein, p. 16.

tise further than upon the subject." But it must be remembered that the "laws" for whose execution he was then appealing must mean the common law of the realm, which of course took cognizance only of concrete injury as basis for a criminal action in the courts. It is true, too, that the new statute, which early in 1563 became a law, mentions still as a ground for the "condign punishment" of such "devilish persons" their witchcrafts "to the destruction of the persons and goods of their neighbors"; but this is no longer the only ground, nor is any *maleficium* longer needed for their conviction. To "use, practise, or exercise any invocations or conjurations of evil and wicked spirits to or for any intent or purpose" is specified first of all as enough by itself to warrant their death as felons; and to their witchcrafts against their neighbors are now assimilated "other lewd intents and purposes contrary to the laws of Almighty God and to the peril of their own souls."[20]

I venture to think that no student familiar with the Erasmian tone of the leaders of church and state in England during the earlier sixteenth century can read the sermon which offered the text for such an outburst, or the statute which thus assumes the old function of the Canon Law and punishes sin as well as crime, without discerning in both alike a new diction and a new spirit, or without recognizing in that diction and that spirit the stamp of what was later to be known as Calvinism. And from this day forward, however individuals prove exceptions either way, the group, the party, which I seem to find always standing in general for a sterner dealing with witches in England is that whose

---

[20] Professor Kittredge (see his note 4) seems wholly to have overlooked, both in the statute of Elizabeth and in that of James, this prescription of death for witchcraft without *maleficium*—witchcraft which wrongs only God and harms only self—and this oversight, I fear, is largely responsible for his whole point of view. Were only *maleficium* to be punished, there was indeed, no need for a special statute: the common law punished, and with severity, both harm to person and harm to goods, whether wrought by witchcraft or in any other wise. Nay, even after there was a special statute, the common law might be invoked to punish *maleficium*, and in one case, at least, it took precedence: a woman who bewitched to death her husband, was burned for husband-murder ("petty treason"), not hanged for witchcraft.

bond of unity was Calvinism.[21]   It was not that Calvinism was more prone to superstition.   I believe it
had to do with the precise converse of this.   What happened now was singularly like what had happened when
Christianity took hold on the Germanic peoples.   The
rational minds of the Swiss and Genevan reformers,
trained in a more critical school than their North German neighbors, discarded at one sweep nearly the whole

----

[21] "The remark," says Professor Kittredge (note 42), "that Calvinism was especially
responsible for witch-trials is a loose assertion which has to reckon with the fact that the
last burning for witchcraft at Geneva took place in 1652." Who may have ventured
such a remark I do not know, and I have no wish to defend it. I should be slow to believe
that Calvinism could be more responsible for witch-trials than was the Dominican theology in its own time and place, or than Lutheranism in the lands where it was most
dominant. That Calvinism was especially responsible for witch-trials *in England is*,
however, a verdict so familiar that, so far as I know, Professor Kittredge is the first to
question it. Principal Lee, a half-century ago, in his *Lectures on the History of the Church
of Scotland* (i, pp. 315-327), undertook to clear the skirts of Scotland and of Presbyterian-
ism, and like Professor Kittredge he refutes many exaggerations; but it is in part at the
cost of English Calvinists, and I doubt if, in general, Professor Kittredge would count
the case advanced by his sometimes startling arguments. If the ascription of especial
responsibility to Calvinism in England has been loosely made, I suspect that it is because
it was supposed an admitted fact or seemed too evident for proof. Such grounds for my
own faith in it as I have space here to present will be found in the text; but let me hasten
to reckon with the date of that last burning at Geneva by asking how many other cities
of the importance or the intelligence of Geneva had a witch-burning so late as 1652. Of
her neighbors Strasburg and Basel seem to have left off a little earlier, Bern and Zurich
a little later. London saw an execution that very year, and perhaps another in the year
that followed; but London was then a very Calvinistic London, and knew nothing of
this sort after the Restoration. It is, of course, to Geneva's honor that she burned no
later, though her witch trials did not cease with her witch-burning; nor will I ask whether
we should attribute the escape of the rest from death to the hesitation of her judges, as
does her historian, Gautier, or to the protest of her physicians, as does Dr. Ladame, who
has edited the documents of that final burning. I am glad to believe it, rather, a civic
advance in which these had only their share. In any case, is it not as irrelevant to the
question of the influence of Calvinism as it would be to question the influence of the medieval theology because witch-burnings ceased early at Rome? Is it not more pertinent
that, while of the one hundred and sixty-two trials whose records are left at Geneva from
the fifteenth century but one was for witchcraft (Ladame, *Procès criminel de la dernière
sorcière brulée à Genève*, p. vi) and while prior to the advent of the reformers it is said
that no death penalty for witchcraft is known to the annals of the city, one hundred and
fifty were burned there for that crime during the next sixty years (Henry, *Leben Calvins*,
ii, p. 75, quoting Picot, *Histoire de Genève*, ii, 280)? I dare not answer for the exactness
of these latter figures, for I do not know on what Picot has based his count; but they gain
much probability from the fact that Dr. Ladame finds still in the Genevan archives the
documents of two hundred witch-trials from the sixteenth century (*Procès*, p. vii), and
that Hansen, who has also sifted these archives, enumerates only a single sixteenth-
century trial there prior to 1540 (*Quellen*, p. 513). As this trial, which ended in a condemnation and therefore probably in an execution, took place in 1527, it might seem in so
far to throw doubt on Picot's figure; but, as the court was the Holy Inquisition and the
witch from an outlying Savoyard village, the case is not strictly a Genevan one. Yet
even for Geneva let me not seem to make Calvinism the only cause of persecution.

mass of the superstitions which had become the heritage
of Christendom—not only those which had to do with
Christian worship, but those as well which clustered
about its alleged counterpart, the ritual of Satan.   As
Calvin's caustic treatise on the need of an inventory
of the relics of the saints, with its shrewd sense and taunt-
ing mockery, rang through the Christian world, translated and read nowhere more eagerly than in England,
so too his contemptuous rejection of a horde of the mar-
vels of witchcraft.   Miracles had ceased, he taught,
with the apostles.   The miracles of the Devil, like those
of the Church, are sham.   The witch-sabbath is a fantastic fiction, the witch's flight through the air a delusion
of Satan.   Luther and his followers took over from
the Middle Ages a host of superstitions to which Calvin
would not listen.   Even of exorcism, whether of babes
or of demoniacs, he would not hear.   And on no side,
I think, did Calvinism more appeal to the practical
common sense of Englishmen.

But on one point Calvin stood firmly with the past
—on the authority of the Bible.   It was in its name
that he condemned all else.   "He that believes more
than the Holy Bible teaches," wrote one of his English
disciples,[22] "he is superstitious, and the use of the thing
is superstition"; and superstition, taught Calvin, is as
bad as atheism.[23]   And to Calvin the Holy Bible meant
Old Testament as well as New.   Luther had denied
that the Old was binding upon Christians; but Calvin
held its legislation still valid and authoritative, and out
of it he drew his scheme of church and state.   It is the
duty of the Christian prince, the Christian magistrate,
he taught, to enforce the law of God as well as that of
man; and the first four Commandments, which define
men's duties to God, should be enforced more zealously
than the other six, which govern their duties to each
other.   "Now the Bible," said Calvin, "teaches that
there are witches and that they must be slain."   "God

[22] Bishop Pilk;ngton.
[23] See h:s sermon on Deut xiii.

expressly commands that all witches and enchantresses be put to death, and this law of God is a universal law," as binding to-day as ever.[24]   To deny that magical arts were ever practised, or that they are so still, would be to accuse God of heedlessness, legislating about things which do not exist.[25]   This is "impudent blasphemy," and they who utter it should be driven out from Christian communities.[26]   Though the Devil's pretended miracles are frauds, "we need not wonder if, by God's permission, he should disturb the elements, or afflict the reprobate with diseases and other evils, or present phantoms to their sight."[27]

Therefore it was that Calvin could take earnest part in the extirpation of those who were charged with spreading the plague at Geneva by anointing with a diabolic unguent the latches of the doors.[28]   Therefore it was that he could appear in person before the Council to insist on the extirpation of the witches (this time not pest-spreaders) in the parish of Peney; and it is to be noticed that the records of the Council make him term them "heretics."[29]   To him it was not their harm to men that was the gist of their offense.   It was that such offenses, however illusory, "carry with them a wicked renunciation of God"; for "God would condemn to

---

[24] See his sermon on the Witch of Endor (*Opera*, ed. Baum *et al.*, xxx, 631-632).

[25] *Opera*, xxiv, 269.

[26] *Opera*, xxx, 632.

[27] *Opera*, xxiv, 269; cf. Eng. transl. of the Calvin Translation Society(*Commentaries on the Four Last Books of Moses*, i, p. 431).

[28] This was *maleficium* with a vengeance; and, if ever a panic of superstitious and cruel terror could be pardoned, it would be in the face of such a mysterious and deadly scourge. Nay, so circumstantial and so rational are the details given us by contemporaries—as by that good Calvinist, Michel Roset—that one could not only credit the guilt of the accused, but could accept the story of its method, were it not for the merciless torture used to win the confessions, and the preposterous tale of league with the Devil which it proved as easy to win from them by the same means.   Those accused of a like crime had been similarly convicted and punished at Geneva a half-dozen years before the coming of Calvin; but in the account we have of it from the good Roset there is this notable difference, that, whereas the first episode is narrated as a case of simple poisoning, without a suggestion of any supernatural influence, in the later he knows that the "more than thirty persons"—thirty-one were put to death—" had leagued together to give themselves body and soul to the Devil in express terms." One catches here both the Calvinist's belief in the guilt of the intent and the Calvinist's doubt as to the reality of the marvel. (See Roset, *Les Chroniques de Genève*, Geneva, 1894, pp. 46–47, 306-308.)

[29] *Opera*, xxi, 365, and A. Roget, *Histoire du Peuple de Genève*, ii, pp. 178-179.

capital punishment all augurs, and magicians, and consulters with familiar spirits, and necromancers and followers of magic arts."[30]

The lawyers, indeed, throughout Europe were not
easy to win to such a departure from the concrete. The
church herself had long jealously restricted them to
non-spiritual offenses, and their own conservatism was
now slow to budge. Those who drew up in the first
decades of the sixteenth century that great criminal
code of Charles V which was promulgated at last in
1532 made the penalty of death for witchcraft depend on
such a concrete mischief. But Lutheran influence in
time changed all this in Saxony, and in 1572 the new code
of the Elector August punished witches with death
"regardless of whether they had by witchcraft done
anybody harm";[31] and in 1582 the new code of the then
Lutheran Palatinate echoed this penalty of death regardless of *maleficium*.[32] But Calvinism had taught
this from the first, and the statute of Elizabeth was
earlier by nearly a decade than even the Saxon code.
And in that same year, 1563, there was enacted in the
neighboring Scotland, where, though Mary was on the
throne, the Calvinists were in the saddle, a similar but
severer statute, punishing with death alike the use of
witchcraft and the consulting of a witch, and without
the slightest mention of a *maleficium*.

But Calvinistic demonology was soon to flow into England through many other channels than the memory
or the correspondence of the exiles. I can take space for
the mention of but one or two. In 1575 there appeared
in English translation the dialogue on witches of the
Genevan professor, Daneau, printed the previous year
in French and soon to be had in Latin as well; and by
1586 there was market for a fresh English translation.[33]
In 1580, however, had appeared the great *Démonomanie*

---

[30] *Opera*, xxiv, 365.
[31] "*Ob sie gleich mit Zauberei niemand Schaden zugefugt*" run the exact words of the Code (pars iv, const. 2).
[32] Titul. ix (p. 9).
[33] See Paul de Félice, *Lambert Daneau*, p. 159.

of Bodin (soon also translated into Latin), whose powerful influence can be traced everywhere in the English
thought of the following years. An open Calvinist
he was not; but so saturated is his book with Calvinistic
thought, and, through Calvinism, with the Old Testament, that he has been suspected not only of crypto-
Calvinism, but sometimes of Judaism.[34]   Yet it was far
less, I think, the influence of any such monograph than
that of Calvin's own commentaries, now on every preacher's shelves, of Calvin's own sermons, the model, if not
the source, of pulpit eloquence,—it was Daneau's *Ethice
Christiana*, the standard treatise of Protestant ethics,
and his *Politice Christiana*, the standard manual of
Protestant rulers,—that impressed this doctrine on the
English conscience.

Not that English demonologic reading was narrow.
In a day when every educated Englishman read Latin
as easily as English and was likely to have a smattering
of French and Italian as well, it should go without saying that the books which shaped in this field the thought
of the Continent were known in England also.   The
bibliography which in 1584 Reginald Scot prefixed to
his *Discoverie of Witchcraft* enumerates well nigh the
whole literature of the subject; and the defenders of the
belief are not chary of displaying a similar learning.   It
is no truer that it is impossible to study New England
thought on witchcraft apart from English than that it
is impossible to study English apart from Continental.
Nay, New England, too, was far from ignorant of Continental thought.   Increase Mather's *Remarkable Providences* shows an amazing acquaintance with the Continental authorities on demonology; and, though it does
not follow, even when he cites them, that that acquaintance was always at first hand, a deal of it is clearly so.[35]

---

[34] See especially the careful study of Friedrich von Bezold on *Jean Bodin als Okkul-
tist und seine Dämonomanie*, in the *Historische Zeitschrift*, Bd. 105 (1910).

[35] Of the books he cites I find only a small proportion listed by Mr. Tuttle in his interesting paper (published last year in our *Proceedings*) on *The Libraries of the Mathers*.
But his study suggests many ways in which this may be explained.

And this wider reading, even the Mathers', included much that was written to question or restrain the persecution. Yet it is not strange that to plain Englishmen, in England or New England, the Calvinistic view should have especial cogency. Not alone what seemed its rationalism, but its discrimination—is it not still the reasoner who discriminates that wins us?—but most of all, I think, its appeal to the Bible, the text-book which now made every man his own theologian, and its acceptance of that literal sense which lay for every man upon the surface, these were the qualities to carry weight with pious men just waking now in every field to self-reliance and self-help. And, if it narrowed superstition, it deepened it as well. Precisely as, by robbing the Puritan of all ritual except the Sabbath, it concentrated on the Sabbath all the devotion which in him still craved ritual, so by denying to the Puritan imagination indulgence in other superstitions it made more keen by far its interest in these deeds of darkness which it was Christian virtue to divine and punish.

What picturesqueness such speculations might take on let me illustrate from a sober law-book put forth in the last years of Elizabeth by a scrivener of that southern Yorkshire whence came so many of the earliest founders of New England. Thus in his *Simboleography*[36] William West defines the crimes of "magicke" and "witcherie":

MAGICKE.

Magitians be those which by uttering of certaine superstitious words conceived, adventure to attempt things above the course of nature, by bringing forth dead mens ghosts, as they fasly [falsely] pretende, in shewing of things either secret or in places far off, and in shewing them in any shape or likenes. These wicked persons by oth or writing written

---

[36] Pp. 87, 88, of pt. 2 in the edition of 1611, which I believe (though I have used no earlier) an unchanged reprint of that of 1592-4. The briefer first edition appeared in 1590. The discerning will, I think, divine that the first sentence of the definition of magic is of older source than the remainder, which savors of the school theology; and it is only the definition of witchery which seems to me to bear a distinctly Calvinistic impress. Note how, though calling it delusion, the author revels in its details. Between these two crimes, as though gradations from one to the other, are described "Southsaying Wizzards," "Divination," "Jugling," and "Inchantings and Charming."

with their own blood, having betaken themselves to the devil, have forsaken God, and broken their covenant made in baptism, and detest the benefits thereof, and worship the [divel only: And setling their only hope in him, doe execute his commandements, and being deade, commend both their bodies and soules unto him.

. . . .

WITCHERIE.

A Witch or hag, is she which being [d]eluded by a league made with the divell through his perswasion, inspiration and jugling thinketh she can designe what moner of evil things soever, either by thogt or imprecation, as to shake the aire with lightnings and thunder, to cause haile and tempests, to remove green corne or trees to another place, to be caried of her familer which hath taken upon him the deceitful shape of a goate, swine, or calf etc. into some mountain far distant, in a wonderfull short space of time. And sometimes to flie upon a staffe or forke, or some other instrument. And to spend all the night after with her sweet hart, in playing, sporting, banqueting, dancing, daliance, and divers other divelish lusts, and lewd disports, and to shew a thousand such monstrous mockeries.

But during these same last years of Elizabeth Calvinism found in England an interpreter whose teachings were of more lasting potency on both sides of the sea. A style more lucid, sensible, straightforward, unpedantic, suited to catch the ear and to convince the mind of sober Englishmen, than that of the great Cambridge preacher, William Perkins, it would not be easy to conceive. And all these winning qualities belong to his "discourse of the damned art of witchcraft," which delivered before his university audience, was circulated in manuscript till his death, in 1602, and then was by his literary executors not only published and republished by itself but embodied in that standard collection of his works which for a century was to be a classic on the shelves of every Puritan divine. Though a fellow of Christ's, his relations were closest with Emmanuel College, that cradle of Puritanism, English and American. John Cotton was his convert. Thomas Hooker, Thomas Shepard, John Harvard, were there his hearers or his readers.

19

Every student of New England witchcraft knows how his dicta are embodied in the books of the Mathers. Nay, Increase Mather quotes with pride the high praise paid New England by a British geographer who wrote that "as to their Religion, the people there are like Mr. Perkins."

Now, the substance of Mr. Perkins's teaching as to witchcraft was that "among us also the sinne of Witchcraft ought as sharply to be punished as in former times; and all Witches . . . ought according to the Law of Moses to be put to death." "The penaltie of Witchcraft being Death by God's appointment . . . binds us, and shall in like sort bind men in all ages"; . . . "for the most notorious traytour and rebell that can be is the Witch, for she renounceth God himselfe," and "as the killing Witch must die by another Lawe, though he were no Witch, so the healing and harmless Witch must die by this Lawe, though he kill not, onely for covenant with Satan." "Death therefore"—thus closes the sermon—"is the just and deserved portion of the good Witch."[37]

It was high time for English Puritanism to find for its witch theory such an advocate. Its opponents, too, were finding voice and in the highest ranks of the Anglican clergy. Certain cases of child illness or child imposture like those which a century later started the Massachusetts panic had not only given rise to charges of bewitchment, but had called into activity, both among the English Catholics and the English Puritans, men who professed to detect the witch and by supernatural aid to cure the bewitched. Against these, and notably against one John Darrel, a Puritan minister who became a sort of itinerant exorcist, the prelates called in the aid of the courts.[38] The controversy soon

---

[37] See his *Discourse of the Damned Art of Witchcraft* (London, 1608), closing pages. Perkins advocated, too, the use of torture. Calvin, as is well known, believed also in this; and nowhere was it used more cruelly or more effectively than at Geneva.

[38] I am, of course, far from ascribing to the Puritans in general Darrel's views as to exorcism; yet how far they were from repudiating him may be gathered from Brook (*Puritans*, ii, 117-122), who tells us how eagerly his books were bought at Cambridge.

aired itself in print, and the spokesman of the Anglicans, Dr. Samuel Harsnett, chaplain of the Bishop of London and accounted the mouthpiece of that prelate, put forth (1599, 1603) two vigorous books, which with amazing boldness pour contempt not only on the exorcists and their claims, but on the belief in possession and witch-craft, and on all the superstitions connected with these. "Horace the Heathen," he declared, "spied long agoe that a Witch, a Wizard, and a Conjurer were but bul-beggers to scare fooles."[39] Now, Samuel Harsnett, from 1602 Archdeacon of Essex, was to become succes-sively Vice-Chancellor of Cambridge, Bishop of Chi-chester, Bishop of Norwich, Archbishop of York; and his backer, Richard Bancroft, Bishop of London, be-came in 1604 Archbishop of Canterbury and primate of the English Church.   With such men at the head of the hierarchy—and supported, as I have found no reason to doubt, by the general opinion of their party—how was it that the persecution of witches was not laughed out of England before the Puritans came to the helm?

Ah, but then came King James.   It is true that James was not a Puritan; but, as everybody knows, he was a Calvinist, and the witch question was one not of church government but of theology.   All his theology was steeped in Calvinism, and everybody knows how, while still in Scotland, he had distinguished himself as a per-secutor of witches.   He had been stirred, too, in 1597, by "the fearful abounding at this time" in Scotland "of these detestable slaves of the divell," to put forth a book, his *Dœmonologie*, in order "to resolve the doubt-ing hearts of manie" as to their guilt and to prove that all, regardless of sex, age, or rank, aye even "bairnes," should be put to death—"for," he says, "it is the highest

---

Two other obscure Puritan ministers (More and Denison) had some part in his doings or in the defense of them, and one tract in his favor has been ascribed to another, James Bamford.   As to all this episode I am happy to be able now to refer to Dr. Notestein's *History of Witchcraft in England* (chapter iv, "The Exorcists").

[39] The rest of this striking passage may be found quoted in Dr. Notestein's work (pp. 88-89).   But Harsnett's tone is the same throughout.   The long titles of his books and of Darrel's may also be learned from Dr. Notestein.

point of Idolatry, wherein no exception is admitted by
the law of God."[40] This book was at once republished
at London when, in 1603, James mounted the English
throne; and his first Parliament, in 1604, replaced the
statute of Elizabeth by one yet sterner. That James's
book, odd mixture of Scotch shrewdness and Scotch
pedantry and full of Scotticisms in its speech, had serious
influence on English thought or action, save as it seemed
to give a key to the king's mind, it is not easy to believe.
But to James's statute or to its colonial echoes all
witches later brought to trial in England or New England
owed their fate.[41] Its purpose was frankly the "more
severe punishing" of the offense. Its first clause re-
enacts the felon's death for all who "shall use, practise,
or exercise any invocation or conjuration of any evil
and wicked spirit"; but this Elizabethan clause—which
seems to have been interpreted to mean, as it was doubtless intended to mean, only the deliberate and formal
conjurer[42]—was now reinforced by one which was clearly
meant to cover all dabbling with witchcraft, and which
may have aimed, like the Scottish statute, to make as
penal the mere consulting of a witch. All should
likewise die, said this clause, who should "consult,
covenant with, entertain, employ, feed, or reward any
evil or wicked spirit," whatever the intent or purpose,

---

[40] *Dæmonologie* (ed. of 1603), preface and p. 76.

[41] The colonial laws were, indeed, no mere echoes. Even more than the statute of James they were to the mind of Calvinism; for they had nothing whatever to say of *maleficium* and wholly identified the crime with the sin. Plymouth, in 1636, enumerated after treason and murder, as an "offence lyable to death," the "solemn compaction or conversing with the divell by way of witchcraft, conjuracion or the like." Massachusetts, in 1641 (and, following her, Connecticut in 1642), brought the crime into more direct connection with the Ten Commandments by enacting, as the second of her "Capitall Laws" (between idolatry, the violation of the First Commandment, and blasphemy, the violation of the Third), that "If any man or woman be a witch (that is hath or consulteth with a familiar spirit), They shall be put to death." And New Haven, in 1655, not only followed the same order, but, as was her wont, made the Mosaic law her own: "If any person be a Witch, he or she shall be put to death, according to *Exod.* xxii, 18, *Levit.* xx, 27, *Deut.* xviii, 10, 11."

[42] Thus, e. g., Edward Hartley perished under it in 1597. How little the clause was in thought or understood in the case of an ordinary witch is suggested by that of Joan Cason, who in 1586 was about to be acquitted, when a lawyer pointed out that the invocation of spirits had been made a capital crime and she was sentenced to death. But see the case, as reported by Holinshed (or rather his continuators), *Chronicles*, ed. of 1807-1808, iv, 893.

or who should for purposes of witchcraft exhume the dead or any part thereof. I need not discuss the superstitions, hideous or nauseous, which underlie this list of possible relations with demons. They betray the lettered demonologist, and opened a door to charges and to evidence hitherto little heard in England. For the witchcraft causing bodily injury the new statute next prescribes death as the penalty for the first offense (instead, as heretofore, for the second); and, for treasure-seeking, the use of love-charms, or the attempt, though unsuccessful, to work ill to the bodies or goods of others, death is to be the penalty of the second offense. Here, then, much more than in Elizabeth's statute, the essence of the crime is made to lie, not in the *maleficium* (which no longer need be charged, and, if charged, no longer need be proved), but in the sin. It is patent how this mirrors the king's own views; yet I could wish we knew more clearly the nature and the measure of his part in it.[43] It is at least to be noted that when, in the later years of his reign, the king's views were believed to have changed, the witch-trials, too, fell off.[44]

Alas, what I had meant for a paper is growing to a treatise. To my grief I must forego the tracing further of the influence of Calvinism. I must not so much as speak of its relation to the most notable of English witch-hunts—that led by Matthew Hopkins in the eastern counties during the period of Presbyterian dominance.[45]

---

[43] Edward Fairfax, the author of that translation of Tasso which James is said to have valued above all other English poetry, tells us that His "Majesty found a defect in the statutes, . . . by which none died for Witchcraft but they only who by that means killed, so that such were executed rather as murderers than as Witches." (See his *Discourse of Witchcraft*, Philobiblon Society's ed., "Preface to the Reader." I owe this passage to Dr. Notestein, having at hand only Grainge's edition, which lacks it.) I find the statement wholly credible; but we do not know the channel of his information.

[44] Dr. Notestein tells us (p. 105) that all but one of the forty or fifty people whom we know to have suffered for the crime during the reign of James perished within his first fifteen years. He has also tried (p. 105) to determine how many of these who suffered death under the law of James would not have suffered under that of Elizabeth. He finds the number known to us under James much greater; but our statistics are probably so incomplete that little importance attaches to these figures.

[45] Yet I cannot forbear, such is their pertinence to the points in question, to transcribe here some of the words with which the official commentary put forth by divines of the Westminster Assembly, in the very year (1645) when this persecution was set on foot, interprets

More gladly yet would I attempt to point out some of
the channels through which this Calvinistic view of
witchcraft made its way across the sea—the men who
took with them to America experience gained in English
witch-trials, the wholesale migrations from regions
committed most deeply to this view, the correspondence
on this theme and those akin to it between the old home
and the new, the return to England for education of
those who were to be New England's teachers—was it
not there, just at the end of the Protectorate, that the
young Increase Mather was drawn into the scheme of
the great Puritan commentator, Matthew Poole, for
the recording on both sides of the Atlantic of those
"remarkable providences" which were so long to keep
alive a moribund credulity?   Yes, and the pressure still
on the New England mind of English sermon and trac-
tate—notably of that Cambridge school whose loyalty
to the witch theory is so well known; has not Mr. Mull-
inger just shown us that to Joseph Mede Cotton Mather
owed even his conviction that the New World had become the special dwelling-place of the Satanic powers,
now driven from the Old by the advance of Christianity?[46]   Above all, I should have liked to inquire
with you into the rôle played by religious party, and by

and applies the Mosaic "Thou shalt not suffer a witch to live" (Exod. xxii, 18): "Witchcraft is here forbidden, Deut. 18, 10 and that upon pain of death, 1 Sam. 28, 9. By *Witch*
is here meant any one that hath any dealings with the Devil, by any compact or confederacy whatsoever. . . Some have thought Witches should not dye, unlesse they had
taken away the life of mankind; but they are mistaken, both for the art of the Witch,
and for the guilt. . . . But why then must the Witch be put to death? *Answ.* Because
of the league and confederacy with the Devill, which is high treason against God; because
he is God's Chiefest enemy, and therefore though no hurt insue this contract at all,
the Witch deserves present and certain death for the contract it self." This commentary
was, it is true, not officially undertaken or revised by the Assembly; but its authors were
chosen by a committee of Parliament from among the Assembly's leading divines (with
but two or three additions from outside) and shared from the first the Assembly's prestige. Nor may it be forgotten that just three years before, in 1642, the great Assembly
of the Kirk of Scotland (whose leaders now sat as its deputies with the Westminster
Assembly) had used its new-won liberty to pass the "Act for the restraining of witchcraft" which revived the persecution in that land; nor yet that these were years when the
Scottish influence was at its height and the Scottish alliance most essential to the Puritan
cause. I must add that my transcript is made from the second edition of the commentary (1651), the first not being within my reach; but the words, if changed, are not likely
to have been made harsher.

    [46] In vol. iii, just published, of his *History of the University of Cambridge.*

its complications, political and social, in New England as in Old. Alas, for this as for so much else, I have discovered how unripe are my studies. If by something of thoroughness where I was best informed I have but shown you that the ascription of an especial responsibility to Calvinism and the Puritans is more than a loose assertion, I am content. But let it again be clearly understood that what I ascribe to the Calvinists, on either side of the sea, is only a leadership and a growing party support—an especial advocacy of the guilt of witchcraft as sin and of the duty of the Christian state to detect and punish sin.

And now for a few paragraphs, without attempt at proof or illustration, and only to give a setting to my thought, let me glance at what is left. I have discussed how the Calvinists believed in witchcraft. But, in the seventeenth century, did not everybody believe in witchcraft, at least everybody except a few of the learned? Again I must dissent, and even more earnestly. The seventeenth century saw vast change as to belief in witchcraft; yet in its darkest day—and the early seventeenth century was confessedly the age of greatest persecution—I do not believe that true. But here again we must discriminate. In *what* witchcraft did everybody believe? Dr. Buckley says—and he has given the matter study—that witchcraft is still believed in by a majority of the citizens of the United States. A month or two ago Mr. Addington Bruce, in the *Outlook*, illustrated the persistence of superstition by studying its survival in the professors at Harvard. Doubtless by a sufficient attenuation of the term the superstitions of the professors of Harvard might be included under witchcraft. Yet I doubt if Mr. Bruce or Dr. Buckley would count the professors of Harvard, or even the majority of the citizens of the United States, on the same side of the question as those who in the seventeenth century put women to death for their league with the Devil. When I hear enumerated among believers in witchcraft the free-thinking Bacon or the incredulous

Hobbes, I confess to the same hesitation. In Bacon's utterances I can find only a cautious skepticism, very thinly veiled. If Hobbes conceded that a witch should be punished, but only for her belief and intent to do mischief, he stopped far short of the Calvinists and of the statute of James, and, by making it necessary to prove against a witch, if not an actual mischief, at least an actual belief and intent, made her conviction almost impossible without the aid of torture. And, as for John Selden, his famous dictum that "if one should profess that by turning the Hat thrice, and crying Buz, he could take away a man's life," it "were a just law . . . that whosoever should turn his Hat thrice, and cry Buz, with an intention to take away a man's life, shall be put to death," was but the formulation of a principle long current in Christian jurisprudence and, however Draconian, would in England have convicted few witches. And, if either Hobbes or Selden thought that witches could thus be convicted, this was not to believe in witchcraft, but only to believe that witches believed in witchcraft—a very different matter.

What was true in the seventeenth century was not less true in the sixteenth. Nay, though to some this may bring surprise, skepticism shows itself more, not less, as one goes back toward its beginning. For—and my own study but confirms the results of other students —the truth is that skepticism had never died. The dogma as to witchcraft was a new one, and the Dominicans had had an up-hill fight to bring it in. In the early years of the sixteenth century it looked much as if they might lose that fight. Over nothing did the all-popular Humanists make more merry than over the credulity and blood-thirstiness of the monkish witch-burners. Agrippa was only the boldest of the group. If then for a time the open protests were hushed, the explanation is simple. The Church had spoken. The Lutheran revolt had discredited Humanism and she fell back on the Dominicans. The Protestant orthodoxies, also a reaction against Humanism, soon also spoke. But doubt was only silenced, not convinced. The Church spoke because skepticism was rampant; and so did the Protestant orthodoxies. Even Calvin, in whose hearing, if anywhere, doubt would have been dumb, tells us of "the notion which some conceited persons entertain that all these things are fabulous and absurd"; and there is not one of the many defenders of the superstition who does not complain of the numbers, the eminence, and the influence of these doubters.

In England, as we have seen, the persecution was slow in asserting itself, and I believe that there, from the first, the doubters were especially numerous. I am not ready to attempt to point them out, nor should I here take space. In Dr. Notestein's book they may be met at every turn; yet by no means all of them, for his gaze has been fixed mainly otherwhere. If any seeker has failed to find them, I fear it is because he has not looked in the right places. Bear with me and I will suggest a few cautions which I should blush to formulate, were they not so often overlooked.

In the first place, I should not look chiefly among the theologians, or even among the jurists. Theirs are the most conservative of professions—each in the field of its own training—and each profession was early committed to a definite doctrine on this subject. If I did look among these, it should not be first at those who have written comprehensive treatises. These are the men of systems. They are the men of soundness. Were they not so, they would hardly have written treatises, or, if they wrote treatises, would not easily have found a publisher. And if among these I did find doubters— and even among them doubters may be found—I should guess that others had led the way. Again—and I trust I may be pardoned this treason to my cloth—I should not look first among teachers, university or other. They are men of books, not of life; and they were more so then than now. They are often doctrinaires; and this question was one for common sense. Too often they too have a position to keep, an orthodoxy to main-

tain. In the sixteenth and the seventeenth century
they were even sworn to that orthodoxy. I would not
look at all among the gossips or the journalists. It was
their business to find stories and to tell them. They
have furnished us much of what we call history; but we
take them much more seriously than did their neighbors.

I would look among the men of practical affairs, the
men in touch with people and with facts; men of business,
men of society, men of politics, men of travel, physicians,
pastors. Yet, even among these, I should not listen
first to those who talk—whether in books or outside
them. Ah, we who fancy ourselves the world's thinkers
because we have fallen upon the knack or the habit of
being its talkers, how do we forget the long pedigree
of common sense!

And, wherever one looks, one must not look for a denial, in so many words, of "the reality of witchcraft."
That would be absurd. Nobody denies that now, however, we have grown used to the careless phrase. All that
anybody denies is the reality of what somebody else
calls witchcraft. Just so it was in that old day; only
the word had to be dealt with more cautiously. Whoever
accepted the authority of the Bible—and who then ventured to question it?—must, of course, have in his mind
a notion of something which deserved the name of witchcraft (or, at least, the Hebrew and Greek names he found
translated by witchcraft) and which—once if not now
—deserved death as its penalty. Of course, to that
extent all Christians believed in witchcraft. It did not
at all follow that they believed witches those whom their
neighbors called so, or believed real what their neighbors
laid to their charge. That was what signified—to them
and us. Even if they did not believe, it did not follow
that they must deny. Sensible men are not given to
denial of what they cannot disprove, but only to doubt
or to suspension of judgment. Nor let us expect that
doubt to be always uttered. Utterance is not the only
way—not always the best—for doubt to be effective,
or for doubt to leave its trace in history. And when

the doubter spoke, it must not mislead if he was not
extreme.   The tactful reasoner does not claim too much,
and they who doubt are oftenest men of caution, to whom
assertion is repugnant.   If he will win to mercy, he may
even make display of sternness on all points except that
which is cardinal—just as, on the other hand, we often
find the harshest making most parade of moderation.
Such rhetorical devices do not deceive us as to our
contemporaries, but they have led historians to some
wild judgments.

Nor need the doubter much indulge in labored logic.
As for "these proofs and arguments," so wrote in 1588
Montaigne, the arch-doubter, of what were urged on
him as proofs of witchcraft, "I do not pretend to unravel
them.   I often cut them, as Alexander did the knot.
After all, it is rating our opinions·high to roast other
people alive for them."   When a Montaigne could
count it prudent to write thus, how long must he and other
level-headed folk have found it wise to act thus?   Can
anybody really suspect Michel de Montaigne of being a
pioneer?   Everybody knows the *mot* of Shaftesbury
when after the Restoration he was asked his religion:
"Madam, wise men are of but one religion."   "And
which is that?"   "Madam, wise men never tell."   It
was often safer in the seventeenth century to tell one's
religion than one's honest opinion of witchcraft.

But such as these, it may be answered, as of Scot and
Webster, were not "scientific rationalists."   I am not
sure that I understand the term.   Universal doubters
they certainly were not.   Such are few to-day—and it
is perhaps as well.   Men who used in their own century
the science of the next they, of course, were not; history
will find none in our day.   But if it be scientific rationalism to trust one's human intellect, one's human heart,
against the dicta of authority in such things as one's
human faculties can test, those old days had many
worthy of the name.

Nor do such doubters as to witchcraft seem to me
mere isolated men of sense.   Largely they can be grouped

under certain great lines of thought. The great Erasmian trend, the heir of Humanism, holding its place between Romanist and Protestant to the century's end, and nowhere more potently than in England; the great lay trend, out of which grew the separatist sects, and, what was more, a growing body of independents or eclectics who trimmed between the faiths or blurred their edges; the great Latitudinarian trend, born of the reaction against Calvinist harshness and spreading with Arminianism to England from that day when John Hales, the ever memorable, listening at the Synod of Dort as England's observer, "bade John Calvin good-night"; the great "natural" movement, which at the hands of jurists and philosophers held so large a place in seventeenth-century thought; the great, albeit so patient, movement of experimental science, of which not Bacon but Harvey was the best English representative: it is along such lines as these that doubt and protest seem to me to cluster. Even the Cambridge Platonists, whose belated credulity has been to some so puzzling, fall into line when one discerns how largely this credulity was but the premise of a philosophic creed. Exceptions of course there were in every group—else might we forget that such groups are only bodies of free men bound by a common purpose.[47] And let not this attempt to classify obscure my conviction that, whatever the pressure of education or environment, there was always room for character, too, to echo or protest.

It will be urged, however, that these doubters were, after all, but a minority. What the majority, counted by the head, may have believed, I do not know. I do not know how to find out. Doubtless those who believed

---

[47] Such an exception among Anglicans was Edward Fairfax, "I intreat you to be assured," he says to his readers, "that for myself I am in religion neither a fantastic Puritan nor superstitious Papist." But his own words suggest that he fears his zeal against those whom he accuses of bewitching his children may stamp him as a Papist or a Puritan; and his complaints of the incredulity of the magistrates, low and high, and of the "divines and physicians" "who attribute too much to natural causes," with his lament that the witches, when examined, "wanted not both counsellors and supporters of the best," show his consciousness of isolation. (See his *Discourse on Witchcraft*, ed. Grainge, Harrogate, 1882—pp. 32, 36, and *passim*.)

made the most noise. I suspect that, counted by the head, the majority was, as usual, on the side of the latest speaker—and most of the speakers were against the witches. Probably it believed in the church and doubted on the street. If "belief" means to believe *something* as to witches, everybody believed; if it means to believe *everything*, everybody doubted. Doubtless there were as many different shades as to belief as there were souls; and, as there was no vote to be given, doubtless few found it necessary to take careful measure of their own opinions.

But what has all this to do with New England? I am sadly aware how little my paper has justified its title. Yet all I have urged has had New England as its goal. It was only a running start I meant to take, and, though I have reached the jumping-off place before I am ready, I am going to make the jump. I cannot acquit our ancestors on the ground that their belief in witchcraft was universal or was not discreditable or was more logical than disbelief. On the contrary I am forced to admit that it was superstitious and bigoted and cruel, even by the standards of their own time; that they clung to it when it was dying out in all but the most belated parts of Christendom; that, though in a few sequestered regions, the trials dribbled on yet for a century, their final panic was the last on such a scale in any Christian land.[48] Their transatlantic home I cannot think an excuse. New homes have always made new men, and no new home has more proved its emancipating power than has America. Its very discovery set men dreaming of freedom. Here Thomas More placed that No Man's Land where all old fetters, social and religious, were unknown. Here the more practical dreamers planted their colonies for the working out of every fresh experiment in human living. Hither came the men who had broken, or were eager to break, the bonds of prejudice and of convention; and four centuries have proved

---

[48] That the latest witch-hanging in England was in 1682, ten years before the Salem outbreak, and that the tales of later executions are but the work of literary shysters, is convincingly shown by Dr. Notestein (pp. 375–382).

the soundness of their hope. One thing is sure: we
must not blow hot and cold with the same breath. If
our fathers were the helpless victims of circumstance,
then they were not its masters. If they were the blame-
less heirs of superstition, then they were not

> "men of present valor, stalwart old iconoclasts,
> Unconvinced by axe or gibbet that all virtue is the past's."

For my part, I cannot plead for them the baby act.
Mitigating elements I can see. If they *must* follow
Old-World fashions, they must be content, of course,
to get them last and keep them latest. If they *could*
believe such crimes of their neighbors, they were at least
men who met them by action. If that action was cruel,
it was but the carrying out, in spirit and letter, of a law
which, within the limits of conscience, they doubtless
counted themselves bound to enforce. I am not asking
you to think them worse than the neighbors who shrank
into the background and took sides for neither justice
nor mercy, belief nor doubt. I am far from arguing
that, take them all in all, they were worse men than they
who bravely stood against them. Their opponents,
too, had doubtless the faults of their own qualities.
But, if this be to acquit them, they would themselves
have scorned the subterfuge. They were disciples of
Him whose message was "Be ye perfect," ancestors of
him who bids us hitch our wagon to a star. When the
light at length dawned on them, not their stubborn
pride, not their fierce convictions, not their predestin-
arian theology, could make them seek excuse in good intentions, in circumstances, or in providence. Confessing
"I have sinned," they made amends as best they could;
and therefore in New England, as nowhere else within
my knowledge, the matter ended—and for good and all.
From that day till this no corner of the earth has been
so free from cruel superstitions.

Ah, "till this." The horizon is by no means free from
clouds. Though the name of "belief in witchcraft"
is now in disrepute, I am not so sure as is Professor

Kittredge as to the superstition and the cruelty for which it stood. That old witch-mania was no survival of the Middle Ages. It was born and came to its prime in centuries which saw the greatest burst of Christian civilization. If I would have History unflinching, it is not because I think we are better than our fathers. It is because deep in ourselves I feel still stirring the impulses which led to their mistakes. It is because I fear that they who begin by excusing their ancestors may end by excusing themselves. May History do so unto us and more also if through blindness tb their failings we repeat their faults.

Underlying Themes in the Witchcraft of Seventeenth-Century New England

John Demos

IT is faintly embarrassing for a historian to summon his colleagues to still another consideration of early New England witchcraft. Here, surely, is a topic that previous generations of writers have sufficiently worked, indeed overworked. Samuel Eliot Morison once commented that the Salem witch-hunt was, after all, "but a small incident in the history of a great superstition"; and Perry Miller noted that with only minor qualifications "the intellectual history of New England can be written as though no such thing ever happened. It had no effect on the ecclesiastical or political situation, it does not figure in the institutional or ideological development."[1] Popular interest in the subject is, then, badly out of proportion to its actual historical significance, and perhaps the sane course for the future would be silence.

This assessment seems, on the face of it, eminently sound. Witchcraft was not an important matter from the standpoint of the larger historical process; it exerted only limited influence on the unfolding sequence of events in colonial New England. Moreover, the literature on the subject seems to have reached a point of diminishing returns. Details of fact have been endlessly canvassed, and the main outlines of the story, particularly the story of Salem, are well and widely known.

There is, to be sure, continuing debate over one set of issues: the roles played by the persons most directly involved. Indeed the historiography of Salem can be viewed, in large measure, as an unending effort to judge the participants—and, above all, to affix blame. A number of verdicts have been fashionable at one time or another. Thus the ministers were really at fault; or Cotton Mather in particular; or the whole culture of Puritanism; or the core group of "afflicted girls" (if their "fits" are construed as conscious fraud).[2] The most recent, and in some ways most so-

▶ *Mr. Demos, whose major field of interest is American social history, is author of* A Little Commonwealth: Family Life in Plymouth Colony *(New York, 1970). He studied with Oscar Handlin and Bernard Bailyn at Harvard and is currently associate professor of history at Brandeis University. An earlier version of this paper was presented at a meeting of the Organization of American Historians in April 1967. The author is grateful to the following for comments and criticism: Robert Middlekauff, Mary Maples Dunn, Robert I. Rotberg, Raphael Demos, Dorothy Lee, Robert A. LeVine, the members of the Group for Applied Psychoanalysis, and, most especially, David Hackett Fischer and Virginia Demos.*

[1] S. E. Morison, *The Intellectual Life of Colonial New England* (Ithaca, 1956), 264; Perry Miller, *The New England Mind: From Colony to Province* (Boston, 1961), 191.

[2] Examples of these varying interpretations may be found in Charles W. Upham, *Salem Witchcraft* (Boston, 1867); Winfield S. Nevins, *Witchcraft in Salem Village* (Salem, 1916); John Fiske, *New*

phisticated, study of the Salem trials plunges right into the middle of the same controversy; the result is yet another conclusion. Not the girls, not the clergy, not Puritanism, but the accused witches themselves are now the chief culprits. For "witchraft actually did exist and was widely · practiced in seventeenth-century New England"; and women like Goody Glover, Bridget Bishop, and Mammy Redd were "in all probability" guilty as charged.[3]

Clearly these questions of personal credit and blame can still generate lively interest, but are they the most fruitful, the most important questions to raise about witchcraft? Will such a debate ever be finally settled? Are its partisan terms and moral tone appropriate to historical scholarship?

The situation is not hopeless if only we are willing to look beyond the limits of our own discipline. There is, in particular, a substantial body of interesting and relevant work by anthropologists. Many recent studies of primitive societies contain chapters about witchcraft, and there are several entire monographs on the subject.[4] The approach they follow differs strikingly from anything in the historical literature. Broadly speaking, the anthropological work is far more analytic, striving always to use materials on witchcraft as a set of clues or "symptoms." The subject is important not in its own right but as a means of exploring certain larger questions about the society. For example, witchcraft throws light on social structure, on the organization of families, and on the inner dynamics of personality. The substance of such investigations, of course, varies greatly from one culture to another, but the framework, the informing purposes are roughly the same. To apply this framework and these purposes to historical materials is not inherently difficult. The data may be inadequate in a given case, but the analytic categories themselves are designed for any society, whether simple or complex, Western or non-Western, past or contemporary. Consider, by way of illustration, the strategy proposed for the main body of this essay.

Our discussion will focus on a set of complex relationships between the alleged witches and their victims. The former group will include all persons accused of practicing witchcraft, and they will be called, simply, witches.[5] The category of victims will comprise everyone who claimed to have suffered from witchcraft,

---

France and New England (Boston and New York, 1902); W. F. Poole, "Witchcraft in Boston," in *The Memorial History of Boston,* ed. Justin Winsor (Boston, 1881); Marion L. Starkey, *The Devil in Massachusetts* (Boston, 1950); Morison, *Intellectual Life of Colonial New England,* 259 ff.

[3] Chadwick Hansen, *Witchcraft at Salem* (New York, 1969). See especially x, 22 ff., 64 ff., 226–67.

[4] Those I have found particularly helpful in developing my own approach toward New England witchcraft are the following: Clyde Kluckhohn, *Navajo Witchcraft* (Boston, 1967); E. E. Evans-Pritchard, *Witchcraft, Oracles, and Magic Among the Azande* (Oxford, 1937); M. G. Marwick, *Sorcery in its Social Setting* (Manchester, 1965); *Witchcraft and Sorcery in East Africa,* ed. John Middleton and E. H. Winter (London, 1963); Beatrice B. Whiting, *Paiute Sorcery* (New York, 1950).

[5] This usage is purely a matter of convenience, and is not meant to convey any judgment as to whether such people actually tried to perform acts of witchcraft. Chadwick Hansen claims to show, from trial records, which of the accused women were indeed "guilty"; but in my opinion his argument is not convincing. The testimony that "proves" guilt in one instance seems quite similar to other testimony brought against women whom Hansen regards as innocent. There may indeed have been "practicing witches" in colonial New England, but the surviving evidence does not decide the issue one way or another.

and they will be divided into two categories to account for an important distinction between different kinds of victims. As every schoolchild knows, some victims experienced fits—bizarre seizures that, in the language of modern psychiatry, closely approximate the clinical picture of hysteria. These people may be called accusers, since their sufferings and their accusations seem to have carried the greatest weight in generating formal proceedings against witches. A second, much larger group of victims includes people who attributed to witchcraft some particular misfortune they had suffered, most typically an injury or illness, the sudden death of domestic animals, the loss of personal property, or repeated failure in important day-to-day activities like farming, fishing, and hunting. This type of evidence was of secondary importance in trials of witches and was usually brought forward after the accusers had pressed their own more damaging charges. For people testifying to such experiences, therefore, the shorthand term witnesses seems reasonably appropriate.

Who were these witches, accusers, and witnesses? How did their lives intersect? Most important, what traits were generally characteristic and what traits were alleged to have been characteristic of each group? These will be the organizing questions in the pages that follow. Answers to these questions will treat both external (or objective) circumstances and internal (or subjective) experiences. In the case of witches, for example, it is important to try to discover their age, marital status, socioeconomic position, and visible personality traits. But it is equally important to examine the characteristics attributed to witches by others—flying about at night, transforming themselves into animals, and the like. In short, one can construct a picture of witches in fact and in fantasy; and comparable efforts can be made with accusers and witnesses. Analysis directed to the level of external reality helps to locate certain points of tension or conflict in the social structure of a community. The fantasy picture, on the other hand, reveals more directly the psychological dimension of life, the inner preoccupations, anxieties, and conflicts of individual members of that community.

Such an outline looks deceptively simple, but in fact it demands an unusual degree of caution, from writer and reader alike. The approach is explicitly cross-disciplinary, reaching out to anthropology for strategy and to psychology for theory. There is, of course, nothing new about the idea of a working relationship between history and the behavioral sciences. It is more than ten years since William Langer's famous summons to his colleagues to consider this their "next assignment";[6] but the record of actual output is still very meager. All such efforts remain quite experimental; they are designed more to stimulate discussion than to prove a definitive case.

There is a final point—about context and the larger purposes of this form of inquiry. Historians have traditionally worked with purposeful, conscious events,

---

[6] William L. Langer, "The Next Assignment" (*AHR*, LXIII [Jan. 1958], 283–304), in *Psychoanalysis and History*, ed. Bruce Mazlish (Englewood Cliffs, N. J., 1963).

"restricting themselves," in Langer's words, "to recorded fact and to strictly rational motivation."[7] They have not necessarily wished to exclude non-rational or irrational behavior, but for the most part they have done so. Surely in our own post-Freudian era there is both need and opportunity to develop a more balanced picture. It is to these long-range ends that further study of witchcraft should be dedicated. For witchcraft is, if nothing else, an open window on the irrational.

The first witchcraft trial of which any record survives occurred at Windsor, Connecticut, in 1647,[8] and during the remainder of the century the total of cases came to nearly one hundred. Thirty-eight people were executed as witches, and a few more, though convicted, managed somehow to escape the death penalty. There were, of course, other outcomes as well: full-dress trials resulting in acquittal, hung juries, convictions reversed on appeal, and "complaints" filed but not followed up. Finally, no doubt, many unrecorded episodes touching on witchcraft, episodes of private suspicion or public gossip, never eventuated in legal action at all.[9]

This long series of witchcraft cases needs emphasis lest the Salem outbreak completely dominate our field of vision. Salem differed radically from previous episodes in sheer scope; it developed a degree of self-reinforcing momentum present in no other instance. But it was very similar in many qualitative aspects: the types of people concerned, the nature of the charges, the fits, and so forth. Indeed, from an analytic standpoint, all these cases can be regarded as roughly equivalent and interchangeable. They are pieces of a single, larger phenomenon, a system of witchcraft belief that was generally prevalent in early New England. The evidence for such a system must, of course, be drawn from a variety of cases to produce representative conclusions. For most questions this is quite feasible; there is more evidence, from a greater range of cases, than can ever be presented in a single study.

Yet in one particular matter the advantages of concentrating on Salem are overwhelming. It affords a unique opportunity to portray the demography of witchcraft, to establish a kind of profile for each of the three basic categories of people involved in witchcraft, in terms of sex, age, and marital status. Thus the statistical tables that follow are drawn entirely from detailed work on the Salem materials.[10] The earlier cases do not yield the breadth of data necessary for this type of quantitative investigation. They do, however, provide many fragments of evidence that are generally consistent with the Salem picture.

There is at least minimal information about 165 people accused as witches during the entire period of the Salem outbreak.[11]

[7] *Ibid.*, 90.

[8] See John M. Taylor, *The Witchcraft Delusion in Colonial Connecticut* (New York, 1908), 145 ff.

[9] Some of these episodes are mentioned, in passing, among the records of witchcraft cases that came before the court. See, for example, the references to Besse Sewall and the widow Marshfield, in the depositions of the Parsons case, published in Samuel G. Drake, *Annals of Witchcraft in New England* (Boston, 1869), 218–57. It is clear, too, that many convicted witches had been the objects of widespread suspicion and gossip for years before they were brought to trial.

[10] These findings are based largely on materials in the vital records of Salem and the surrounding towns.

[11] In some cases the information is not complete—hence the variation in the size of sample among the different tables. Still the total for each table is large enough to lend overall credence to the results.

Sex	Total
Male	42
Female	120
Total	162

Marital Status	Male	Female	Total
Single	8	29	37
Married	15	61	76
Widowed	1	20	21
Total	24	110	134

Age	Male	Female	Total
Under 20	6	18	24
21–30	3	7	10
31–40	3	8	11
41–50	6	18	24
51–60	5	23	28
61–70	4	8	12
Over 70	3	6	9
Total	30	88	118

These figures point to an important general conclusion: the witches were predominantly married or widowed women, between the ages of forty-one and sixty. While the exceptions add up to a considerable number, most of them belonged to the families of middle-aged, female witches. Virtually all the young persons in the group can be identified as children of witches and most of the men as husbands of witches. In fact this pattern conformed to an assumption then widely prevalent, that the transmission of witchcraft would naturally follow the lines of family or of close friendship. An official statement from the government of Connecticut included among the "grounds for Examination of a Witch" the following:

if ye party suspected be ye son or daughter the servt or familiar friend; neer Neighbor or old Companion of a Knowne or Convicted witch this alsoe a presumton for witchcraft is an art yt may be learned & Convayd from man to man & oft it falleth out yt a witch dying leaveth som of ye aforesd. heirs of her witchcraft.[12]

In short, young witches and male witches belonged to a kind of derivative category. They were not the prime targets in these situations; they were, in a literal sense, rendered suspect by association. The deepest suspicions, the most intense anxieties, remained fixed on middle-aged women.

Thirty-four persons experienced fits of one sort or another during the Salem trials and qualify thereby as accusers.

Sex	Total
Male	5
Female	29
Total	34

Marital Status	Male	Female	Total
Single	5	23	28
Married	0	6	6
Widowed	0	0	0
Total	5	29	34

Age	Male	Female	Total
Under 11	0	1	1
11–15	1	7	8
16–20	1	13	14
21–25	0	1	1
26–30	0	1	1
Over 30	0	4	4
Total	2	27	29

Here again the sample shows a powerful cluster. The vast majority of the accusers were single girls between the ages of eleven and twenty. The exceptions in this case (two boys, three males of undetermined age, and four adult women) are rather difficult to explain, for there is little evidence about any of them. By and large, however, they played only a minor role in the trials. Perhaps the matter can

[12] An early copy of this statement (undated) is in the Ann Mary Brown Memorial Collection, Brown University.

be left this way: the core group of accusers was entirely composed of adolescent girls, but the inner conflicts so manifest in their fits found an echo in at least a few persons of other ages or of the opposite sex.

Eighty-four persons came forward as witnesses at one time or another during the Salem trials.

Sex	Total		Marital Status	Male	Female	Total		Age	Male	Female	Total
Male	63		Single	11	3	14		Under 20	3	2	5
Female	21		Married	39	16	55		21–30	13	4	17
			Widowed	3	1	4		31–40	14	6	20
Total	84							41–50	18	7	25
			Total	53	20	73		51–60	11	1	12
								61–70	2	1	3
								Over 70	2	0	2
								Total	63	21	84

Here the results seem relatively inconclusive. Three-fourths of the witnesses were men, but a close examination of the trial records suggests a simple reason for this: men were more likely, in seventeenth-century New England, to take an active part in legal proceedings of any type. When a husband and wife were victimized together by some sort of witchcraft, it was the former who would normally come forward to testify. As to the ages of the witnesses, there is a fairly broad distribution between twenty and sixty years. Probably, then, this category reflects the generalized belief in witchcraft among all elements of the community in a way that makes it qualitatively different from the groupings of witches and accusers.

There is much more to ask about external realities in the lives of such people, particularly with regard to their social and economic position. Unfortunately, however, the evidence is somewhat limited here and permits only a few impressionistic observations. It seems that many witches came from the lower levels of the social structure, but there were too many exceptions to see in this a really significant pattern. The first three accused at Salem were Tituba, a Negro slave, Sarah Good, the wife of a poor laborer, and Sarah Osbourne, who possessed a very considerable estate.[13] Elizabeth Godman, tried at New Haven in 1653, seems to have been poor and perhaps a beggar;[14] but Nathaniel and Rebecca Greensmith, who were convicted and executed at Hartford eight years later, were quite well-to-do;[15] and

[13] The proceedings against these three defendants are included in the typescript volumes, *Salem Witchcraft, 1692*, compiled from the original records by the Works Progress Administration in 1938. These volumes—an absolutely invaluable source—are on file in the Essex County Courthouse, Salem.

[14] See *Records of the Colony of New Haven*, ed. C. J. Hoadly (Hartford, 1858), II, 29–36, 151–52, and *New Haven Town Records 1649–1662*, ed. Franklin B. Dexter (New Haven, 1917), I, 249–52, 256–57.

[15] Some original records from this trial are in the Willys Papers, Connecticut State Library, Hartford. For good short accounts see Increase Mather, *An Essay for the Recording of Illustrious Providences*, in *Narratives of the Witchcraft Cases*, ed. G. L. Burr (New York, 1914), 18–21, and a letter from John Whiting to Increase Mather, Dec. 10, 1682, entitled "An account of a Remarkable passage of Divine providence that happened in Hartford, in the yeare of our Lord 1662," in *Massachusetts Historical Society Collections*, 4th Ser., VIII (Boston, 1868), 466–69.

"Mistress" Ann Hibbens, executed at Boston in 1656, was the widow of a wealthy merchant and former magistrate of the Bay Colony.[16]

What appears to have been common to nearly all these people, irrespective of their economic position, was some kind of personal eccentricity, some deviant or even criminal behavior that had long since marked them out as suspect. Some of them had previously been tried for theft or battery or slander;[17] others were known for their interest in dubious activities like fortunetelling or certain kinds of folk-healing.[18] The "witch Glover" of Boston, on whom Cotton Mather reports at some length, was Irish and Catholic, and spoke Gaelic; and a Dutch family in Hartford came under suspicion at the time the Greensmiths were tried.[19]

More generally, many of the accused seem to have been unusually irascible and contentious in their personal relations. Years before her conviction for witchcraft Mrs. Hibbens had obtained a reputation for "natural crabbedness of . . . temper"; indeed she had been excommunicated by the Boston church in 1640, following a long and acrimonious ecclesiastical trial. William Hubbard, whose *General History of New England* was published in 1680, cited her case to make the general point that "persons of hard favor and turbulent passions are apt to be condemned by the common people as witches, upon very slight grounds." In the trial of Mercy Desborough, at Fairfield, Connecticut, in 1692, the court received numerous reports of her quarrelsome behavior. She had, for example, told one neighbor "yt shee would make him bare as a bird's tale," and to another she had repeatedly said "many hard words." Goodwife Clawson, tried at the same time, was confronted with testimony like the following:

Abigail Wescot saith that as shee was going along the street goody Clasen came out to her and they had some words together and goody Clason took up stones and threw at her: and at another time as shee went along the street before sd Clasons dore goody Clason caled to mee and asked mee what was in my Chamber last Sabbath day night; and I doe afirme that I was not there that night: and at another time as I was in her sone Steephens house being neere her one hous shee folowed me in and contended with me becase I did not com into her hous caling of me proud slut what—are you

---

[16] See *Records of Massachusetts Bay*, ed. Nathaniel B. Shirtleff, IV, Pt. I (Boston, 1854), 269; William Hubbard, *A General History of New England* (Boston, 1848), 574; Thomas Hutchinson, *The History of the Colony and Province of Massachusetts Bay*, ed. Lawrence S. Mayo (Cambridge, Mass., 1936), I, 160–61.

[17] For example, Giles Corey, executed as one of the Salem witches, had been before the courts several times, charged with such offenses as theft and battery. Mary Parsons of Springfield was convicted of slander not long before her trial for witchcraft.

[18] For example, Katherine Harrison, prosecuted for witchcraft at Weathersfield, Connecticut, in 1668, was reported to have been given to fortunetelling; and a group of ministers called to advise the court in her case contended that such activity did "argue familiarity with the Devil." See John M. Taylor, *The Witchcraft Delusion in Colonial Connecticut* (New York, 1908), 56–58. Evidence of the same kind was offered against Samuel Wardwell of Andover, Massachusetts, in 1692. See the proceedings in his case in the typescript volumes by the Works Progress Administration, *Salem Witchcraft, 1692*, in the Essex County Courthouse, Salem. Margaret Jones, convicted and executed at Boston in 1648, was involved in "practising physic." See Winthrop's *Journal*, ed. J. K. Hosmer (New York, 1908), II, 344–45. Elizabeth Morse, prosecuted at Newbury, Massachusetts, in 1679, was alleged to have possessed certain occult powers to heal the sick. See the depositions published in Drake, *Annals of Witchcraft*, 258–96.

[19] Cotton Mather, *Memorable Providences, Relating to Witchcraft and Possessions, in Narratives*, ed. Burr, 103–06; Increase Mather, *An Essay* etc., 18.

proud of your fine cloths and you love to be mistres but you neuer shal be and several other provoking speeches.[20]

The case of Mary and Hugh Parsons, tried at Springfield in 1651, affords a further look at the external aspects of our subject. A tax rating taken at Springfield in 1646 records the landholdings of most of the principals in the witchcraft prosecutions of five years later. When the list is arranged according to wealth, Parsons falls near the middle (twenty-fourth out of forty-two), and those who testified against him come from the top, middle, and bottom. This outcome tends to confirm the general point that economic position is not, for present purposes, a significant datum. What seems, on the basis of the actual testimonies at the trial, to have been much more important was the whole dimension of eccentric and anti-social behavior. Mary Parsons, who succumbed repeatedly to periods of massive depression, was very nearly insane. During the witchcraft investigations she began by testifying against her husband and ended by convicting herself of the murder of their infant child. Hugh Parsons was a sawyer and brickmaker by trade, and there are indications that in performing these services he was sometimes suspected of charging extortionate rates.[21] But what may have weighed most heavily against him was his propensity for prolonged and bitter quarreling; many examples of his "threatening speeches" were reported in court.

One other aspect of this particular episode is worth noting, namely, the apparent influence of spatial proximity. When the names of Parsons and his "victims" are checked against a map of Springfield in this period, it becomes very clear that the latter were mostly his nearest neighbors. In fact nearly all of the people who took direct part in the trial came from the southern half of the town. No other witchcraft episode yields such a detailed picture in this respect, but many separate pieces of evidence suggest that neighborhood antagonism was usually an aggravating factor.[22]

We can summarize the major characteristics of the external side of New England witchcraft as follows: First, the witches themselves were chiefly women of middle age whose accusers were girls about one full generation younger. This may reflect the kind of situation that anthropologists would call a structural conflict—that is, some focus of tension created by the specific ways in which a community arranges the lives of its members. In a broad sense it is quite probable that adolescent girls in early New England were particularly subject to the con-

[20] Hutchinson, *History of the Colony and Province of Massachusetts Bay,* I, 160; Hubbard, 574. There is a verbatim account of the church proceedings against Mrs. Hibbens in the journal of Robert Keayne, in the Massachusetts Historical Society, Boston. I am grateful to Anita Rutman for lending me her transcription of this nearly illegible document. Manuscript deposition, trial of Mercy Desborough, Willys Papers; manuscript deposition, trial of Elizabeth Clawson, Willys Papers.

[21] The tax list is published in Henry Burt, *The First Century of the History of Springfield* (Springfield, Mass., 1898), I, 190–91; a long set of depositions from the Parsons case is published in Drake, *Annals of Witchcraft,* 219–56; see also 224, 228, 242. Mary Parsons herself offered some testimony reflecting her husband's inordinate desire "for Luker and Gaine."

[22] See Burt, *First Century of the History of Springfield,* I, for just such a map; see Increase Mather, *An Essay* etc., 18 ff., on the case of the Greensmiths. Also Richard Chamberlain, *Lithobolia,* in *Narratives,* ed. Burr, 61, on the case of Hannah Jones at Great Island, New Hampshire, in 1682.

trol of older women, and this may well have given rise to a powerful underlying resentment. By contrast, the situation must have been less difficult for boys, since their work often took them out of the household and their behavior generally was less restricted.

There are, moreover, direct intimations of generational conflict in the witchcraft records themselves. Consider a little speech by one of the afflicted girls during a fit, a speech meticulously recorded by Cotton Mather. The words are addressed to the "specter" of a witch, with whom the girl has been having a heated argument:

What's that? Must the younger Women, do yee say, hearken to the Elder?—They must be another Sort of Elder Women than You then! they must not bee Elder Witches, I am sure. Pray, do you for once Hearken to mee.—What a dreadful Sight are You! An Old Woman, an Old Servant of the Divel![23]

Second, it is notable that most witches were deviant persons—eccentric or conspicuously anti-social or both. This suggests very clearly the impact of belief in witchcraft as a form of control in the social ordering of New England communities. Here indeed is one of the most widely-found social functions of witchcraft; its importance has been documented for many societies all over the world.[24] Any individual who contemplates actions of which the community disapproves knows that if he performs such acts, he will become more vulnerable either to a direct attack by witches or to the charge that he is himself a witch. Such knowledge is a powerful inducement to self-constraint.

What can be said of the third basic conclusion, that witchcraft charges particularly involved neighbors? Very briefly, it must be fitted with other aspects of the social setting in these early New England communities. That there was a great deal of contentiousness among these people is suggested by innumerable court cases from the period dealing with disputes about land, lost cattle, trespass, debt, and so forth. Most men seem to have felt that the New World offered them a unique opportunity to increase their properties,[25] and this may have heightened competitive feelings and pressures. On the other hand, cooperation was still the norm in many areas of life, not only in local government but for a variety of agricultural tasks as well. In such ambivalent circumstances it is hardly surprising that relations between close neighbors were often tense or downright abrasive.

"In all the Witchcraft which now Grievously Vexes us, I know not whether any thing be more Unaccountable, than the Trick which the Witches have, to

---

[23] See Cotton Mather, *A Brand Pluck'd Out of the Burning*, in *Narratives*, ed. Burr, 270.

[24] See, for example, Whiting, *Paiute Sorcery*; Evans-Pritchard, *Witchcraft, Oracles, and Magic Among the Azande*, 117 ff.; and *Witchcraft and Sorcery in East Africa*, ed. Middleton and Winter.

[25] For material bearing on the growth of these acquisitive tendencies, see Philip J. Greven, Jr., "Old Patterns in the New World: The Distribution of Land in 17th Century Andover," *Essex Institute Historical Collections*, CI (April, 1965), 133–48; and John Demos, "Notes on Life in Plymouth Colony," *William and Mary Quarterly*, 3d Ser., XXII (Apr. 1965), 264–86. It is possible that the voluntary mechanism of colonization had selected unusually aggressive and competitive persons at the outset.

render themselves and their Tools Invisible."[26] Thus wrote Cotton Mather in 1692; and three centuries later it is still the "invisible" part of witchcraft that holds a special fascination. Time has greatly altered the language for such phenomena— "shapes" and "specters" have become "hallucinations"; "enchantments" are a form of "suggestion"; the Devil himself seems a fantasy—and there is a corresponding change of meanings. Yet here was something truly remarkable, a kind of irreducible core of the entire range of witchcraft phenomena. How much of it remains "unaccountable"? To ask the question is to face directly the other side of our subject: witchcraft viewed as psychic process, as a function of internal reality.

The biggest obstacles to the study of psycho-history ordinarily are practical ones involving severe limitations of historical data. Yet for witchcraft the situation is uniquely promising on these very grounds. Even a casual look at writings like Cotton Mather's *Memorable Providences* or Samuel Willard's *A briefe account* etc.[27] discloses material so rich in psychological detail as to be nearly the equivalent of clinical case reports. The court records on witchcraft are also remarkably full in this respect. The clergy, the judges, all the leaders whose positions carried special responsibility for combatting witchcraft, regarded publicity as a most important weapon. Witchcraft would yield to careful study and the written exchange of information. Both Mather and Willard received "afflicted girls" into their own homes and recorded "possession" behavior over long periods of time.

A wealth of evidence does not, of course, by itself win the case for a psychological approach to witchcraft. Further problems remain, problems of language and of validation.[28] There is, moreover, the very basic problem of selecting from among a variety of different theoretical models. Psychology is not a monolith, and every psycho-historian must declare a preference. In opting for psychoanalytic theory, for example, he performs, in part, an act of faith, faith that this theory provides deeper, fuller insights into human behavior than any other. In the long run the merit of such choices will probably be measured on pragmatic grounds. Does the interpretation explain materials that would otherwise remain unused? Is it consistent with evidence in related subject areas?

If, then, the proof lies in the doing, let us turn back to the New England witches and especially to their "Trick . . . to render themselves and their tools Invisible." What characterized these spectral witches? What qualities were attributed to them by the culture at large?

The most striking observation about witches is that they gave free rein to a whole gamut of hostile and aggressive feelings. In fact most witchcraft episodes

[26] Cotton Mather, *The Wonders of the Invisible World*, in *Narratives*, ed. Burr, 246.

[27] Cotton Mather, *Memorable Providences* etc., 93–143; Samuel Willard, *A briefe account of a strange & unusuall Providence of God befallen to Elizabeth Knap of Groton*, in Samuel A. Green, *Groton in the Witchcraft Times* (Groton, Mass., 1883), 7–21.

[28] The best group of essays dealing with such issues is *Psychoanalysis and History*, ed. Mazlish. See also the interesting statement in Alexander L. George and Juliette L. George, *Woodrow Wilson and Colonel House* (New York, 1964), v–xiv.

44

began after some sort of actual quarrel. The fits of Mercy Short followed an abusive encounter with the convicted witch Sarah Good. The witch Glover was thought to have attacked Martha Goodwin after an argument about some missing clothes.[29] Many such examples could be accumulated here, but the central message seems immediately obvious: never antagonize witches, for they will invariably strike back hard. Their compulsion to attack was, of course, most dramatically visible in the fits experienced by some of their victims. These fits were treated as tortures imposed directly and in every detail by witches or by the Devil himself. It is also significant that witches often assumed the shape of animals in order to carry out their attacks. Animals, presumably, are not subject to constraints of either an internal or external kind; their aggressive impulses are immediately translated into action.

Another important facet of the lives of witches was their activity in company with each other. In part this consisted of long and earnest conferences on plans to overthrow the kingdom of God and replace it with the reign of the Devil. Often, however, these meetings merged with feasts, the witches' main form of self-indulgence. Details are a bit thin here, but we know that the usual beverage was beer or wine (occasionally described as bearing a suspicious resemblance to blood), and the food was bread or meat. It is also worth noting what did not happen on these occasions. There were a few reports of dancing and "sport," but very little of the wild excitements associated with witch revels in continental Europe. Most striking of all is the absence of allusions to sex; there is no nakedness, no promiscuity, no obscene contact with the Devil. This seems to provide strong support for the general proposition that the psychological conflicts underlying the early New England belief in witchcraft had much more to do with aggressive impulses than with libidinal ones.

The persons who acted as accusers also merit the closest possible attention, for the descriptions of what they suffered in their fits are perhaps the most revealing of all source materials for present purposes. They experienced, in the first place, severe pressures to go over to the Devil's side themselves. Witches approached them again and again, mixing threats and bribes in an effort to break down their Christian loyalties. Elizabeth Knapp, bewitched at Groton, Massachusetts, in 1671, was alternately tortured and plied with offers of "money, silkes, fine cloaths, ease from labor"; in 1692 Ann Foster of Andover confessed to being won over by a general promise of "prosperity," and in the same year Andrew Carrier accepted the lure of "a house and land in Andover." The same pattern appears most vividly in Cotton Mather's record of another of Mercy Short's confrontations with a spectral witch:

"Fine promises!" she says, "You'l bestow an Husband upon mee, if I'l bee your Servant. An Husband! What? A Divel! I shall then bee finely fitted with an Husband:

---

[29] See Cotton Mather, *A Brand Pluck'd Out of the Burning,* 259–60, and *Memorable Providences* etc., 100.

. . . Fine Clothes! What? Such as Your Friend Sarah Good had, who hardly had Rags to cover her! . . . Never Dy! What? Is my Life in Your Hands? No, if it had, You had killed mee long before this Time!—What's that?—So you can!—Do it then, if You can. Come, I dare you: Here, I challenge You to do it. Kill mee if you can. . . ."[30]

Some of these promises attributed to the Devil touch the most basic human concerns (like death) and others reflect the special preoccupations (with future husbands, for example) of adolescent girls. All of them imply a kind of covetousness generally consistent with the pattern of neighborhood conflict and tension mentioned earlier.

But the fits express other themes more powerfully still, the vital problem of aggression being of central importance. The seizures themselves have the essential character of attacks: in one sense, physical attacks by the witches on the persons of the accusers and in another sense, verbal attacks by the accusers on the reputations and indeed the very lives of the witches. This points directly toward one of the most important inner processes involved in witchcraft, the process psychologists call "projection," defined roughly as "escape from repressed conflict by attributing . . . emotional drives to the external world."[31] In short, the dynamic core of belief in witchcraft in early New England was the difficulty experienced by many individuals in finding ways to handle their own aggressive impulses. Witchcraft accusations provided one of the few approved outlets for such impulses in Puritan culture. Aggression was thus denied in the self and attributed directly to others. The accuser says, in effect: "I am not attacking you; you are attacking me!" In reality, however, the accuser is attacking the witch, and in an extremely dangerous manner, too. Witchcraft enables him to have it both ways; the impulse is denied and gratified at the same time.

The seizures of the afflicted children also permitted them to engage in a considerable amount of direct aggression. They were not, of course, held personally responsible; it was always the fault of the Devil at work inside them. Sometimes these impulses were aimed against the most important—and obvious—figures of authority. A child in a fit might behave very disobediently toward his parents or revile the clergy who came to pray for his recovery.[32] The Reverend Samuel Willard of Groton, who ministered to Elizabeth Knapp during the time of her most severe fits, noted that the Devil "urged upon her constant temptations to murder her p'rents, her neighbors, our children . . . and even to make away with herselfe & once she was going to drowne herself in ye well." The attacking impulses were quite random here, so much so that the girl herself was not safe. Cotton Mather

[30] Willard, *A briefe account* etc., in *Groton in the Witchcraft Times*, ed. Green, 8; deposition by Ann Foster, case of Ann Foster, deposition by Andrew Carrier, case of Mary Lacy, Jr., in Works Progress Administration, *Salem Witchcraft, 1692*; Cotton Mather, *A Brand Pluck'd Out of the Burning*, in *Narratives*, ed. Burr, 269.

[31] This is the definition suggested by Clyde Kluckhohn in his own exemplary monograph, *Navajo Witchcraft*, 239, n. 37.

[32] See, for example, the descriptions of the Goodwin children during the time of their affliction, in Cotton Mather, *Memorable Providences* etc., 109 ff., 119.

reports a slight variation on this type of behavior in connection with the fits of Martha Goodwin. She would, he writes, "fetch very terrible Blowes with her Fist, and Kicks with her Foot at the man that prayed; but still . . . her Fist and Foot would alwaies recoil, when they came within a few hairs breadths of him just as if Rebounding against a Wall."[33] This little paradigm of aggression attempted and then at the last moment inhibited expresses perfectly the severe inner conflict that many of these people were acting out.

One last, pervasive theme in witchcraft is more difficult to handle than the others without having direct recourse to clinical models; the summary word for it is orality. It is helpful to recall at this point the importance of feasts in the standard imaginary picture of witches, but the experience of the accusers speaks even more powerfully to the same point. The evidence is of several kinds. First, the character of the "tortures" inflicted by the witches was most often described in terms of biting, pinching, and pricking; in a psychiatric sense, these modes of attack all have an oral foundation. The pattern showed up with great vividness, for example, in the trial of George Burroughs:

It was Remarkable that whereas Biting was one of the ways which the Witches used for the vexing of the Sufferers, when they cry'd out of G.B. biting them, the print of the Teeth would be seen on the Flesh of the Complainers, and just such a sett of Teeth as G.B.'s would then appear upon them, which could be distinguished from those of some other mens.[34]

Second, the accusers repeatedly charged that they could see the witches suckling certain animal "familiars." The following testimony by one of the Salem girls, in reference to an unidentified witch, was quite typical: "She had two little things like young cats and she put them to her brest and suckled them they had no hair on them and had ears like a man." It was assumed that witches were specially equipped for these purposes, and their bodies were searched for the evidence. In 1656 the constable of Salisbury, New Hampshire, deposed in the case of Eunice Cole,

That being about to stripp [her] to bee whipt (by the judgment of the Court att Salisbury) looking uppon hir brests under one of hir breasts (I thinke hir left brest) I saw a blew thing like unto a teate hanging downeward about three quarters of an inche longe not very thick, and haveing a great suspition in my mind about it (she being suspected for a witche) desiered the Court to sende some women to looke of it.

The court accepted this proposal and appointed a committee of three women to administer to Goodwife Cole the standard, very intimate, examination. Their report made no mention of a "teate" under her breast, but noted instead "a place in her leg which was proveable wher she Had bin sucktt by Imps or the like." The women also stated "thatt they Heard the whining of puppies or such like under Her Coats as though they Had a desire to sucke."[35]

[33] Willard, *A briefe account* etc., 9; Cotton Mather, *Memorable Providences* etc., 108, 120.
[34] Cotton Mather, *Wonders of the Invisible World*, 216–17.
[35] Deposition by Susannah Sheldon, case of Philip English, in Works Progress Administration, *Salem Witchcraft, 1692;* manuscript deposition by Richard Ormsbey, case of Eunice Cole, in Massachusetts Archives, Vol. 135, 3; manuscript record, case of Eunice Cole, in *ibid.*, 13.

Third, many of the accusers underwent serious eating disturbances during and after their fits. "Long fastings" were frequently imposed on them. Cotton Mather writes of one such episode in his account of the bewitching of Margaret Rule: "tho she had a very eager Hunger upon her Stomach, yet if any refreshment were brought unto her, her teeth would be set, and she would be thrown into many Miseries." But also she would "sometimes have her Jaws forcibly pulled open, whereupon something invisible would be poured down her throat ... She cried out of it as of Scalding Brimstone poured into her."[36] These descriptions and others like them would repay a much more detailed analysis than can be offered here, but the general point should be obvious. Among the zones of the body, the mouth seems to have been charged with a special kind of importance for victims of witchcraft.

In closing, it may be appropriate to offer a few suggestions of a more theoretical nature to indicate both the way in which an interpretation of New England witchcraft might be attempted and what it is that one can hope to learn from witchcraft materials about the culture at large. But let it be said with some emphasis that this is meant only as the most tentative beginning of a new approach to such questions.

Consider an interesting set of findings included by two anthropologists in a broad survey of child-rearing practices in over fifty cultures around the world. They report that belief in witchcraft is powerfully correlated with the training a society imposes on young children in regard to the control of aggressive impulses.[37] That is, wherever this training is severe and restrictive, there is a strong likelihood that the culture will make much of witchcraft. The correlation seems to suggest that suppressed aggression will seek indirect outlets of the kind that belief in witchcraft provides. Unfortunately there is relatively little concrete evidence about child-rearing practices in early New England; but it seems at least consistent with what is known of Puritan culture generally to imagine that quite a harsh attitude would have been taken toward any substantial show of aggression in the young.[38]

Now, some further considerations. There were only a very few cases of witchcraft accusations among members of the same family. But, as we have seen, the typical pattern involved accusations by adolescent girls against middle-aged women. It seems plausible, at least from a clinical standpoint, to think that this pattern masked deep problems stemming ultimately from the relationship of

[36] Cotton Mather, *Memorable Providences* etc., 131.
[37] John W. M. Whiting and Irvin L. Child, *Child Training and Personality* (New Haven, 1953), Chap. 12.
[38] John Robinson, the pastor of the original "Pilgrim" congregation, wrote as follows in an essay on "Children and Their Education": "Surely there is in all children . . . a stubbornness, and stoutness of mind arising from natural pride, which must be broken and beaten down. . . . Children should not know, if it could be kept from them, that they have a will in their own: neither should these words be heard from them, save by way of consent, 'I will' or 'I will not.'" Robinson, *Works* (Boston, 1851), I, 246-47. This point of view would not appear to leave much room for the free expression of aggressive impulses, but of course it tells us nothing certain about actual practice in Puritan families.

mother and daughter. Perhaps, then, the afflicted girls were both projecting their aggression and diverting or "displacing" it from its real target. Considered from this perspective, displacement represents another form of avoidance or denial; and so the charges of the accusers may be seen as a kind of double defense against the actual conflicts.

How can we locate the source of these conflicts? This is a more difficult and frankly speculative question. Indeed the question leads farther and farther from the usual canons of historical explanation; such proof as there is must come by way of parallels to findings of recent psychological research and, above all, to a great mass of clinical data. More specifically, it is to psychoanalytic theory that one may turn for insights of an especially helpful sort.

The prominence of oral themes in the historical record suggests that the disturbances that culminated in charges of witchcraft must be traced to the earliest phase of personality development. It would be very convenient to have some shred of information to insert here about breast-feeding practices among early New Englanders. Possibly their methods of weaning were highly traumatic,[39] but as no hard evidence exists we simply cannot be sure. It seems plausible, however, that many New England children were faced with some unspecified but extremely difficult psychic tasks in the first year or so of life. The outcome was that their aggressive drives were tied especially closely to the oral mode and driven underground.[40] Years later, in accordance with changes normal for adolescence, instinctual energies of all types were greatly augmented; and this tended, as it so often does, to reactivate the earliest conflicts[41]—the process that Freud vividly described as "the return of the repressed." But these conflicts were no easier to deal with in adolescence than they had been earlier; hence the need for the twin defenses of projection and displacement.[42]

[39] However, we can determine with some confidence the usual time of weaning. Since lactation normally creates an impediment to a new conception, and since the average interval between births in New England families was approximately two years, it seems likely that most infants were weaned between the ages of twelve and fifteen months. The nursing process would therefore overlap the arrival of baby teeth (and accompanying biting wishes); and this might well give rise to considerable tension between mother and child. I have found only one direct reference to weaning in all the documentary evidence from seventeenth-century New England, an entry in the journal of John Hull: "1659, 11th of 2d. My daughter Hannah was taken from her mother's breast, and, through the favor of God, weaned without any trouble; only about fifteen days after, she did not eat her meat well." *American Antiquarian Society, Transactions,* III (Boston, 1857), 149. Hannah Hull was born on February 14, 1658, making her thirteen months and four weeks on the day of the above entry. Hull's choice of words creates some temptation to speculate further. Was it perhaps unusual for Puritan infants to be "weaned without any trouble"? Also, does it not seem that in this case the process was quite abrupt— that is, accomplished entirely at one point in time? (Generally speaking, this is more traumatic for an infant than gradual weaning is.) For a longer discussion of infancy in Puritan New England see John Demos, *A Little Commonwealth: Family-Life in Plymouth Colony* (New York, 1970), Chap. 8.

[40] I have found the work of Melanie Klein on the origins of psychic conflict in infancy to be particularly helpful. See her *The Psycho-Analysis of Children* (London, 1932) and the papers collected in her *Contributions to Psycho-Analysis* (London, 1950). See also Joan Riviere, "On the Genesis of Psychical Conflict in Earliest Infancy," in Melanie Klein *et al., Developments in Psycho-Analysis* (London, 1952), 37–66.

[41] See Peter Blos, *On Adolescence* (New York, 1962). This (basically psychoanalytic) study provides a wealth of case materials and some very shrewd interpretations, which seem to bear strongly on certain of the phenomena connected with early New England witchcraft.

[42] It is no coincidence that projection was so important among the defenses employed by the afflicted girls in their efforts to combat their own aggressive drives. For projection is the earliest of all defenses, and indeed it takes shape under the influence of the oral phase. On this point see Sig-

One final problem must be recognized. The conflicts on which this discussion has focused were, of course, most vividly expressed in the fits of the accusers. The vast majority of people in early New England—subjected, one assumes, to roughly similar influences as children—managed to reach adulthood without experiencing fits. Does this pose serious difficulties for the above interpretations? The question can be argued to a negative conclusion, in at least two different but complementary ways. First, the materials on witchcraft, and in particular on the fits of the accusers, span a considerable length of time in New England's early history. It seems clear, therefore, that aggression and orality were more or less constant themes in the pathology of the period. Second, even in the far less bizarre testimonies of the witnesses—those who have been taken to represent the community at large—the same sort of focus appears. It is, above all, significant that the specific complaints of the accusers were so completely credible to so many others around them. The accusers, then, can be viewed as those individuals who were somehow especially sensitive to the problems created by their environment; they were the ones who were pushed over the line, so to speak, into serious illness. But their behavior clearly struck an answering chord in a much larger group of people. In this sense, nearly everyone in seventeenth-century New England was at some level an accuser.

---

mund Freud, "Negation," *The Standard Edition of the Complete Works of Sigmund Freud*, ed. J. Strachey (London, 1960), XIX, 237, and Paula Heimann, "Certain Functions of Introjection and Projection in Early Infancy," in Klein *et al.*, *Developments in Psycho-Analysis*, 122–68.

FREDERICK C. DRAKE

University of Wales, Aberystwyth

Witchcraft in the American Colonies, 1647-62

THE WITCHCRAFT EVENTS THAT SHATTERED SALEM SOCIETY IN 1692 LED directly to nineteen human executions by hanging, one by pressing with heavy weights, and the imprisonment of scores of people. Since that date they have also inspired a multitude of narrative accounts and stimulated at least three different controversies among historians.

The first of these controversies dealt with the role of Cotton and Increase Mather in the trials of 1692. Attacks upon the Mathers have varied from insinuations of responsibility for guiding the hysteria, in order to drive people back to church, to open condemnation for being slow to speak out against spectral evidence, a charge of ignoring the rules in judging the presence of witchcraft.[1] During the last quarter of the 19th century a second argument developed over the legality of the courts which

[1] The Mathers have been charged with much more than this. Robert Calef, *More Wonders of the Invisible World*, in *Narratives of the Witchcraft Cases: 1647-1706*, ed. George Lincoln Burr (New York, 1914), pp. 296-393; George Bancroft, *History of the United States* (Boston, 1857), III, 75-99; Vernon Louis Parrington, *Main Currents of American Thought* (New York, 1927), I, 115-17; and C. W. Upham, *Salem Witchcraft* (Boston, 1867), *passim*, all placed the Mathers in the forefront of those who contributed to the hysteria of the time. For the whole controversy see Charles W. Upham, *Salem Witchcraft with an Account of Salem Village, and a History of Opinion on Witchcraft and Kindred Subjects* (Boston, 1867) and his *Salem Witchcraft and Cotton Mather: A Reply* (Morrisana, N.Y., 1869); W. F. Poole, "Cotton Mather and Salem Witchcraft," *North American Review*, CVIII (Apr. 1869), 337-97; Poole, *Cotton Mather and Salem Witchcraft: two Notices of Mr. Upham his Reply* (1870); Poole, "Witchcraft at Boston," in *The Memorial History of Boston: 1630-1880*, ed. Justin Winsor (Boston, 1881) II, 131-72; *Narratives*, ed. Burr, pp. 291-93; and G. H. Moore's review of the respective parts played by Calef and the Mathers in "Bibliographical Notes on Witchcraft in Massachusetts," American Antiquarian Society, *Proceedings*, n. s., V (1888), 245-73. For more recent sympathetic views of Mather see Clifford K. Shipton, "New England Clergy of the 'Glacial Age,'" Colonial Society of Massachusetts, *Publications*, XXXII (Dec. 1933), 23-54; M. L. Starkey, *The Devil in Massachusetts* (New York, 1949), chap. 20. On Calef one should consult W. S. Harris, "Robert Calef, Merchant of Boston," *Granite Monthly*, n. s., XXXIX (May 1907), 157-63.

dealt with the indictments of 1692 and the adequacy of the compensa-tion awarded to the dependents of those who suffered in the trials. Two of the foremost witchcraft historians of the 1880s, George H. Moore and Albert Goodell Jr., were the chief protagonists in this debate.[2] Yet a third dispute, which arose in the first decade of the 20th century, between George Lyman Kittredge of Harvard and George Lincoln Burr of Cor-nell, concentrated more intently upon establishing the significance of witchcraft in America. The echoes of this debate, which evaluated the Salem outburst of 1692 within the overall context of European witch-craft, can still be heard today.

Professor Kittredge pointed out that belief in witchcraft was a con-stant quality in mankind; it was "the common heritage of humanity."[3] Professor Burr dissented sharply from this view, claiming that witchcraft rose and fell in less than five centuries during "the greatest burst of Christian civilization."[4] For Burr witchcraft meant the practice of wor-shiping the Devil thrown down from Heaven, and using powers gained from him to work evil. As the witch hunters justified their activities by reference to chapters from the Old Testament, it followed that witch-craft was a phenomenon within the Christian religion embracing both New and Old Testament doctrine. Necromancing, spiritualism and types of voodoo lay beyond the scope of this definition, and Burr accordingly rejected Kittredge's more universal view of witchcraft. Obviously, these respective definitions of the phenomenon led toward totally different conclusions. When both historians examined the New England record on witchcraft they differed considerably. Kittredge drew up a list of 21

[2] George H. Moore, "Notes on the History of Witchcraft in Massachusetts," Amer-ican Antiquarian Society, *Proceedings*, n. s., II (Oct. 1882), 162-92; Moore, "Supple-mentary Notes on Witchcraft in Massachusetts: a Critical Examination of the Alleged Law of 1711 for Reversing the Attainder of the Witches of 1692," Massachusetts His-torical Society, *Proceedings*, 2nd ser., I (1884), 77-98; Moore, *Final Notes on Witch-craft in Massachusetts: a Summary Vindication of the Laws and Liberties concerning Attainders with Corruption of Blood, Escheats, Forfeitures for Crime, and Pardon of Offenders in Reply to the "Reasons," etc. of A. C. Goodell* (New York, 1885); Abner C. Goodell Jr., "The Trial of the Witches in Massachusetts," Massachusetts Historical Society, *Proceedings*, XX (June 1883), 280-326; Goodell, *Further Notes on the History of Witchcraft in Massachusetts* (Cambridge, 1884) and his rebuttal to Moore's "Sup-plementary Notes . . ." in Massachusetts Historical Society, *Proceedings*, 2nd ser., I (1884), 99-118. The meeting of the Massachusetts Historical Society in Sept. 1883 had several letters and a debate upon Goodell's paper, *Proceedings*, XX (Sept. 1883), 327-33. There is a survey of the controversy in Justin Winsor, "The Literature of Witchcraft in New England," American Antiquarian Society, *Proceedings*, n. s., X (Oct. 1895), 371-73. With it should be read Henry W. Belknap, "Philip English, Commerce Builder," American Antiquarian Society, *Proceedings*, n. s., XLI (Apr. 1931), 17-24.

[3] G. L. Kittredge, "Notes on Witchcraft," American Antiquarian Society, *Proceed-ings*, n. s., XVII (Apr. 1907), 210.

[4] G. L. Burr, "New England's Place in the History of Witchcraft," American Anti-quarian Society, *Proceedings*, n. s., XXI (Oct. 1911), 186-87, 217.

theses on the subject, the twentieth of which stated: "the record of New England in the matter of witchcraft is highly creditable, when considered as a whole and from the comparative point of view."[5] Burr, however, was unable to acquit his own ancestors upon the grounds that their belief in witchcraft was universal, or was more logical than disbelief. He affirmed that:

> it was superstitious and bigoted and cruel, even by the standards of their own time . . . their final panic [Salem] was the last on such a scale in any Christian land. Their transatlantic home I cannot think an excuse. . . . One thing is sure: we must not blow hot and cold with the same breath. If our fathers were the helpless victims of circumstance, then they were not its masters.[6]

The multiple effect of these three controversies has been to elevate Salem to a position of being the only significant point of reference in colonial witchcraft literature. The prelude to the hysteria of 1692 is usually acknowledged to be the Goodwin case of 1688, when Goodwife Glover was executed in Boston after accusations that she had bewitched four young Goodwin children suffering from convulsions.[7] Cases of witchcraft prior to 1692 have generally served merely as introductory material for the main discussion on Salem. John M. Taylor, an historian who provided evidence of early cases in Connecticut, nevertheless clung to this approach.[8] References to earlier cases are often incorrect on numbers and important details. For example, W. N. Gemmill wrote of "over twenty trials for witchcraft" before 1692, when "many people were convicted and several hung [sic]."[9] This estimate alone reduced the numbers indicted to 25% of the actual total and vaguely underestimated the numbers convicted and executed. Rossell Hope Robbins in the excellent *Encyclopedia of Witchcraft and Demonology* concentrated so intently upon Salem that he termed it "the best known name in the entire history of witchcraft." He asserted that the colonial witchcraft delusion was "sporadic and mild and, compared with the holocausts in sixteenth and seventeenth century Europe," it was largely "insignificant." Robbins affirmed, moreover, that the "relative freedom" from witchcraft for the 40 pre-

5 Kittredge, American Antiquarian Society, *Proceedings*, XVII, 211-12.

6 Burr, American Antiquarian Society, *Proceedings*, XXI, 215-16.

7 For estimates of the importance of this case for the Salem trials see the works cited above, or Samuel E. Morison, "Charles Morton," Colonial Society of Massachusetts, *Publications*, XXXII (1940), xxvi.

8 John M. Taylor, *The Witchcraft Delusion in Colonial Connecticut: 1647-1697* (New York, 1908), pp. 24-25.

9 W. N. Gemmill, *The Salem Witch Trials, a chapter of New England History* (Chicago, 1924), p. 45. Compare also with Caroline E. Upham, *Salem Witchcraft in Outline* (Salem, 1891), p. 6.

ceding years made the Salem trials overshadow everything else to such an extent that "it may be said the history of American witchcraft is Salem."[10]

In some cases a tendency has developed to dismiss the crisis of 1692 as "a mere bubble in Massachusetts history."[11] Thus Ola E. Winslow in her biography of Samuel Sewall, Salem judge in 1692, has commented that the "sporadic" witchcraft cases before the Salem troubles, were "surprisingly few in comparison with the disasters that might so naturally have been attributed to evil spirits in human flesh."[12] A further example can be found in an essay by Stuart Henry upon Puritan character displayed in the Salem crisis. Henry generalized about the entire Puritan response to witchcraft from the one example at Salem. Closely following Kittredge's arguments to exonerate Puritanism, he flatly asserted that "the first vibration of the acute, high-strung Puritan mind to the demons of the spirit world was in Boston, 1688." Consequently, the Salem story polarizes as "one of the few chapters of American history which seems to have a definite beginning, middle and end." In searching for the source of the Salem story Henry observed that some English cases in 1683, "were instances of witchcraft, not in America, but in England, the memory of which might have been in the minds of the American colonists."[13]

Salem has thus become the focal point of historical analysis of colonial witchcraft. The outburst of 1692 has been effectively separated from its American ancestry, and its origins located somewhere in the 1680s. Earlier cases have been ignored and miscounted. For there were over 95 incidents involving colonial people with witchcraft before 1692. Nearly 60 of these incidents occurred between the adoption of the Cambridge platform of 1648 and the acceptance of the Half-Way Covenant of 1662. These incidents led to at least 83 trials between 1647 and 1691 in which 22 people were executed, and many others suffered banishment, whipping and financial loss. Yet, of the 22 executions 20 had taken place between 1647 and 1662, and the first eight occurred in less than four years. The following table lists the witchcraft trials which directly involved the colonies from 1647 to 1662.

[10] Rossell H. Robbins, *The Encyclopedia of Witchcraft and Demonology* (New York, 1959), pp. 519-20.

[11] John Noble, "Some Documentary Fragments touching the Witchcraft Episode of 1692," Colonial Society of Massachusetts, *Publications*, X (Dec. 1904), 12-26.

[12] Ola Elizabeth Winslow, *Samuel Sewall of Boston* (New York, 1964), p. 115, wrote also that not one of the earlier cases "aroused widespread hysteria." A similar comment was made by Perry Miller, *The New England Mind from Colony to Province* (Cambridge, 1953), p. 179.

[13] Stuart C. Henry, "Puritan Character in the Witchcraft Episode of Salem," in *A Miscellany of American Christianity: Essays in Honor of H. Shelton Smith*, ed. Stuart C. Henry (Durham, N. C., 1963), pp. 148, 165, 142.

A Table of Witchcraft Cases and Incidents in the American Colonies: 1645-62

Name of Witch	Date	Accusers	Victims	Town	Colony	Verdict of the Jury	Final Verdict, Date and Sentence
Mary and Hugh Parsons?[a]	1645	Not known	Rev. Moxon's children	Springfield	Mass.		Not accused in 1645, but several were disturbed.
Alse Young[b]	1647	Not known	Not known	Windsor	Conn.	Guilty	Executed, May 25, 1647.
Margaret Jones[c]	1648	A Neighbor	Neighbor's children	Charlestown	Mass.	Guilty	Executed at Boston, June 15, 1648.
Thomas Jones[d]	1648	A Neighbor	Neighbor's children	Charlestown	Mass.	Not known	Arrested, fate unknown, possibly released.

[a] Edward Johnson, *Wonder-Working Providence: 1628-1651*, ed. J. Franklin Jameson (New York, 1910), p. 237, mentioned that in 1645 "there hath of late been more then [sic] one or two in this Town greatly suspected of witchcraft [who] . . . bewitched not a few persons, among whom two of the reverend Elders [Reverend Moxon's] children." Later in 1651 Hugh and Mary Parsons were accused of bewitching Moxon's children, and this charge almost certainly applied to the 1645 incident.

[b] John Winthrop, *Journal: 1630-49*, ed. James K. Hosmer (New York, 1908), II, 323, merely cited the fact of execution: "One . . . of Windsor arraigned and executed at Hartford for a Witch." John M. Taylor, *Witchcraft Delusion*, pp. 35, 145-47, 156, synthesizes the best and most thorough evidence in determining the name; see also *Narratives*, ed. G. L. Burr, p. 408, n2; C. H. Levermore, "Witchcraft in Connecticut: 1647-1697," *New Englander and Yale Review*, XLIV (Nov. 1885), 792-93.

[c] Instructions of the Court, May 13, 1648, in *Records of the Massachusetts Bay in New Eng-land*, ed. Nathaniel B. Shurtleff (Boston, 1854), III, 126, and II, 242. The references to this case are extensive. It is mentioned by William Hubbard, "History of New England, Part II, 1635-1660," Massachusetts Historical Society, *Collections*, 2nd ser., VI (c. 1816-17), 530; John Winthrop, *Journal*, II, 344-45: Emanuel Downing wrote to John Winthrop Jr.: "Boston 13.4.48 [June in the Puritan calendar], A Witche is condemned, and to be hanged to-morrow, being Lecture Day," Massachusetts Historical Society, *Collections*, 4th scr., VI (1863), 68; Gov. Thomas Hutchinson, "The Witchcraft Delusion of 1692," communicated with notes by William F. Poole in *New England Historical and Genealogical Register and Antiquarian Journal*, XXIV (1870), 384, n4; William D. Northend, "Address before the Essex Bar Association, Part II," *Historical Collections of the Essex Institute*, XXII (Oct.-Dec. 1885), 266, n16; S. G. Drake, *Annals of Witchcraft in New England and elsewhere in the United States from their first settlement* (Boston, 1869), pp. 59, 58-61 for a detailed review of the case.

[d] John Winthrop, *Journal*, II, 344-45: Drake, *Annals of Witchcraft*, pp. 59-61.

Name of Witch	Date	Accusers	Victims	Town	Colony	Verdict of the jury	Final Verdict, Date and Sentence
Mary Johnson[e]	1648	Her Employer	Animals in the fields	Wethersfield	Conn.	Guilty	Guilty, Dec. 7, 1648, and executed at Hartford.
Mary Oliver[f]	1649	Not known	Not known	Boston	Mass.	Not known	Confessed to witchcraft, fate not known but probably executed.
Mrs. H. Lake[g]	1650	Not known	Not known	Dorchester	Mass.	Guilty	Executed at Boston.
Hostile Indians[h]	1651	Not known	Uncas, Mohegan Indian				Inquiry by the Commissioners of the United Colonies.

[e] Particular Court, Dec. 7, 1648, in *The Public Records of the Colony of Connecticut, prior to the Union with New Haven Colony, May, 1665*, ed. J. Hammond Trumbull (Hartford, 1850), I, 171; Cotton Mather, *Magnalia Christi Americana* (Hartford, 1853), II, 456-57, who listed this case as his eighth example of witchcraft; S. G. Drake, *Annals of Witchcraft*, pp. 62-63; Levermore, *New Englander and Yale Review*, XLIV, 792.

[f] Drake, *Annals of Witchcraft*, p. 64. Her fate is unknown but her confession, and her known trouble making as a supporter of Anne Hutchinson, would be enough proof of witchcraft for execution. See also John Winthrop, *Journal*, I, 285-86; and the particulars of the Quarter Court at Boston, "the 4th day of the 10th month, 1638" where she was committed to prison for disturbing the Church of Salem, given in *Records of the Court of Assistants of the Colony of the Massachusetts Bay: 1630-1692*, comp. Jack Noble (Boston, 1904), II, 80.

[g] Nathaniel Mather to Increase Mather, Dec. 31, 1684, mentioned Mrs. Lake when he wrote "I have also received by way of London one of your books of Remarkable Providences. . . Why did you not put in the story of Mrs. Hibbens witchcrafts, & the discovery thereof, as also H. Lake's wife, of Dorchester, whom, as I have heard, the devill drew in by appearing to her in the likenes, & acting the part of a child of hers then lately dead, on whom her heart was much set: as also another of a girl in Connecticut who was judged to dye a reall convert, tho she dyed for the same crime?" *The Mather Papers*, Massachusetts Historical Society, *Collections*, 4th ser., VIII (1868), 58-59. This clue was found in W. F. Poole, ed. *Governor T. Hutchinson's Witchcraft Delusion*, p. 384, n5.

[h] In Connecticut, the Commissioners of the United Colonies advised that the colony should appoint a committee of examination when Uncas, the Mohegan Indian friendly to the settlers, reported that hostile Indians were bedeviling him. The general fear of the Indians being upon familiar terms with the Devil formed part of the theological rationale of the settlers, and the importance attached by the leaders to the "children of Satan" becoming active with witchcraft can be judged from the careful attention they gave to the affair. Levermore, *New Englander and Yale Review*, XLIV, 793, and *New England's First Fruits* (London, 1643), I, which mentioned "those poor Indians, who have ever sate in hellish darknesse, adoring the *Divell* himselfe for their GOD."

Name of Witch	Date	Accusers	Victims	Town	Colony	Verdict of the Jury	Final Verdict, Date and Sentence
John Carrington[1]	Feb. 20 1651	Not known	Not known	Wethers-field	Conn.	Guilty March 6, 1651	Executed after March 6, 1651.
Joan Carrington[1]	Feb. 20 1651	Not known	Not known	Wethers-field	Conn.	Guilty March 6, 1651	Executed after March 6, 1651.
Goodwife Bassett[j]	May 1651	Many people	Not known	Strat-ford	Conn.	Guilty	Guilty after a review by the Governor and Magistrates, and executed.
Mary Parsons[k]	1651	Neighbors	Her own children and the Rev. Moxon's children	Spring-field	Mass.	Guilty	Imprisoned at Boston, May 1, Acquitted of witchcraft by the General Court on May 7, 1651, but guilty of the murder of her child. Between May 7 and 27 confessed to witchcraft, and executed May 29, 1651, at Boston.

[1] Both John and Joan Carrington were accused of having "Intertained flamiliarity with Sathan, the Great Enemy of God and Mankinde"; and both were condemned to death by a jury on Mar. 6, 1651. Taylor, *Witchcraft Delusion*, pp. 38, 147; Levermore, *New Englander and Yale Review*, XLIV, 793.

[j] A delegation consisting of the governor and two magistrates was authorized to go to Stratford just after May 15, "to keepe Courte vppon the tryall of Goody Bassett for her life, and, if the Gouernor cannot goe, then Mr. Wells is to go in his roome." There is a reference in another witchcraft case, that of Goodwife Staplies in 1654, to "*goodwife* Bassett, when she was condemned . . . ," and it is certain that she was executed. *See* General Court of Election in Hartford, May 15, 1651, in *The Public Records . . .*

Connecticut, ed. Trumbull, I, 220; Drake, *Annals of Witchcraft*, pp. 73-74; Taylor, *Witchcraft Delusion*, pp. 148-49; and Record of the trial of Goodwife Staplies in *Records of the Colony or Jurisdiction of New Haven, from May 1653, to the Union. Together with the New Haven Code of 1656*, ed. Charles J. Hoadley (Hartford, 1858), II, 81.

[k] Court Records and indictments of Mary Parsons dated "13. 3mo. 1651; May 22nd, 1651; and October 24th, 1651," are given in *Records of the Governor and Company of Massachusetts Bay*, ed. Shurtleff, IV, Pt. I, 47; III, 229; and IV, Pt. I, 73 respectively. Mention is made of the Rev. Mr. Moxon's children being bewitched.

Name of Witch	Date	Accusers	Victims	Town	Colony	Verdict of the jury	Final Verdict, Date and Sentence
Hugh Parsons[l]	1651	Neighbors and Mary Parsons	Rev. Moxon's children	Springfield	Mass.	Guilty	The jury verdict was set aside by the Magistrates, and the case went to the General Court in Boston, Acquitted May 31, 1651.
John Bradstreet[m]	1651	Not known	Not known	Rowley	Mass.	Guilty	A fine of 20 shillings or a whipping.
Mrs. Kendal[n]	1651	Godman Genings' nurse	Godman Genings' child	Cambridge	Mass.	Guilty	Executed.
Elizabeth Godman[o] (First case)	1653(?)	The Mrs. Goodyeare, Atwater, Bishop Thorp and Rev. Hooke	As Accusers	New Haven	New Haven		The Court of Magistrates issued a warning to Mrs. Godman that she was suspected as a witch, and she was informed that if she appeared in court again her evidence and case would be reconsidered.
Goodwife Knapp[p]	1653	Roger Ludlow, Mrs. Lockwood and seven others	Not known but several	Fairfield	Conn.		Executed at Fairfield.

[l] The Documents of indictment and release of Hugh Parsons, dated May 27, 1652, and May 31, 1652, are given in *ibid.*, III, 273; and IV, Pt. I, 96 respectively. Drake, *Annals of Witchcraft*, pp. 64-73, has a long review of the case, including an attack on Cotton Mather for excluding it from his compilation of cases.

[m] John Bradstreet was indicted for having familiarity with the Devil, which consisted of hearing a voice telling him to make a bridge of sand over the sea and a ladder of sand to heaven. He was sentenced for "fanciful delusions" and "telling a lie." Drake, *Annals of Witchcraft*, pp. 74-75; Joseph B. Felt, *History of Ipswich, Essex, and Hamilton* (Cambridge, 1834), p. 267.

[n] Governor T. Hutchinson's *Witchcraft Delusion*, ed. Poole, p. 385, n6.

[o] The examination of Elizabeth Godman, May 21, 1653, in *Records of ... New Haven ... 1653 to the Union*, ed. Hoadley, p. 31; the examination of Elizabeth Godman, May 24, 1653 given at a Court of Magistrates held at "New Hauen for the jurisdiction," Aug. 4, 1653, *ibid.*, pp. 30-36; Levermore, *New Englander and Yale Review*, XLIV, 796-97; Drake, *Annals of Witchcraft*, pp. 88-97; Taylor, *Witchcraft Delusion*, pp. 85-96.

[p] *Records of ... New Haven ... 1653 to the Union*, ed. Hoadley, p. 81; Taylor, *Witchcraft Delusion*, p. 132.

Name of Witch	Date	Accusers	Victims	Town	Colony	Verdict of the jury	Final Verdict, Date and Sentence
Mrs. T. Staples^q	1653	Roger Ludlow	Not known but several	Fairfield	Conn.	Not Guilty	Released, and her accuser Roger Ludlow surrendered a total of £25 for defamation.
John Godfrey^r	1653	Job and Moses Tyler	Mary Tyler	Andover	Mass.		Deposition and evidence not presented until 1659.
Mary Lee^s	1654	Sailors on the Charity	Sailors and the vessel	En route to the Chesapeake	Md.		Mary Lee was hanged at sea: no verdict found on John Bosworth, master of the Charity.
Mrs. R. Manship^t	Oct. 16, 1654	Peter Godson	Peter Godson		Md.	Not Guilty	Released, and Peter Godson was judged to have defamed and slandered Mrs. Manship.

q *Records of . . . New Haven . . . 1653 to the Union*, ed. Hoadley, pp. 77-89, "the court of Magistrates held at New Haven, for the jurisdiction, 29th of May, 1654"; Taylor, *Witchcraft Delusion*, pp. 121-41, 149, 156; Levermore, "Witchcraft in Connecticut," *New England Magazine*, n. s., VI (July 1892), 640; also *New Englander and Yale Review*, XLIV, 798-801; Drake, *Annals of Witchcraft*, pp. 76-86.

r *Ibid.*, pp. 87-88, 114-15.

s "Depositions of Henry Corbyn, merchant; and Francis Darby, gentleman, sworne and examined in the Province of Maryland before the Governor & Councell . . 23 day of June, 1654," in *Archives of Maryland: Proceedings of the Council of Maryland 1636-1667*, ed. William Hand Brown (Baltimore, 1885), I, 306-8. This hanging took place on board ship from England. Before the ship *Charity* had reached the Chesapeake she had been caught in a storm. The seamen believed that Mary Lee, a passenger, was responsible for bewitching the vessel, and blamed her for its unseaworthiness. Two sailors searched her and claimed to have found a witch's mark. Next day, faced with another search, she confessed, and the sailors demanded her death from the Master, John Bosworth. He had no stomach to stop or assist in the execution and retired to his cabin, whereupon the crew hanged her. The Maryland Court heard the depositions from the passengers but no verdict is known. The depositions are also given in E. S. Riley, "Witchcraft in Early Maryland," *Southern Magazine*, XII (Apr. 1873), 453; and the case is mentioned by F. N. Parke, "Witchcraft in Maryland," *Maryland Historical Magazine*, XXXI (Dec. 1936), 271-98; and Anna Siousat, "Colonial Women of Maryland," *Ibid.*, II (1907), 219-20.

t Riley, *Southern Magazine*, XII, 453; Parke, *Maryland Historical Magazine*, XXXI, 272. Peter Godson claimed to become lame after seeing Richard Manship's wife, and his wife joined in the accusation of witchcraft. The Court, however, ruled that Mrs. Manship had been defamed and slandered, and the Godsons were forced to apologize and pay costs.

Name of Witch	Date	Accusers	Victims	Town	Colony	Verdict of the jury	Final Verdict, Date and Sentence
Lydia Gilbert[u]	Sept. or Oct. 1654	Not known	Henry Stiles	Windsor	Mass.	Guilty	Executed.
Nicholas Bayly[v]	July-Oct. 1655	Not known but several	Not known	New Haven	New Haven	Suspicious of witchcraft	Released, but banished from the colony.
Mrs. N. Bayly[v]	July-Oct. 1655	Not known but several	Not known	New Haven	New Haven	Suspicious of witchcraft	Released, but banished from the colony, for "Impudent and notorious lying."
Elizabeth Godman[w] (Second case)	1655	See the first Godman case, and Allen Ball	Stephen Goodyeare's step-daughters, and several animals		New Haven	Suspicious of witchcraft	Bound over to another court meeting on October 4, 1655.

[u] In 1651 Henry Stiles of Windsor, Massachusetts, had been killed by an accidental discharge of a gun held by Thomas Allyn. The latter had been indicted, pleaded guilty and was fined £20 for "sinful neglect and careless carriage" and placed under a £10 bond for good behaviour for a year. Two years later Lydia Gilbert of Windsor was charged with the crime that "thou ... still dost give entertainment to Sathan ... and by his helpe hast killed the body of Henry Styles, besides other witchcrafts." She was indicted, tried in September or November 1654 and was found guilty by the jury. There is no written record of her fate, but all indications such as the absence of any meeting by the Court of Magistrates to review the case point to the jury decision being acceptable, and implemented by execution. Henry R. Stiles, *The History of Ancient Windsor, Connecticut* (New York, 1859), p. 779; and Taylor, *Witchcraft Delusion*, pp. 148, 156.

[v] In New Haven, Nicholas Bayly and his wife were called before the court and informed that "sundrie passages taken in writing ... doth render them both, but especially the woman, very suspitious in poynt of witchcraft, but for matters of that nature the Court intends not to proceed at this time." After this judgment the Baylys appeared repeatedly before the courts between July and October 1655, in order for the magistrates to admonish Mrs. Bayly for "impudent and notorious lying; endeauouring to make discord among neighbours; and filthy & Vncleane speeches vttered by her." The couple were warned to remove themselves from the colony, and they took the advice; present banishment being preferable to future execution. The Baylys' appearances before the New Haven Courts on July 3, Aug. 7, Sept. 4 and Oct. 2, 1655, are recorded in *Ancient Town Records: New Haven Town Records 1649-1662*, ed. F. Bowditch Dexter (New Haven, 1917), I, 244-46, 249, 256-58, respectively; Levermore, *New Englander and Yale Review*, XLIV, 801.

[w] Testimonies given at courts held at New Haven, Aug. 7, and Sept. 4, 1655, in *New Haven Town Records*, ed. Dexter, I, 249-52, 256; court sentence given at a Court of Magistrates held at New Haven, Oct. 17, 1655, given in *Records of ... New Haven ... 1653 to the Union*, ed. Hoadley, pp. 151-52. See also Levermore, *New Englander and Yale Review*, XLIV, 803.

Name of Witch	Date	Accusers	Victims	Town	Colony	Verdict of the Jury	Final Verdict, Date and Sentence
Elizabeth Godman[w] (Third case)	Oct. 4, 1655	As above	As above		New Haven	Suspicious of witchcraft	Released upon payment of £50 security for future good conduct.
Anne Hibbins[x]	1656	Not known	Not known	Salem	Mass.	Guilty	A Court of Magistrates set aside the verdict but the General Court found her guilty on May 14, 1656 and she was hanged June 19, 1656.
Jane Welford[y]	1656	Several Not known	Not known	Dover	New Hamp.	Acquitted	Freed upon condition of future good behaviour.
Eunice Cole[z]	1656	Goodman Robe, Thomas Coleman, Abraham Drake	A cow and a sheep	Hampton	New Hamp.	Discharged	Released.

[x] Anne Hibbins was the sister of Deputy-Governor Richard Bellingham, and widow of late magistrate William Hibbins. A jury of life and death found her guilty; a court of magistrates set aside the verdict, and it fell to the General Court of May 14, 1656, to decide by vote that she was guilty. Joshua Scottow, who came to her defense following her conviction, was forced to apologize most humbly to the court. Verdict of the General Court, May 14, 1656, in *Records of the Governor and Company of Massachusetts Bay*, ed. Shurtleff, IV, Pt. I, 269; also Northend. *Historical Collections of the Essex Institute*, XXII, 266, n16: *Governor T. Hutchinson's Witchcraft Delusion*, ed. Poole, p. 385, n7; Thomas Hutchinson, *The History of the Colony of Massachu-*

setts Bay, from the first Settlement thereof in 1628, until its Incorporation with the Colony of Plimouth, Province of Main, &c (2nd ed.; London, 1760), I, 187-88: Drake, *Annals of Witchcraft*, pp. 98-99; Robbins, *Encyclopedia*, p. 520: *Narratives*, ed. Burr. p. 410, n1: and Emory Washburn, *Sketches of the Judicial History of Massachusetts from 1630 to The Revolution in 1775* (Boston, 1840), p. 45.

[y] Everett Hall Pendleton, *Brian Pendleton and His Massachusetts: 1634-1681* (n.p-p., 1951), pp. 112-16 claimed several were accused but only one bound over; Drake, *Annals of Witchcraft*, pp. 103-7.

[z] *Ibid*., pp. 99-103.

Name of Witch	Date	Accusers	Victims	Town	Colony	Verdict of the jury	Final Verdict, Date and Sentence
William Harding[aa]	1656	Mr. David Lindsaye	Not known	Northumberland County	Va.	Guilty	Ten stripes upon his bare back, and forever banished from the county, as well as paying all the costs of the trial.
William Meaker[bb]	1657	Thomas Mullener	Not known		New Haven	Not Guilty	The Court found against Mullener and ordered him to pay £50 estate security or removal from the colony.
Jane Hogg[cc]	1657	Not known	Not known		Mass.	Not known	Unknown.
—— Knape[ee]	1657	Not known	Not known		Mass.	Not known	Unknown.
Goodwife Batchelor[ee]	1657	Not known	Not known		Mass.	Not known	Unknown.
Ann Pope[ee]	1657	Not known	Not known		Mass.	Not known	Unknown.
Elizabeth Garlick[dd]	1657-1658	A fellow servant	Servant's child	Easthampton, Long Island	Conn.	Acquitted	Released, but had to pay the costs of transport to and from the trial.

[aa] In Northumberland County, Va., a jury of 24 men found evidence of witchcraft exhibited to the court by Mr. David Lindsaye, a minister, against the accused William Harding, was proved by several depositions. Accordingly Harding was sentenced. "Witchcraft in Virginia," *William and Mary Quarterly,* I, No. 3 (Jan. 1893), 69, "Books of Northumberland County, November 20, 1656."

[bb] Mullener's use of a witchcraft charge in an attempt to gain personal revenge upon Meaker reveals the potentialities of that crime. "At a Court of Magistrates, New Haven, 30. 4mo., 1657" in *Records of . . . New Haven . . 1653 to the Union,* ed. Hoadley, pp. 224-26; *New Haven Town Records,* ed. Dexter, I, 317-18; Tay-

lor, *Witchcraft Delusion,* pp. 149-50; Levermore, *New Englander and Yale Review,* XLIV, 803-4.

[cc] John Hull mentions at least four afflicted women in 1657, in *Some Observable Passages of Providence Toward the Country, and specially in these parts of the Massachusetts Bay,* in American Antiquarian Society, *Transactions and Collections,* III (1857), 191-92.

[dd] Letter to Easthampton in Town and Lands Vol. I, Doc. No. 8 in *The Public Records . . . Connecticut,* ed. Trumbull, I, 572-73; Levermore, *New England Magazine,* VI, 641-42; Drake, *Annals of Witchcraft,* pp. 110-12.

Name of Witch	Date	Accusers	Victims	Town	Colony	Verdict of the Jury	Final Verdict, Date and Sentence
Elizabeth Richardson**	1658	The Ship's company of the Sarah Artch	Ship's Master and company	At Sea	Md.		Executed. Edward Prescott, the Ship's Owner, was released and freed from a charge of allowing the hanging to take place on his vessel.
Katherine Grade**	1659	Captain Bennett	Not known	At Sea and Jamestown	Va.		Executed. Captain Bennett summoned before a General Court at Jamestown, but the verdict is not known.
Mrs. N. Robinson**	1659	Ann Godby	Not known		Va.	Acquitted	Mrs. Godby's husband had to pay 300 pounds of tobacco, the cost of the suit, and the witnesses' charges at the rate of 20 pounds of tobacco per day, for the slander.
John Godfrey** (Second case)	1659	Job, Moses, Mary, and Mary Tyler	Mary Tyler	Andover	Mass.		Depositions were made before the Governor, Simon Bradstreet, and six years later, in 1665, Godfrey was tried in Boston for witchcraft.
Mrs. W. Holmes**	1660	Dinah Sylvester	Not known	Scituate	Old Plymouth Colony	Not Guilty	Dinah Sylvester had to make public acknowledgement for a false accusation.

** In another Maryland case identical to the Mary Lee case of 1654, a witch, Elizabeth Richardson, was hanged at sea. John Washington of Westmoreland County, Virginia, great-grandfather of George Washington, charged Edward Prescott, a merchant, with a felony for allowing the hanging on board the *Sarah Artch*, bound for the colonies. Governor Fendall had Prescott arrested. In the court case, held in September and October 1658, Prescott did not deny that the execution had taken place, but declared that it had been performed by John Greene, Voyage Master. Though Prescott was both merchant and owner of the vessel, he affirmed that the ship's Master and company were ready to mutiny if she was not hanged. Prescott was acquitted at the bar for no one came forward to give evidence. John Washington was unable to attend for the baptism of his son took place at the same time

as the verdict. Parke, *Maryland Historical Magazine,* XXXI, 272-74; Sioussat, *Maryland Historical Magazine,* XXXI, 220; Charles H. Browning, "The Washington Pedigree; Corrigenda and Addenda," *Pennsylvania Magazine of Historical and Biography,* XLV (1921), 325; Edward D. Neill, "The Ancestry and Earlier Life of George Washington," *ibid,* XVI (1892), 263-64.

** Tom Peete Cross, "Witchcraft in North Carolina," *Studies in Philology,* XVI, No. 3 (July 1919), 219, n6.

** Several depositions testified to Mrs. Godby's loose tongue "At a Court held ye 15 December, 1659 pscnt att. Savill Gaskins," in Edward W. James, "Witchcraft in Virginia," *William and Mary Quarterly,* II (July 1893), 59.

** Drake, *Annals of Witchcraft,* pp. 86-88, 113.

** *Ibid.,* pp. 117-19, 113-16.

Name of Witch	Date	Accusers	Victims	Town	Colony	Verdict of the jury	Final Verdict, Date and Sentence
Mary Wright[jj]	1660	Not known	Not known		Long Island	Suspected of Witchcraft	Arraigned before the General Court of Mass., and acquitted of witchcraft, though convicted of being a Quaker, and banished.
Winifred Holman[kk]	1660	Not known	Rebecca Stearns	Cambridge	Mass.	Not known	Two affidavits signed by 7 and 18 persons respectively were produced to clear her, though the verdict is not known.
Nicholas Jennings[ll]	1661 Sept. 5	Not known	Several people	Sea Brook	Conn.	Disagreed	Freed after a jury disagreement "the major part thinking them guilty, and the rest strongly suspect it that they are guilty."
Margaret Jennings[ll]	Sept. 5, 1661	Not known	Several people	Sea Brook	Conn.	Disagreed	See verdict on Nicholas Jennings.
Nathaniel Greensmith[mm]	1662	Rebecca Greensmith, and the daughter of John Kelley	Anne Cole	Hartford	Conn.	Guilty	Executed.

jj *Ibid.*, pp. 117-18.

kk *Governor T. Hutchinson's Witchcraft Delusion*, ed. Poole, p. 385, n6; Robbins, *Encyclopedia*, p. 520.

ll *The Public Records . . . Connecticut*, ed. Trumbull, I, 338; Taylor, *Witchcraft Delusion*, p. 112; Drake, *Annals of Witchcraft*, pp. 150, 156. Mr. Samuel Willis was requested "to goe downe to Sea Brook, to assist ye Maior [Major] in examininge the suspitions about witchery, and to act therein as may be requisite." The Jennings were indicted on Sept. 5, 1661 for having caused the death of several people but they were freed after a jury disagreement. The General Court of Connecticut at Hartford declared that "they do not see cause to allow pay to witnesses for time and travaile, nor to any other upon such accounts for the future." See Levermore, *New Englander and Yale Review*, XLIV, 806.

mm Increase Mather, *An Essay for the Recording of Illustrious Providences* in *Narratives*, ed. Burr, pp. 18-21, 18n1; C. Mather, *Magnalia Christi Americana*, II, 448; Letter of John Whiting to Increase Mather, Apr. 10, 1682, entitled "An Account of a Remarkable passage of Divine providence that happened in Hartford, in the year of our Lord 1662," in *The Mather Papers*, Massachusetts Historical Society, *Collections*, 4th ser., VII (Boston, 1868), 466-69; Charles J. Hoadley, "A Case of Witchcraft in Hartford," *Connecticut Magazine*, V (Nov. 1899), 557-61; Drake, *Annals of Witchcraft*, pp. 119-25; Taylor, *Witchcraft Delusion*, pp. 96-100, 151, 156, 157; Levermore, *New Englander and Yale Review*, XLIV, 808-9.

Name of Witch	Date	Accusers	Victims	Town	Colony	Verdict of the jury	Final Verdict, Date and Sentence
Rebecca Greensmith mm	1662	Anne Cole, William Ayres	Anne Cole	Hartford	Conn.	Guilty	Executed.
Andrew Sanford mm	1662	Not known	Anne Cole or the daughter of John Kelley	Hartford	Conn.	Not known	Not known.
Mary Sanford mm	1662	Not known	Not known	Hartford	Conn.	Guilty	Executed, sometime after June 13.
William Ayres mm	1662	Daughter of John Kelley	Anne Cole	Hartford	Conn.	Guilty	The water test was applied and confirmed witchcraft; he escaped prison and fled the colony.
Goodwife Ayres mm	1662	Daughter of John Kelley	Anne Cole	Hartford	Conn.	Guilty	The water test was applied and confirmed witchcraft; she fled the colony with her husband.
Mary Barnes mm	1662	Not known	Not known	Farm-ington	Conn.	Guilty	Executed.
Judith Varleth mm	1662	Daughter of John Kelley	Not known	Hartford	Conn.	Guilty	Found guilty, Jan. 6, but released after the personal intervention of Peter Stuyvesant, Governor of New Amsterdam and brother-in-law of the accused.
Elizabeth Seager mm (First case)	1662	Anne Cole	Anne Cole	Hartford	Conn.	Guilty	Discharged.
Elizabeth Seager mm (Second case)	1662	Anne Cole	Anne Cole	Hartford	Conn.		Discharged, but under suspicion.
James Walkley mm	1662	Daughter of John Kelley	Not known	Hartford	Conn.	Not known	Probably guilty, because he fled to Rhode Island.
Katherine Palmer mm	1662	Not known	Not known	Hartford	Conn.	Not known	Not known.
Mrs. Peter Grant mm	1662	Not known	Not known	Hartford	Conn.	Not known	Not known.

The two questions upon which this table can cast no light are, firstly, why did so many cases occur and, secondly, what characteristics did they possess? Both questions may be approached through an analysis of the three factors most likely to contribute to the occurrence of witchcraft activity in a society, namely the theological (or ideological) background of the people suspecting witchcraft, the presence of external stimuli and evidence of internal pressures in society likely to produce an active awareness of witches.[14]

In his monumental survey of the theological framework of Puritan New England, Perry Miller wondered why no more cases of witchcraft had occurred before 1692, "for it was axiomatic that the Devil would try hard to corrupt regions famous for religion." He accepted without reservation, however, that cases of witchcraft before 1692 were "sporadic" but speculated that:

Perhaps the reason there were so few witches in New England . . . is . . . the people were good enough Calvinists to resist temptation. They might not always be able to refuse an extra tankard of rum, but this sin—although it was the most plausible and the most enticing—they withstood.[15]

Many of those indicted for witchcraft were judged to have failed in withstanding the sin. This was relatively easy to do for a covenant could be applied with equal diligence to a relationship with the Devil or with God, and the American Puritans were openly confronted with the Indians as positive instruments of Satan's power and determination to conquer New England for himself, permitted to torment all because of God's terrible judgments against his wayward people. Once it had been decided that the assumption of redemption through God's grace no longer applied to an individual, the twin assumption of original sin worked against him with devastating effect. The next step backward was seduction by the Devil, then open covenanting with him. For example, the indictments

---

[14] There is another area of witchcraft analysis based upon the collection of colorful tales, legends and folklore of witches and witchcraft, rather than court records, in the manner of the epic songs examined by A. B. Lord, *The Singer of Tales* (Cambridge, 1960). The best examples are Joseph F. Folsom, "Witches in New Jersey," New Jersey Historical Society, *Proceedings*, n. s., VII (1922), 293-305; Tom Peete Cross, *Studies in Philology*, XVI, 217-87; Mary L. Deaver, "Witchcraft in Buttermaking," *Ross County Historical Society* Pamphlet (Chillicothe, Ohio, 1958); Nelson E. Jones, "Witchcraft in Lawrence County," from his book *The Squirrel Hunters of Ohio, or, Glimpses of Pioneer Life* (Ohio Valley Folk Publications, n. s., p. 100); Albert Douglas, "Ohio's only Witchcraft Case," *Ohio Archaeological and Historical Publications*, XXXIII (1924), 205-14.

[15] Perry Miller, *The New England Mind: From Colony to Province* (Cambridge, 1953), p. 179.

against Mary Johnson indicated that she was an allegedly lazy servant girl who prayed to the Devil for aid, and "by her own confession shee is guilty of familliarity with the Deuill." The evidence against her cited the fact that she had been able to command the services of a goblin to perform her household duties. When she was chastised for not carrying out the ashes "a Devil afterwards would clear the Hearth of Ashes for her," and when she was sent into the fields to chase out marauding hogs "a Devil would scowre the Hogs away, and make her laugh to see how he scared them." In her confession she admitted uncleanness "both with men and with Devils." At Wethersfield, Connecticut, the indictment against the Carringtons claimed they had "Intertained ffamiliarity with Sathan, the Great Enemy of God and Mankinde," and in the Mary Parsons case the indictment accused her of not having fear of God before her eyes, nor in her heart, seduction by the Devil, familiarity and covenanting with the Devil while having used several devilish practices by witchcraft "to the hurt of the persons of Martha and Rebeckah Moxon," and yielding to the Devil's instigations and "malitious motion." Similarly, in the cases where people were released they were warned, generally, that they were "suspitious of witchcraft." These warnings were given to Mrs. Godman, the Baylys and the Jennings.[16]

Evidence of witchcraft was accumulated in three ways: by confession, by searchings for witchmarks and by the collection of testimonies and accusations of witchcraft. The first two alone meant automatic proof of guilt followed by execution. Margaret Jones was examined and found to possess a Devil's mark, "a teat, as fresh as if [it] had been newly sucked." This revealed where an imp or animal of the Devil had fastened on to her, a physical affirmation of the reversal of the covenant. Both the Staplies and Knapp cases in Connecticut were concerned with the discovery of witchmarks on Mrs. Knapp's body, and her fate was sealed by seven neighbors who claimed to have seen them. Mrs. Staplies refused to believe Goodwife Knapp was a witch, and suspicion fell on her also. As Mrs. Knapp's body was brought off the gallows, Mrs. Staplies examined it for the alleged witchmarks and found none. Mrs. Lockwood, one of the seven accusers, declared that they had been there; "she had them, and she confessed she was a witch; that is sufficient."[17]

16 For the examples see notes e, i, k, v, w and ll.

17 Readers familiar only with the procedure at Salem in 1692, where confession was followed by release should note that confession by witches was proof of guilt, and led to execution under the Statute of James, 1604. Salem judges reversed this process. Witchmarks revealed where a witch had allowed a devil or an imp to "fasten" on to her, a physical reaffirmation of the reverse covenant. See Joseph Glanvil, *Saducisimus Triumphant* (London, 1689), pp. 75-76, and for the examples, notes c, p and q.

The majority who did withstand the sin of witchcraft did not do so merely as a passive exercise. As the Elect they were presented with Biblical evidence of the existence of witchcraft. They would hardly be good Calvinists if they did not seek out witches, for Calvin stood explicitly by the Old Testament book of Exodus which declared "Thou shalt not suffer a witch to live" and this decree was written into the laws of Massachusetts, Connecticut, New Haven and Plymouth. Upon witchcraft itself Calvin had declared: "now the Bible teaches that there are witches and that they must be slain. God expressly commands that all witches and enchantresses be put to death, and this law of God is a universal law." For this reason the early colonists of New England were good Calvinists precisely because they did search out witches. Witchcraft was not only a "temptation" to resist; it was an evil requiring positive eradication before God.[18]

Consequently, colonial leaders became increasingly concerned during the 1640s with the emergence of witchcraft activity as a manifestation of the Devil's desire to subvert God's Commonwealth. Puritan, Anglican, Pilgrim and Catholic alike took steps to arm themselves with legal protection against his agents. In 1636 Plymouth included in its Summary Offences "lyable to Death," the action of "Solemn Compaction or conversing with the devil by way of Witchcraft, conjuration or the like." The 1641 Massachusetts Bay Body of Liberties and the 1642 Connecticut Capital Code both included, as their second law: "Yf any man or woman be a witch (that is) hath or consulteth with a familiar spirit, they shall be put to death." All three colonies re-enacted these laws in 1646. Rhode Island accepted a witchcraft law on May 19th, 1647, after its charter had been granted. The law stated that "witchcraft is forbidden by this present Assembly to be used in this colony, and the penalty imposed by the authority that we are subjected to, is felony of death." New Haven possessed a law similar to Connecticut's. Armed thus, the colonies were prepared to deal with outbreaks of witchcraft, as well as conform to the laws of England on the subject. By 1662 they had made good use of their legal provisions in a fifteen-year campaign against the Devil's agents in nearly all of the colonies.[19]

[18] Calvin's pronouncements upon witchcraft are clearly analyzed in Burr, American Antiquarian Society, *Proceedings*, XXI, 198-99.

[19] *Records of the Colony of New Plymouth in New England*, ed. David Pulsifer (Boston, 1861), XI, 12, 95, 172; *The Public Records . . . Connecticut*, ed. Trumbull, I, 77; Drake, *Annals of Witchcraft*, p. 56; Taylor, *Witchcraft Delusion*, pp. 23-24; "Laws of Rhode Island," Massachusetts Historical Society, *Collections*, 2nd ser., VII (Boston, 1818), 79, n2. Samuel G. Drake believed that early activity led to the Plymouth laws. John Winthrop in 1639 noted that "the Indians near Aquiday being pawwawing in this tempest, the devil came and fetched away five of them." See John

While New England laws and religion attempted to undermine the "Great Enemy of God and Mankind," the pressure for an outbreak of witchcraft activity came from overseas. In England, against a background of mounting tension, and later warfare, between King and Parliament, hundreds of witchcraft accusations were made. Between 1645 and 1647 over two hundred witches were executed. The period of greatest slaughter was in the summer of 1645 when Matthew Hopkins, Witch Finder General, was at the height of his campaign to find witches. Altogether, the decade between 1637 and 1647 produced the greatest percentage of hangings per. indictment, 42%, of any period in English witchcraft history. Later still, outbreaks were recorded in Scotland, 1643-50; East Anglia, 1645; Newcastle, 1648; Kent, 1652 and Scotland, 1661. In Europe, the Swedish case of bewitched children, sometimes referred to as the possible inspiration for the Goodwin case of 1688 and the Salem episode of 1692, occurred in 1661.[20]

These persecutions undoubtedly troubled the colonists in New England. Certainly the colonial magistrates knew of English methods of examining suspected witches. In their search for "familiars," witchmarks and imps they were adopting the same practices as Matthew Hopkins. In the very first case brought before the bench at Boston, the Court was "desireows that the same course which hath ben taken in England for the discouery of witches, by watchinge, may also be taken here with the witch now in question." Thus for Margaret Jones the Court ordered that "a strict watch be set about her every night, & that her husband be confined to a priuat roome, & watched also." In Hartford, in 1662, William Ayres and his wife were given the water test, a common European method of determining witchcraft. They failed the test which was suffi-

---

Winthrop, *Journal*, I, 297; Edward Johnson, *Wonder-Working Providence*, p. 237; Josiah Gilbert Holland, *History of Western Massachusetts, The Counties of Hampden, Hampshire, Franklin and Berkshire* (Springfield, 1885), I, Pt. I, 40-41; Cross, *Studies in Philology*, XVI, 221, n9, who pointed out that "accusations of witchcraft are found in Virginia records as early as 1641." James R. Jacob, *"The Phantastick Air": The Idea of the Praeternatural in Colonial New England* (Master's thesis, Rice University, May 1964), gives an excellent treatment of the bases and assumptions of colonial attitudes to witchcraft theory, especially pp. 21-22, 47-67 and 69-87.

20 For the European background see *Narratives*, ed. Burr, pp. xv-xvi; Burr, "The Literature of Witchcraft," *Papers of the American Historical Association*, IV (July 1890), 37-66 and American Antiquarian Society, *Proceedings*, XXI, 185-217; Kittredge, American Antiquarian Society, *Proceedings*, XVII, 8, 148-212 and his *Witchcraft in Old and New England* (New York, 1928); *Materials toward a History of Witchcraft*, ed. Henry C. Lea (Philadelphia, 1939) gives great detail of cases all over Europe and C. L'Estrange Ewen, *Witch Hunting and Witch Trials: the indictments for Witchcraft from the Records of 1373 Assizes held for the Home Circuit, A. D. 1559-1736* (London, 1929), pp. 1-115, esp. 31, 42, 100, 112-13. Ewen's statistical tables will cause many revisions of witchcraft estimates, especially in the corrections of exaggerated claims of witch executions in the Commonwealth period.

cient evidence of guilt to warrant execution, and they were in prison after it when they escaped with the aid of friends. The executions at sea in 1654, 1658 and 1659 indicated not only common denominators in the search for witches, but also stimulated witchcraft incidents in the colonies where the vessels landed.[21]

As a series of distressing internal upheavals combined with Old Testament theology in England to generate the witchcraft cases, so too in the colonies did Puritan theology serve as a catalyst to the extraordinary number of distressing events which affected colonial society in the 1640s. A similar state of affairs had prevailed in Salem before the outburst of 1692. Samuel E. Morison has observed that the 1692 episode needed little clerical belief in witchcraft for it arose, "as witchcraft epidemics had usually arisen in Europe, during a troubled period, the *Decennium Luctuosum* of New England History."[22] Morison noted the uneasiness of the people with rebellions, changes of government, fear of Indian attacks, and factional strife within the community. The unsettled state of the colony was further agitated when Increase Mather, after long negotiations, failed to win back the old charter revoked by James II; the colony had to accept a Royal Governor; a boundary dispute broke out with neighboring Topsfield;[23] and the new Governor had to leave for the frontier to lead an expedition against the Indians.

This unrest of the 1692 period was a replica of the distress in the 1640s, particularly in Massachusetts, Connecticut and Plymouth. William Bradford commented upon the wickedness that had grown and broken forth "in a land wher the same was so much witnessed against, and so narrowly looked into, and severly punished." Despite these punishments, Bradford observed "sundrie notorious sins" prevailed in Plymouth, "oftener than once." In analyzing the outbreak of wickedness, he feared that:

The Divell may carry a greater spite against the churches of Christ and the gospell hear, by how much the more the indeaour to preserve holynes and puritie amongst them. . . . I would rather thinke thus,

[21] The water test, whereby a suspected witch was thrown into a pond with the thumbs cross-tied to the opposite big toes, was a common European method of determining witchcraft. It was based upon the assumption that the pure element would not receive an agent of the devil. If one floated one was regarded as a witch, and if one sank one was innocent, though often drowned! For references see notes c and mm.

[22] Samuel E. Morison, *The Puritan Pronaos* (New York, 1963), p. 259.

[23] Abbie W. Towne, "William Towne, his daughters and the Witchcraft Delusion," Topsfield Historical Society, *Collections*, I (1895), 12-14; Abbie Peterson Towne & Marietta Clark, "Topsfield in the Witchcraft Delusion," *ibid.*, XIII (1908), 23-38; George Francis Dow, "Witchcraft Records Relating to Topsfield," *ibid.*, pp. 39-143.

then that Satane hath more power in these heathen lands, as some have thought, then in more Christian nations espetially over God's servants in them.[24]

Even greater evidence of unrest existed in Massachusetts. On September 22, 1642, the year after the colony's promulgation of its witchcraft law, John Winthrop drew attention in his journal to the "unsettled frame of spirit" which had led many people to emigrate to the West Indies, to New Amsterdam, Long Island or even back to England. He blamed the "sudden fall of land and cattle"; the scarcity of money and foreign commodities, and people fleeing from the colony, for the unrest in Massachusetts.[25] From that date forward evidence of Satanic intervention in the colony's affairs fills his pages. The corn crop of 1643 was spoiled by pigeons and mice; a great storm swept over Newberry, darkening the air with dirt on July 5, 1643; lights were seen near Boston and over the North East point in January 1644, at the place where Captain Chaddock's pinnace had been blown up, reputedly by a necromancer. A voice was heard calling across the water several times. At Hingham, a man named Painter, who turned Anabaptist and prevented his wife from baptizing their child, even though she was a member of the church, disturbed the Church leaders sufficiently in July for them to have the man whipped for "reproaching the Lord's ordinance." Out of just such small beginnings arose the great tensions leading to the Half-Way Covenant as a solution for the baptismal problems of the children of non-church members. In 1645 the wife of Hartford's Governor, Mrs. Hopkins, lost her reason and understanding. Externally, preparations were made for a second war against the Pequot Indians, for "Sathan may stir up & combine many of his instruments against the Churches of Christ." The Hingham militia had to be lectured by Winthrop on the meanings of liberty to obey their leaders. On August 28, 1645, a day of fasting and humiliation for troubles in Old and New England was held, the third such day to be set aside since 1643. By 1646 the General Court of Massachusetts was inundated with petitions of grievances. Then came two monumental calamities in 1646-47. The colonies were just struggling back to prosperity after the depression of 1642-43 when the corn, wheat and barley crops were ruined by black worms and caterpillars, which ate the blades and tassels and left the rest to wither. The churches held a day of humiliation. Secondly, in 1647, an epidemic swept the country among Indians, English and Dutch. It weakened the people so much that the

[24] William Bradford, *History of Plymouth Plantation* (Boston, 1912), II, 308-9.
[25] John Winthrop, *Journal*, II, 82, 83-84. He noted "they fled from fear of want, and many of them fell into it, even to extremity, as if they had hastened into the misery which they feared and fled from."

gathering of the remaining crops was lost for want of help, even though few died in Massachusetts and Connecticut.[26]

The pessimism that was generated by these plagues was aptly described in the almanacs of a young Harvard intellectual, Samuel Danforth. In 1647 the Harvard "philomathemat" recorded the ordinary occurrences in the colony—the arrival of ships, the coming of winter, and the debilitating effects of the late sickness—in epigrammatic verse. To his first almanac was appended a list of events which optimistically expressed the hopes of the settlers in converting the Indians, and illustrated the expansion of New England towns. In 1648, however, the contents of his verse underwent a marked change. With a painstaking tribute to classical allusion and allegory he ran through all the blessings of the New England scene; a pleasant land in which the Puritan plant, tended by a faithful husbandman, could survive. All of the advantages of Justice, Liberty, Peace, Unity, Truth, Plenty, a Nursery [Harvard College], and the conversion of the Indians, were meticulously spelled out. On the surface this appears to be a hymn of praise to a beneficent providence. But the verses should be examined alongside the chronological table of "some few memorable occurrences" that are listed at the end of the almanac. There Danforth summarized every melancholy event and disaster that had hit the colonies from 1636 to 1647. Nothing was omitted, and the whole checks off exactly with Winthrop's observations. Far from being a hymn of praise, Danforth's verses of 1648 represent an antidote to social, economic and religious distress by referring to classical abstract virtues. With the issue of the 1649 almanac he even removed this escapist cloak. Both his verse content and his table of occurrences list one long series of unhappy events. With intended irony, the young intellectual informed his readers that, even in the midst of their host of troubles, things could still be worse. With England, Ireland, Scotland and Barbadoes racked by war and pestilence, "the worthless Orphan may sit still and blesse, That yet it sleeps in peace and quietness."[27]

In the presence of so many other troubles, the absence of war may have seemed small consolation to New Englanders. For when the synod of 1648 met at Cambridge to settle "such errors, objections, and scruples as

[26] *Ibid.*, II, 92, 126, 155-56, 177, 225, 229-39. See also John Winthrop, *A Declaration of Former Passages and Proceedings Between the English and the Narragansets* (Boston, 1645), p. 7; George Parker Winship, *The Cambridge Press: 1638-1692* (Philadelphia, 1945), pp. 64-65; Edward Johnson, *Wonder-Working Providence*, p. 237, n2, p. 238, n1, pp. 240-41 and Samuel Danforth, *An Almanac for 1647* (Cambridge, 1647), list of notable events for the years 1646 and 1647; Danforth, *An Almanac for 1648* (Cambridge, 1648), A chronological table of some few memorable instances, years 1646 and 1647.

[27] Danforth, *Almanacs* for 1646, 1647, 1648 and *An Almanac for 1649* (Cambridge, 1649), lines 87-88.

had been raised about it by some young heads in the country," the barriers of resistance to the realities of the Devil's work were going down in Connecticut and Massachusetts. While Winthrop glorified the synod as the triumphant representative of the churches of Christ in New England, his fellow magistrates in Boston and Hartford were finding fresh confirmation of the Devil's malignant concern. As Mary Johnson and Margaret Jones went to their respective scaffolds the whole formula of religious ferment added to social distress and natural disasters, which later characterized the Salem episode, was present in 1647.[28]

Once underway, the witchcraft cases of 1647 to 1662 added to the tension from which they sprang. They did this in a steady stream of cases, year by year, rather than in one frenzied outburst such as occurred in 1692. Yet many of the characteristics of the Salem trials were in evidence in the earlier trials. The indictments were often concerned with the bewitchment of children and animals. Mary Johnson and Mary Parsons were accused of killing their own children by witchcraft. The former had smothered her child, and before execution left another baby, born in prison, to the care of Nathaniel Rescew, the jailer. Mary Parsons, after marrying Hugh Parsons on October 27, 1645, had two sons to him, born October 4, 1649, and October 26, 1650. Both died in less than a year of their births, and the evidence suggests that after the death of the second one, on March 1, 1651, the mother lost her reason. Although denunciations of witchcraft were leveled against Hugh Parsons by his neighbors, it was Mary Parsons who was imprisoned at Boston on May 1, and her case came before the General Court six days later. Later still the cases involving Mrs. Kendal and Goodwife Garlick concerned the deaths of other people's children. Mrs. Kendal was executed for bewitching to death a young child belonging to Goodman Genings of Watertown. The child's nurse testified that Mrs. Kendal had fondled the child, that soon afterward it changed color and died. The Court received this evidence without bothering to call the child's parents. After Mrs. Kendal's execu-

28 John Winthrop, *Journal,* II, 347. There is a remarkable observation by Charles Francis Adams in *Massachusetts: Its Historians and Its History* (Boston, 1893), pp. 85-86. Writing upon the witch cases at Salem in 1692, he noted, "The New England historians have usually regarded this curious and interesting period as an isolated phenomenon, to be described as such, and then palliated it by references to the far more ferocious and unthinking maniacal outbreaks of like nature in other lands at about the same time. . . . The mania of 1691-92 in Massachusetts was no isolated or inexplicable manifestation . . . given John Winthrop's journal in 1630-40, Salem witchcraft at a somewhat later period might with safety be predicted. The community was predisposed to the epidemic. . . ." This single reference to Salem and Winthrop's *Journal* indicated that Adams had made the connection between witchcraft and the unrest of the 1640s. All he lacked was the specific information of the cases in these years.

tion the parents testified that the child had died of exposure caused by the neglect of the nurse. By this time the latter was in prison for adultery, and she died there. The case ended with no further recantations; striking evidence of how the stigma of witchcraft tainted the innocent and muted inquiry. Further afield, in Easthampton, in the winter of 1657-58, Goodwife Garlick escaped from an identical accusation by a fellow servant, who claimed she had bewitched her child. The head of the household, Lion Gardiner, gave evidence that the baby died from the neglect of the mother, yet the magistrates at Easthampton ordered two men, Thomas Baker and John Hand, to go "into Kenicut for to bring us under their government . . . and also to carry Goodwife Garlick, that she may be delivered up into the authorities there for the triall of the cause of witchcraft [of] which she is suspected."[29]

Some of the evidence in many of the cases concerned the illnesses of witnesses and animals, and accidental occurrences. In Maryland, Peter Godson and his wife alleged that he became lame after seeing the wife of Richard Manship. In the first Mrs. Godman case of 1653, in New Haven, she was accused on May 21, of knowing whatever was done at church meetings, muttering to herself, being responsible for the sickness of the Rev. Mr. Hooke's son, and for the "verey strang fitts wch hath continewed at times ever since," of Mrs. Bishop, who had lost her own children. Later Mrs. Godman quarreled with the wife of the Colonial Treasurer, Mrs. Atwater, who then blamed her when she found Betty Brewster, a servant, ill "in a most misserable case, heareing a most dreadfull noise wch put her in great feare and trembling, wch put her into such a sweate . . . and in ye morning she looked as one yt had bine allmost dead." Three days later, on May 24, 1653, further depositions were made regarding the cause of Mrs. Bishop's fainting fits. As early as 1648 this type of evidence had brought about the conviction of Margaret Jones, blamed when her neighbor's children fell ill.[30]

---

[29] In 1651 Massachusetts held a solemn day of prayer "to consider how far Satan prevails amongst us in respect of witchcraft." See Robbins, *Encyclopedia of Witchcraft*, p. 520. Exactly the same decision was made in 1688, following the Goodwin case, but then it was confined only to Boston and Charlestown. See Cotton Mather, *Magnalia Christi Americana*, II, 457. Fifty years after Mary Johnson's death, Cotton Mather concluded with unintended irony that "she dy'd in a frame extreamly to the satisfaction of them that were spectators of it," which meant that she repented under the guidance of the Rev. Mr. Stone, her minister. See *The Public Records . . . Connecticut*, ed. Trumbull, I, 209, 222, 226 and 232. In 1646 Mary Johnson had been whipped for thievery and sentenced at the Particular Court, Aug. 21, 1646, *ibid.*, I, 143. For the reference to Mather see *Magnalia Christi Americana*, II, 456.

[30] For the clique gathered around "Mr. Goodyeare, Mris. Goodyeare, Mr. Hooke, Mris. Hooke, Mris. Bishop, Mris. Atwater, Hanah and Elizabeth Lamberton [sisters of Mrs. Bishop], and Mary Miles, Mris. Atwater's maide," see *Records of New Haven . . . 1653 to the Union*, ed. Hoadley, pp. 31-34.

Illness among animals was often blamed upon the activities of witches. In New Haven, during the first Mrs. Godman case, Mrs. Thorp swore that after she had refused to sell or give some chickens to Mrs. Godman she feared they would be struck down by witchcraft:

> she thought then that if this woman was naught as folkes suspect, may be she will smite my chickens, and quickly after one chicken dyed, and she remembred she had heard if they were bewitched they would consume wthin, and she opened it and it was consumed in ye gisard to water & wormes, and divers others of them droped, and now they are missing and it is likely dead, and she neuer saw either hen or chicken that was so consumed w'hin wth wormes.[31]

Later, in the second and third Godman cases, the testimonies of new witnesses included similar examples. Allen Ball spoke of strange happenings with his calf; Mrs. Thorp added fresh complaints about her cow; and others mentioned troubles with pigs and calves. In Hartford, the Mary Johnson case involved the frightening of hogs by a goblin. During 1659 a deposition was made before Governor Bradstreet of Massachusetts that the Tyler family in Andover had received a visitation from the Devil in the form of a "Thing like a Bird" six years earlier. In 1665 the Tylers renewed their testimonies. The second case in New Hampshire, involving Eunice Cole, was brought before the courts by Goodman Robe who had lost a cow and a sheep.[32]

Even more trivial evidence was accepted as proof of the Devil's evil influences on his agents. Part of the charges against Mrs. Godman dealt with her ability to smell figs in the pockets of Mrs. Atwater when no one else could. The main evidence against Hugh Parsons was given by his wife after she had confessed to witchcraft in May 1651. Her charges included his knowing all of the secrets that she had revealed only to her intimate friend Mrs. Smith; being out late at night; his arrival in a bad temper; putting out the fire; throwing peas about; talking in his sleep and fighting with the Devil. The Jury convicted him on this testimony, but he was acquitted by the General Court. In the Lydia Gilbert case execution followed evidence that she had caused the accidental death of Henry Stiles, two years previously. Any strange occurrence could thus be laid at the witches' doors. In 1657, Thomas Mullener's use of a witchcraft charge, in an attempt to gain personal revenge upon William Meaker, backfired upon the accuser, but the potentialities of the charge remained.

[31] Complaint of Goodwife Thorp, June 16, 1653, after the examination of Mrs. Godman, May 24, 1653, *ibid.*, p. 36.
[32] See notes r, w, z, hh.

Dissatisfaction with a neighbor could easily be converted into accusations of witchcraft.[33]

As the evidence presented to the courts covered a wide range of accusations it also concerned a large number of people. In the trial of Hugh Parsons 39 testimonies were presented to Edward Rawson, clerk of the court. Only nine of these bore the same surname as other witnesses, and at least 30 families were involved in this case at Springfield in 1651. During 1653 and 1654, the Staplies and Knapp trials recorded the names of at least seven people who had accused Mrs. Knapp and then accused Mrs. Staplies of witchcraft. For the latter case 18 more added their contributions to the evidence. In addition five people went to see Mrs. Knapp in prison. Altogether 30 people were involved in this case, 22 of whom possessed different surnames. Two of the witnesses, Deborah Lockwood and Bethia Brundish were seventeen and sixteen years old respectively. In New Haven, Nicholas Bayly and his wife were called before a court and informed that "sundrie passages taken in writing . . . doth render them both, but especially the woman, very suspitious in poynt of witchcraft. . . ."[34]

With large numbers in small communities that were closely clustered, the news of witchcraft was carried from one region to another on the wings of gossip. This gossip was often sufficient to stimulate a search for other witches. Mary Parsons' charges against her husband included a declaration that "you tould her that you were at a Neighbor's Howse a little before Lecture, when they were speaking of Carrington and his Wife, that were now apprhended for Witches," thus establishing a direct link with the execution of the Carringtons of Wethersfield. In the Staplies' case, Goodwife Sherwood's written testimony against Staplies revealed much of the preoccupation with witchcraft, as well as intercommunity awareness:

> so the next day she went in againe to see the witch with other neighbours, there was Mr. Jones, Mris. Pell & her two daughters, Mris. Ward and goodwife Lockwood . . . Elizabeth [Mrs. Pell's daughter] bid her [Knapp] doe as the witch at the other towne [Bassett] did, that is, discouer all she knew to be witches.[35]

The spread of tragic examples from New England implicated other areas in witchcraft activity. Virginia experienced the first effects of the dangers

---

33 See notes k, l, o, u, bb.
34 See notes l, p, q, v.
35 Testimony of Mrs. Parsons in Drake, *Annals of Witchcraft*, p. 233. Mrs. Parsons continued "I hope that God will find all such wicked Psons and purge New England of all Witches ere it be long" (p. 234); Taylor, *Witchcraft Delusion*, p. 136, for Goodwife Sherwood's testimony.

inherent in gossiping over witches in May 1655. At a private court in Linhaven, the following resolution was passed:

> Whereas divrs dangerous & scandalous speeches have been raised by some psons concerning sevrall women in this Countie, termeing them to be Witches, whereby theire reputacons have been much impaired and their lives brought in question (ffor avoydeing the like offence). It is by this Cort ordered that what pson soever shall hereafter raise any such like scandall, concerninge any partie whatsor, and shall not be able to pve the same, both upon oath, and by sufficient witness, such pson soe offending shall in the first place paie a thousand pounds of tob: and likewise by lyable to further Censure of the Cort.[36]

It was in the face of this resolution that the Rev. David Lindsaye proved his case against William Harding in 1656, and Ann Godby failed to prove her case against Mrs. Nicholas Robinson in 1659. Virginia and Maryland's first cases followed immediately after the excitements of the shipboard hangings that were brought to light in their courts, but the cases resembled New England cases so closely that it is difficult to say which was the major cause of witchcraft spreading to these areas. From the colonists' point of view it was not important. What had occurred was an extension of the Devil's activities. While still interested primarily in Puritan New England, the "Great Enemy" was conducting flanking operations along the shores of Catholic Maryland and Anglican Virginia. He also appeared across the New Hampshire border.[37]

In addition to large numbers of people generating the searches for witches in their own communities, leading to inquiries in other towns, many of these cases reveal a curious comparison with the Salem outburst of 1692. That frenzy had occurred in the absence of the Governor, away fighting the Indians. Similarly, the cases of 1647-62 often developed in the absence of the colonial governors, and were directly connected with the Deputy Governors, leading officials and prominent clergymen. In 1653, all of the eminent citizens of New Haven society were implicated when Elizabeth Godman, a woman possessing a quick temper and the ability to antagonize her own sex, became the subject of malicious gossip by a clique gathered around the wives of Deputy Governor Stephen Goodyeare, Colonial Treasurer, Mr. Atwater, and the Rev. Mr. Hooke. As she was attached to the Goodyeare household, Mrs. Godman was easily accessible as the center of attraction and the rumors spread. After being locked out of the Atwater house one day, Mrs. Godman proceeded to alarm the Rev. Mr. Hooke by maintaining that witches should not be

---

[36] "Lower Norff: At a private Cort held the 23 day of May, 1655, at the home of Mr. Edward Hall in Linhaven. . . ." in James, *William & Mary Quarterly*, I, 58-60.

[37] See notes s, aa, ee, ff, gg.

provoked but, instead, brought into the church. This doctrine shocked Hooke, and as he was troubled in his sleep about witches at the time of his son's sickness he centered his uneasiness upon Mrs. Godman. She proved as resourceful as her adversaries, and won the day by carrying the fight to them by summoning all of her tormentors before the magistrates, and complaining of them for suspecting her of being a witch. After reviewing all of the evidence, which included a claim that "Hobbamocke" [the Indian Devil] was her husband, the Court pointed out that Mrs. Godman was known as a liar, and it found the defendants not guilty. Moreover, it warned her that she had "vnjustly called heither the seuerall psons before named, being she can proue nothing against them, and that her cariage doth justly render her suspitious of witchcraft, wch she herselfe in so many words confesseth." The Court warned her to watch her conduct afterward, for in the event of further proof being presented, "these passages will not be forgotten." Credit has been given to the Court of Magistrates for its forbearance in withstanding the force of contemporary pressure, and to Governor Eaton for judiciously distinguishing between "a cross grained temper and possession by a devil," but Mrs. Godman also deserves credit for her astute legal move as opinion began to build against her. It became exceedingly difficult to find her guilty of witchcraft when she was the plaintiff, however much the Court might pass opinions upon her.[38]

The Knapp and Staplies cases developed in New Haven and Connecticut in 1653 when Deputy Governor Roger Ludlow of Connecticut accused the two women. In the course of the trial Ludlow reported that Goodwife Knapp had revealed that Mrs. Staplies was her accomplice. Mrs. Knapp had refused to incriminate anyone, especially when seven of her neighbors constantly placed Mrs. Staplies' name before her. Mrs. Staplies refused to believe that Knapp had witchmarks, or was a witch. When she protested against the searchings for witchmarks she was howled down by the seven old harridans, and then accused by Ludlow. Her husband, Thomas, cross-sued for defamation. Before the court met at New Haven, May 29, 1654, Mrs. Staplies gained an ally, the Rev. Mr. Davenport, who testified that Ludlow had told him that Mrs. Knapp had come down from the gallows and revealed Mrs. Staplies as a witch. Ludlow protested that he had told this to Davenport in strictest confidence, but Davenport testified on oath that he had been careful to make no unlawful promises to Ludlow to keep any confidences and secrets, and that with God's help he would keep only lawful promises. His evidence thus meant that Ludlow had been guilty of defaming Mrs. Staplies. Even

---

38 See notes o and w.

though Ludlow marshaled impressive evidence that Mrs. Staplies admitted to possessing witchmarks if Goodwife Knapp did, the Court, pressed by Staplies' lawyer, would not accept unsworn testimony for Ludlow, and the case went against him. But it had needed the active intervention of one of the founding fathers of New Haven, invoking the righteousness of his oaths before God, to thwart Ludlow's charges.[39]

In other areas witches were not as fortunate. Deputy Governor Richard Bellingham of Salem was powerless to save his sister, Anne Hibbins, in 1656. But the Hartford case of 1662, when a whole coven of witches was condemned, proved the most disastrous for the accused, when Governor Winthrop was absent in England gaining a charter. The case had a further similarity to Salem in 1692, for the accusations were inspired by two young children. In spring 1662, the eight-year-old daughter of John Kelley cried out in delirium before she died that Goodwife Ayres had bewitched her. William Ayres and his wife were arrested and given the water test. Then James Walkley fled to Rhode Island. The net gathered in Judith Varleth, sister-in-law of the Governor of New Amsterdam, Peter Stuyvesant. On May 13, 1662, Nathaniel Greensmith filed suit against the Ayres for slander of witchcraft, but then the Greensmiths were arrested. Mary Sanford was indicted for the same offense. Nathaniel Greensmith had a criminal record for stealing, and his wife, married twice previously, was described by the Rev. John Whiting as a "lewd, ignorant and considerably aged woman." After the daughter of John Kelley died, the accusations were maintained by Ann Cole, daughter of John Cole, a neighbor of the Greensmiths. She was afflicted with fits, muttering in a Dutch tongue when she did not know the language, and cried out that a company of devils was conspiring to ruin her. She then denounced Goodwife Seager for bewitching her. This woman was indicted for witchcraft three times between 1662 and 1665, and was only released when Governor Winthrop postponed a death sentence upon her, releasing her in 1666. Rebecca Greensmith, under the promptings of the Rev. Mr. Hooke of Farmington, admitted the charges against her, implicated her husband, and set in motion the train of events that led to the executions of four people, the fleeing of several others and the disruption of Hartford society.[40]

Why the Deputy Governors and more prominent religious leaders should be active as participants within the witchcraft cases, and not

[39] The instances of vindictiveness and crowd consensus about witchcraft and witchmarks are shown clearly in the testimonies of the witnesses presented to the court of magistrates "held at New Hauen, for the Jurisdiction, 29 of May, 1654." See notes p and q.

[40] See notes x and mm.

merely concerned with stamping them out, is difficult to discern. One possibility is that the frustrations attached to a position one level removed from actual power in the colonies concerned may have spilled over into energetic involvement with witch searches. The absence of superior authorities would have given them their chances. Furthermore, they had a compelling desire to prove their worthiness to lead the colonists at a time when the first-generation leaders were dying.[41] They were being called on to lead at a time of spiritual depression. As liberty of conscience was becoming a subject for acrimonious debate, Charles Chauncey complained in 1665 that there was to be found in New England "the contempt of the word of God and his Ordinancies, and listening to lying books & pamphlets, that are brought over into the country whereby multitudes are poysoned amongst us." The next year Thomas Shepherd Jr. worried that "this land which sometimes flourished: Shall in a dying state be found." By 1662, Michael Wigglesworth was ready to condemn, among the hosts who trembled on the day of judgment, those "Witches, Inchanters and Ale-House-haunters" who faced their final doom. In offering reasons for the Truth of the Doctrine of God, John Higginson, pastor at Salem, warned his audience that "Satan from the beginning hath had an old grudge against the seed of the Woman, and he never wanted instruments, who either by force or fraud or both, have done what mischief they could against the Church and cause of God." Well might Edward Johnson declare, therefore, that "now N. E. that had such heaps upon heaps of the riches of Christ's tender compassionate mercies, being turn'd off from his dandling knees, began to read their approaching rod in the bend of his brows and frowns of his former favourable countenance toward them."[42]

---

[41] In 1643 Plymouth lost William Brewster, a stalwart of "this poore persecuted church above 36. years in England, Holand, and in this wildernes." William Bradford, *History of Plymouth Plantation*, II, 342; and in 1644 George Philips, pastor of the church at Watertown died. By 1647 the Connecticut Valley flock had been left leaderless by the death of Thomas Hooker, pastor of the church at Hartford. Hooker was soon followed by Mr. Green, pastor of the church at Reading, and by the end of the decade Massachusetts had lost Governor Winthrop and Thomas Shepherd, pastor at Cambridge. The cream of colonial leadership was skimmed further in the 1650s: John Cotton died in 1652; William Bradford and John Wilson, pastor of the first church in Boston in 1657; and the remote, but still "Lord Protector" Cromwell in 1658.

[42] Charles Chauncey, *God's Mercy Shewed to His People in Giving Them A Faithful Ministry and Schooles of Learning for the Continual Supplyes Thereof* (Cambridge, 1655), p. 19; Thomas Shepherd Jr., *An Almanac for the year 1656* (Cambridge, 1656), verse for February; Michael Wigglesworth, *The Day of Doom*, verse 33; John Higginson, *The Cause of God and His People in New England . . . in a sermon preached before the . . . General Court of the Massachusetts Colony, 27 May 1663* (Cambridge, 1663), p. 7; and Johnson, *Wonder-Working Providence*, p. 252.

From 1647 to 1662 witchcraft incidents and cases spread across the colonies into Maryland, New Hampshire, New Haven, old Plymouth Colony and Virginia, from the original bases in Connecticut and Massachusetts. After 1663 there was still a steady progression of cases, year by year, and they spread still further into New York, Pennsylvania, North and South Carolina.[43] But only two executions took place between 1662 and 1691, and it is evident that the colonial magistrates and governors seriously questioned the wisdom of executions as a remedy for control after 1662. Before 1662, however, it is equally evident that they used executions as a legitimate weapon against the Devil's handmaidens. Their aim was to suppress the work of those covenanting with the Devil. Consequently, this sixteen-year period from 1647 to 1662 produced over 50 indictments and 20 executions, three banishments, three people fleeing to Rhode Island, two water tests, three long-term imprisonments, and at least two whippings, one of which could be prevented by paying a fine. In terms of executions alone, the percentage returns of 40% compare as highly as the witchcraft execution rate in England at the height of the 1637-47 period. By 1662 the English percentage rate was well below that figure.

This period of witchcraft has several obvious similarities with the Salem episode. But two differences also stand out. By 1692 evidence of witchcraft had been before the public eye for 45 years. The Devil had a solid footing, and to rout him it would require a tremendous effort. In 1647, by contrast, there was no colonial reservoir of cases and prosecutions. The Great Enemy of God and Mankind was then attempting to gain a footing in order to subvert God's Commonwealth in the wilderness, and the early leaders were just as grimly determined that he would not succeed. That they failed is evident from the chain of events culminating in 1692. But in documenting the Devil's advance, the New England ministers, especially the Mathers, went out of their way to record some, though not all, of the earlier cases. To them the urge to provide some background for their own dilemma was compelling. Yet they started out with the Ann Cole case involving the Greensmiths in 1662, in order to illustrate the wonderful providences of the invisible world. Nathaniel Mather chided Increase in 1684 for omitting earlier examples as evidence, but the authors were more concerned with presenting earlier cases merely as evidence that the Devil did exist; thus atheists would be refuted. Consequently, historians relying upon them have accepted their intention and missed an opportunity to demonstrate that their ancestors were faced with an

---

[43] Cases and incidents of witchcraft occurred at different places in the colonies for all but the years 1666-67, 1672, 1677-78, 1687 and 1689-90, before Salem.

outbreak before 1692, and that they dealt with it severely. Salem should be studied as part of the witchcraft in America, and not as an isolated example. The background, as well as the peculiarities of 1692, is worth examining. Because Salem judges were to deal with their witches in the strange way of hanging those protesting their innocence and releasing those admitting their guilt, the reverse logic of covenant theology applied in 1692 has always attracted historians. The cases of 1647-62 followed a more normal pattern; confession was followed by execution. From that point of view the earlier period of witchcraft was the more orthodox one in the colonies, and Salem was the aberration.

John Godfrey and His Neighbors:
Witchcraft and the Social Web
in Colonial Massachusetts

John Demos

I N the long roster of early New Englanders accused of witchcraft, John
Godfrey invites attention for one special reason: he was *male*. To be
sure, other men were accused at various times, and four or five were
executed, but most of them were husbands of female "witches."[1] Given the
overall prominence of women in witchcraft cases, it thus seems probable that
the charges against these men arose as a secondary or derivative matter.
Traditional lore suggested that the power to effect witchcraft was most easily
transmitted from one family member, or close friend, to another; there was,
in short, a literal process of "guilt by association."[2] And among such
associations, clearly the marital one was most telling. To recognize this is not,
of course, to foreclose all questions, for many husbands of convicted witches
were never the object of similar suspicions. It seems that some men, more

Mr. Demos is a member of the Department of History, Brandeis University.
Earlier drafts of this essay were read and criticized by Stanley N. Katz, Kenneth
Lockridge, Philip Greven, David Rothman, Sheila Rothman, Oscar Handlin, Ernest
Wolf, M.D., and Virginia Demos. The author is most grateful for their assist-
ance and encouragement.

[1] For example, Hugh Parsons of Springfield, Massachusetts, was prosecuted for
witchcraft soon after the trial and execution of his wife Mary in 1651. Nathaniel
Greensmith, husband of the confessing "witch" Rebecca, was himself convicted of
"familiarity with the Devil" at Hartford in 1662. John Carrington and his wife Joan,
of Farmington, Connecticut, were tried and executed together in 1651. The only male
"witch," besides Godfrey, *not* married to a woman similarly accused, was James
Wakeley, who fled from his home at Hartford in 1663 in order to escape prosecution.
Unfortunately, the documentation of Wakeley's case is very scattered and
fragmentary.

[2] Among the "grounds for examination of a witch" cited in an official statement
from the government of Connecticut was the following: "If the party suspected be
the son or daughter, the servant or familiar friend, near neighbor or old companion
of a known or convicted witch, this also [is] a presumption; for witchcraft is an art
that may be learned and conveyed from man to man, and oft it falleth out that a
witch dying leaveth some of the aforesaid heirs of her witchcraft." An early copy of
this statement (undated) is in the Ann Mary Brown Memorial Collection, Brown
University, Providence, R. I.

than others, could plausibly be viewed as implicated in the guilt of their wives.

But John Godfrey cannot be fitted to this pattern, for he had no witch-wife; in fact, he had no wife at all. What was it, then, that made him suspect? Why should this particular man have been singled out for such special disfavor from virtually all of his masculine peers? Does his career perhaps reflect an intensification of certain themes which, in the lives of women, created a strong presumption of guilt?

In 1659 William Osgood, of Salisbury, Massachusetts, made the following deposition at the quarterly court of Essex County:

in the year '40, in the month of August, he being then building a barn for Mr. Spencer [and] John Godfrey being then Mr. Spencer's herdsman, he on an evening came to the frame where diverse men were at work and said that he had gotten a new master against the time he had done keeping cows. The said William Osgood asked him who it was. He answered [that] he knew not. He again asked him where he dwelt. He answered [that] he knew not. He asked him what his name was. He answered [that] he knew not. He then said to him, "How then wilt thou go to him when thy time is out?" He said, "The man will come and fetch me." . . . I asked him, "Hast thou made an absolute bargain?" He answered that a covenant was made [and] he had set his hand to it. He then asked of him whether he had not a counter covenant. Godfrey answered, "No." William Osgood said, "What a mad fellow are thou to make a covenant in this manner." He said, 'He's an honest man." "How knowest thou?" said William Osgood. John Godfrey answered, "He looks like one." William Osgood then answered, "I am persuaded thou hast made a covenant with the devil." He then skipped about and said, "I protest, I protest."[3]

This episode, recounted nearly twenty years after the fact, marks the first certain appearance of John Godfrey in New England. The place was

[3] This deposition is printed in full in *Records and Files of the Quarterly Courts of Essex County, Massachusetts, 1656–1683* (Salem, 1912–1921), II, 160, hereafter cited as *Records of Quarterly Courts, Essex County*. In 1666, at a later trial for witchcraft, William Howard of Hampton, New Hampshire, gave testimony which partially corroborates the Osgood deposition. Howard recalled an incident "about 26 years ago," when he met a person "like John Godfrey" ("and as I suppose he did then name himself by that name") who was "following of cattle . . . on Newbury plain." The man had identified himself as "Mr. Spencer's apprentice" and had offered to serve Howard when "his time was . . . out." *Records of the Court of Assistants of the Colony of the Massachusetts Bay, 1630–1692*, III (Boston, 1928), 159. Here and elsewhere in the pages that follow, quotations from the manuscript sources have been "modernized" as to spelling and punctuation. Word order has not been changed, though occasional words have been added in brackets in order to clarify meaning or sentence structure.

Newbury, Massachusetts—then a community barely five years old. The deponent, Osgood, was a young carpenter and millright, who would later become a founder of the town of Salisbury. "Mr. Spencer" (first name, John) was a local gentleman and heir to a large estate in Newbury; both Godfrey and Osgood were temporarily in his employ.

Of Godfrey's background and origins nothing definite can be learned. Even the date of his birth is in question. Twice later on, in the course of legal proceedings, he made reference to his age: in 1660 he deposed "aged about 40 years," and in 1661 "aged about 30 years."[4] Imprecision or ignorance as to chronology was not unusual among the early New Englanders, but *this* discrepancy seems particularly large. As such, it accords nicely with other will-of-the-wisp elements in Godfrey's personal history. Upon reflection, the first estimate seems far more plausible, since by 1640 Godfrey was established as a "herdsman" and this was normally a job for a young man. Thus 1620 will serve as a best possible approximation of the year of Godfrey's birth.

Actually, there is one very early notation of the name John Godfrey—on a passenger list for the ship *Mary and John,* which left London for New England in March 1634. We cannot be sure that this emigrant and the later "witch" were one and the same, but the probability seems strong, for John Spencer and others prominent in the founding of Newbury were also among the passengers for this sailing. Most of the group had come from a tier of counties on or near the south coast of England (Dorsetshire, Somersetshire, Berkshire, Hampshire, and Surrey), and it is tempting to think that Godfrey's roots were likewise in that part of the country.[5] Perhaps, then, his beginning in New England was as a boy in his mid-teens, fresh from a springtime voyage, unaccompanied by family, and "bound" in service to a gentleman from the region of his birth. If so, it was a beginning that held no forecast of the unusual career that lay ahead.[6]

---

[4] *Records of Quarterly Courts, Essex County,* I, 250, II, 288.

[5] *New England Historical and Genealogical Register,* IX (1885), 267. The identifications with place of origin have been developed largely by reference to Charles Edward Banks, *Topographical Dictionary of 2885 English Emigrants to New England, 1620–1650* (Philadelphia, 1937).

[6] There is one detail about this beginning that may deserve mention. The original John Spencer—presumably Godfrey's master—had a brief and unhappy career in New England. A founder of the town of Newbury, he quickly became a leading citizen there, as well as a magistrate and representative to the General Court of the Massachusetts Bay Colony. However, he was implicated in the Antinomian heresy and returned to England in 1638. His estate was left to a nephew and namesake. (It was the younger "Mr. Spencer" for whom Godfrey was working as herdsman at the time of the episode described in Osgood's deposition.) One wonders about the effect of this outcome—high status and esteem, followed by deviance and disgrace—on a young and perhaps impressionable member of Spencer's household.

If the Osgood deposition is creditable, then Godfrey was suspected of conniving with the Devil at least as early as 1640. There is no other comparable information from this period, but it is worth noticing the first court cases in which Godfrey took part as a principal. In the summer of 1642 he sued Richard Kent of Newbury for slander, and Kent was found "greatly criminal." In 1649 he won a similar complaint against Richard Jones of Salisbury.[7] Depositions from these cases do not survive, so the substance of the slander remains unknown. But allegations of witchcraft seem an obvious possibility. At a minimum, such events reveal Godfrey as someone about whom others were tempted to speak in strong and sharply hostile terms.

There were additional cases during the 1640s in which Godfrey appeared as *defendant:* in 1648 for "subborning a witness"; in 1649 for "lying"; again in 1649 for some unspecified charge. Gradually, it seems, he assumed a position outside the moral center of his community. Yet for most of the next decade, from 1650 to 1658, he did not come to court at all. Scattered references in land deeds and later legal proceedings show him moving out of Newbury and appearing briefly in Rowley, Haverhill, and Andover; but otherwise he left no tracks.[8]

The absence of Godfrey's name from court dockets during this long interval is all the more striking in light of the pattern that developed immediately thereafter. From 1658 until his death in 1675 Godfrey was in court at least once each year and in some years many times. As suit and counter-suit piled one on top of another, his record of legal actions became extraordinary even by the standards of a highly litigious society. Most of these actions dealt with property—land, money, bonds, wheat, corn, rye, oxen, sheep, cloth—and most involved relatively small values. Nearly all of Godfrey's opponents at court were other Essex County residents, of modest wealth and status. Taken as a whole, the records depict a man continually at odds with his peers, over a host of quite specific, personal, and mundane affairs.

In the spring of 1658 Godfrey lodged a suit for debt—his first of this type—against one Abraham Whitaker of Haverhill, and within months he had begun additional actions against other persons from Haverhill.[9] It appears that these cases were in some way interrelated and that Godfrey's position was fully supported by the verdicts. Almost immediately, however, the issue of witchcraft was raised and formally presented to the court. The exact sequence is unclear, but two actions were evidently pressed more or less simultaneously. A petition, signed by eleven persons and submitted at Ipswich in March 1659, alleged that "diverse [persons] of esteem with us, and,

[7] *Records of Quarterly Courts, Essex County*, I, 43, 53, 164.
[8] *Ibid.*, 142, 162, 168, 179, II, 39, 159.
[9] *Ibid.*, II, 65, 66, 143, 157, 158, 160.

as we hear, in other places also, have for some time suffered losses in their estates and some afflictions on their bodies also."[10] Moreover, these events, which defied explanation by reference to "any natural cause," had usually followed "upon differences had betwixt themselves and one John Godfrey, resident at Andover or elsewhere at his pleasure." Under the circumstances an official inquiry seemed necessary. Unfortunately, there is no record of the court's further proceedings in this matter, but almost certainly Godfrey was indicted, tried in Boston, and acquitted.[11] Meanwhile the accused was mounting a counter-suit on grounds of slander, "for charging him to be a witch." A local jury sustained this complaint, "notwithstanding [we] do conceive that by the testimonies he is rendered suspicious."[12] Thus was Godfrey vindicated in the short run, but clearly put on notice for the future.

A variety of depositions, from either or both of these actions, survive in the files of the county courts.[13] Twenty-four different witnesses are included, and probably there were others whose testimony has disappeared. Efforts to trace these people reveal a considerable geographic spread—no less than six different towns were represented[14]—but clearly the most detailed and telling evidence came from residents of Haverhill. The four men with whom Godfrey was concurrently involved in property suits all participated in the witchcraft inquiry—one as a signer of the original petition, the other three as deponents. Yet there was more to this than the simple extension of a personal quarrel. If Godfrey's debtors played a significant role, so too did others who had no such immediate interest in the outcome. If some witnesses were people of small means and humble status, at least a few held leading positions in their community. William Osgood, who recalled for the court that curious episode on "Mr. Spencer's" farm long before, was among the wealthiest inhabitants (and most frequent officeholders) in the town of Salisbury. And Henry Palmer, a comparably important figure at Haverhill, also entered the lists against Godfrey.

The full corpus of testimony supplied many particulars on the difficulties

---

[10] *Ibid.*, 157-158.

[11] The basis for this conclusion is as follows. In June 1659 Godfrey was bound by the county court for an appearance at the General Court in Boston. Witchcraft, as a capital crime, could only be tried in the General Court; and no other court actions in which Godfrey was then involved were sufficiently serious to warrant this procedure. *Ibid.*, 166. Moreover, there is independent evidence that Godfrey was imprisoned during some part of this year—for example, the testimony in a later case that he had engaged to work for Francis Urselton of Topsfield when "he came out of Ipswich jail" in the summer of 1659. See Urselton v. Godfrey, *ibid.*, 175.

[12] *Ibid.*, 157.

[13] Some of these depositions are printed *ibid.*, 157-162. Other testimony, in manuscript, is in Suffolk Files, II, no. 322, Office of the Clerk of the Suffolk County Court, Boston, Mass.

[14] Haverhill, Andover, Rowley, Amesbury, Ipswich, and Salisbury.

that Godfrey experienced (or caused?) in his personal relations. Henry Palmer, for instance, recounted an episode "3 or 4 years since," when he had been serving as a selectman at Haverhill. Godfrey "did often speak to me to join with the rest of the selectmen to hire the said Godfrey to keep the cows at Haverhill." When refused, Godfrey "showed himself much displeased," and soon thereafter cattle from the herds of both Palmer and his son-in-law vanished "quite away."[15] A similar sequence, described in a deposition from Elizabeth Whitaker, throws more light on Godfrey's personal style—or at least the style attributed to him by his adversaries. Since the details are presented with special vividness, this document is worth quoting at length:

I being at my father's house, one day [there] came in John Godfrey, and my father entertained him and gave him victuals and [bedding?]. And the next morning after, as the said Godfrey was [*illeg.*] a pair of shoes, he fell out very bitterly with me, and told me that my husband owed him more than he was worth and also that all the cloth I had was his. Then said my father to him, "That is not true, Godfrey, for she had them clothes of me when she was married." Then Godfrey rose up in a great rage and knocked his head against the manteltree and threatened my father and I that we should neither of us get nothing by it before that summer passed. Then presently upon it I went and gave my father's three swine some meat, and the swine was taken with foaming and reeling and turned around and did die. Then, after this, when I came home, the said Godfrey came [on] a Sabbath day in the morning next after Salisbury court, and demanded charges for witnessing that week before at Salisbury court. And my husband told him [to] come another time and he would pay him. Then, as Godfrey stood at the door of the house, my husband and my brother was driving our oxen out at the barn. Said Godfrey, "Where are you going with them oxen?" Then said my husband, "I have hired my brother to keep them in the woods today." Said Godfrey, "I will keep them for you, if you will." Then said my husband, "No, my brother shall keep them." Then said Godfrey, "One of them oxen should never come home alive anymore." And that day they were lost, and one of them did never come home alive anymore. And the next day, when my husband was gone to look [for] the oxen, the said Godfrey came to our house and asked for my husband, and I told him he was gone to look [for] his oxen. Said Godfrey, "If Abraham had hired me, I would have looked [for] them and brought them home. For," said Godfrey, "he may seek them, but he will not find them." And when my husband came home, I told him what Godfrey had said, and my husband went that night to seek Godfrey to hire him. But Godfrey went away, and I saw him no more till after the one of the oxen was found dead. And after this, upon Godfrey falling out and threatening, we had many strange losses in our swine and cows and calves, and sore weakness of my body [such] that I could not go up and down all summer.[16]

[15] MS, Suffolk Files, II, no. 322.
[16] *Ibid.*

The abrasive, grasping qualities so prominent in this account of Godfrey appear throughout the testimony presented against him. Indebtedness, threats, angry accusations, and "losses" of property or health—such were the central ingredients of an oft-repeated sequence.

In fact this sequence deserves very careful consideration. Consider Godfrey's response—"one of them oxen should never come home alive anymore"—when his services as cowherd had been refused in favor of Whitaker's brother. Were those his exact words? Or had they been slightly altered, in the process of recollection, so as to exaggerate the element of danger? Even if correctly quoted, they leave room for varying interpretations. Perhaps this was simply a petulant reflection on the brother's competence, with the implied meaning: "your brother is such a poor herdsman that probably he will lose one of your oxen." If so, there was a vital difference between what Godfrey *meant* and what Whitaker *heard*—and it was precisely the difference between a casual and defensive slur and a bona fide threat. There is no way now to recover the intent behind such a remark, and Whitaker's interpretation of it was, in any case, what counted most at court. But it is important to recognize the possibilities for misunderstanding and subtle distortion that must have attended any dealings with a reputed witch.

Two other aspects of the evidence seem worthy of comment for what they suggest about Godfrey's character and social circumstances. First, there was something odd, and disturbingly suspect, about his conversation. It was not merely his frequent resort to "threatening" statements (though this was an obvious and important count against him). There was also his tendency to say things that would startle, confuse, or annoy his listeners. His comments to Osgood about his "new master" have the look of deliberate provocation. The same could be said of another episode reported at court, involving a visit by Godfrey to the house of an Andover resident named Job Tyler.[17] According to the Tylers, an odd-looking bird came in at their door with Godfrey. Efforts to catch it proving unsuccessful, the bird then "vanished" quite suddenly. And Godfrey, "being asked by the man of the house wherefore it came . . . answered 'it came to suck your wife.'" There were, moreover, times when Godfrey was given to "speaking about the power of witches." For example, "The said Godfrey spoke that if witches were not kindly entertained, the Devil will appear unto them and ask them if they were grieved or vexed with anybody, and ask them what he should do for them. And if they would not give them beer or victuals, they might let all the beer run out of the cellar. And if they looked steadfastly upon any creature, it would die. And it were hard to some witches to take away life, either of man

[17] See the MS depositions from Tyler and members of his family, *ibid.* The statement attributed to Godfrey that the bird "came to suck [Tyler's] wife" carried an imputation of witchcraft, for, according to traditional lore, witches were attended by "familiars"—animals or birds given to sucking on preternatural "teats."

or beast; yet when they once begin it, then it is easy to them."[18] Repeatedly, then—and in all sorts of ways—John Godfrey flouted his community's standards of discreet conversation.

Another recurrent theme in the testimony on Godfrey is his special association with cattle. He was, of course, an experienced "herdsman": he had worked in this capacity during his servant-years, and later he was hired for a time to "keep the cows" at Haverhill.[19] Yet these arrangements were distinctly problematic. As noted above, Godfrey was forever putting himself forward as a herdsman—and was frequently rebuffed. His interest in cattle seemed beyond doubt, but there was something strange about it. Perhaps, indeed, he was *too* interested. One witness reported a curious incident when Godfrey, "hearing her call [her] calf, . . . [asked] what it was she called. She told him, this calf. He asked if she gave it milk still. And, as the calf was drinking the milk, the said Godfrey stroked the calf on the back, calling it 'poor rogue' and 'poor rascal,' and said it was very fat. And that night it died, and we could none of us find anything it ailed."[20] Another witness described rumors that Godfrey had "come to places where some cattle were bewitched . . . and said, 'I will unwitch them,' and presently they were well."[21] Here, then, was a truly remarkable, even supernatural, talent, and yet it could not be trusted. *Un*witching and *be*witching were too closely related—in cow-keeping, as in any other activity. When joined in a man of bad temperament, such powers assumed a highly menacing aspect. It was no coincidence that most of the damage attributed to Godfrey's witchcraft involved domestic animals.

What seems most striking about Godfrey's life following the witchcraft litigation of 1659 is his immediate return to the same community, to a familiar network of personal relationships, and to a highly similar pattern of activities. It was almost as if nothing had happened. A court case in September brought judgment against him "for not performing a summer's work." Witnesses testified that Godfrey had engaged to work for Francis Urselton of Topsfield "when he came out of Ipswich jail," had taken money, and had then reneged on his part of the arrangement.[22] But never mind this outcome; the important thing is that someone had wished to hire

[18] MS, Charles Browne, *ibid.*
[19] MS, Elizabeth Ayres, *ibid.*
[20] *Ibid.*
[21] MS, Thomas Fowler, *ibid.* Godfrey's relation to cattle calls to mind a child's attachment to favorite pets, where tenderness is usually based on some form of "identification" (with "alter ego" qualities). Perhaps this man, seemingly so tough in his inter*personal* life, showed a softer, more empathic side in his care of domestic animals.
[22] *Records of Quarterly Courts, Essex County,* II, 175.

Godfrey in the first place. An accused witch—formally acquitted of the charges against him but "rendered suspicious" by much testimony—was considered employable!

With the Urselton case Godfrey began a new and intense round of legal involvements.[23] The matters at issue were largely as before: land, cows, crops, and debt. Most of his opponents were drawn from the circle of his neighbors and associates (if not exactly his friends) in Haverhill, Andover, and the surrounding area. In 1661, for example, he initiated a complicated suit for debt against his old adversary Job Tyler. His claims included payment for twenty-seven days of labor on Tyler's farm, for many additional errands, for back loans, and much more. Meanwhile a counter-suit by Tyler alleged debts on Godfrey's side as well, mainly for "washing, dress, and diet [during] a summer." Witnesses spelled out the particulars. "Moses Tyler deposed that his mother dressed John Godfrey and washed his clothes above twenty weeks in one year, and that his father found Godfrey's diet for eleven weeks, which was never satisfied."[24] The Tylers, be it recalled, had supplied damaging evidence against Godfrey in the witchcraft inquiry. Yet here are all parties, just a short while later—their lives densely intertwined. The evidence makes clear that for a period in 1661 Godfrey had been working as Tyler's hired man and most probably staying in Tyler's house. For whatever reasons, the Tylers had taken into their home a man whom they regarded as a witch.

The following year Godfrey became involved in new litigation with still another Haverhill family. His chief antagonist this time was one Jonathan Singletary, aged twenty-two, son of a modest "planter," recently married, and father of an infant daughter who had died soon after birth. The records depict Singletary as a young man overwhelmed by sudden adversities. Repeatedly in debt and in trouble during these years, he would subsequently leave the area altogether for a new start in the colony of East Jersey.

The earliest Godfrey-Singletary litigation involved the latter's use of a certain bond, but this was soon followed by claims and counter-claims for debt ("50 shillings in silver" and "£8 in wheat and corn"). The depositional evidence reveals a tangled skein of interaction between the two men—in which Singletary was consistently at a disadvantage.[25] The court decided against him; he was temporarily jailed; his father made a further unsuccessful attempt to settle with Godfrey; and, finally, accusations of

[23] Ibid., 185, 209, 212, 216, 222, 250, 274, 277, 279, 297, 299, 301, 327, 328, 343, 353, 366, 367, 376, 377, 385, 408, 409, 412, 430, 437, 438.

[24] Ibid., 328, 343, 353, 366.

[25] The same evidence offers some pithy examples of Godfrey's speech style—for instance, this comment on a debt of corn allegedly withheld from him by a friend of Singletary's: "I had rather it were in a heap in the street and all the town hogs should eat it, than [that] he should keep it in his hands." Ibid., III, 10, 27, 39.

witchcraft were made.[26] Once again, there is no certain record that Godfrey was formally tried on this charge, but the probability seems strong.[27] We *do* know that Godfrey sued for slander, charging Singletary with "calling him a witch, and saying 'is this witch on this side of Boston gallows yet?' "[28] There is only one substantial deposition that survives from the case—a statement by Singletary recounting a bizarre experience during his stay in Ipswich prison. Sitting alone late one evening, he heard loud noises, "as if many cats had been climbing up the prison walls . . . and . . . boards or stools had been thrown about, and men [were] walking in the chambers, and a crackling and shaking as if the house would have fallen upon me." Almost immediately his thoughts ran to witchery and, more especially, to an acquaintance who "upon some difference with John Godfrey . . . [had been] several nights in a strange manner troubled." Whereupon Godfrey himself appeared in the doorway (having magically unbolted the lock), and said, " 'Jonathan, Jonathan.' So I looked on him [and] said 'What have you to do with me?' He said, 'I come to see you; are you weary of your place yet?' I answered, 'I take no delight in being here, but I will be out as soon as I can.' He said, 'If you will pay me in corn, you shall come out.' I answered, 'No, if that had been my intent, I would have paid the marshal and never have come hither.' He, knocking of his fist at me in a kind of a threatening way, said he would make me weary of my part and so went away." Soon he was back, and the discussion continued in a similar vein. At last Singletary took a rock and lunged at his tormentor, "but there was nothing to strike, and how he went away I know not, for I could . . . not see which way he went."[29] There was only one means of explaining such an episode—at least from the standpoint of the "victim."

There is no doubt about Godfrey's next trial for witchcraft. Prosecuted during the winter of 1665-1666, this case is duly noted in records still on file from the Court of Assistants in Boston.[30] The initial complaint was lodged by Job Tyler and John Remington. Eighteen witnesses were summoned, from whose testimony seven depositions survive. The indictment charged that

---

[26] *Ibid.*, 74, 120ff.

[27] The evidential difficulty here arises from the fragmentary nature of the records of the General Court. Slander, by contrast, was a matter for the county courts, from which excellent records survive. Two things suggest that Godfrey was at least indicted. (1) The Singletary deposition of his experience in Ipswich jail was copied from the original in Salem and filed with various Boston records at the Suffolk court. (Such material would not ordinarily be needed in Boston, except in connection with a capital case.) (2) Singletary's alleged comment—"is this witch on this side Boston gallows yet?"—also suggests a trial proceeding. (Again the reference to Boston is indicative.) See Suffolk Files, II, no. 543.

[28] *Records of Quarterly Courts, Essex County*, III, 120.

[29] *Ibid.*, 121–122.

[30] *Records of Court of Assistants*, III, 151–152, 158–161.

Godfrey had "consulted with a familiar spirit" and had "done much hurt and mischief by several acts of witchcraft to the bodies and goods of several persons." The jury's verdict was an obviously reluctant acquittal: "We find him not to have the fear of God in his heart. He has made himself suspiciously guilty of witchcraft, but not legally guilty according to law and evidence we have received." The magistrates "accepted" this decision but aimed a backhanded swipe at Godfrey in obliging him to pay all the costs of the trial.[31]

The depositions were a mixture of old and new material. The Whitakers and Tylers recounted their various misadventures with Godfrey, going back a full ten years, and presumably other witnesses did likewise. But John Remington had a fresh contribution—and a telling one, as the proceedings unfolded. A carpenter who had moved to Haverhill from Andover some five years before, Remington testified concerning an injury recently sustained by his fifteen-year-old son. Unsurprisingly, the point of departure was a quarrel with Godfrey over the care of the family cows. Remington had decided to winter his herd on land some miles distant from his home, and this had apparently provoked Godfrey to "great rage and passion." Indeed, Godfrey had sworn that "he should have cause to repent it before the winter was out." The actual tending of the animals was "for the most part" left to John Remington, Jr., and it was he who allegedly suffered the consequences of Godfrey's anger.[32]

Riding home alone through the woods one day, the boy noticed sudden signs of apprehension in both his horse and his dog. Soon there appeared in the middle of the path a crow "with a very great and quick eye, and . . . a very great bill." Young Remington "began to mistrust and think it was no crow, and "as I was a-thinking this to myself," the horse fell heavily "on one side" with one of the boy's legs underneath. Eventually he reached home— though not without further harassment from the pseudo-crow—and recounted the experience to his parents. Two days later Godfrey visited the house and began the following conversation (as recalled by John Jr.):

He asked me how I did, and I told him, pretty well, only I was lame with the horse falling on me. Then said Godfrey: "Every cock-eating boy must ride. I unhorsed one boy the other day, and I will unhorse thee, too, if thee rides." . . . Then said I: "I am not able to carry victuals on my back." Then said Godfrey: " 'tis a sorry horse that cannot carry his own provender."

[31] *Ibid.*, 151–152. There were substantial expenses for those who had come to Boston to give evidence.

[32] MS, John Remington in Suffolk Files, II, no. 322. Depositions by his wife Abigail and his son John Remington, Jr., are printed in *Records of Court of Assistants*, III, 160–161.

Then said Godfrey to me: "John, if thee had been a man, thee had died on the spot where thee got the fall." Then said my mother: "How can thee tell that? There is none but God can tell that, and except thee be more than an ordinary man, thee cannot tell that." Then Godfrey bade my mother hold her tongue; he knew what he said better than she. And [he] said: "I say again, had he been a man, . . . he had died on the spot where he fell."[33]

John Remington, Jr., had witnessed the original quarrel between Godfrey and his father, and the power of his own fear while carrying out his duties with the herd can easily be imagined. Weeks later his father testified that "the boy is very ill . . . and swells in the body every night [so] that I fear he will die of it."[34] As to Godfrey's motives in all this, there is much less clarity; but the bitter comment—"every cock-eating boy must ride"—suggests his long-standing concern to protect his particular vocation. (If boys did *not* ride, perhaps there would be more work for a herdsman?) Godfrey's reference to "unhorsing" seemed, of course, directly incriminating, and most suspect of all was the statement that but for his age young Remington would have died on the spot. This was knowledge not vouchsafed to "ordinary" men. No suspected witch could afford to make comments that even hinted at such knowledge.

Acquitted in such a narrow and grudging way, Godfrey had little to look forward to in the spring of 1666. At least twice, and probably three times, he had faced the possibility of conviction and death on the gallows; few, if any, of his peers believed in his innocence; and his notoriety extended throughout Essex County and perhaps beyond.[35] Indeed, his name had become something of a byword, mentioned in situations where Godfrey himself played no direct part whatsoever. A lawsuit from Newbury in 1668 produced the following bit of testimony: "He [the defendant] further said that he could have as good dealing from a Turk or pagan or Indian as from Mr. Newman [the plaintiff]—yea, saith he, from Godfrey himself—with many such like words."[36] In another case, several months later, a defendant was alleged to have slandered a county magistrate by asserting that "he was as bad as Godfrey in usury." When the deponents had asked "what that God-

---

[33] *Records of Court of Assistants,* III, 160.

[34] MS, Suffolk Files, II, no. 322.

[35] The range of John Godfrey's legal entanglements extended at least as far as Plymouth colony, where in 1666 he appeared before the General Court as plaintiff in a probate case. Nathaniel B. Shurtleff, ed., *Records of the Colony of New Plymouth in New England,* II (Boston, 1855), 130–131.

[36] Deposition of Elizabeth Gott, Mar. 31, 1668, in the case of Mr. Antipas Newman v. Thomas White. *Records of Quarterly Courts, Essex County,* IV, 9.

frey was," they were told that "he was an evil-looked fellow, and that he was a great usuror; and if he came before a judge, his looks would hang him."[37]

It is striking, too, that some men not particularly involved in Godfrey's legal and business affairs could feel—and express—a bitter rage when confronting him in person. One particularly violent episode was described in court by a local constable:

I, going to Job Tyler's house to serve an attachment, did take John Godfrey with me. And when I came to the said Tyler's house, John Carr being there said, "What come you hither for, Godfrey, you witching rogue? I will," said John Carr, "set you out of doors." This deponent said to the said John Carr, "Let John Godfrey alone." The said Carr said he would not, but said, "What had you to do, to bring such a rogue with you?" And the said Carr immediately ran his fist in the said Godfrey's breast, and drove the said Godfrey up against the chimney-stock which was very rugged. Then I charged the said Carr to be quiet and let the said Godfrey alone. But the said Carr said he would turn the said Godfrey out of doors and kick him down the hill. And again this deponent charged the said Carr to let the said Godfrey alone, and so Carr did forbear, and called the said Godfrey many bad names.[38]

Much of this had been true long before, yet now one senses a cumulative effect that was new and compelling. The records of the late 1660s suggest a changing set of relationships—a different balance of forces—between Godfrey and the people among whom he lived. Whatever his earlier difficulties, there had been no mistaking the force of his aggressive energy, his determination to fight on, his ability to outmaneuver opponents, and the apprehension he aroused on all sides. But after 1666 he seemed an altogether less menacing and more vulnerable figure.

There was, for example, a marked shift in the record of Godfrey's court appearances. The vigorous and frequently successful plaintiff of former years was cast more and more in the role of defendant. In the period 1660-1664 he had appeared thirteen times as defendant and thirty-four as plaintiff; for 1665-1669 the comparable figures were nineteen and twenty-three. Moreover, Godfrey could no longer be sure of obtaining fair treatment from the legal process. The court docket from the late 1660s contains several notations like the following: "John Godfrey vs. Henry Salter. For refusing to give him an acquitance as promised for a deed of sale of land at Haverhill. Verdict for the

---

[37] Deposition of Thomas Wells, Nov. 24, 1668, in the prosecution of Stephen Cross, *ibid.*, 78. The reference to Godfrey's appearance is singular and most intriguing. As litigant, as "usuror"—and perhaps as "witch"—he evidently looked the part.
[38] Deposition of Thomas Chandler, June 24, 1662, *ibid.*, II, 410.

defendant, but the Court did not accept the verdict."[39] (What this meant was that the magistrates in charge detected prejudice in the decision of the jury.) Similarly, court and community officers sometimes balked at executing judgments in Godfrey's favor. His only recourse in such cases was a further appeal to the magistrates: for example, "John Godfrey vs. Abraham Whitaker. For refusing, though the marshal's deputy, to levy executions against John Remington and Edward Yeomans."[40] Thus the same court which had once served Godfrey as a forum for the exercise of his peculiar talents now became the protector of his weakness.

But protection from this source was incomplete and inconsistent, and Godfrey's troubles continued to mount. In 1669 he was accused of "firing" the house of a Haverhill neighbor and causing the death by burning of the neighbor's wife.[41] Convicted by the county court, he eventually won a reversal through an appeal to the Court of Assistants in Boston. Also during these years he was twice convicted of theft[42] and once for "subborning witnesses ... by hindering persons from giving evidence and sometimes instigating some to give false evidence."[43] The penalties in the latter instance included a fine of a full £100. Still other cases traced a line of personal deterioration. There were repeated fines for drunkenness, for "taking tobacco in the streets," for "cursing speeches," and for "prophaning the sabbath."[44] Godfrey had never cared much for the social and moral conventions of his community; now, one feels, he no longer cared for himself.

[39] Godfrey v. Salter, *ibid.*, III, 423. For other cases in which verdicts against Godfrey were not accepted see Godfrey v. Whitaker, *ibid.*, 454; Godfrey v. Whitaker, *ibid.*, IV, 28; Godfrey v. Button, *ibid.*, 29; Todd v. Godfrey, *ibid.*, 71; Godfrey v. Button, *ibid.*, 152; and Godfrey v. Ela, *ibid.*, 181.

[40] Godfrey v. Whitaker, *ibid.*, III, 421ff. For other instances in which Godfrey's interests were apparently abused by officers of the court see Godfrey v. Ela, *ibid.*, IV, 178; Godfrey v. Skerry, *ibid.*, 372; and Godfrey v. Clark, *ibid.*, V, 182. Parallel evidence on Godfrey's difficulties with the court came from several witnesses in the case of Godfrey v. Ela (for defamation) in 1669. James Ordway testified that he had intended to post bond on Godfrey's behalf, "but the matter was made so odious by the Court ... [that] he would not. ... The Judge of the Court said he did believe that no man will have the face to appear in this case to be bound for him." Abiel Somerby quoted the same judge as saying, "We shall not take a thousand pounds bond in this case [and] then the voice of the people that stood by was that there should be no bond taken for him, which did discourage those that was intended to be bound for him." *Records of Court of Assistants,* III, 155.

[41] *Records of Quarterly Courts, Essex County,* IV, 130, 185, 186, 372–373.

[42] *Ibid.*, 130, 153. These prosecutions for theft involved incidents in Boston and were tried in Suffolk County Court. See *Records of Court of Assistants,* III, 154–155.

[43] *Records of Quarterly Courts, Essex County,* IV, 132. Similar charges were made against Godfrey—but apparently not prosecuted—a few years later. *Ibid.*, 372–373.

[44] *Ibid.*, III, 251, 352, IV, 119, 187, 239.

There was one final court case of special interest here. In 1669 Godfrey filed suit against Daniel Ela, still another resident of Haverhill, charging defamation "for reporting that he, the said Godfrey, was seen at Ipswich and at Salisbury at the same time."[45] On this occasion, in contrast to the earlier ones, there is no hint of a criminal charge against Godfrey; the comments attributed to Ela were a matter of personal conversation. Indeed, the word witchcraft is not mentioned in any of the documents from Godfrey's suit— though the implication was very clear.[46]

Some of the testimony simply confirmed that Ela had spoken as alleged, but a far larger portion aimed to show the grounds for such a statement. Ela called as defense witnesses several persons who had seen Godfrey in Ipswich, and others who had seen him in Salisbury, on the day in question. Moreover, there were reports of similar occurrences in the past. A deposition from one John Griffin may stand for the rest:

About seven years ago the last winter John Godfrey and this deponent went over Merrimac River on the ice . . . to Andover—Godfrey on foot, and this deponent on horseback, and the horse was as good a one as ever I rode on. And when I was at Goodman Gage's field, I saw John Godfrey in the same field a little before me. . . . But when I had ridden a little further—not seeing Godfrey or any tracks at all (and it was at a time when there had fallen a middling snow overnight)—I ran my horse all the way to Andover. And the first house I came into at Andover was Goodman Rust's house, and when I came in I saw John Godfrey sitting in the corner, and Goody Rust told me that he had been there so long that a maid that was in the house had made clean a kettle and hung on peas and pork to boil for Godfrey. And the peas and pork were ready to boil, and the maid was skimming the kettle.[47]

This picture of wintertime life in early New England conveys a homely charm that is strengthened by the passage of three hundred years. The fresh snow, the river crossing, the fast ride on horseback, the snug house, the peas and pork warming in the fireplace: here are all the ingredients of a vintage Norman Rockwell painting. But, more important, there is a calmness, a factual tone, an absence of dread and loathing, *in the participants themselves.* In fact, the same quality characterizes most of the other evidence presented in *Godfrey* v. *Ela* and sets this case apart from all of the earlier ones. That a man should be capable of appearing in two places simultaneously, or of outracing a fast horse, seemed literally incredible, but it was not equivalent to magical acts of destruction against life or property. And it is most significant that none of the witnesses in 1669 imputed such acts, or threats to perform

[45] *Ibid.,* IV, 152.
[46] Depositions from this case are in *Records of Court of Assistants,* III, 154–158.
[47] *Ibid.,* 155–156.

such acts, to Godfrey. In this final public consideration of his alleged witchcraft, there was much less at stake; as a result, the proceedings were both less intense and less involved.

Following the conclusion of this case—a conclusion, incidentally, that favored the defendant—six years of life remained to John Godfrey. There was no significant change in his experience during these years, at least nothing that the extant records can be made to reveal. Suits and counter-suits over questions of property, minor criminal offenses, a restless moving about: so his life wound down. The end came in the summer of 1675, apparently at Boston. There is no certain record of Godfrey's death,[48] but legal documents from the settlement of his estate are pertinent. In September 1675 the court appointed a schoolteacher named Benjamin Thompson, of Charlestown, as his administrator; it appeared, too, that Thompson would be his chief beneficiary.[49] But this arrangement was soon challenged by others with claims on Godfrey's property. Though there was no will, a statement signed with the dead man's mark appeared to undermine Thompson's position. In addition to its substantive interest, it affords a last look at Godfrey's personal style:

That whereas there was formerly a deed of gift of my estate, drawn from me John Godfrey unto Benjamin Thompson of Charlestown. . . . [I declare that this was] done by fraudulent means, myself and most of the company being drunk at the same time. He engaging to pay unto me for my yearly maintenance the full and just sum of ten pounds in silver, the which was never paid to me to the value of one farthing, though the said ten pounds was yearly engaged to be paid during my life. . . . All that he ever did for me [was], once when I was in Boston prison, he was an occasion of my being let out. The truth of which, I being in perfect sense and memory, I do protest upon my soul before God as I am a dying man.[50]

The estate was not large, but included personal effects, several oxen, and 100 acres of land in Haverhill. Additional papers show death-bed bequests to two

[48] There is, however, an intriguing notation in an almanac belonging to Samuel Sewall of Boston: "1675: July 27, 3. John Godfrey." "Diary of Samuel Sewall" Massachusetts Historical Society, *Collections*, 5th Ser., V (Boston, 1878), 9. Sewall's connection with Godfrey is otherwise undocumented; however, it is tempting to interpret this as a reference to Godfrey's death (or perhaps his burial).

[49] There was a prior "indenture" between Godfrey and "Benjamin Thompson of Boston . . . schoolmaster" which spelled out certain particulars. Dated July 3, 1670, this deed granted to Thompson all of Godfrey's estate ("as well this side as beyond seas"), to take effect "immediately after the said Godfrey's decease." I have not been able to locate the original copy of this document, but it is quoted in Sarah Loring Bailey, *Historical Sketches of Andover* (Boston, 1880), 54.

[50] *Records of Quarterly Courts, Essex County*, V, 71, 88, 248ff.

men (not including Thompson) who had assisted Godfrey during his last illness. The issue dragged on in the local courts for at least two years, and its final resolution went unrecorded. Probate litigation was not uncommon in colonial New England; but it seems particularly fitting, given all we know about the *life* of John Godfrey, that his *death* should have occasioned one more quarrel.

We have managed to follow John Godfrey through some thirty years of his personal history. The picture is necessarily incomplete—less a filled canvas than a collection of fragments—but certain thematic continuities do come clear. The following summary is an effort to stress these continuities more forcefully than has been possible heretofore. They are presented as six distinct, although obviously overlapping, attributes of Godfrey's life and career. Taken altogether, they go far toward explaining his singular position, given the sociocultural context, and the logic of his selection as a potential (or actual) witch.

(1) It is striking that Godfrey was without family, and virtually without relatives of any kind, during all his years in New England. The only person who may have been his kin was one Peter Godfrey of Newbury; but even here the evidence is limited to a shared surname and a modest amount of personal contact.[51] Was Peter a younger brother? a cousin? a nephew? Perhaps, but the records do not say. Apart from this single possibility, there was no one at all: no parents, no spouse, no children. Lifelong bachelors were an extreme rarity in colonial New England; in this respect alone Godfrey must have seemed conspicuous.

The singular fact of Godfrey's bachelorhood suggests a hypothesis which, while highly speculative, forges links with other bits and pieces of his

[51] Peter Godfrey was born in England in about 1631, came to Massachusetts as a boy, married Mary Browne (daughter of Thomas), spent his entire adult life in the town of Newbury, and died in 1697. He was a "yeoman" of average means. His estate was inventoried at £252 after his death. None of these personal data would appear to tilt the case for or against the possibility of a blood-relation to John Godfrey. There is, however, one intriguing piece of evidence that connects the two men in *some* fashion—in the file bearing on the administration of John Godfrey's estate. The court took testimony from Peter and his wife to the effect that John had been at their house a month before he died and had discussed with them certain particulars of his estate. Peter seems to have initiated the conversation: "Said I to him, 'you may die and leave your things to you know not who.' " Was Peter angling for a legacy—perhaps on the basis of kinship? If so, he must have been disappointed by the eventual settlement. *Ibid.*, 71. It should be said that this is the only datum showing close contact between John and Peter Godfrey; otherwise the evidence is fragmentary and indirect. There is no warrant whatsoever for inferring a continuous pattern of interaction between the two men; on a day-to-day basis John Godfrey was much more deeply involved with many other people.

life. Was he homosexual—perhaps not actively but latently so? Consider the following: Godfrey's pursuit of work as a herdsman meant that he was continually presenting himself to men and displaying his talent for their approval. And there was a passive side to this; he was, in effect, saying "choose me." Often these approaches involved him in triangular situations, in which the object of his attentions was a mature man. (His rival in such instances was usually an adolescent boy. The bitter reference to "cock-eating boys," quoted in the deposition by John Remington, also comes to mind here.) Moreover, the pattern of multiple litigation with a variety of men in his community—a pattern which seems to have a compulsive aspect—may reflect a defense against homosexuality. The strategy would be the one known to psychoanalysis as "reaction formation:" that is, in order to suppress a culturally forbidden wish to *love* other men, ego *attacks* them continually. Finally, the bitter, tenacious style with which he waged his personal battles has a distinctly paranoid cast—and homosexuality has long been associated with paranoia in psychiatric theory and practice.[52]

(2) Lacking family, he also lacked a home. Many plots of land passed through his hands, either by regular sales or in payment of debts, but he did not maintain any settled habitation. His domestic arrangements were haphazard, and in part he depended on others. Thus one glimpses him staying overnight with the Whitakers in 1656; spending the summer of 1661 at Job Tyler's; eating a meal in 1668 at the home of Matthias Button ("he said to Goody Button . . . 'woman, weigh me out some meat,' and she arose and gave him meat and brought in water"); declaring in court, in 1669, that "his usual abode was at Francis Skerry's in Salem;" and spending his last days, in 1675, under the care of a certin "Dr." Daniel Weed and Richard Croade.[53]

(3) By the standards of his time and culture John Godfrey was extremely mobile. His life seemed to violate the usual gravitational forces—social ones for certain, perhaps physical ones as well. The following is a list of his places of residence arranged in chronological sequence (though probably not a complete list, since some of his movements went unrecorded):

1640:	living in Newbury as "Mr. Spencer's herdsman"
1648:	called "of Andover"
1649:	called "of Newbury"

[52] Of course, there is no way to prove this hypothesis by reference to the usual canons of historical scholarship; certainly there is nothing in the records to suggest that John Godfrey had any overtly homosexual relationships. But, from a clinical standpoint, the picture seems to hint at an underlying, perhaps unconscious, orientation of this kind. I am grateful to Virginia Demos for suggesting this interpretation, and to Ernest S. Wolf, M.D., for confirming its plausibility on the basis of long experience in psychoanalytic practice.

[53] *Records of Quarterly Courts, Essex County*, II, 366ff., IV, 186, 132, V, 88ff.

1652–1653:	probably living in Rowley
mid-1650s:	living in Haverhill
1657:	called "of Dover"
1658:	called "of Newbury"; then "of Haverhill"
1659, 1661:	called "of Andover"
1666:	called "of Newbury"
1668:	called "of Ipswich"; then "of Newbury"
1669:	called "of Salem"
1671:	called "of Haverhill"
1675:	probably living in Boston at time of death

Many early New Englanders changed residence during the course of a lifetime, and some made several such changes. But few people felt comfortable in so doing, for their values consistently affirmed stability. And virtually no one amassed a record of movement to approach John Godfrey's.

There is little doubt that this record was explicitly recognized, and condemned, by Godfrey's peers. The petition which opened the witchcraft inquiry of 1659 referred to "John Godfrey, resident of Andover or elsewhere at his pleasure"[54]—a quite unusual notation. In later years his propensity for Sabbath-breaking was described in terms of "travelling from town to town."[55] Most striking of all in this connection was the evidence presented in *Godfrey v. Ela,* the defamation case of 1669. The defendant's statement that Godfrey had been seen in two places at the same time found credence with many witnesses; such a feat seemed quite plausible on the part of a man whose reputation for moving about was already beyond question. The testimony of John Griffin, quoted above, shows that this reputation had long encompassed some "supernatural" elements.

The three aspects of Godfrey's life considered so far have an important underlying affinity. The dearth of kin, the casual dependency on others for bed and board, the frequent changes of residence—these are all manifestations of an extreme rootlessness. Perhaps it seemed to those who knew him that Godfrey was scarcely touched by the elemental ties that controlled the lives of average folk. And being thus unbound, what might he not think and feel and do? The answer was manifest in three additional elements of his character: his abrasive personal style, his greed, and his contentiousness. These things, too, formed an overlapping triad of signal consequence.

(4) Of Godfrey's manner in dealing with others the surviving evidence yields an entirely consistent picture. He was rough, provocative, and unpredictable. He paid little heed to accepted conventions; he would try, for

---

[54] *Ibid.,* II, 157–158.
[55] *Ibid.,* IV, 187, 239.

instance, to collect debts on the Sabbath when decent men were otherwise preoccupied.[56] He cursed; he threatened; he was given to sudden "rages." He never once admitted fault, never—so far as one can tell—allowed himself those moments of ritual self-abasement so familiar to the Puritans.

(5) His greed was equally plain. Time and again the records show him grasping for something—whether for work as a herdsman, or for property, or for revenge. Many of his demands seemed excessive in amount and inappropriate in character, but he never stopped pressing. Jonathan Singletary, petitioning the court for relief from Godfrey's importunate claims, expressed a widely held view: "still he goes on with me, as with many other poor men, and saith he is resolved utterly to undo me, although he undo himself also."[57] There is a quality of relentless pursuit here, no matter what the cost or consequences. With Godfrey, so it seemed, a wish became a need and finally an imperative demand.

(6) Conflict was the normal condition of Godfrey's life. His instincts were deeply combative, and he made little effort to curb their expression. Once again Jonathan Singletary can serve as spokesman for views that were widely held in the community. "Why do you come dissembling and playing the Devil's part?" asked Singletary, midway through his quarrel with Godfrey at Ipswich prison. "Your nature is nothing but envy and malice, which you will vent though to your own loss, and you seek peace with no man."[58]

It was, of course, in court that Godfrey's "nature" found its appropriate outlet. Beginning in 1658, his involvement in litigation of one sort of another was virtually continuous. This pattern has been sampled extensively in the preceding pages; it remains to add an overall summary, a score-sheet of court cases in which Godfrey participated as one of the principals. The total of such cases is staggering—132 by a conservative count. (This figure is the sum of actions explicitly noted on a court docket. Almost certainly there were additional cases for which records have been lost.) In eighty-nine of these cases (some 67 percent of the total) Godfrey appeared as plaintiff; in thirty he was the defendant in a civil suit (23 percent); and in a further thirteen instances he was indicted on criminal charges (10 percent).[59]

---

[56] MS, Elizabeth Whitaker, Suffolk Files, II, no. 322. See also the deposition of John Carr and Moses Tyler, Nov. 26, 1661: "John Godfrey came to the house of Job Tyler on a Sabbath day, after afternoon meeting, and demanded a reckoning of said Tyler. The latter said he thought it strange that he should be so earnest, not being a convenient time, and that he would reckon with him in the morning. Whereupon the said Godfrey was in a rage, and said he would take a sudden course . . ." *Records of Quarterly Courts, Essex County*, II, 328.

[57] MS, Jonathan Singletary, Suffolk Files, V, no. 543.

[58] *Records of Quarterly Courts, Essex County*, III, 121–122.

[59] More than one hundred years ago the historian Charles W. Upham noted Godfrey's extraordinary contentiousness: "he had more lawsuits, it is probable, than

The matter of outcomes also deserves notice. When Godfrey brought suit against others, a verdict in his favor was returned in 55 percent of all cases. (The remainder included verdicts for the defendant, nonsuits, and cases reported without reference to result.) When others brought suit against Godfrey, they were victorious only 30 percent of the time. He was, then, not only an aggressive litigant (far more appearances as plaintiff than as defendant), but also a notably successful one (a high rate of favorable verdicts, relative to his opponents).

Godfrey's combative instincts remained active to the end of his life, but they became in a sense less consequential. He continued the vigorous pursuit of his interests in the courts, but more and more often he was himself a defendant. His rate of successful prosecutions did not drop significantly, but only because the magistrates reversed several decisions by juries that seemed prejudiced against him. His involvement in petty misdemeanors increased, but he was less subject to charges of witchcraft. And, to the extent that his reputation as witch hung on, his accusers showed less fear, less anger, less deep-down dread. There developed around him a new balance of forces which perceptibly reduced his social influence. From malevolent foe to clever trickster, from witch to eccentric: such was the direction of the change.

The foregoing list of significant themes in the life and career of John Godfrey yields a final opportunity to assess his position in the larger history of New England witchcraft. He was in some ways distinctive even among accused witches—for example, in his gender and in his detachment from family and kin.[60] (The hints of latent homosexuality suggest a further area of possible singularity.) But at least as striking are the various traits and experiences which Godfrey shared with others accused of "familiarity with the Devil." The blunt, assertive style; the appearance of envious and vengeful motive; the unrestrained expression of an aggressive impulse—in all this Godfrey epitomized the character New Englanders expected in their

---

any other man in the colony." C. W. Upham, *Salem Witchcraft*, I (Boston, 1867), 436. This judgment is impossible to verify by broad statistical samples, but four of Godfrey's Essex County neighbors have been studied as to the extent of their own activity at court. The results are as follows. Job Tyler appears in 17 cases (7 as plaintiff, 10 as defendant); John Remington in 7 cases (1 as plaintiff, 6 as defendant); Abraham Whitaker in 29 cases (6 as plaintiff, 23 as defendant); and William Holdridge in 3 cases (2 as plaintiff, 1 as defendant). These figures, crude and limited as they are, strongly support the notion that Godfrey was litigious far beyond prevailing norms.

[60] However, at least a few of the female "witches" were similarly detached—as widows or as childless women.

witches.[61] Of course, this character was manifest in a social context; always and everywhere, witchcraft charges reflected disturbances in human relationships. And this part of Godfrey's experience is documented for us with truly remarkable clarity.

In another sense, however, witches and their accusers interacted on a deeply reciprocal basis; disturbances and disharmony were themselves an epiphenomenon, the paradoxical sign of inner bond. Here, too, Godfrey's case is instructive. Even in moments of bitter antagonism he and his peers were inextricably joined. Theirs was a relationship of functional dependence, with implicit gains for each side.

For average folk in Essex County, Godfrey's presence was frequently adaptive, helping them to relieve and resolve significant elements of inner tension. He offered, most conspicuously, a ready target for anger, a focus of indignation. An attack on Godfrey was understandable, even commendable, if not always within the terms of the law. Moreover, his special malign agency served to explain and excuse a variety of misadventures which must otherwise have been attributed to personal incompetence. When cows were lost or food was spoiled, when a boy was injured in a fall from a horse, the people involved could fix the blame on witchcraft. There was a kind of comfort here. Finally and most broadly, Godfrey defined for his community a spectrum of unacceptable behaviors. Like deviant figures everywhere, he served to sharpen the boundaries between "good" and "bad," "moral" and "immoral," "legitimate" and "illegitimate."[62]

Godfrey himself seems to have derived covert gratification from the special notoriety he gained as an accused witch. His response to accusation, and even to formal indictment, was to continue the very pattern of activity that had brought him into difficulty in the first place. He became in this way a man of consequence, someone known—and feared—throughout Essex County. His compulsive involvement in conflict implies as well a psychological need on Godfrey's part. Something deep inside urged him insistently to challenge, to provoke, to contend.

Even as he tested the normative frontiers of his community, Godfrey was never far from its organizing center. Thus to describe him as an outsider—a common sociological view of accused witches—would be substantially misleading. He was, after all, a familiar participant in a variety of everyday

[61] See John Demos, "Underlying Themes in the Witchcraft of Seventeenth-Century New England," *American Historical Review*, LXXV (1970), 1311–1326. In a forthcoming monograph I hope to present additional case studies exemplifying the aggressive stereotype of the New England "witch."

[62] For a helpful discussion of this "boundary-setting" function see Kai T. Erikson, *Wayward Puritans: A Study in the Sociology of Deviance* (New York, 1966).

situations. At one time or another he had his bed and board from many of his neighbors; he worked alongside, and for, other men; he accompanied the constable in serving attachments; and so forth. Indeed it might well be argued that he was a special sort of *in*sider, so deeply did he penetrate the thoughts and feelings of his peers.

And did they, for their part, have a sense of this underlying affinity? Godfrey was not an "ordinary" man by the standards they customarily applied, but could they feel confident that his life and behavior were totally at variance with their own? Did his rootlessness, for example, serve in the end to separate him from the mass of his fellow New Englanders— or did it merely exaggerate a central tendency in their own lives? Had not many of these men and women undergone, quite willingly, a process of uprooting beyond anything experienced by most of their English contemporaries? And did they not feel repeated temptations to move about in the American "wilderness," as new towns were established and new lands opened to settlement?[63] There was, too, the matter of Godfrey's conduct towards others. Aggressive, angry, grasping he certainly seemed; but were the others entirely free of such traits themselves? Their sermons, charters, and private devotions affirmed harmony and peaceableness as preeminent values; but the records of their courts and governments tell a different story. Petty disputes among neighbors and "heart-burning contentions" within whole towns or religious congregations were endemic in the history of early New England.[64]

These pathways of identification suggest how fully John Godfrey and his neighbors served and used—one might even say, needed—each other. They afford, moreover, a new point of approach to questions which at an earlier

[63] The scope and predominant forms of geographic mobility in early New England are subjects of some dispute among historians. Studies such as Darrett B. Rutman, *Winthrop's Boston: Portrait of a Puritan Town, 1630–1649* (Chapel Hill, N. C., 1965); John Demos, *A Little Commonwealth: Family Life in Plymouth Colony* (New York, 1970); Kenneth A. Lockridge, *A New England Town, The First Hundred Years: Dedham, Massachusetts, 1636–1736* (New York, 1970); Philip J. Greven, Jr., *Four Generations: Population, Land, and Family in Colonial Andover, Massachusetts* (Ithaca, N. Y., 1970); and Linda Auwers Bissell, "From One Generation to Another: Mobility in Seventeenth-Century Windsor, Connecticut," *William and Mary Quarterly*, 3d Ser., XXXI (1974), 79–110, seem in this regard to reach rather different conclusions. My own (revised) impression—based on incomplete studies of towns such as Springfield and Northampton, Massachusetts, and Hampton and Exeter, New Hampshire—is that mobility was extremely high among the settler generation but dropped off markedly among their descendants. All studies to date agree on one point: namely, the value placed on stable residence and the normative opposition to moving about.

[64] For a careful study of factional strife in one particular town see Paul Boyer and Stephen Nissenbaum, *Salem Possessed: The Social Origins of Witchcraft* (Cambridge, Mass., 1974).

stage in our discussion seemed baffling. Recall that Godfrey was suspected of practicing witchcraft during a span of at least fifteen years. Two or three times he was prosecuted on charges that might have brought the death penalty. After each trial, no matter how narrow his escape, he returned to the same locale and was reincorporated into the same network of ongoing relationships. The problem of John Godfrey simply would not go away. Perhaps now we can begin to understand why. For this was a problem deeply rooted in the collective life of the community and in the individual lives of its members. It is not too much to say that there was a little of Godfrey in many of the Essex County settlers; so his fate and theirs remained deeply intertwined.

Essay Review

WITCHCRAFT AND THE LIMITS OF INTERPRETATION

DAVID D. HALL

THE great European witch-hunts rose and vanished in little more than three centuries. This cycle had nearly run its course by the time the colonists in New England undertook to find and punish witches. Belated though it was, witchcraft and witch-hunting in New England had the same structure as witchcraft in England and, taking due account of certain differences, as witchcraft on the Continent. The road that leads to Salem in 1692 originates in Europe. So too the road to an understanding of our native witches and witch-hunters originates in the historiography of their European counterparts.

A turning point in the historiography of European witchcraft came when it was realized that the "rational" or scientific historians had failed to make sense of the phenomenon.[1] According to Henry C. Lea and others of his persuasion, witchcraft was entirely irrational, a superstition that violated common sense. Lea blamed the witch-hunts on a clergy that wanted to enhance or maintain its power. Transforming witchcraft into heresy, clerics had encouraged the slaughtering of innocent victims, many of whom confessed under torture to crimes they had never committed. The alternative to this interpretation originated with social anthropologists who studied witchcraft in preliterate societies. In those communities, belief in witches was endemic, not sporadic, and "real" in meeting certain social needs. Witchcraft was functional, either because it affirmed village solidarity or because it relieved social strain. Accusations

[1] The historiography is reviewed and criticized by E. William Monter, in "The Historiography of European Witchcraft: Progress and Prospects," *Journal of Interdisciplinary History* 2 (1972): 435–51; H. C. Erik Midelfort, "Witchcraft, Magic, and the Occult," in *Reformation Europe: A Guide to Research*, ed. Steven Ozment (St. Louis: Center for Reformation Research, 1982), pp. 183–209; M. J. Kephart, "Rationalists vs. Romantics among Scholars of Witchcraft," in *Witchcraft and Sorcery*, ed. Max Marwick, 2d ed. (Harmondsworth, England: Penguin Books, 1982), pp. 326–42; and Christina Larner, *Enemies of God: The Witch-hunt in Scotland* (London: Chatto & Windus, 1981), chap. 2.

253

were not random but patterned; that is, certain types of persons were singled out as "witches." The structure of witchcraft in preliterate societies provided the basis for reappraising witchcraft in the village communities of early modern Europe, and it was found that here too witchcraft was socially functional and "real," not some obscurantist belief that would vanish with the rise of science. [2]

Two historians, Keith Thomas and Alan Macfarlane, would apply anthropology to European witchcraft in the books each wrote, *Religion and the Decline of Magic* and *Witchcraft in Tudor and Stuart England*. These books were closely linked; Thomas had supervised Macfarlane's thesis, and Macfarlane had read his mentor's work-in-progress. Using to advantage the anthropological literature on witchcraft in Africa, Macfarlane and Thomas argued that witchcraft in the form of maleficium (occult means of doing evil or harm) was endemic and arose from the very "roots of society." For those who were variously victims, accusers, and witches residing in the same close-knit community, witchcraft was a form of social interaction among neighbors. Macfarlane and Thomas suggested that accusations of witchcraft sprang from one particular mode of interaction: the accuser had angered someone else and then, expecting retribution, experienced a misfortune that he attributed to maleficium. Witchcraft was thus an outgrowth of conflict and its psychic consequences, including guilt. It was also, Thomas argued, a means of making sense out of misfortune for which there was no other obvious cause. [3]

Like other students of witchcraft in early modern Europe, Thomas and Macfarlane wanted to explain why accusations increased sharply during that period. Thomas linked the upsurge in cases to the Protestant Reformation, which, he argued, had discredited most of the countermagic that villagers had previously employed to protect themselves against maleficium. More important, however, was the social strain resulting from the onset of a market economy. The traditional economy of the village had sustained an ethic of charity to one's neighbors, but when the individualism of the

[2] Lucy Mair, *Witchcraft* (New York: McGraw-Hill, 1969), pp. 199–200; Keith Thomas, "The Relevance of Social Anthropology to the Historical Study of English Witchcraft," in *Witchcraft Confessions and Accusations*, ed. Mary Douglas (London: Tavistock, 1970), pp. 47–79.

[3] Keith Thomas, *Religion and the Decline of Magic* (London: Weidenfeld and Nicolson, 1971), chap. 17, and Alan Macfarlane, *Witchcraft in Tudor and Stuart England* (New York: Harper & Row, 1970), pp. 111–12.

market economy undermined this obligation, every village became an arena of conflict between old values and new. This conflict emerged whenever someone rejected a neighbor's request for aid. Hence, said Thomas, the sequence of rejection, anger, guilt, and accusations of witchcraft. Guilt turned into accusations of maleficium when and if misfortune followed, for misfortune lent itself to interpretation as revenge by the offended party.[4]

Along the way, Thomas disposed of Margaret Murray's hypothesis that witchcraft was actually being practiced by a pagan cult that had survived the Christianization of Europe.[5] He also questioned Russell Hope Robbins's argument that "the theological concept of witchcraft" as heresy was "imposed" on the people. Thomas observed that "the great bulk of witchcraft accusations in England did not relate to any alleged heretical activities upon the part of the witch."[6] In this regard the prosecution of witches in England differed markedly from the prosecution of witches in Scotland and parts of continental Europe. Indeed there were other substantial differences. The actual incidence of witchcraft cases in England was much lower than in contemporary Scotland or southwestern Germany, where canon law sanctioned inquisitorial justice and the use of torture; in common-law England, torture was infrequent and witches were hanged, not burned as heretics. For the most part English witches did not confess to participating in sexual orgies or the witches' sabbat. Nor did they say that they had signed compacts with the devil. Only in the famous Essex witch-hunt of 1645 did the devil's pact become significant.[7]

The English materials were instructive in several other respects. English witches tended to be slightly poorer than most of their neighbors. This finding precluded any interpretation of witch-hunting as a form of social protest by the poor or an agrarian peasantry against their betters, as some historians had suggested was the case

[4] Thomas, *Religion and Magic*, pp. 490–98, 560, chap. 17, pp. 553–62.

[5] Thomas, *Religion and Magic*, pp. 514–16. Virtually every recent historian dismisses Margaret Murray. An important critique of her work that also takes in Montague Summers, Carlo Ginzburg, and others is Norman Cohn's *Europe's Inner Demons: An Enquiry Inspired by the Great Witch-Hunt* (1975; reprinted New York: New American Library, 1977), pp. 107–15, 119–21.

[6] Thomas, *Religion and Magic*, pp. 456–58, 450.

[7] Thomas, *Religion and Magic*, chap. 14; Macfarlane, *Witchcraft in England*, pp. 18, 20; Cohn, *Europe's Inner Demons*, p. 254. On the Essex witch-hunt, see Macfarlane, *Witchcraft in England*, p. 139.

in France.[8] The English judicial system, like that of other regions, seemed able to differentiate between convincing and unconvincing evidence of witchcraft; many more than half of all the persons brought to trial were acquitted, a ratio that increased sharply after 1620. Like other historians before and after them, Thomas and Macfarlane found that the machinery of enforcement ceased to function long before accusations disappeared.[9]

The chapters on witchcraft in *Religion and the Decline of Magic* are masterful. Yet some readers found them wanting. One important critic was Norman Cohn, who felt that Thomas had not really explained the timing of the witch-hunts. Cohn pointed out that "a fund of popular suspicion," that is, maleficium, antedated the witch-hunts of the early modern period. Precisely for this reason, he insisted, maleficium in and of itself was insufficient to explain the rhythm of prosecutions on the Continent. The question that concerned him, therefore, was the transformation of maleficium into an ideology that allowed, or made necessary, the mass pursuit of witches. The answer lay in the emergence of a complex demonology that turned witches into heretics and magic into something understood as threatening to religion. Cohn sketched the convergence in the late middle ages of certain themes and fantasies—night-flying heretical sects, the witches' sabbat, compacts with the devil. Out of this potent combination came a new understanding of witches as engaged in a conspiracy against the Christian church. Contemporaries found ample proof of this conspiracy in the confessions that inquisitorial procedures drew out of hundreds of suspects. These inquisitors, Cohn declared, were an elite group, the bishops, magistrates, and lawyers who were set apart from the people by literacy and social rank. Using their powers to advantage, this elite conducted the great witch-hunts in order to eradicate real or imagined opposition to authority. Cohn stressed, therefore, the significance of a new demonology and of organized, political authority. "Left to themselves," he concluded, "peasants would never have created mass witch hunts—these occurred only where and when the authorities

[8] Emmanuel Le Roy Ladurie, *The Peasants of Languedoc* (1966; reprinted, Chicago: University of Chicago Press, 1974), pt. 2, chap. 5.

[9] No single factor seems to explain the "decline" of witch-hunting, and interpretations vary from one historian to the next. Certainly a loss of confidence among the magistrates in trial procedures, and a corresponding reluctance to prosecute, was crucial. An outstanding study is Robert Mandrou's *Magistrats et Sorciers en France au xvii* Siècle* (1968; reprinted, Paris: Editions du Seuil, 1980).

had become convinced of the reality of the sabbat and of nocturnal flights to the sabbat."[10]

Christina Larner supported this interpretation in *Enemies of God*, a careful study of witchcraft and witch-hunting in Scotland. Witchcraft prosecutions in Scotland were of a different order of magnitude than those in England; in the same decades that saw some 300 English witches executed, the Scottish authorities put to death an estimated 1,300 persons out of a much smaller population. Witchcraft prosecutions on this scale deserved the title of "witch-hunt," the term she preferred. Larner had a second reason for referring to the Scottish experience as a witch-hunt. She linked the onset of prosecution in the late sixteenth century with the emergence of a new kind of civil state that was attempting to assert its legitimacy and extend its range of control. In her view, "witchcraft was an activity fostered by the ruling class; it was not a spontaneous movement on the part of the peasantry." A crucial factor in Scotland was the evolution of legal machinery in the direction of "abstract, rational bureaucratic justice with repressive sanctions." Legal rationality became the instrument of a national state bent on imposing ideological conformity. [11]

A political interpretation of witchcraft was not new, of course, for the "rationalist" or scientific historians of the late nineteenth century had also described ordinary people as victims of an elite-led crusade. Larner and Cohn departed from this frame of reference in several respects. For them there was no conspiracy, no backstage machinations by a priesthood. More important, no one had to invent the demonology that turned witches into heretics. A medley of fantasies and concepts, some originating in Scripture, others in pre-Christian myth or paganism, and still others vaguely folkloric, had converged in the late middle ages. Cohn and Larner discriminated between popular and learned culture but also—and in Larner's case quite strongly—argued for an intermingling. In doing so, they distanced themselves from an alternative political interpretation, the one much favored by some French historians of popular culture, that an urban bourgeoisie used witch-hunting as one weapon

[10] Cohn, *Europe's Inner Demons*, pp. 154, 238–39, 246–78, 252.

[11] Larner, *Enemies of God*, pp. 1, 21–23. See also, Mair, *Witchcraft*, p. 198: "The elaboration of the ideology of witchcraft goes with the development of a tradition of scholastic learning such as was only possible in a literate society, and of religious and political institutions seeking to make effective a centralized authority over an area much wider than was ever covered by any African polity."

in a broader campaign to suppress the culture of the peasants. [12]

Larner filled out her interpretation with a critique of Thomas and Macfarlane. Like Cohn, she dissented from their functionalism because it did not seem to explain the increased incidence of witchcraft. If conflict were endemic in the peasant community before the late sixteenth century, as surely it had been, then its later presence did not account for the upsurge in prosecutions. Nor did Larner accept the argument that witchcraft was an outgrowth of "social strain." In her view there was no obvious way of demonstrating greater strain in one period or community than in another. [13] She and Cohn would have a surprising ally in Alan Macfarlane when, on further reflection, it seemed to him that the great transition from small-scale "peasant communities" to "individualism" had occurred several centuries earlier than at first he had supposed. [14] Historians of witchcraft on the Continent were critical of functionalism for other reasons. Erik Midelfort, reflecting on the functionalist assumption that witchcraft prosecutions helped to strengthen a society, concluded that in southwestern Germany they had made matters worse, not better. William Monter, writing on witchcraft in France and Switzerland, found other social dynamics in the villages he studied than those Thomas and Macfarlane had specified. [15]

[12] Larner, *Enemies of God*, p. 23, chap. 11; Cohn, *Europe's Inner Demons*, passim. Larner *(Enemies of God*, p. 25) summarizes the interpretation of Jean Delumeau; see also, Robert Muchembled, "Sorcellerie, culture populaire et christianisme au xvi⁰ siècle, principalement en Flandre et Artois," *Annales: ESC* 28 (1973): 271–84.

[13] Larner, *Enemies of God*, pp. 21–23. Marwick's argument for witchcraft as a "gauge" of social strain is included in his *Witchcraft and Sorcery*, pp. 300–313. Mary Douglas has observed that "The general proposition that an increase in witchcraft accusations occurs as a symptom of disorder and moral collapse was superbly untestable" ("Introduction: Thirty Years after *Witchcraft, Oracles and Magic*," in her *Witchcraft Confessions*, p. xx).

[14] Alan Macfarlane, *The Origins of English Individualism* (Oxford: Basil Blackwell, 1978), pp. 1, 59–60.

[15] H. C. Erik Midelfort, *Witch Hunting in Southwestern Germany, 1562–1684: The Social and Intellectual Foundations* (Stanford, Calif.: Stanford University Press, 1972), pp. 1–2; E. William Monter, *Witchcraft in France and Switzerland: The Borderlands during the Reformation* (Ithaca, N.Y.: Cornell University Press, 1976). Here may be the place to mention H. R. Trevor-Roper, "The European Witch-craze of the Sixteenth and Seventeenth Centuries," in *Religion, the Reformation and Social Change and other Essays* (London: Macmillan, 1967) and his famous argument that witchcraft accusations arose out of the antagonism between lowlands and highlands, the latter associated with heresy. Monter joins Macfarlane in criticizing this argument. Here may also be the place to point out that anthropologists are vigorously reexamining the uses they have made of functionalism. See, e.g., Douglas, "Introduction: Thirty Years after *Witchcraft, Oracles and Magic*," pp. xiii–xxxviii;

We should not take this conflict of opinion to mean that we must always prefer functionalism to the political interpretation or vice versa. Each is important. It is beyond doubt that witchcraft was heresy in the eyes of the church and persecuted accordingly in some regions. Everywhere, even in England by the middle of the seventeenth century, the notion of the devil's compact circulated widely, and everywhere this idea prepared the way for confessions that implicated large numbers of the innocent. It is also beyond doubt that Thomas, Macfarlane, and, before them, George Lyman Kittredge, were right to emphasize the role of maleficium. Jeffrey Burton Russell, in the course of elucidating the connections between witchcraft and heresy in the middle ages, has insisted that the majority of cases involved sorcery and "folk tradition" and relatively few the "formal definitions" laid down by "inquisitors and scholastics." The same often seems true of later centuries. Thomas was surely on firm ground, moreover, in assuming, like the anthropologists, that witchcraft accusations fell into patterns that revealed "ambiguous social relations" or "tensions between neighboring rivals [that] could not otherwise be resolved." As Mary Douglas has observed, in offering a tempered defense of functionalism, "People are trying to control one another, albeit with small success. The idea of witch is used to whip their own consciences or those of their friends."[16]

For Larner and Cohn, the significant process of control began with elites and not with villagers. But what really distanced Cohn from the functionalists was their assumption that witchcraft was normal and sane. In keeping with the anthropological literature, Macfarlane and Thomas argued that witchcraft was socially useful. Cohn disagreed. To him, the witch-hunts were a "vast holocaust," a "horrid picture." Witch-hunting was a form of social pathology, a process that lay quite outside the boundaries of the normal and was based, like that other dark vision of the Jew as conspirator, upon "fantasy." The less agitated tone of *Religion and the Decline of Magic* was linked with Thomas's assertion that large numbers of "cunning folk" were actually practicing magic and sorcery in sixteenth- and

Marwick, introduction to his *Witchcraft and Sorcery*, and the essay by Kephart, "Rationalists vs. Romantics."

[16] George Lyman Kittredge, *Witchcraft in Old and New England* (Cambridge, Mass.: Harvard University Press, 1929); Jeffrey Burton Russell, *Witchcraft in the Middle Ages* (Ithaca, N.Y.: Cornell University Press, 1972), pp. 18–19; Douglas, "Introduction: Thirty Years after *Witchcraft, Oracles and Magic*," pp. xvii, xxv.

seventeenth-century England. [17] Though Cohn conceded that some sorcery was being practiced, he preferred to emphasize the slaughter of the innocent—which the cunning folk were not, or at least not entirely.

For some historians, the presence of these cunning folk had another significance. Their way of life betokened a widespread credulity in magic, a credulity that enabled the practice of magic to "work." The curse or blessing muttered by a village healer had real consequences because so many persons assumed, without thinking twice about it, that certain individuals possessed occult powers. The mental world that linked the cunning folk with their patrons and victims was a world that ignored the distinctions we have since imposed between the real and the imaginary, the natural and the supernatural. [18] As William Monter has pointedly remarked, twentieth-century historians of witchcraft must acknowledge "the relativism of their own concept of 'reality' " before they explain away what was seen and felt as real four hundred years ago. [19] The people of early modern Europe believed that matter and spirit were interchangeable. Nature was invested with occult or spiritual forces; any physical effect or symptom could result from something as intangible as a dream, a few spoken words, a lapse into sin, or the presence of a ghostly spirit. The world of man and nature was ultimately a moral order, with good contending against evil. Witchcraft and religion were but points along a spectrum, each dramatizing this great conflict. [20]

This line of interpretation carries us to the opposite extreme from

[17] Norman Cohn, "The Myth of Satan and His Human Servants," in Douglas, *Witchcraft Confessions and Accusations*, pp. 12–13; Thomas, *Religion and Magic*, chap. 8; Macfarlane, *Witchcraft in England*, chap. 8.

[18] Julio Caro Baroja, *The World of the Witches*, trans. O. N. V. Glendinning (Chicago: University of Chicago Press, 1965), pp. xxx, xi; Thomas, *Religion and Magic*, pp. 522–24, chap. 8.

[19] Monter, "The Historiography of European Witchcraft," p. 447. This point has prompted various sociologists and anthropologists to elaborate a "sociology of perception." A disappointing exercise of this kind is Dennis E. Owen's "Spectral Evidence: The Witchcraft Cosmology of Salem Village in 1692," in *Essays in the Sociology of Perception*, ed. Mary Douglas (London: Routledge & Kegan Paul, 1982), pp. 275–301.

[20] The most sophisticated explication of this world view is Michael MacDonald's *Mystical Bedlam: Madness, Anxiety, and Healing in Seventeenth-Century England* (Cambridge: Cambridge University Press, 1981), chap. 5 and passim. See also Thomas, *Religion and Magic*, chap. 8; Stuart Clark, "Inversion, Misrule and the Meaning of Witchcraft," *Past and Present* 87 (May 1980): 98–127; Sydney Anglo, ed., *The Damned Art: Essays in the Literature of Witchcraft* (London: Routledge & Kegan Paul, 1977).

the rationalist historiography of the nineteenth century. One of the premises of that historiography, and a premise still worth recalling, was that witchcraft beliefs were not "universal" but intermittent and selectively distributed. [21] Indeed it is well established that certain contemporaries questioned the procedures for discovering witches and scoffed at popular beliefs. We may go further and assert that skepticism and credulity were intermixed, even in the mental world of those who readily accused others of the crime of witchcraft. Exactly how this intermixture functioned is not clear. Nor do we understand how "ideas that attract belief but are inactive in human affairs"—and witchcraft beliefs were very often inert or latent—become activated. [22] The contradictions that pervaded witchcraft certainly worked to inhibit the judicial system from pursuing every single person suspected of the practice. For its part, the medical community endeavored to distinguish "true" demonic possession from forms of mental illness. [23] Excluding phases of real panic, the history of witch-hunting in early modern Europe and America reveals a surprising capacity to suspend judgment and to discriminate. The more we explicate and make persuasive the functional and mental intelligibility of witchcraft, the more we also have to recognize that inconsistency and contradiction figure in the ideology that sustained both the witch-hunts and the cunning folk.

What then of witchcraft in New England? A century ago, no one could approach the subject without stumbling upon the twin issues of Puritanism and the role of the clergy. Charles Upham was but the most vehement of the antiquarians who insisted that Calvinism, or the Puritan version of it, perpetuated a literal belief in witchcraft that clergy such as Cotton Mather put to devastating use. The rebuttals were equally vehement and had the better of the evidence. The foremost rebutter, William L. Poole, contributed a chapter to *The Memorial History of Boston* summing up his point of view and narrating several of the most important cases to occur before Salem.

[21] George Lincoln Burr, "New England's Place in the History of Witchcraft," *American Antiquarian Society Proceedings*, n.s. 21 (1911): 185–217. As E. E. Evans-Pritchard remarks in his preface to Macfarlane's *Witchcraft in England*, "it is a problem why . . . some misfortunes are attributed to witches and others not" (p. xvi).

[22] Douglas, "Introduction: Thirty Years after *Witchcraft, Oracles and Magic*," p. xxiv. Several of the essays in Anglo, *The Damned Art*, bear on the history of skepticism. See also Wallace Notestein, *A History of Witchcraft in England from 1558 to 1718* (1911; reprinted New York: Russell and Russell, 1965), chaps. 3, 10–12.

[23] Sanford J. Fox, Jr., *Science and Justice: The Massachusetts Witchcraft Trials* (Baltimore: Johns Hopkins University Press, 1968).

Half a century later, Kittredge was still caught up in these old battles. He would argue in his eccentric masterpiece, *Witchcraft in Old and New England*, that English and American demonology differed from continental theories and insist that Calvinism bore no responsibility for the witch-hunts in England and America. With him one great phase of interpretation came to a dead end. Sensing the exhaustion of these issues, Perry Miller would break with tradition by insisting that "the intellectual history of New England can be written as though no such thing [as Salem] ever happened. It had no effect on the ecclesiastical or political situation, it does not figure in the institutional or ideological development."[24]

Despite Kittredge and Poole, myth and error remain stubbornly embedded in "popular tradition," to borrow Chadwick Hansen's useful phrase. Hansen blames the nineteenth-century historian George Bancroft for perpetuating the story of a domineering clergy and a duped populace. Tracing the repetitions of this story down to the present, Hansen divides it into six separate propositions. Two of these propositions remain controversial: the behavior of the afflicted girls at Salem and the practice of witchcraft. The other four are utterly without substance, as Hansen demonstrates convincingly: the "afflicted persons were inspired, stimulated, and encouraged by the clergy"; the "clergy whipped the general populace into a state of 'mass hysteria' with their sermons and writings on witchcraft"; the "only significant opposition" to Salem "came from the merchant class"; and "the executions were unique . . . and attributable to some narrowness or fanaticism or repressiveness peculiar to Puritans."[25] I shall repeat: each of these propositions is wrong. Originating in the malice of Robert Calef or in a deep hostility to Puritanism, such notions are now the subject matter of the folklorist but no longer, thanks to Hansen, Kittredge, and Poole, the concern of the historian. To this general statement I must note one minor exception. Debate continues on the attitude and role of Cotton Mather, and

[24] Charles Upham, *Salem Witchcraft: With an Account of Salem Village and a History of Opinions on Witchcraft and Kindred Subjects*, 2 vols. (1867; reprinted New York: Frederick Ungar, 1966); William L. Poole, "Witchcraft in Boston," in *The Memorial History of Boston*, ed. Justin Winsor, 4 vols. (Boston: James R. Osgood, 1881), 2:131–72; Perry Miller, *The New England Mind: From Colony to Province* (Cambridge, Mass.: Harvard University Press, 1954), p. 191. Miller subsumed the Salem tragedy into his narrative of the rise and fall of the covenantal conception of New England's identity.

[25] Chadwick Hansen, *Witchcraft at Salem* (New York: George Braziller, 1969), pp. ix–x.

though none of his recent biographers is at all interested in making him responsible for Salem, David Levin and Kenneth Silverman disagree sharply, Levin interpreting the evidence in a liberal and forgiving manner, Silverman much more critical.[26]

Fifty years after Kittredge, the history of witchcraft in New England finally entered a new phase with the publication of *Salem Possessed*, by Paul Boyer and Stephen Nissenbaum.[27] This book escaped the stalemate of the 1920s by applying the procedures of the town study to Salem Village, an agricultural community that lay to the west of the seaport and the locale of the initial accusations in 1692. The stimulus behind *Salem Possessed* was not in any direct sense Macfarlane's work, though his interpretation shaped the final chapter of the book. Its authors were responsive, rather, to the wider vogue of social history, family reconstitution, and Kenneth Lockridge's provocative hypothesis of increasing (or portending) deprivation as communities outgrew their reserves of land.

The argument of *Salem Possessed* is too well known to need restating in detail. Boyer and Nissenbaum described a factionalism in Salem Village that erupted whenever one group pressed for ecclesiastical independence from Salem proper or brought in candidates for the ministry of a church that finally, after much dispute, was officially organized in 1688. This sort of factionalism was routine in colonial New England, yet Boyer and Nissenbaum perceived a deeper resonance to conflict in the Village. One group of residents was advancing economically even as another group faced the prospect or reality of decline. Boyer and Nissenbaum expanded this difference into one of attitude or consciousness: the prosperous were

[26] David Levin, *Cotton Mather: The Young Life of the Lord's Remembrancer* (Cambridge, Mass.: Harvard University Press, 1978); Kenneth Silverman, *The Life and Times of Cotton Mather* (New York: Harper & Row, 1984), pt. 2, chap. 4. See also Richard Werking, "'Reformation Is Our Only Preservation': Cotton Mather and Salem Witchcraft," *William and Mary Quarterly*, 3d ser. 29 (1972): 281–90; Thomas G. Holmes, *Cotton Mather: A Bibliography of His Works*, 3 vols. (Cambridge, Mass.: Harvard University Press, 1940), 3:1234–66; Robert Middlekauff, *The Mathers: Three Generations of Puritan Intellectuals* (New York: Oxford University Press, 1971). These are only the most recent contributions to a very extensive literature. Miller's account of Cotton Mather's role in *The New England Mind: From Colony to Province* remains an impressive piece of analysis.

[27] Paul Boyer and Stephen Nissenbaum, *Salem Possessed: The Social Origins of Witchcraft* (Cambridge, Mass.: Harvard University Press, 1974). Boyer and Nissenbaum also edited *The Salem Witchcraft Papers: Verbatim Transcripts of the Legal Documents of the Salem Witchcraft Outbreak of 1692*, 3 vols. (New York: Da Capo Press, 1977).

at ease with mercantile capitalism, the less prosperous hostile or, at best, extremely uneasy, envious, and critical at one and the same time. Village factionalism seemed to align with the clustering of victims, accusers, and witches. Six of the nineteen persons executed in 1692 were residents of Salem Village, and most of them were "outsiders" to the agrarian community in one manner or another. Looking one more time at their materials, Boyer and Nissenbaum turned to psychological language to explain what had occurred. The people who set out after witches were moved by guilt and rage; ambivalent in their own response to change, they sought to exorcise confusion and, in doing so, to express their anger at losing out in the pursuit of gain. Also suggesting that the young people of the Village were especially restless and disturbed, Boyer and Nissenbaum would liken the attacks of possession that some of them experienced to the religious enthusiasm of the 1740s.

This web of evidence and assumption continues to provoke critical response as well as strong approval. Elsewhere I have challenged the assumption, itself derived from other scholarship, that religion stood in opposition to emerging capitalism. [28] Boyer and Nissenbaum view Samuel Parris, the man who was minister as the crisis unfolded, as archetypal in his mixture of feelings; they argue, moreover, that he projected his anxieties onto witchcraft. But a recent study of all his extant sermons makes him out to be conventional and sincere in his evangelism. [29] Other critics have identified alternative patterns among victims, accusers, and witches. Christine Heyrman, in the course of challenging the premise that capitalists turned away from Puritanism, has pointed to religious dissent, and especially Quakerism, as a significant cause of tension between accusers and witches. [30] David Konig has argued that being designated "witches" had much to do with the "extralegal behavior" of certain persons. He perceives the early 1690s as a period when the colonists were ex-

[28] See my "Religion and Society: Problems and Reconsiderations," in *Colonial British America*, ed. Jack P. Greene and J. R. Pole (Baltimore: Johns Hopkins University Press, 1984), pp. 334–36.

[29] Larry P. Gregg, "Samuel Parris: Portrait of a Puritan Clergyman," *Essex Institute Historical Collections* 119 (1983): 209–37, an essay that, by failing to address the question of changes over time in the preaching of Samuel Parris, may not refute Boyer and Nissenbaum's contention.

[30] Christine L. Heyrman, "Spectres of Subversion, Societies of Friends: Dissent and the Devil in Provincial Essex County, Massachusetts," in *Saints and Revolutionaries: Essays on Early American History*, ed. David D. Hall et al. (New York: W. W. Norton, 1984), pp. 38–74. See also Mair, *Witchcraft*, p. 232.

tremely anxious to reaffirm "established authority patterns," especially the authority of the judicial system, in the aftermath of the Dominion of New England. Anyone who was openly defiant of the judges in 1692, Konig notes, was executed, and several other condemned witches had been involved in larceny, family conflicts, or incidents of trespass. Witchcraft, whether real or imagined, betokened contempt for established rules. Rejecting, therefore, the assumption that Salem Village was undergoing acute and sudden social strain, Konig concludes that "most of the charges brought to the Court . . . reflected long-term terrors, uncertainties, and fears."[31] One other critic, Chadwick Hansen, has repeatedly pointed out that the great majority of accusers, victims, and confessing witches came from communities other than Salem Village, a circumstance left unexplained in *Salem Possessed*.[32]

Also missing from the book was the anthropological perspective of Macfarlane and Thomas. *Salem Possessed* took its motif of deeply anxious, ambivalent Puritans more from Michael Walzer than from social anthropology. It is useful to return to Thomas's observation that cunning folk were active in the English village and apply it to New England. Were any cunning folk at work in Salem Village and its environs? Were any of the "witches" practitioners of "magic"? Chadwick Hansen insists, contrary to another proposition of the "traditional interpretation," that *real* witchcraft was being practiced in New England. His argument remains controversial, though certainly some of the accused in the Salem panic were fortune-tellers in the manner of the cunning folk.[33]

[31] David Thomas Konig, *Law and Society in Puritan Massachusetts: Essex County, 1629–1692* (Chapel Hill: University of North Carolina Press, 1979), chap. 7.

[32] Chadwick Hansen, "Andover Witchcraft and the Causes of the Salem Witchcraft Trials," in *The Occult in America: New Historical Perspectives*, ed. Howard Kerr and Charles L. Crow (Urbana: University of Illinois Press, 1983), pp. 38–57. Richard P. Gildrie, studying Salem from its founding to the eve of the witchcraft panic, has argued that the mercantile and agrarian interests were not at odds. *Salem, Massachusetts, 1626–1683: A Covenant Community* (Charlottesville: University of Virginia Press, 1975). A central premise of the Boyer-Nissenbaum interpretation, the crunch of diminishing resources, must be qualified in the light of more recent work demonstrating the colonists' capacity for adaptation.

[33] Hansen, *Witchcraft at Salem*, chap. 5. John Demos was briefly critical in "Underlying Themes in the Witchcraft of Seventeenth-Century New England," *American Historical Review* 76 (1971): 1312 n. 5, and repeats his skepticism in *Entertaining Satan: Witchcraft and the Culture of Early New England* (New York: Oxford University Press, 1982), pp. 80–84. Yet in both places (see "Underlying Themes," p. 1317 n. 18) he describes activities of accused witches that were characteristic of the cunning folk.

The English situation was duplicated in another respect. Some of the depositions by accusers and hostile witnesses at Salem indicate that accusations originated in petty conflicts, misfortune, and rejections of requests for help. *Salem Possessed* was akin to *Religion and the Decline of Magic* in depicting a community under stress from competing norms. But in giving the impression that stress induced extraordinary, out-of-bounds behavior, Boyer and Nissenbaum resisted the insight that witchcraft accusations were routine, even normal, in the village context. Theirs was not a history of maleficium; nor was it a political interpretation, save in the sense of linking witchcraft with village factionalism. No outside elite manipulated the system, as Cohn and Larner both had argued was the case in Europe.

In the wake of *Salem Possessed*, further progress lay in undertaking more community studies of witch-hunting. Alternatively, progress depended upon a search for patterns within the entire body of accusations, indictments, and executions. In 1965 Frederick S. Drake called attention to the cases that had occurred in the fifteen years between 1647 and 1662, the most active period of witch-hunting in New England before 1692.[34] Aside from his brief listing, the tasks of local study and broad survey were neglected until John Demos started down the path that led to *Entertaining Satan*. Demos included data from the Salem cases in an essay of 1971, "Underlying Themes in the Witchcraft of Seventeenth-Century New England." But in *Entertaining Satan*, limiting himself to the episodes that occurred before 1692, he allows data from Salem to intrude only in support of one crucial argument, the sex and age distribution of the witches. *Entertaining Satan* has three main objectives: to explore, à la Thomas and Macfarlane, the social relationships that engendered witchcraft accusations; to pursue the inner history of witchcraft, the "deeper levels of experience" that it drew on and made manifest; and to explain the rhythm of witch-hunting in relation to the ebb and flow of conflict. I want to pass by the last of these topics in order to focus on the two other questions he addresses.

Before Salem, sixteen persons were executed as witches in Connecticut and Massachusetts, another eighty-odd indicted or accused of the crime, and as in England, the majority of accusations that went to court resulted in acquittals of one kind or another. Recon-

[34] Frederick S. Drake, "Witchcraft in the American Colonies, 1647–1662," *American Quarterly* 20 (1968): 694–725.

structing the life histories of the accused, Demos finds that gender and age were significant factors affecting an individual's vulnerability to witch-hunting. Most witches were women, by a ratio of 4:1, and in age, these women clustered around "midlife." Other characteristics, none of them as consistent as these two, include a "domestic experience" that was "often marred by trouble and conflict" and a history of disputes that ended up in court. In social position, "witches were recruited, to a greatly disproportionate extent, among the most humble, least powerful of New England's citizens."[35] Demos's is a tale of the *menu peuple* of New England, with the magistrates and ministers often looking on askance.

In interpreting this data, Demos moves in two directions, the social and the psychological. He looks closely at two communities, Easthampton, Long Island, and Springfield, Massachusetts,[36] before summing up his conclusions in a separate chapter. Thomas and Macfarlane provide the essentials of the interpretative framework. Defending their functionalism, Demos argues that New England was but Old writ small—or large, if we assume, as he does, that the incidence of witchcraft accusations was greater in Massachusetts and Connecticut than in Essex County, England. Here, as in England, witchcraft was a phenomenon of one neighbor suspecting another. Here, as in England, it operated as a "'conservative,' cohesive force," reinforcing social boundaries and the social norms of "kindness," "charity," and "harmony."[37] Here, as well, Demos argues, witchcraft exposed a fundamental contradiction. The ground or source of conflict in New England was the intermixture of order and disorder in the social experience of the colonists. On the one hand, people lived within the confines of the town or village. Quoting the opening sentence of John Winthrop's "Modell of Christian Charity," Demos evokes communalism and hierarchy as operative, dominant values in the making of the town. But these same communities were beset by "individualism" and "mobility." His case histories seem to demonstrate that many of the persons identified as witches had experienced "social dislocation," some of them descend-

[35] Demos, *Entertaining Satan*, chap. 3.

[36] See also Stephen Innes, *Labor in a New Land: Economy and Society in Seventeenth-Century Springfield* (Princeton: Princeton University Press, 1983), pp. 136–41.

[37] Demos, *Entertaining Satan*, pp. 276–78, 300–305. See also Kai T. Erikson, *Wayward Puritans: A Study in the Sociology of Deviance* (New York: John Wiley, 1966), pp. 137–59.

ing in their social status, others becoming unusually "mobile" or "rootless." Yet these processes or, more generally, the incursion of "individualism" had affected all of the colonists. Demos echoes the authors of *Salem Possessed* as well as Thomas and Macfarlane in regarding the seventeenth-century village as caught between the old and the new. Unlike Thomas, he does not feel that the refusal to perform traditional acts of charity was where this conflict became manifest. Instead, the colonists quarrelled over the "transfer of goods, services, and information." All of these conflicts somehow came to embody "neighborliness" versus "individualism."[38]

Remarking that "the association of witchcraft and community" is "hardly a novel finding," Demos turns in the longest section of the book to psychology. Here he is on ground that is uniquely his own, for no one else has pursued the inner history of witchcraft with such care or with the same mastery of psychoanalytic theory. The behavior of the afflicted girls at Salem, and their role as witch-finders, has attracted much psychological interpretation. Marion Starkey keyed her interpretation of the Salem panic to a psychological theme, the "hysterical" behavior of these girls. Loosely used, the word "hysterical" lends itself to the final proposition of the traditional interpretation, that the girls faked their fits and were not really ill. To the contrary, Chadwick Hansen has insisted that certain of their symptoms, like convulsive fits, indicate the presence of a pathological hysteria. Were the girls at Salem sick or not? To this question, alas, *Entertaining Satan* contains no answer. But Demos asserts unequivocally of Elizabeth Knapp (of whom more in a moment) that she was "ill." Where he departs from the Starkey-Hansen debate is in his attitude toward the term "hysteria." He regards it as "too elastic" in meaning and therefore prefers other categories.[39]

Demos's interpretation unfolds in two case studies and a long chapter, "Accusers, Victims, Bystanders: The Innerlife Dimension." Elizabeth Knapp, the first of the case studies, was a girl of sixteen when she began having fits of demonic possession in 1671. The minister of Groton, Massachusetts, Samuel Willard, with whom she lived as a servant, took careful notes on and wrote out a narrative of her behavior. This extraordinary text provides Demos with his point of departure. No other case is quite so richly documented, so "inner"

---

[38] Demos, *Entertaining Satan*, pp. 298–300, 86, 266.

[39] Marion Starkey, *The Devil in Massachusetts* (New York: Alfred Knopf, 1949), chap. 3; Hansen, *Witchcraft at Salem*, pp. ix, 34–45; Demos, *Entertaining Satan*, p. 441.

in its feeling. But in this as in every other instance, Demos has discovered many clues to the life histories of his people. The search for these clues in wills, genealogies, local histories, and court records is exemplary, as is the care with which they are interpreted. Intrinsic limitations on the data stand in the way, he tells us, of "formal causal connections." What he offers is a sequence of inferences, in which he always indicates the line between fact and hypothesis. [40] Any brief summary must oversimplify, but so be it.

Demos regards the behavior of Elizabeth Knapp as evidence of regression. In her fits she reenacted certain experiences of infancy and childhood. The first born in her family, she was displaced at the age of two "in the infant world of narcissistic indulgence" by a brother, whose death a few months later taught her that her "anger was too dangerous, too effectual—and must be entirely suppressed." Her parents led troubled lives, the father charged with but not convicted of adultery, the mother lapsing into insanity. These circumstances—the second of them an inference—may have prompted deep feelings of vulnerability in Elizabeth. There was no one she could idealize, not even Samuel Willard. Denied the ego satisfactions of power and recognition, Elizabeth expressed in her fits "all these threads of narcissistic imbalance: rage, archaic grandiosity and the demand for mirroring, attachment to a figure of eminence." Demonic possession became the means of manifesting the "deep, intrapsychic lesions" she had acquired in the earliest years of life. She blamed her fits on Satan in order to escape "personal responsibility" for feelings that society (or her own defense system) wished to keep repressed. [41]

The fantasies in other cases also rest on or express a core of rage and fear. But with Elizabeth Morse, the second case study, the source of anger shifts to menopause and its associations. Elizabeth Morse was at midlife herself when her house became bewitched. The persons she afflicted were also, for the most part, at midlife. [42] Demos reintroduces menopause, or midlife, in his collective portrait of suspected witches, most of them women between the ages of forty and sixty. Victims and accusers, on the other hand, tended to be young men or adolescent girls, all of them at other stages of development that left them feeling vulnerable. From these groups, and the

[40] Demos, *Entertaining Satan*, p. 124.

[41] Demos, *Entertaining Satan*, chap. 4.

[42] Demos, *Entertaining Satan*, chap. 5.

inner significance that witchcraft had for them, Demos turns to analyzing symptoms of witchcraft and fantasies about witches, here, as always, searching for the psychoanalytic basis of behavior and images. Moving on, he surveys his materials for how they display "affect" and finds that the most prevalent emotional experiences were fear, anger, and the wish to attack. Struggling to control unwelcome or forbidden feelings, the colonists engaged in denial and projection. Demos argues that the fantasy of witches thereby functioned as a "negative identity," a means of projecting and externalizing certain unconscious wishes. Concluding his interpretation, he returns once more to the theme of "attack-aggression-rage, which looms so large throughout the witchcraft material." He connects this theme to the development of the "self-system." Witchcraft, he suggests, was rooted in the profound ambivalence of the infant-mother relationship. Fantasies of witchcraft tapped into infantile experience of a powerful mother. Alternatively, these fantasies indicate regression to the age of two, a period of time when the self is achieving autonomy yet also undergoing sibling rivalry and the "breaking of the will." Generalizing beyond the group of witches and their victims, Demos asserts that the entire community of colonists shared in these processes, these areas of vulnerability: "every attack by witchcraft summoned deeply responsive echoes in a host of 'bystanders,' for the victim was acting out—although (sometimes) to an 'extremity'—pressure-points and vulnerabilities that were widely shared."[43]

Demos wants to persuade us that witchcraft and the inner structure of the self are as readily associated as witchcraft and community. In either instance, the historian is applying to the past a set of categories originating in a "wholly different social culture." E. P. Thompson, whom I have just quoted, has warned of the "danger" of this transfer of categories in his critical response to Thomas, Macfarlane, and their appropriation of social anthropology.[44] The same warning applies to Demos. We do not know whether structures of the self in the seventeenth century were the same as they are today. Categories such as narcissistic rage arise out of the practice of psychoanalysis in the second half of the twentieth century. While they may very well suit the colonists, there is also a good chance that they do not.[45] Demos asserts from time to time that the structure of the

[43] Demos, *Entertaining Satan*, chap. 6.

[44] E. P. Thompson, "Anthropology and the Discipline of Historical Context," *Midland History* 1 (1972): 43.

[45] Demos had relied on the developmental psychology of Erik Erikson in his earlier

self is unchanging: psychology (or psychoanalysis) elucidates "universal" laws. Such was Freud's position. Demos speaks of a "virtually universal 'antagonism to women,' a misogynous substrate of transcultural dimensions," and in his preface refers to witchcraft as a problem of "transcultural significance." On the other hand, he is explicitly historical in his analysis of New England witchcraft, especially when he ties the development of the self-system to one particular mode of child-rearing, the "breaking of the will" that he described some years ago in *A Little Commonwealth*. In *this* particular society, moreover, children were "mother-raised."[46] The more Demos moves in the direction of historical context, the less appropriate it is for him to invoke categories imported from another time and place. The opposite is also true. Demos can defend himself by asserting that "theory" has driven him to ferret out new information, as in the case of Elizabeth Knapp; in other words, theory works because it fits the data. Most readers would agree up to a point, though another reviewer has noted that the themes of the "maternal function" and of malice toward children are not borne out by the data on ages of victims.[47]

Let me turn to the relationship between the normal and the pathological. I have already noted that Demos regards Elizabeth Knapp as pathologically "ill." The critical task of *Entertaining Satan* is to negotiate the transition from Elizabeth to the colonists at large. The bridging category is "vulnerable": the colonists become furious, they go on the attack because they feel so endangered. I cannot avoid feeling that this proposition is tautological, or self-evident: people become angry because they feel vulnerable. But why were these people so angry, and why did their anger take the form of witch-hunting? Demos reverts to social history and to a relatively commonsense psychology in answering the first of these questions. It was the push and pull of community versus individualism or, more

---

study of the Puritan family, *A Little Commonwealth: Family Life in Plymouth County* (New York: Oxford University Press, 1970), and the question I raise here had previously been asked in reviews of that book. The analysis in *Entertaining Satan* depends substantially upon the work of Heinz Kohut, as Demos makes explicit in his text and footnotes. Demos follows Kohut and other revisionists of classical theory in deemphasizing the role of sexual instinct. But he leaves unquestioned the premise that experiences of infancy and the earliest years of childhood exert a determining influence on the development of the self.

[46] Demos, *Entertaining Satan*, pp. 204–5, vii, 207–8.

[47] Michael MacDonald, "New England's Inner Demons," *Reviews in American History* 11 (1983): 323.

particularly, the prevailing experience of "dislocation," that made the colonists feel vulnerable and angry. A second explanation lies in the child-rearing practices of the colonists. In the end, *Entertaining Satan* comes to rest upon two straightforward propositions, that the colonists experienced a social "rootlessness" that chafed against the norm of community, and that a mother-centered family structure led to a certain type of self-system and its attendant (repressed) anger.

One of these arguments is quite widely shared among historians of seventeenth-century New England; the other, at least in any precise form, has much less of a following. I must profess myself a radical skeptic on both counts. I do not think that the colonists were especially rootless, mobile, or dislocated. I have the same suspicion of these words that Demos has of hysteria and that Mary Douglas has of social strain: they are too general, too connotative, to be of real use to the social historian. Rootlessness implies a state of fundamental disorientation. Mobility, or changing place, was, we know, a very widespread process in seventeenth-century England and New England; the immigrants were not unique in this regard and, like many other persons of their century, had become adapted to change. Adaptation, not deep psychological disturbance—is this not a better way of understanding the social experience of the people who moved readily about within England and, for that matter, within New England? As for communalism, no twentieth-century historian has any means of measuring the quality of the colonists' commitment to this ideal, provided, of course, we assume that it was at the center of their system of social values. Two different lines of thinking converge in *Entertaining Satan*, an older social history of uprooted Americans, and a newer one of stability and communalism. I regard the first as discredited, and the second as severely overstated.

I am skeptical about the second point for reasons that apply directly to the thesis of *Entertaining Satan*. Puritanism, which is invoked in several instances, is taken to be the key to communalism and the family structure that prevailed among the colonists. There is a wonderful irony to this emphasis on Puritanism, given that the main thrust of social history has been to limit sharply the significance of the term, whatever it may represent, and to discredit the hegemony of the church or ministry. But in *Entertaining Satan* the Puritan sermon makes its return as evidence for the social functions of witchcraft and the experience of communalism; sermons also provide key evidence for the "breaking of the will."[48] Any considered reflection on cause and effect relationships seems lacking as well as reflection on what weight the sermon or the category "Puritan" will bear. The fact that witch-hunting and witchcraft flourished in very different religious cultures should make us wary of imputing great significance to any one set of beliefs. It seems far from obvious, moreover, that Puritanism inspired a particular mode of child-rearing or family structure that, in turn, became responsible for a disproportionate share of victims, accusers, and witches.[49] Certainly the evidence from Scotland is equivocal. Larner's measured assessment of Calvinism and its significance strikes a very different tone than does *Entertaining Satan*.[50]

To what point, then, does Demos take us in our understanding of witchcraft? He provides us with a detailed portrait of the persons labeled "witches." He catalogues the types of conflict between witches and their victims. He demonstrates the intricacy of neighborhood relationships and their bearing on some cases. His is a story of conflict and anger in social relations; a worthy sequel would be a history of anger-making and anger-releasing processes in early modern Europe and America. *Entertaining Satan* explicates difficult and confusing material, like the fits of a young girl and the depositions of enraged witnesses. It insists on the importance of the age-clustering of the witches as well as their gender. Finally, it offers us a careful, systematic reading of age, gender, and verbal themes from the standpoint of psychoanalytic theory. Many readers will admire, as I do, the intelligence and clarity of this analysis, yet many readers may also prefer a commonsense psychology of guilt and projection and, in the end, the social history Demos offers us. Speaking of the "rites of violence" in sixteenth-century France, Natalie Z. Davis has written, "The violence is explained not in terms of how crazy, hungry, or sexually frustrated the violent people are (though they may sometimes have such characteristics), but in terms of the goals of their actions and in terms of the roles and patterns of behavior allowed by

[48] Demos, *Entertaining Satan*, p. 466 nn. 225–27. On other occasions Demos has been among the first to insist that ordinary people paid little heed to the church and did not share the world view of the ministers.

[49] Compare Keith Wrightson, *English Society, 1580–1680* (London: Hutchinson, 1982), pp. 106–18.

[50] Larner, *Enemies of God*, chap. 12. See also, Macfarlane, *Witchcraft in England*, pp. 186–88; Thomas, *Religion and Magic*, pp. 499–500.

their culture." This statement is equally suited to fits of possession and other witch-related behavior.[51]

Three other issues in the history of New England witchcraft deserve brief comment: gender, the relationship between learned and popular belief, and the role of religion.

Witches were women. Gender is the most reliable of all predictors of who would be singled out and labeled "witch." Explanations vary for this pattern, which holds for preliterate societies as well as for early modern Europe and America. The "traditional misogyny" of European culture is a factor,[52] including the long-held belief that women possessed dangerous (sexual) powers. Historians have learned that suspicion fell most readily on women who were older or deviant in some respect—poorer, and perhaps not unwilling to play on rumors of their occult powers. The data in *Entertaining Satan* support these patterns. In keeping with his social and economic analysis, Keith Thomas has argued that older women were more vulnerable because they were "the most dependent members of the community," the persons most likely to invoke "the old tradition of mutual charity and help" and therefore to provoke the "guilt" and "tensions" that found release in accusations of witchcraft.[53] Disagreeing, Christina Larner believes that witch-hunting was "women hunting," an explicit effort to enforce a patriarchical ideal that was threatened by the changing status of women newly empowered by the Reformation with responsibility for their souls.[54] What then of the fact, duly noted by Thomas and Macfarlane, that so many women participated as victims and accusers? Any alignment of men versus women, or hypothesis of women-hating, would seem to oversimplify. Demos is reluctant as well to equate witch-hunting with women-hating; "no single line in the extant materials," he remarks,

[51] Natalie Z. Davis, *Society and Culture in Early Modern France* (Stanford, Calif.: Stanford University Press, 1975), p. 186. See also I. M. Lewis, *Ecstatic Religion: An Anthropological Study of Spirit Possession and Shamanism* (New York: Penguin Books, 1971) for a social interpretation of the role of the possessed. The wider cultural tradition that sustained this role is described in D. P. Walker's *Unclean Spirits: Possession and Exorcism in France and England in the Late Sixteenth and Early Seventeenth Centuries* (Philadelphia: University of Pennsylvania Press, 1981). See also, Thomas, *Religion and Magic*, pp. 480–81.

[52] Monter, "The Historiography of European Witchcraft," p. 450. A brief but illuminating survey is Clarke Garrett, "Women and Witches: Patterns of Analysis," *Signs: Journal of Women in Culture and Society* 3 (1977): 461–70.

[53] Thomas, *Religion and Magic*, pp. 562–69; Macfarlane, *Witchcraft in England*, pp. 160–61.

[54] Larner, *Enemies of God*, pp. 3, 100–102.

"raises the issue of sex-defined patterns of authority." His interpretation omits the politics of domination and is keyed, instead, to menopause and reverberations in the role of mother. [55]

Two historians nonetheless insist on viewing witchcraft as related to the politics of domination, Lyle Koehler in *A Search for Power: The "Weaker Sex" in Seventeenth-Century New England,* and Carol Karlsen in her forthcoming book, *The Devil in the Shape of a Woman.* [56] Karlsen's is the more convincing of the two interpretations. She demonstrates anew two familiar facts: most witches were women, and most male witches were close relatives of female suspects. Witchcraft was a family affair, or so the colonists assumed. Karlsen questions the statistical basis of the psychoanalytic interpretation, that is, the tight age clustering around "midlife." She denies, as Demos does also, that religious dissent was particularly significant in the lives of the witches. Where she breaks new ground is in her discovery that a "remarkable proportion" of the suspects were lacking brothers or sons to share in an inheritance. Not poverty or wealth considered in the abstract but access to property via inheritance differentiated certain women from others and made those so distinguished extraordinarily vulnerable. Anomalies within the patriarchal system, these women were frequently drawn into lawsuits aimed at depriving them of their estates—or into a web of witchcraft accusations that in certain cases had the same effect. Eunice Cole, Katherine Harrison, and Rachel Clinton, three persons whose life histories are narrated in *Entertaining Satan,* were victims of this process. As for the apparent silence on women's issues in the records, Karlsen declares that silence is deceptive. Using Mary Douglas's concept of "implicit meaning" to advantage, Karlsen insists on the presence of gender-based conflict. To explain the timing of the witch-hunts, she argues that a number of circumstances specific to seventeenth-century New England, among them a new role for women as spiritual leaders of the household, intersected with old myths to give the illusion that women were threatening male dominance. Witchcraft, she concludes, was women-hating in the context of shifting values and uncertain property relationships.

Karlsen suggests in passing that the Salem panic was distinctive because the idea of the devil's compact, a "learned" idea reiterated

[55] Demos, *Entertaining Satan,* pp. 63–64.

[56] Lyle Koehler, *A Search for Power: The "Weaker Sex" in Seventeenth-Century New England* (Urbana: University of Illinois Press, 1980). For Carol Karlsen's argument, I refer to her Ph.D. diss. (Yale University, 1981).

by the clergy, had finally passed over into popular belief. Here and elsewhere in some recent interpretations, [57] the distinction between learned and popular belief serves to renew debate on the clergy and their relationship to witch-hunting. The influence of the clergy, or of religion (and the two were not exactly synonymous), was large, as I will suggest in a moment. But I also believe that the distinction between popular and learned belief does not serve us well in understanding New England witchcraft. According to conventional wisdom, belief in maleficium was "popular" and in diabolism, or the idea of the devil's compact, "learned." Keith Thomas, who borrowed the distinction from earlier interpretations, used it to support his general proposition that witchcraft in England arose out of village politics, where maleficium was plausible, and not out of an elite-led crusade against heresy. His evidence was of two sorts: the court records, which overwhelmingly indicated that the basis of conviction was maleficium (or, if the devil's compact, almost always in association with maleficium), and statute law, where diabolism became specified very late, long after the idea had taken hold among witch-hunters in Germany. [58] Thomas notes, however, that by 1600 or thereabouts, English treatises or commentaries on witchcraft ordinarily mention or describe diabolism. By the 1640s, the theme had gained sufficient currency to support the witch-hunting of Matthew Hopkins in Essex in 1645. We are dealing, therefore, with a theme or belief that circulated relatively widely by the second quarter of the seventeenth century, reiterated not only in sermons (of which we have little direct evidence) but also in statute law, broadsides, ballads, and treatises on witchcraft. [59] This chronology gives reason to assume that the two traditions, which *may* have been sharply differentiated in the late middle ages, had begun to converge. Indeed, Larner argues that the Scottish documents indicate a "mutual

[57] Richard Weisman, *Witchcraft, Magic, and Religion in Seventeenth-Century Massachusetts* (Amherst: University of Massachusetts Press, 1984).

[58] The distinction is drawn—for medieval witch trials—in Richard Kieckhefer, *European Witch Trials: Their Foundations in Popular and Learned Culture, 1300–1500* (Berkeley: University of California Press, 1976). See also, Thomas, *Religion and Magic*, pp. 438–49.

[59] James VI of Scotland had included the idea of the devil's compact in his *Demonology* of 1597. The English statute of 1604 embodied "the full continental doctrine," though Thomas discounts the significance of this law (*Religion and Magic*, p. 443). A vast, amorphous lore circulated in popular modes of print in the seventeenth century, as many of the references in *Religion and Magic* indicate. It seems wiser to assume that the colonists were familiar with most of this lore, including the idea of the devil's compact, than to assume their ignorance.

influence," not strict separation. Accordingly, she prefers to speak of a "new popular demonic" that included the compact—which figures in the Scottish trials of the 1590s—and that by the *early seventeenth* century had replaced previous traditions. [60] Other historians who have studied the evolution of witch beliefs remark repeatedly on the syncretism of European culture. As I have previously noted, Cohn and Russell indicate that elite fantasies of the witches' sabbat, devil's compact, and night-flying demons drew on folk and popular sources. Clarke Garrett has characterized the mental world of the cunning folk as a "conglomeration of Roman Catholic doctrine, magical practices, animism, paganism, and common sense," a mixture that does not yield to rapid labeling as either popular or learned. [61] Bearing this rich jumble of beliefs in mind, it should not surprise us that Mary Johnson of Hartford confessed in 1648 to "familiarity with the Devil." Half a century before Salem, something resembling Larner's "new popular demonic" was being echoed in New England. [62]

The role of the clergy in transmitting belief is not easy to separate from the role of printed sources, some of them distinctly "popular." What seems clear is that, like George Gifford, William Perkins, and Richard Bernard, all three of whom wrote treatises on which the colonists relied, the clergy in New England wished to clarify the grounds for distinguishing between real and pretended witchcraft. The outcome of this effort was a distinct narrowing of acceptable criteria. The clergy in New England were at one and the same time critics of received wisdom (whether popular or learned) and defenders of the concept of witchcraft, the alternative to which, in their view, was atheism. In any event their concern with the devil was closely allied with their understanding of the spiritual dynamics of conversion, or of resistance to conversion. It was this relationship that so many of the colonists absorbed and that played so critical a part in the mentality of the confessing witches.

The testimony of the confessing witches is deeply expressive of

[60] Larner, *Enemies of God*, pp. 138, 145.

[61] Clarke Garrett, "Witches and Cunning Folk in the Old Regime," in *The Wolf and the Lamb: Popular Culture in France from the Old Regime to the Twentieth Century*, ed. Jacques Beauroy, Marc Bertrand, and Edward T. Gargan, Stanford French and Italian Studies, no. 3 (Saratoga, Calif.: Anma Libri, 1977), p. 57.

[62] Demos, *Entertaining Satan*, p. 346. Mary Parsons of Springfield confessed c. 1650 to entering into covenant with the devil. In his ideal law code, prepared in the mid-1630s, John Cotton defined witchcraft as "fellowship by covenant with a familiare spirit." *The Hutchinson Papers*, 2 vols. (Boston: Prince Society, 1865), 1:196.

religious belief and spiritual needs.[63] One great need is for relief from the burden of spiritual distress: feelings of inadequacy, guilt, or melancholy. The devil had promised Elizabeth Johnson "all glory and happiness and joy" and to her daughter "that she should be saved." He had promised Mary Barker "to pardon her sins" and to her father that "all his people should live bravely that all persons should be equal; that there should be no day of resurrection or of judgment, and neither punishment nor shame for sin." The fantasy of compacting with the devil became an instrument of self-assertion against the pressures of the cultural system. These confessions also bespeak a commitment to the idea of secret sins and to the kindred idea that such sins, unless brought to light, will result in damnation. The persons who confessed at Salem or in other trials somehow felt extraordinarily guilty. Why this should be so remains a mystery. Only in one or two instances did they confess to committing real crimes that had gone undetected; for most, it was a matter of acknowledging an indifference to the ordinances or to the Sabbath or simply their wish to have more material success.[64] Confession became a means of reconciliation with the church (or dominant culture) and of reconciliation within themselves between competing voices. This dialogue of voices is singularly evident in Elizabeth Knapp. Speaking repeatedly to Willard of her sense of guilt at not being a good Christian, she complained "against herself of many sins, disobedience to parents, neglect of attendance upon ordinances, attempts to murder herself and others." In effect, Elizabeth was on the

[63] The religious dimensions of witchcraft demand much fuller explication than I can give them here, especially in view of the reductionism that prevails in most psychological and sociological interpretations. Thomas has written perceptively on the relationship between religious need and fantasies of witchcraft in *Religion and Magic*, chap. 15. Alan Macfarlane is enlightening on the religious understanding of misfortune in "A Tudor Anthropologist: George Gifford's *Discourse* and *Dialogue*," in *The Damned Art*, pp. 140–55; in passing, Macfarlane notes that Puritanism is not a useful term of analysis. The religious mentality that accepted witchcraft as real and incorporated it within the framework of divine providence was a mentality that also accorded prophetic significance to dreams, voices, visions, and other "wonders." Thomas has described this mentality at length in *Religion and Magic*. I describe it from a different vantage point in "A World of Wonders: The Mentality of the Supernatural in Seventeenth-Century New England," in *Seventeenth-Century New England*, ed. David D. Hall and David Grayson Allen (Boston: Colonial Society of Massachusetts, 1985), pp. 239–74. An interesting but speculative essay on the relationship between conceptions of the devil and conceptions of God is Ann Kibbey, "Mutations of the Supernatural: Witchcraft, Remarkable Providences, and the Power of Puritan Men," *American Quarterly* 34 (1982): 125–48.

[64] Boyer and Nissenbaum, *Salem Witchcraft Papers*, 2:501, 1:59, 66.

threshold of conversion, but first she had to confess her sins and confess them fully, to the point of fantasizing that she had committed that most horrible of acts, covenanting with the devil. Resisting even as she confessed, she acted out her resistance in the form of her alter-ego, the devil-voice that saucily defied the minister. [65] It may be said in general of the lay colonists that they sought some psychological and social middle ground between resistance and submission. In seeking that ground, some experienced more stress than others. We may speculate that confessions of covenanting with the devil grew out of this search. They express, as well, the importance of confession and repentance within this religious culture, an importance that is elsewhere evident in the procedures of the civil courts. [66] Confession brought immense benefits even though it also jeopardized one's future. Poor Martha Tyler faced this dilemma in 1692 as she listened to her minister plead with her to confess: "Well I see you will not confess! Well, I will now leave you, and then you are undone, body and soul, for ever." [67]

Enough. Let me draw together the major strands of interpretation by way of summary, beginning with those interpretations on which there is consensus. We may safely conclude that witchcraft accusations originated in local conflict and personal misfortune. No modern historian has surpassed the Rev. John Hale, a contemporary witness of the Salem panic, in articulating the relationships among conflict, misfortune, and witch-naming: "In many of these cases," Hale remarked of Salem, "there had been antecedent personal quarrels, and so occasions of revenge; for some of those condemned, had been suspected by their neighbours several years, because after quarreling with their neighbours, evils had befallen those neighbours." [68] Victims, accusers, and "witches" lived in close proximity. Witches were predominantly older women, many of them marginal

---

[65] John Demos, ed., *Remarkable Providences, 1600–1760* (New York: George Braziller, 1972), pp. 358–71.

[66] The role of confession in court procedures is described in Gail Sussman Marcus, " 'Due Execution of the Generall Rules of Righteousnesse': Criminal Procedure in New Haven Town and Colony," in *Saints and Revolutionaries*, pp. 99–137. The European materials contain the same structure of guilt, confession, and repentance, a circumstance that should make us wary once again of overemphasizing Puritanism. See Etienne Delcambre, "The Psychology of Lourraine Witchcraft Suspects," in *European Witchcraft*, ed. E. William Monter (New York: John Wiley, 1969), pp. 95–109.

[67] Boyer and Nissenbaum, *Salem Witchcraft Papers*, 3:777.

[68] John Hale, *A Modest Enquiry into the Nature of Witchcraft* (Boston, 1702),

or deviant in some respect: in social or economic position, sexual behavior, or possibly religious attitude. Anyone who practiced folk healing or fortune-telling became vulnerable to accusations of witchcraft.

Beneath these points lie certain deeper truths. Anthropology has furnished several of the most important: belief in witchcraft is not "irrational"; accusations are a function of misfortune; witch-naming reflects social relationships. To speak more abstractly, "certain social structures will focus tension between certain categories of persons."[69] Thanks to the anthropologists, moreover, historians of early modern Europe have realized that accusations of witchcraft were a constant feature of the village community. In drawing attention to endemic circumstances, these historians minimize the significance of the mass panics that loom so large in the literary evidence. Similarly, in drawing attention to a popular culture that nourished many sorts of occult beliefs, these historians minimize the significance of ideas circulating within learned culture or animating the elite. Assuming, as we do, that New England towns replicated English village life and that English (or European) popular culture crossed the Atlantic with the immigrants, we must therefore assume that these discoveries and assumptions apply to witchcraft in New England. Indeed, *Entertaining Satan* and *Salem Possessed* derive in broad measure from the European historiography. They make witchcraft and witch-hunting credible as functions and processes of a world very different from our own; they make us realize the *otherness* of life in the seventeenth century. But they do not see witchcraft and witch-hunting as political save in the context of the village. It bears repeating, therefore, that witch-hunting is open to interpretation as the politics of patriarchy or the politics of cultural domination.

If the fundamental choice in witchcraft studies lies between a history of witchcraft as witch-hunting or a history of conflict and consensus in the village community, other issues seem nearly as

---

p. 37. As Hale indicates, some of the persons named as witches at Salem and elsewhere had been suspected of the crime for a long time. Susannah Martin, executed at Salem in 1692, had been accused of witchcraft as early as 1669, and suspicion accumulated around Bridget Bishop for twenty years before she fell victim to the Salem panic. (Demos, *Entertaining Satan*, provides many other examples.) Such life histories imply that objective patterns of behavior, and not simply fantasy or projection on the part of witch-hunters, may have been at issue. See also, Macfarlane, *Witchcraft in England*, p. 159.

[69] Marwick, *Witchcraft and Sorcery*, p. 331.

significant. The religious factor, and for New England in particular, the role of Puritanism, continues to provoke debate. The relationship between religion and "magic" may not be fully understood, in part because it is difficult to describe a relationship that was not fixed but fluid and shifting, as I have elsewhere tried to demonstrate. We do not know whether to credit the cunning folk with a world view of their own[70] or how seriously to take the themes and motifs deemed "occult" that circulated widely in the seventeenth century. Is Larner correct in identifying a "new popular demonic," and can we trace its passage to these shores? Last, but far from least, is the task of understanding the collective fantasies and experiences of possession that figure in the witchcraft materials. Where can we draw the line between the pathological and the normal, that is, if any line can be drawn at all? How do these fantasies reflect or make manifest the structure of the self?

Mystery remains, and will never vanish altogether. What is satisfying about the recent flood of books on witchcraft is that they do not simplify. As in the historiography of chattel slavery and master-slave relations in the antebellum South, they reimagine and re-create a world made up out of multiple and overlapping realms of meaning and behavior. This world was rife with contradiction. It requires of us, therefore, a tolerance of alternatives, an awareness of our finite understanding, even as it summons us to press against the limits of interpretation.

[70] Hildred Geertz, "An Anthropology of Religion and Magic, I," and Keith Thomas, "An Anthropology of Religion and Magic, II," both in *Journal of Interdisciplinary History* 6 (1975): 71–109.

David D. Hall, *Professor of History at Boston University, is completing a book on popular religion and popular belief in early New England.*

2

Andover Witchcraft and the Causes of the Salem Witchcraft Trials

CHADWICK HANSEN

I

OVER THE PAST THIRTEEN YEARS American scholars have offered an extraordinary number of explanations of that most grotesque episode in our colonial history, the Salem witchcraft trials. John Demos has suggested that generational hostility was the "underlying" cause. Richard Slotkin has suggested that it was racial hostility: demonic possession in his view becomes merely a neurotic parody of the experience of Indian captivity. Paul Boyer and Stephen Nissenbaum have suggested factional hostility. Linnda R. Caporeal has suggested that ergotism, a kind of food poisoning occasioned by a fungus infestation of the rye from which bread was made, was responsible for the seizures, hallucinations, and other symptoms of the "afflicted" persons. David Thomas Konig has seen malefic witchcraft as one of several means by which "opponents of law" might take the law into their own hands, and has suggested that servants constitute a class to which such extralegal power might seem particularly attractive. Lyle Koehler has suggested sexual hostility and the resulting anxieties as the cause of much feminine hysteria, including the hysterical seizures at Salem. And Cedric B. Cowing has suggested hostilities between persons with origins in the southeast of England and those from the northwest as "the roots" of Salem witchcraft.[1]

There is considerable merit in some of these explanations. Konig's view of witchcraft as one of several extralegal avenues to power is particularly illuminating. If Cowing's regional characterizations are valid, his statistics are impressive. Certainly there was abundant factional hos-

138

tility in Salem Village. And sexual hostility, or at least conjugal hostility, is very clearly present in many of the more important cases. Bridget Bishop was alleged to have bewitched her first husband to death. Edward Bishop accused his wife Sarah of being "familiar with the Devil." Martha Corey's, Sarah Good's, and Sarah Osburn's husbands testified against them at their hearings. "Indeed," said Sarah Good's husband, in one of the more memorable lines in the legal testimony, "I may say with tears that she is an enemy to all good." John Procter was alleged to have contemplated suicide because of his wife's quarreling with him, and he left her out of the will that he made in prison. George Burroughs was alleged to have been cruel to his wives, and John Willard to have beaten his wife.[2]

With any single explanation, however, there is always the temptation to see it as comprehensive and sufficient in itself. Witchcraft is so alien to the experience of twentieth-century American scholars, so medieval, so primitive a matter, that it is tempting to dismiss all the evidence of folk belief and folk behavior at Salem and to account for the events there in terms that are modern, and thus comfortable and familiar, to say, for example, "Oh, so that's all it was—just something they ate." Boyer and Nissenbaum, among others, yield temporarily to this temptation. Having described the two main Salem Village factions as allied to the mercantile-capitalist economy of Salem Town on the one hand and to the agrarian economy of Salem Village on the other, they announce that "a superhuman force" was loose in Essex County and conclude, "We have chosen to construe this force as emergent mercantile capitalism. Mather, and Salem Village, called it witchcraft."[3]

The purpose of this essay, however, is less to review the recent scholarship than to return to the documents in the light of it, to see whether there is anything more that they can tell us about the causes of the Salem trials. Such a return has been made more convenient by Boyer and Nissenbaum, chiefly by their publication of *The Salem Witchcraft Papers*,[4] which is a much more comprehensive collection of the basic legal documents than Woodward's nineteenth-century collection, but also by their various lists and maps, which make it easier to find one's way around in the documents. Here their "List of All Persons Accused of Witchcraft in 1692"[5] will be particularly useful. It gives the names of the accused, the town in which they were living at the time of the trials, and the date of the complaint against them or the warrant for their arrest. It is not complete, but of course no modern list could be. And it does contain a number of inaccuracies.[6] But it is complete enough, and accurate enough, for the present purposes.

There are 141 names on the list. One each come from Amesbury, Boston, Chelmsford, Marblehead, Rumney Marsh, Salisbury, Wells (Maine), and Wenham. Two each come from Billerica, Charlestown, Ipswich, Malden, Manchester, and Piscataqua (Maine). Three come from Woburn and four from Beverly. Five each come from Haverhill, Lynn, and Reading. Six each come from Gloucester, Rowley, and Topsfield. Nineteen come from Salem Town (now Salem). Twenty come from Salem Village (now Danvers). Forty-three come from Andover.

One's first reaction to this simple analysis of the list of the accused is that we have been remiss in talking about the Salem witchcraft. If we want to be geographically comprehensive, we ought to call it the Essex County, Middlesex County, Suffolk County, and Maine witchcraft. Or if we want to name it after the town where it was at its worst, we ought to call it the Andover witchcraft, relegating to a subtitle or a footnote the information that it began in Salem Village and that the trials were held in Salem Town, the Essex County seat.

These statistics are all the more surprising because recent studies of seventeenth-century New England communities have portrayed Salem Town and Salem Village as subject to extraordinary social stress of one kind or another, and thus as thoroughly unstable,[7] while Andover has been seen as virtually devoid of stress. Richard P. Gildrie, the author of a recent community study of Salem (both Town and Village), contrasted Dedham and Andover to his own stress-torn subject as "Puritan utopia[s]," "organic and stable agricultural commune[s]."[8] Philip J. Greven, Jr., the author of the groundbreaking demographic study of Andover, said of that community in the second half of the seventeenth century that "during this period, the evidence reveals that people were extraordinarily healthy, lives were unusually long, and women were exceedingly fecund. . . . What the basic demographic characteristics of life in seventeenth-century Andover imply . . . seems clear enough: stability and health. . . . [T]he small rural agricultural towns like Andover probably proved to be excellent places in which to realize the [Puritan] goals of order, hierarchy, and the closely-knit community." He adds that "in no significant sense were the lives of the first and second generations in disorder, once their permanent roots had been firmly established in early Andover."[9] Yet Andover, at the height of its second generation, produced 30 percent of the accused persons during the witchcraft trials, more than Salem Village (14 percent) and Salem Town (13 percent) put together. What had gone wrong in this orderly agricultural utopia?

II

It is more difficult to tell what happened at Andover than what happened at Salem Village and Salem Town. In part this is because so many of the accused persons from Andover confessed. When the magistrates had obtained a confession, they seem to have stopped looking for further evidence. As a consequence it is generally impossible to tell, with confessors, what brought them under suspicion in the first place. With most of them one has only the confession (or the report of it) and the names of some of the accusers. Another difficulty is that many of the Andover accused were first examined in Andover by Dudley Bradstreet, the local magistrate. The accounts of these examinations are much more sketchy than the accounts of examinations at the county seat in Salem.[10] Andover is poorly documented in the contemporary narratives as well as in the surviving legal evidence. Nevertheless, it is possible to sketch at least a broad outline of what took place there.

The witchcraft proceedings began with the issuing of warrants for three Salem Village women on February 29, 1692. It was not until almost three months later, on May 28, when matters were well underway and dozens of persons had been arrested, that the first warrant was issued for a resident of Andover. It was for Martha Carrier. Her accusers were several of the afflicted girls of Salem Village, and at her examination they went into convulsive seizures and began hallucinating, complaining that her "specter" was biting, pinching, pricking, and choking them, and accusing her of looking "upon the black man." When the examining magistrate (presumably John Hathorne) asked her, "What black man did you see?" her reply was, "I saw no black man but your own presence." Twentieth-century readers are bound to applaud such words, but they may have struck seventeenth-century hearers as impudent or even malicious. Shortly afterward she said to Hathorne one of the most sensible things, from a twentieth-century point of view, that he was to hear during the entire proceedings: "It is a shameful thing that you should mind these folks that are out of their wits." Her defiance evoked even more violent seizures from the afflicted girls. According to the anonymous court reporter, "The tortures of the afflicted was so great that there was no enduring of it, so that she was ordered away and to be bound hand and foot with all expedition, the afflicted in the meanwhile almost killed, to the great trouble of all spectators, magistrates, and others." "Note," he added, "As soon as she was well bound they all had strange and sudden ease."[11]

By the time of her trial in August there were other kinds of testimony against her, and some of it, from her former neighbors, suggests why she first came under suspicion. John Roger of Billerica testified, "That about seven years since, Martha Carrier, being a nigh neighbor unto this deponent, and there happening some difference betwixt us she gave forth several threatening words, as she often used to do." Shortly afterward Roger missed two of his sows. One he never found. The other he found "dead, nigh the said Carrier's house, with both ears cut off." During the same summer one of his cows for no apparent reason suddenly stopped giving milk in the mornings for about a month's time. Roger concluded by saying, "I did in my conscience believe, then in the day of it, and have so done ever since, and do yet believe, that Martha Carrier was the occasion of those ill accidents by means of witchcraft, she being a very malicious woman."[12]

The importance of the dead sow with the ears cut off is that taking a part of the body, or a body product, and subjecting it to occult manipulation was one of the commonest means of working either white or black magic on a person or an animal. With a person you took some of their hair, or their nail parings, or their urine or feces. The hair and nail parings and urine were most commonly boiled; the urine and feces might also be stopped up tight in a container. With an animal it was most common to cut off one or both ears, and boil or burn them. (For a proposal to cut a piece off of a sick mare and burn it, as white magic, see the hilarious affair of the mare's fart.)[13]

There were others of her neighbors who thought that Martha Carrier was a witch. Samuel Preston testified that "about two years since I had some difference with Martha Carrier, which also had happened several times before, and soon after I lost a cow [i.e., it died] in a strange manner. . . . Within about a month after this the said Martha and I had some difference again, at which time she told me I had lost a cow lately, and it would not or should not be long before I should lose another, which accordingly came to pass."

The implication here, of course, is that Martha Carrier predicted the death of the cow because she intended to kill it with a charm or a spell. A similar implication is present in the threats she made against human beings. Benjamin Abbott testified that a little over a year before, when the town of Andover had granted him some land next to Goodman Carrier's,

> Goodwife Carrier was very angry, and said that she would stick as close to Benjamin Abbott as the bark stuck to the tree, and that I

should repent of it afore seven years came to an end, and that Doctor Prescott could never cure me. . . . Presently after I was taken with a swelling in my foot, and then was taken with a pain in my side, exceedingly tormented, which bred to a sore which was lanced by Dr. Prescott, and several gallons of corruption did run out, as was judged, and so continued about six weeks very bad. And then one other sore did breed in my groin which was lanced by Doctor Prescott also and continued very bad a while. And then one other sore bred in my groin which was also cut, and put me to very great misery, so that it brought me almost to death's door, and continued until Goodwife Carrier was taken and carried away by the constable. And that very day I began to grow better. My sores grew well and I grew better every day, and so have been well ever since, and have great cause to think that the said Carrier had a great hand in my sickness and misery.

It should be kept in mind that Goodwife Carrier's threat would have been understood as something more than an ill wish in the seventeenth century. Such words were a curse. In and of themselves they were believed to be a dangerous weapon. One would not utter them lightly. It is most unlikely, of course, that they had anything to do with Benjamin Abbott's actual physical condition. But that is not the point. Benjamin Abbott believed they did, and the chances are that so did Martha Carrier.

Martha Carrier's own nephew, Allen Toothaker, testified that he had been a witness to her cursing of Benjamin Abbott. She had once cursed Toothaker as well: "I was wounded in the war. Martha Carrier told me I would never be cured. Afore she was apprehended I could thrust in my wound a knitting needle four inches deep, but since she have been taken I am thoroughly healed." He was so afraid of his aunt that once, during a fight with her son, Richard Carrier, he had suffered an attack of hysterical paralysis, followed by a hallucination: "I fell down flat upon my back to the ground, and had not power to stir hand nor foot. Then I told said Richard I would yield to him and own him the best man. And then I saw Martha Carrier go off from my breast, but when I was risen up I saw none of her." The sudden appearance and disappearance of his aunt's shape meant, of course, to Allen Toothaker, that it was her "specter" that had been restraining him. He concluded by saying that several of his animals had died after his aunt had threatened him. "And I know not of any natural causes of the death of the above-said creatures, but have always feared it hath been the effect of my Aunt Martha Carrier her malice."

Toothaker was not the only Andover resident whose fear of Martha

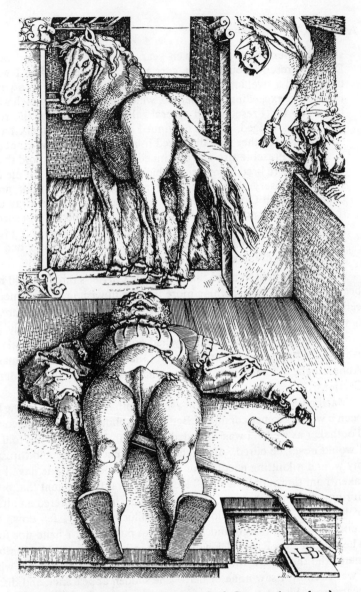

Hans Baldung Grien, *The Bewitched Groom* (woodcut).
National Gallery of Art, Washington, D.C. Gift of W. G.
Russell Allen. Like Allen Toothaker in seventeenth-century
Andover, Baldung Grien's sixteenth-century German be-
twitched groom has fallen flat on his back, without the
"power to stir hand nor foot."

Carrier produced psychogenic disorders. Phoebe Chandler, "aged about twelve years," testified that

> about a fortnight before Martha Carrier was sent for to Salem to be examined, upon the Sabbath Day when the psalm was singing, said Martha Carrier took me, said deponent, by the shoulder and shaked me, in the Meeting House, and asked me where I lived. But I made her no answer (not doubting but that she knew me, having lived some time the next door to my father's house, on one side of the way). And that day that said Martha Carrier was seized, my mother sent me to carry some beer to the folks that were at work in the lot, and when I came within the fence there was a voice in the bushes (which I thought was Martha Carrier's voice, which I know well) but saw nobody. And the voice asked me what I did there and whither I was going, which greatly frighted me, so that I run as fast as I could to those at work and told them what I had heard. About an hour and [a] half, or two hours after, my mother sent me again upon the same occasion, to the workmen abovesaid. Coming home, near the place abovesaid where I heard that voice before, I heard the same voice, as I judged, over my head, saying I should be poisoned within two or three days, which accordingly happened, as I conceive. For I went to my Sister Allen's farm the same day, and on Friday following about one half of my right hand was greatly swollen and exceeding painful, and also part of my face, which I can give no account how it came, and continued very bad some days. And several times since I have been troubled with a great weight upon my breast, and upon my legs when I have been going about, so that I could hardly go, which I have told my mother of. And the last Sabbath Day, was seven night, I went to meeting very well in the morning and went to my place where I used to sit (the ministers not being come). And Richard Carrier, son of abovesaid Martha, looked very earnestly upon me and immediately my hand, which had formerly been poisoned, as abovesaid, began to pain me greatly, and I had a strange burning at my stomach, and then was struck deaf, that I could not hear any of the prayer nor singing till the two or three last words of the singing.

She believed, of course, that Richard Carrier had "overlooked" her, given her the evil eye. Her hysterical deafness was one consequence. The "strange burning" in her stomach was probably the lower body pain with which the *globus hystericus* typically begins. And since the pain in her hand followed so immediately on Richard Carrier's look, one wonders whether it too may not have been psychogenic. One wonders even to what extent her earlier pains may have been a consequence of her aural hallucination of Martha Carrier. In any case, it is clear that some of the citizens of Andover had been living in fear of the supposed occult powers of Martha Carrier for a period of up to seven years before her trial.

A little over two weeks after Martha Carrier's arrest, on July 15, another Andover woman, Ann Foster, was arrested, but little is known about her except for her confessions.

It was John Ballard, an Andover constable, who had served the warrant and warned the witnesses in the Martha Carrier case, and although the documents are missing he may have done the same in the Foster case. At any rate, Ballard's wife had been "this several months sorely afflicted and visited with strange pains and pressures."[14] He thought her bewitched, and thus had several of the hallucinating girls of Salem brought to Andover to see whose specters were afflicting her.[15] As a consequence Mary Lacey, Sr., and Mary Lacey, Jr., the daughter and granddaughter of Ann Foster, were arrested on July 20. Both confessed. The next day three sons of Martha Carrier were arrested, and they confessed as well.

It was a week later, on July 28, that a warrant was issued for the next citizen of Andover, Mary Bridges, Sr. This time the accuser was not one of the afflicted girls of Salem but Timothy Swan, of Andover. From that time on the names of the Salem girls are only infrequently found in indictments against citizens of Andover. That town had developed its own group of hallucinating afflicted persons, who were responsible for the overwhelming majority of the Andover accusations. The names one sees most often in the indictments, besides that of Timothy Swan, are Rose Foster, of Andover; Abigail Martin, of Andover, "aged about sixteen years";[16] Sarah Phelps, of Andover; and Martha Sprague, alias Tyler, of neighboring Boxford, "aged sixteen years."[17] Among them they accused an extraordinary number of persons, and most of those whom they accused confessed. But before we look at the confessors we should look at two more cases in which, because the persons did not confess, the magistrates accumulated sufficient evidence so that we can tell what had brought them under suspicion.

The first is that of Mary Parker, who was arrested toward the end of August. Besides the behavior of afflicted persons, who went into seizures at the mention of her name and were "recovered . . . out of their fits"[18] by the touch of her hand, and besides the evidence given by confessors, there were three witnesses against her. John Westgate testified that "about eight years since" he had been at the public house of Samuel

Beadle when John Parker was among those present. Goodwife Parker then

> came into the company and scolded at and called her husband all to naught, whereupon I, the said deponent, took her husband's part, telling of her it was an unbeseeming thing for her to come after him to the tavern and rail after that rate. With that she came up to me and called me rogue, and bid me mind my own business, and told me I had better have said nothing. Sometime afterwards· I, the said deponent, going from the house of Mr. Daniel King, when I came over against John Robinson's house I heard a great noise coming from towards Mr. Babbidge his house. Then there appeared a black hog running towards me with open mouth as though he would have devoured me.

He fell on his hip, driving his knife into it, and had to crawl home with the hog worrying him all the way. He had a "stout" dog with him that ran from the hog, "leaping over the fence and crying much, which at other times used to worry any hog well or sufficiently, which hog I then apprehended was either the Devil or some evil thing, not a real hog, and did then really judge or determine in my mind that it was either Goody Parker or by her means, and procuring fearing that she is a witch."

It seems an idle tale, or would seem so in most contexts. But it shows how little it took for a colonial American to convince himself that his neighbor's wife was a witch, and how his fear of her, festering over eight years, would be enough to bring him into court to testify that she was what he had feared her to be.

The second witness, John Bullock, had helped to get Goodwife Parker home when she had been lying out of doors in winter in what was apparently a catatonic state, since the man carrying her "let her fall upon a place of stones, which did not awake her, which caused me to think she was really dead." But when they got her home and "were taking off her clothes to put her into bed, she rises up and laughs in our faces." Martha Dutch confirmed Bullock's testimony and added "that I have seen said Parker in such a condition several other times." Again, it seems an idle tale, and one's first reaction is to wonder why it was offered as testimony in a witchcraft case. Apparently Bullock and Dutch believed that Mary Parker's catatonic seizures were evidence that she possessed occult powers. Once more one has to be impressed at how little it took to make people afraid of their neighbors.

The third witness was Samuel Shattuck, a Quaker who was a hatter and dyer in Salem Town. He testified that in the year 1685 Goodwife Parker, wife to John Parker, Mariner, came to my house and went into the room where my wife and children were and fawned upon my wife with very smooth words. In a short time after, that child which was supposed to have been under an ill hand for several years before was taken in a strange and unusual manner, as if his vitals would have broke out, his breast bone drawn up together to the upper part of his breast, his neck and eyes drawn so much aside as if they would never come to right again. He lay in so strange a manner that the doctor and others did believe he was bewitched. Some days after some of the visitors cut some of his hair off to boil, which they said, although they did [it] with great tenderness, the child would shriek out as if he had been tormented. They put his hair in a skillet over a fire which stood plain on the hearth, and it was thrown down, and I came immediately into the room as soon as they were gone out of the room, and could see no creature in the room. They put it on again, and after it had boiled some time the abovesaid Goodwife Parker came in and asked if I would buy some chickens.

Shattuck's visitors had themselves been practicing malefic witchcraft here, since boiling the victim's hair was a charm intended either to harm the witch or compel her presence. Since it turned out on later investigation that Goodwife Parker had had no chickens to sell, it must have been considered a success, in spite of the spectral casting down of the skillet on the first attempt.

Here as elsewhere it should be noted that New England witchcraft cannot be considered a temporary insanity confined to 1692. Shattuck's suspicions of Mary Parker dated back seven years, to a time when she had lived in Salem Town. Why hadn't he prosecuted her then? Perhaps he was one of Professor Konig's "opponents of law"; certainly he had been willing to take the law into his own hands. Or perhaps he had realized that although his suspicions were strong his evidence was incomplete. Nobody had heard Mary Parker curse the child, or seen her work a charm against it, or even look at it fixedly with an evil eye. And if you took a witch to court, and the court did not put her to death, surely she would find some way to have her revenge. But in 1692, when the Court of Oyer and Terminer was doing its best to rid the country of witches, and when the afflicting specter of Mary Parker had appeared in the hallucinations of three of her present neighbors (Sarah Phelps of Andover, Hannah Bigsby of Andover, and Martha Sprague of Boxford), Samuel Shattuck was willing to come forward and offer his testimony.

Our third case is that of Samuel Wardwell, and in some ways it is

The indictment of Mary Parker of Andover for "witchcraft and sorceries wickedly, maliciously, and feloniously . . . used, practiced, and exercised at and in the Town of Andover . . . in, upon, and against one Sarah Phelps of Andover." Courtesy of Massachusetts Historical Society.

the most interesting, if only because it is so very insubstantial. His specter had appeared in several persons' hallucinations, afflicting Martha
Sprague of Boxford. He had been "much addicted" to fortune telling,
so much so that several of his neighbors were clearly in awe of his supposedly occult abilities in predicting the future. And he had boasted
"that he could make cattle come to him when he pleased."[19] When he
was first examined he confessed "that he had been foolishly led along
with telling of fortunes, which sometimes came to pass. He used also
when any creature came into his field to bid the Devil take it, and it
may be the Devil took advantage of him by that." He went on to provide an account of meetings with the Devil, and of making a covenant
with him. But he later repudiated his confession. Whether he had ever
actually practiced malefic magic remains in doubt, of course. But the
evidence we have seen against him so far is "specter" evidence and evidence about his practicing white magic. So it would be a little surprising
to learn that he, Mary Parker, and Martha Carrier were the three citizens of Andover who were executed for witchcraft if it were not for the
fact that there was another kind of evidence against him. His name, like
that of Martha Carrier and Mary Parker, turns up repeatedly in the
testimony of the Andover confessors.

John Hale, whose *Modest Enquiry into the Nature of Witchcraft* is
the most reliable contemporary account of the Salem trials, tells us that
the "matter was carried on . . . chiefly by the complaints and accusations of the afflicted . . . and . . . by the confessions of the accused, condemning themselves and others."[20] Of the forty-three Andover names
on Boyer and Nissenbaum's list of accused witches, it is not known how
seven pled. Of the remaining thirty-six, only six denied the accusations;
thirty confessed. If Hale and Calef are correct in saying that there were
"about fifty"[21] confessors altogether, that would mean that Andover
supplied at least 60 percent of them. Whether they are correct or not, it
is clear that the number of Andover confessors is out of all proportion
both to the relative size of the community and to the number of the
Andover accused.

One can find several motives for the Andover confessions in the surviving documents. Two of the confessors clearly enjoyed the attention
paid them in their hearings. Mary Lacey, Jr., responded readily to the
magistrates in her several examinations, frequently supplying colorful
details for which she had not been asked. It was she who volunteered
that "Goody Carrier told me the Devil said to her that she should be a
queen in Hell,"[22] a detail that so impressed the Massachusetts magistrates and ministers that it found its way into Cotton Mather's account

of the Carrier case in *Wonders of the Invisible World*. She later joined the ranks of the afflicted persons, although she does not seem to have initiated any accusations. William Barker, Sr., also enjoyed confessing, so much so that courtroom appearances were not enough for him: John Hale prints a confession "which he wrote himself in prison, and sent to the magistrates to confirm his former confession to them."[23]

A very different motive for confession is found in the case of Sarah Wilson, Sr. When the Reverend Increase Mather interviewed several of the confessing Andover women in prison, she told him "that, knowingly, she never had familiarity with the Devil; that, knowingly, she never consented to the afflicting of any person, &c. However, she said that truly she was in the dark as to the matter of her being a witch. And being asked how she was in the dark, she replied that the afflicted persons crying out of her as afflicting them made her fearful of herself."[24]

Neither her examination nor her confession survives, but it is easy to reconstruct what happened. Affliction took two main forms. In the first, the afflicted person went into seizures and hallucinations at the glance of the accused person, and could be recovered by her touch. The cause of the affliction was then believed to be the evil eye. In the second form the afflicted also went into seizures and hallucinations, complaining that the "specter" or spirit of the accused was the cause of her convulsions, or was pinching, pricking, biting, or choking her. Goodwife Wilson had seen the awe-inspiring behavior of the afflicted persons in her presence, and, hearing their accusations and unable to think of any other cause, was afraid that she might possess the evil eye without being aware of it, or that her spirit might be responsible for the afflictions without her knowledge.

A third motive for confession was that by the time arrests became general in Andover, it was clear that confessors were not being executed. As the Reverend Francis Dane, the senior minister of Andover, wrote to an anonymous "reverend sir," "I fear the common speech that was frequently spread among us, of their liberty if they would confess, have brought many into a snare" (i.e., of false confession).

But by far the greatest reason for the large number of confessions at Andover appears to have been the bullying of the accused by their own friends and relatives. A particularly chilling instance was discovered by Increase Mather when he interviewed Martha Tyler in prison. She told him

that when she was first apprehended she had no fears upon her, and did think that nothing could have made her confess against herself. But since she had found, to her great grief, that she had wronged the truth and falsely accused herself. She said that when she was brought to Salem her brother Bridges rode with her, and that all along the way from Andover to Salem her brother kept telling her that she must needs be a witch, since the afflicted accused her and at her touch were raised out of their fits, and urging her to confess herself a witch. She as constantly told him that she was no witch, that she knew nothing of witchcraft, and begged him not to urge her to confess. However, when she came to Salem she was carried to a room where her brother on one side, and Mr. John Emerson on the other side, did tell her that she was certainly a witch, and that she saw the Devil before her eyes at that time (and accordingly the said Emerson would attempt with his hand to beat Him away from her eyes); and they so urged her to confess that she wished herself in any dungeon rather than to be so treated. Mr. Emerson told her, once and again, "Well, I see you will not confess! Well, I will now leave you, and then you are undone, body and soul, forever." Her brother urged her to confess, and told her that in so doing she could not lie, to which she answered, "Good brother, do not say so, for I shall lie if I confess, and then who shall answer unto God for my lie?" He still asserted it, and said that God would not suffer so many good men to be in such an error about it, and that she would be hanged if she did not confess, and continued so long and so violently to urge and press her to confess that she thought, verily, that her life would have gone from her, and became so terrified in her mind that she owned, at length, almost anything that they propounded to her; that she had wronged her conscience in so doing; she was guilty of a great sin in belying of herself, and desired to mourn for it so long as she lived. This she said, and a great deal more of the like nature; and all with such affection, sorrow, relenting, grief, and mourning, as that it exceeds any pen to describe and express the same.[25]

Indeed, Andover became notorious for the ease and thoroughness with which family and community bonds were broken in the face of witchcraft accusations. Brattle speaks of the "husbands who, having taken up that corrupt and highly pernicious opinion that whoever were accused by the afflicted were guilty, did break charity with their dear wives upon their being accused and urge them to confess their guilt."[26] Calef says of Andover, "Here it was that many accused themselves of riding upon poles through the air, many parents believing their children to be witches, and many husbands their wives."[27] And Andover's senior minister, Francis Dane, lamented that "the conceit of specter evidence as an infallible mark did too far prevail with us. Hence we so easily parted with our neighbors of honest and good report, and [church] members in full communion. Hence we so easily parted with our children, when we knew nothing in their lives, nor any of our neighbors to suspect them. And thus things were hurried on, hence such strange breaches in families. . . ."[28]

Why did Andover's family and community loyalties break down so thoroughly in the face of witchcraft accusations? It may not be possible, of course, to find a fully satisfactory explanation. Perhaps it was their very devotion to Puritan ideals of communal unity which made Andover citizens prefer to think their wives, children, and neighbors witches rather than accept the idea that, as Martha Tyler's brother put it, God would permit "so many good men to be in such an error about it." .

Factional hostility has been the most persuasive of the recent explanations of the Salem trials. But it does seem clear, in the light of Andover's experience, that we cannot account for those trials by suggesting that Salem had a history of factional hostility and Andover had not. Even without the Andover experience, it ought to be clear that factional hostility does not in itself provide a comprehensive explanation for the Salem trials. There are departments in twentieth-century American universities with as long and as vicious a history of factional hatreds as any to be found in Salem, and the parties to these hatreds accuse each other of all sorts of absurdities, but witchcraft is not one of them. If we want to understand what happened at Salem, we shall have to begin by acknowledging as causes of the trials some of the ways in which seventeenth-century American culture was different from our own.

III

The first, or one might say the underlying, cause was that seventeenth-century Americans, like seventeenth-century Europeans, believed in witchcraft. That is to say, they believed it possible to affect the course of events, including doing good or evil to other persons, through occult means. Belief in witchcraft was virtually universal, but the practice of it was limited, because it was seen not simply as an appeal to occult forces but to specifically anti-Christian occult forces. Therefore it was practiced only by certain kinds of people: the ignorant, who did not understand that their charms or spells were anti-Christian, and the powerless, the desperate, and the malicious, who did not care. None of these kinds of people are apt to put themselves on the historical record, and most of them are apt to try to keep themselves off it, so we hear of colonial American witchcraft only when it reached the attention of the authorities. But this happened far more frequently than most American historians, or even most historians of American witchcraft, have recognized. Frederick C. Drake lists fifty-eight "cases and incidents" of witchcraft in the American colonies in the eighteen years from 1645 to 1662,[29] and when we remember that colonial records, especially outside New England, are very incomplete, it seems clear that witchcraft cases were a regular feature of American colonial experience. Only some of these cases, of course, were instances of the actual practice of witchcraft; many of them were instances of the fear of it. But if we keep in mind that the "cases and incidents" in the surviving records must be only a very small proportion of the total number, it seems clear that belief in and fear of witchcraft were endemic in the American colonies. From the evidence of the surviving documents it also seems clear that white witchcraft was commonly practiced and that black witchcraft was not uncommon. We have one instance of openly avowed black witchcraft above, in the boiling of the Shattuck child's hair. Without the near-universal belief in witchcraft and the regular practice of it, it is hard to see how witchcraft could have remained a capital crime, as it did in both England and English America until a generation after the Salem trials.[30]

But in the typical colonial witchcraft trial only one or two persons were accused. What distinguishes the Salem trials from all the others is their scale. The total number of the accused is unknown, but a conservative estimate would put the figure over 200. Calef claims that it was more than 350.[31] Nineteen people were hanged, and one was pressed to death for refusing to plead to his indictment. In one sense, then, when we ask the causes of the Salem trials, we are really asking why, on this occasion, a fairly common kind of judicial proceeding got out of hand. Community studies will not help us much here because the accused, the accusers, and the judges of the Court of Oyer and Terminer came from many different communities. Nor will the various hostility theories help us, although servile hostility, sexual hostility, regional hostility, and factional hostility may all be useful in an analysis of why particular persons were accusers or accused. A number of explanations can be found, however, all of them more or less familiar.

Let us start with John Hale's statement that the "matter was carried on . . . chiefly by the complaints and accusations of the afflicted . . . and . . . by the confessions of the accused, condemning themselves and others." "The complaints and accusations of the afflicted" depended chiefly on their hallucinations of the "specters" of the accused, that is, on so-called spectral evidence. The Boston clergy advised the court early, and throughout the proceedings, not to place too much weight on spectral evidence, and it is clear that the court did not take this advice seriously enough. Why they did not do so can only be a matter for conjecture, because no record was kept and no report made of the court's deliberations.[32] One possible explanation may lie in the characters of the magistrate who conducted most of the preliminary examinations, John Hathorne, and of the chief justice, William Stoughton. Both of them, through most of the proceedings, seem to have been much more anxious to obtain evidence of guilt—any kind of evidence of guilt— than to weigh the evidence impartially. It is not only possible but probable that with a different leadership the proceedings would have turned out very differently.

As for confessions, it was here that the Salem court's procedure differed from that of all other colonial American courts, as Drake has pointed out,[33] and from all English courts as well. The ordinary procedure was to execute confessors, since confession was often the best possible proof of guilt in witchcraft cases. The Salem court did not bring them to trial; it even stayed the executions of condemned witches who subsequently confessed. Again we do not know the reasons for the court's procedure. They may have been following Cotton Mather's early advice that "lesser criminals be only scourged with lesser punishments, and also put upon some solemn, open, public and explicit renunciation of the Devil."[34] Or they may have been attracted to the drama of redemption that the confession presented, and reluctant to execute those they had redeemed. Or they may have been hungry for guilt, and pleased that the confessors incriminated not only themselves but others. In any case, the court's policy toward confessors was a major cause of the escalation of accusations.

And of course, as many scholars have pointed out, 1692 was a time of extraordinary troubles for Massachusetts. She had finally and irrevocably lost her Old Charter, which had been the very basis of her identity. There were serious troubles with the French and the Indians on the frontier. It was precisely the sort of time in which even the best of men are apt to feel that unnamed evils are abroad in the land, and that it would be a public service to root them out.

We cannot know, in our present state of knowledge, which of these causes were the more compelling. But we can recognize that the causes of the Salem trials were extraordinarily complex. No single explanation is going to sweep them under the historical rug; we can expect the debate over them to continue.

NOTES

1. John Demos, "Underlying Themes in the Witchcraft of Seventeenth-Century New England," *American Historical Review*, 75 (1970): 1311–26; Richard Slotkin, *Regeneration through Violence* (Middletown, Conn.: Wesleyan University Press, 1973), ch. 5; Paul Boyer and Stephen Nissenbaum, *Salem Possessed* (Cambridge, Mass.: Harvard University Press, 1974); Linnda R. Caporeal, "Ergotism: The Satan Loosed in Salem?" *Science*, 192 (Apr. 2, 1976): 21–26; David Thomas Konig, *Law and Society in Puritan Massachusetts* (Chapel Hill: University of North Carolina Press, 1979), chs. 6 and 7; Lyle Koehler, *A Search for Power* (Urbana: University of Illinois Press, 1980), chs. 10–13; Cedric B. Cowing, "The Roots of Salem Witchcraft." I am indebted to Professor Cowing for his kind permission to read his essay in typescript and to refer to it here.

2. Paul Boyer and Stephen Nissenbaum, *The Salem Witchcraft Papers*, 3 vols. (New York: Da Capo, 1977), pp. 83; 112; 249, 259–60; 357; 611; 797–98, 963; 162–63, 176; 824, 842. This collection is cited hereafter as *SWP*.

3. Boyer and Nissenbaum, *Salem Possessed*, p. 209.

4. See n. 2.

5. Boyer and Nissenbaum, *Salem-Village Witchcraft* (Belmont, Calif.: Wadsworth, 1972), pp. 376–78.

6. If one takes the table of contents of *SWP* as a revised list, some omissions and errors are corrected there, but new omissions and errors are introduced. Either list would do for the present purposes, but the later one would have to be corrected.

7. Richard P. Gildrie, *Salem, Massachusetts, 1626–1683* (Charlottesville: University of Virginia Press, 1975), and Boyer and Nissenbaum, *Salem Possessed*.

8. Gildrie, *Salem*, p. 179.

9. Philip J. Greven, Jr., *Four Generations: Population, Land, and Family in Colonial Andover, Massachusetts* (Ithaca, N.Y.: Cornell University Press, 1970), pp. 269–71.

10. See, for example, the Andover and Salem examinations of Elizabeth Johnson, Jr. (*SWP*, pp. 503–5).

11. *SWP*, pp. 185–86. Because of the extreme irregularity of spelling, punctuation, and capitalization in the legal documents, I have modernized all three.

12. The testimony of Martha Carrier's neighbors is in *SWP*, pp. 189–94.

13. *SWP*, pp. 444–46.

14. Ibid., p. 513.

15. The account of Ballard's sending to Salem for witchfinders is to be found both in Thomas Brattle's "Letter" and in Robert Calef's *More Wonders of the Invisible World*, in George Lincoln Burr, ed., *Narratives of the Witchcraft Cases* (New York: Barnes & Noble, 1959), pp. 180–81 and 371–72. Both Brattle and Calef seem to have been working from very incomplete evidence, as their brief accounts of Andover demonstrate.

16. *SWP*, p. 788.

17. Ibid., p. 786.

18. The legal documents of the Mary Parker case are in *SWP*, pp. 629–37.

19. The legal documents of the Samuel Wardwell case are in *SWP*, pp. 783–89.

20. Burr, *Narratives*, p. 421.

21. Ibid., pp. 416, 373.

22. The legal documents of the Mary Lacey, Jr., case are in *SWP*, pp. 520–29.

23. Hale, *Modest Enquiry* in Burr, *Narratives*, p. 419.

24. An account of Mather's visit, presumably from Thomas Brattle's papers, is in the *Massachusetts Historical Society Collections*, 2d ser., 3: 221–25.

25. Ibid.

26. Burr, *Narratives*, p. 181.

27. Ibid., p. 372.

28. *SWP*, p. 882.

29. Frederick C. Drake, "Witchcraft in the American Colonies, 1647–62," *American Quarterly*, 20 (1968): 694–725. A recent article on the widespread existence of various kinds of occultism in colonial America is Jon Butler, "Magic, Astrology, and the Early American Religious Heritage, 1600–1760," *American Historical Review*, 84 (1979): 317–46.

30. For the Old Charter law, see Section 94 of the *Body of Liberties*, reprinted in Edwin Powers, *Crime and Punishment in Early Massachusetts* (Boston: Beacon, 1966), pp. 533–48. The English law in effect at the time is 1 *Jacob*. Cap. 12.

31. Burr, *Narratives*, p. 373.

32. For a discussion of the court's and the clergy's disagreements on this issue, see Chadwick Hansen, *Witchcraft at Salem* (New York: George Braziller, 1969), especially those passages indexed under "spectral evidence."

33. Drake, "Witchcraft," p. 725.

34. Cotton Mather, "Letter to John Richards," *Collections of the Massachusetts Historical Society*, 4th ser., 8: 397.

Some Unexplored Relationships of Essex County Witchcraft to the Indian Wars of 1675 and 1689

By JAMES E. KENCES*

NEW ENGLAND "was miserably briar'd in the perplexities of an Indian war," a conflict with the Indians and French that is now known as King William's War and that was but six months away from its fourth year when the first accusations of witchcraft were made during the spring and summer of 1692. Public morale was poor in Massachusetts Colony at the time, in the wake of periodic massacres in isolated communities and as a result of the rampant inflation which had followed an expensive expedition to Quebec in the autumn of 1690.[1]

Further, the proximity of the towns of Essex County, situated in the northeastern section of Massachusetts to the "eastward"—the regions of New Hampshire and Maine where the heaviest fighting occurred—meant not only that they were expected to support the struggle by providing militia men as well as tax monies, but that they were highly vulnerable to the dreadful massacres. Andover and Billerica, for example, two of the towns directly involved in the witch hunts, became targets. The attack upon Billerica on 1 August 1692, in which six members of the Shed and Dutton families were killed, occurred within two weeks of the executions of six witches on Gallows Hill.[2]

The contiguousness of the two events is further underscored by the

* James Kences is a former student of the University of Massachusetts/Amherst. He is working on a chronological encyclopedia on the causes of American wars from 1575 to 1860.

1. Douglas Edward Leach, *Arms for Empire: A Military History of the British Colonies in North America, 1607–1763*, The Macmillan Wars of the United States (New York: Macmillan, 1973), p. 112fn.

2. Samuel Adams Drake, *The Border Wars of New England* (1897; reprint ed., Williamstown, Massachusetts: Corner House, 1973), p. 86.

179

confession of Billerica's Martha Toothaker, who stated that she had made a pact with the devil while "under great discontentedness & troubled w^h feare about the Indians," because he promised her "if she would serve him she would be safe from the Indians." On 5 August 1695 the Indians actually attacked the farms of the Toothaker, Rogers, and Leviston families, indicating that she had reason for being phobic about the heathen.[3]

How many other people in Essex County feared the Indians? How did casualties, the burden of taxes, and wartime tensions affect the towns that were close to the fighting? How did the attitudes of Puritanism influence the way in which Essex County perceived the Indian wars of 1675 and 1689? These are questions that merit thoughtful consideration.

I

In the final decade of the seventeenth century it was still very much apparent that Essex County, like much of New England, was originally Indian land that the English had acquired through both legitimate and illegitimate means. The three rivers that flowed to the east of Salem Village possessed the Indian names; Pouomeneuhcant, Conamabsquenooncant, and Soewamapenessett.[4]

Less than a decade before the witchcraft outbreak, the political leaders of the towns of Salem, Beverly, and Marblehead felt that it was necessary to demonstrate their formal right to the lands they occupied with a legal document signed by the Indian representatives. On 11 October 1686 six men of Salem, including Israel Porter of Salem Village, became the trustees of the land for a payment of £20 presented to David Nonnuphanohow, Sam Wuttaanoh, Jno. Tontohquenne, Cicely Petaghuncksq, Sarah Wuttaquatinnusk, Thomas Usqueakufsennum (alias Captain Tom), James Quonophkownatt (alias James Rumney Marsh), Israell Quonophkownatt, Joane Quonophkownatt, Yawataw Wattawtinnusk.[5]

3. Paul Boyer and Stephen Nissenbaum, eds., *The Salem Witchcraft Papers*, 3 vols. (New York: Da Capo Press, 1977), 3:767; Drake, *Border Wars*, p. 107.

4. See "Map of Indian Lands and Localities in Essex County Massachusetts," in Sidney Perley, *The Indian Land Titles of Essex County Massachusetts*, Publications of the Essex Book and Print Club, no. 3 (Salem: Essex Book and Print Club, 1912), p. 13.

5. Sidney Perley, *Indian Land Titles*, pp. 78–84.

The conspicuous mixture of Christian and Indian names, as well as the language that was used in the transfer, indicate that these Indians were quite civilized and that the ceremony was a symbolic act intended to reinforce the colonists' claims to the land during a period of challenge by royal authority. The episode reflected a continuing awareness of the local Indian influence by the inhabitants of Essex County some ten years after the close of King Philip's War.

In every community of the county, veterans of that destructive conflict and survivors of the massacres still carried memories of their experiences; in Salem Village, Thomas Putnam, Jr. and Nathaniel Ingersoll had formerly been members of Capt. Thomas Prentice's and Capt. Nicholas Page's troops of horse during Philip's War and had participated in the Mount Hope and Narragansett campaigns of 1675. Thomas Flint, another village veteran, was wounded during the second of these campaigns. The village and all adjacent towns had also contributed soldiers to Capt. Thomas Lathrop's company and thus had suffered in the aftermath of the battle of 18 September 1675, which the Reverend William Hubbard described as "the Saddest day that ever befell New England." Seventy soldiers, including Lathrop, died that day at Bloody Brook outside Deerfield. The "ruine of a choice Company of young Men," lamented Hubbard, "the very Flower of the County of Essex all called out of the towns belonging to that county."[6]

In the late winter and early spring of 1676, the towns of western Essex and northern Middlesex Counties were repeatedly attacked by Nipmuck Indian war parties. Andover and Billerica were attacked in April and May; on 2 May Indians led by Simon burned the house of Thomas Kimball at Rowley. The head of the family was killed, and Kimball's wife and five children were taken captive.[7]

Indians destroyed the towns of Lancaster and Groton on the Merrimack River, just forty miles to the west of Salem Village (fig. 1). On 10 February 1676 fifty persons were killed at Lancaster, in a display which Mrs. Mary Rowlandson characterized as wild and violent:

---

6. George M. Bodge, *Soldiers in King Philip's War* (Leominster, Massachusetts: Rockwell and Churchill Press, 1896), pp. 167, 83, 291; Douglas Edward Leach, *Flint-Lock and Tomahawk: New England in King Philip's War* (New York: Macmillan Company, 1958), p. 88.

7. George W. Ellis and John E. Morris, *King Philip's War*, The Grafton Historical Series (New York: The Grafton Press, 1906), p. 221.

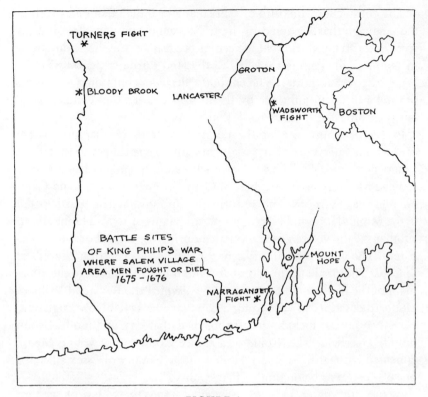

FIGURE 1

It is a solemn sight to see so many Christians lying in their blood, some here and some there, like a company of sheep torn by wolves, all of them stripped naked by a company of hell-hounds, roaring, singing, ranting and insulting as if they would have tore our very hearts out.[8]

A bizarre incident at Marblehead in 1677 expressed the effect of the pressures of Indian war upon colonial women of the same generation as Mrs. Rowlandson:

A group of women emerging from church set upon two In-dian prisoners from Maine and with their bare hands literally

8. Mary Rowlandson, "The Sovereignty and Goodness of God," in *Puritans Among the Indians; Accounts of Captivity and Redemption, 1676–1724,* ed. Alden T. Vaughan and Ed-ward W. Clark (Cambridge, Massachusetts: Belknap Press of Harvard University Press, 1981), p. 35.

tore them apart. An eyewitness reported that "we found the Indians with their heads off and gone, and their flesh in a manner pulled from their bones."[9]

The violent actions of another woman, Hannah Dustin of Haverhill, occurred only five years after the 1692 witchcraft outbreak. On 30 April 1697 Mrs. Dustin, her nurse, and a small boy murdered nine Indians in their sleep because she "thought she was not forbidden by any law to take away the life of the murderers by whom her child had been butchered." Mrs. Dustin very quickly attained celebrity status and was applauded by her contemporaries for this brutal act of vengeance.[10]

By the late 1690s, the enthusiasm for experiments in assimilation which had been exemplified by the missionary John Eliot had been replaced by "an emerging racism based on fear of the Indian and suspicion that he would never accept Christianity or English ways." The New England Indian population of the 1690s was represented by the once-bellicose southern tribes shorn of military power and forced into the periphery of society and by the alienated northern tribes who had turned to the French.[11]

The military alliance of the Indians and the French in the 1690s added a terrifying dimension to Indian war, because the Puritans were taught from childhood of the evils of Catholicism. The captive John Gyles showed how the papists preyed on Puritan superstitions:

> My Indian master made a visit to the Jesuit and carried me with him. I saw the Jesuit show him pieces of gold and understood afterward he tendered them for me. The Jesuit gave me a biscuit which I put into my pocket and dare not eat but buried it under a log fearing that he had put something into it to make me love him, for I was very young and heard much of the Papists torturing the Protestants etc. so that I hated the sight of the Jesuit. When my mother heard the talk of my being sold to the Jesuit she said to me "Oh my dear child, if it were God's will I had rather fol-

9. James Axtell, "The Indian Impact on English Colonial Culture," in Axtell, *The European and the Indian; Essays in the Ethnohistory of Colonial North America* (New York: Oxford University Press, 1981), p. 312.

10. Cotton Mather, "A Narrative of Hannah Dustin's Notable Deliverance from Captivity," in *Puritans Among the Indians,* ed. Vaughan and Clark, p. 164.

11. Francis J. Bremer, *The Puritan Experiment: New England Society from Bradford to Edwards* (New York: St. Martin's Press, 1976), p. 204.

low you to your grave, or never see you more in this world then you should be sold to a Jesuit, for a Jesuit will ruin you body and soul."[12]

Antipapist prejudices of a different kind were heard from the pulpit of the Reverend Samuel Parris in the Salem Village meeting house. Parris's primary concern was the Catholic communion ritual and the belief that the communion bread "must be put into the mouths of the common people by the priest," because the people were unworthy to touch the bread with their hands. Parris also declared that "the Papists are arraigned of Sacriledge in their robbing the common People of the Cup. They will allow them the Bread . . . but they deny them the cup."[13]

The false sense of self-importance and love for gold, jewels, and finery that comprised much of Catholic stereotype in the Puritan mind was evidently an important element of the stereotypical devil which the Puritan both feared and envied. Capitulation to the devil often occurred due to his "wheedling through glittering promises of material gain and economic betterment." In 1692 the devil promised "new clothes," "a piece of money," and "a pair of French fall shoes," and the "afflicted" girl Mercy Lewis was offered "gold and many fine things" if she would write in his book.[14]

And, as John Gyles revealed in his memoirs, Jesuits and papists were most feared because of their capacity for deceit. It will be shown later that the Puritans were predisposed to regard the Indians as natural worshipers of the devil; an organized plot or conspiracy formed by the Indians and a major European power hostile to the English—French or even the Dutch—was a psychologically decisive event for the Puritans of New England and one that inevitably encouraged comparison with the supernatural alliance of the devil and the witch. This factor was not only the basis for the 1692 outbreak, but can be recognized in witchcraft episodes which occurred earlier during the seventeenth century.

12. John Gyles, "Memoirs of Odd Adventures, Strange Deliverances etc.," in *Puritans Among the Indians*, ed. Vaughan and Clark, p. 99.

13. Larry D. Gragg, "Samuel Parris: Portrait of a Puritan Clergyman," *Essex Institute Historical Collections* 119(1983):214 (hereafter referred to as *EIHC*).

14. Paul Boyer and Stephen Nissenbaum, *Salem Possessed: The Social Origins of Witchcraft* (Cambridge: Harvard University Press, 1974), p. 210; see also John Putnam Demos, *Entertaining Satan: Witchcraft and the Culture of Early New England* (New York: Oxford University Press, 1982), p. 178.

The quarter century that preceded King Philip's War was characterized by occasional war scares involving the Indians of southern New England. The scares of 1667, 1669, and 1671–72 were especially grave because they had developed in an atmosphere of Anglo-Dutch tension and threatened armed conflict. The anxiety that was experienced by the inhabitants of coastal settlements was conveyed by the energy which they exerted to install fortifications designed to repulse seaborne invasion.[15]

A pattern, albeit a tenuous one, might be suggested by the occurrence of witchcraft accusations in the coastal towns of both Massachusetts and Connecticut during the same years that an invasion or raid was thought imminent. In Essex County the 1653 Gloucester witchcraft outbreak that implicated Agnes Evans, Grace Dutch, Elizabeth Perkins, and Sarah Vinson, as well as the 1667 Marblehead and Salem episodes which involved Jane James and Edith Crawford, took place during Anglo-Dutch war scares.[16]

The only Dutch woman who was ever actually accused of witchcraft in New England was Judith Varlet, who was among the first individuals to be charged in the Hartford, Connecticut, outbreak of 1662–63. Varlet, the daughter of a merchant and related through marriage to Governor Peter Stuyvesant, was accused of witchcraft by Ann Cole, who was "given to Dutch-toned discourse when overtaken by 'fits'." The coastal towns of Connecticut like those in Massachusetts appeared to experience visitations of witchcraft during times of major war scares—Saybrook and New Haven in 1654–55, Stamford and Saybrook in 1667.[17]

The scares imposed a significant strain upon society; daily the inhabitants scanned the horizon for signs of enemy ships and were alert to detect any suspicious activity among the local Indian tribes, such as unexplained movement or very large gatherings. The crisis diminished the colonists' tolerance for antisocial behavior, and they interpreted verbal attacks against life and property as being extremely dangerous and symbolically in conformity with the actions of an enemy that had yet failed to appear.

15. Douglas Edward Leach, *Flintlock and Tomahawk*, pp. 24–25.
16. Based on data from "List of Known Witchcraft Cases in Seventeenth Century New England," in John P. Demos, *Entertaining Satan*, pp. 402–409.
17. John P. Demos, *Entertaining Satan*, pp. 71, 403, 406.

The persons accused of witchcraft functioned as ideal surrogates for that "enemy;" the discovery of a covenant with the devil helped the populace to rationalize the alliance between the Indians and the Europeans. Thus the witch was basically both a microcosm and a test created by a community that was reacting to war. The elimination of a supposed witch within a community eased the fear that the community would become a magnet for agents of destruction.

John Demos has argued recently that the witch recognized by the Puritans was not simple or monolithic, but displayed "at least four leading forms or guises—those of attacker, envier, intruder, and nurse."[18] The same set of contradictory traits were observable in the Indians who were encountered by the captives Mary Rowlandson and John Gyles; side by side with stories of torture and cruelty occurred stories of kindness and self-sacrifice often performed by the same individual. Much of the confusion and ambivalence that was generated by witches and Indians in the seventeenth century could be attributed to this nonstereotypical dimension of their personalities.

One reliable measure of Puritan ambivalence toward the Indian was the large number of persons taken into captivity who could not be induced to return. Anywhere "from 25 to 71 percent of the English captives" taken between 1689 and 1713 made that decision largely because "they found Indian life morally superior to English civilization and Catholicism more satisfying than Puritanism." The rejection of Puritan religion by a major portion of approximately 600 individuals was evidence of the many problems that were plaguing the churches of New England in the 1690s, a generation after Puritan leadership submitted to the Half-Way Covenant.[19]

The Half-Way Covenant was something of a contrivance that had been formulated to preserve church membership regardless of its diluted quality. The reform helped to:

> further weaken the homogeneity of the New England Way by
> opening the floodgates to all forms of membership extension and
> by setting the clergy in fierce debate among themselves with a
> resulting loss of prestige for the ministerial class.[20]

18. John P. Demos, *Entertaining Satan*, p. 174.
19. James Axtell, "The Scholastic Philosophy of the Wilderness," in Axtell, *The European and the Indian*, pp. 162–66.
20. Francis J. Bremer, *The Puritan Experiment*, p. 149.

The church at Salem Village rejected this reform in favor of a more traditional baptism policy that was promoted by the Reverend Samuel Parris. Membership in the village church could be earned only through a confession from applicants of a work of faith and repentence wrought in their souls. Samuel Parris was also committed to probing into the affairs of village families. On 20 October 1690 while Massachusetts awaited the outcome of the Phips expedition to Quebec, Parris attended a meeting of the Cambridge Association of ministers which had been convened to discuss the reasons for the current "heavy judgement of God." Samuel Parris was apparently responsible for both the framing of the question on what steps should be taken for social and moral reform, and the answer, which was:

> that the ministers of the several congregations do endeavor with utmost industry and faithfulness personally to visit the several families in their places, and inquire, instruct, and warn and charge, according to the circumstances of the families.[21]

This neurotic clerical response to defeat in an Indian war supplied neither comfort nor security and was in itself an indication of why it was within Parris's own household that the witchcraft outbreak first erupted in 1692.

II

On 23 May 1690, three days after the surrender of the garrison at Falmouth, Maine, to the French and Indian attackers, Bartholomew Gedney, a successful Salem merchant and military officer, visited Salem Village on a recruiting mission only to find that field work made the farmers reluctant to depart "on such a sodaine [sic]." Gedney did persuade, however, the son of Jonathan Walcott, the local militia captain, to go in his father's place, accompanied by the "stout young men."[22]

Two months earlier, in March, Gedney had probably been in attendance at the Salem Town meeting which had rejected the request by many of these same farmers for independent status as a separate township. Having been one of three men selected in February 1687 to arbitrate over Rev. Deodat Lawson's contested ordination, he understood the nature of the local conflicts. The May encounter of the merchant

21. Larry D. Gragg, "Samuel Parris," *EIHC* 119(1983):228–29.
22. Massachusetts Archives 36:89.

and farmers would have made clear many of the contrasts that helped to promote those conflicts.[23]

Salem Village did not possess a large defense apparatus, and what little it did have had been obtained with difficulty because the town frequently interfered. In the autumn of 1677, a year following the conclusion of King Philip's War, the villagers were given permission by the colonial government to establish a militia company so that they would no longer be required to participate in training sessions held several miles from their homes.[24]

Early in King William's War, a new element was added to the village defenses with the construction of a watch house, but as the village artisans labored building this structure, their time and skill was required to repair the Salem fort on Winter Island. Because these fortifications had been constructed during the Anglo-Dutch war in 1666, they demanded perpetual maintenance and large outlays of tax money for their upkeep. Throughout the 1680s the Massachusetts government remonstrated with Salem to undertake the restoration of these works; and in 1681 immediate attention was prescribed just to keep the fort functional as it had become "altogether unserviceable & deffective." At the opening of William's War, the fort was in such bad condition that residents warned the legislature of the danger of its easy capture by the French, who might then make use of its cannon to destroy Salem Town.[25]

The fort was especially important in the history of the village's grievances against the town, because only a year after it had been constructed, it produced an anxious admission of vulnerability as well as a plea for some independence. In a petition to the legislature, the farmers explained that while the fort would deter an attack directly upon the town, it would not prevent a seaborne attack upon them, because at the sparsely settled village, the enemy would "meet neither with fforte, nor 400 men under warning of an Alarm to oppose them."[26]

The fort may also have been partly responsible for Salem Town's reluctance to permit the village to become a legally distinct entity, ow-

---

23. Massachusetts Archives 11:57–60; Boyer and Nissenbaum, *Salem Possessed*, p. 58.

24. Nathaniel B. Shurtleff ed., *Records of the Governor and Company of Massachusetts Bay in New England*, vol. 5 (Boston: William B. White, 1854), p. 172.

25. On Salem Village watch house see *Town Records of Salem, Massachusetts*, vol. 3, 1680–1691 (Salem: Essex Institute, 1934), p. 221; fort repairs, *Salem Town Records*, vol. 3, p. 240; Massachusetts Archives 52:42, 48; 36:231, 58.

26. Massachusetts Archives 112:175–177.

ing to the fact that it was reluctant to forfeit tax monies that it could levy from the farmers. Even when the town did make concessions they proved to be slight or symbolic; however, one major concession made in March of 1672 relieved the villagers of their obligation to pay a church tax. Instead, a five-member village committee would determine how much money would be allocated to support the minister and the meetinghouse, which came into existence that same year.[27]

From 1672 until 1689, the year that the Reverend Samuel Parris was ordained, Salem Village had hired and fired three ministers due to the influence of inhabitants who opposed the choice of a minister and customarily withheld payment of the tax used for his salary. The Reverends James Bayley, George Burroughs, and Deodat Lawson had all been forced to resign in the years 1679, 1683, and 1688 because of these pressures.[28]

On 10 October 1689, four months after Parris was hired, Nathaniel Ingersoll, Nathaniel Putnam, John Putnam, Jonathan Walcott, and Thomas Flint were appointed to supervise the transfer of the village parsonage, barn, and two acres of land to Parris as a gift after a 1681 rule preventing such an outright donation had been rescinded. It is interesting to note at this point that the appointments of these five men demonstrated how closely the ecclesiastical and military histories of Salem Village had been intertwined prior to the witch hunts; Walcott, Ingersoll, and Flint were officers in the militia company and war veterans, and the Putnams had supplied the land on which a blockhouse had been built in 1676.[29]

Further, during the same year that Lt. Thomas Putnam, Sr., had helped to improve the village's security, Joseph Hutchinson, an avowed enemy of the church, was accused of limiting egress to the meeting house by building stone walls so that the villagers "were all forced to go [out] at one gate." The obstruction, which would hinder any attempt at escape during an Indian attack, was representative of the tactics that were employed by the opponents of the church. Later, in October of 1691, while in the midst of a second Indian war, the church was abruptly crippled by the elections of Joseph Porter, Hutchinson, Joseph Putnam,

27. Boyer and Nissenbaum, *Salem Possessed*, pp. 41–42.
28. Boyer and Nissenbaum, *Salem Possessed*, pp. 46–47.
29. Boyer and Nissenbaum, *Salem Possessed*, pp. 61–62.

Daniel Andrew, and Francis Nurse to the village committee. The enemies of the church had effectively taken control.[30]

III

On 25 January 1692 a messenger conveying news of a catastrophe galloped south toward Boston on the Ipswich Road, which passed Salem Village; earlier that day, and only forty miles distant, a war party comprised of 150 Abanaki Indians had attacked "wretchedly secure" York, Maine, on the Agamenticus River. The homes of 300 or 400 persons had been burned, and the community's minister, Shubael Dummer, had perished with about 50 other persons. The Reverend George Burroughs, minister at neighboring Wells, Maine, supplied authorities at Boston with a graphic report of the "pillours of smoke, ye raging of ye merciless flames, ye insultations of ye heathen enemy, shouting, shooting, hacking . . . & dragging away [80] others [to Canada]."[31]

Contemporary observers felt that York had not been sufficiently vigilant, "dwelling in unguarded houses." Actually, one of the reasons York fell was that as a typical agricultural village of late seventeenth-century New England, its homes and farms were too widely scattered to be adequately protected if attacked. Salem Village was clearly aware of the dangers of this type of scattering, having addressed this problem in its previously mentioned 1667 petition to the Massachusetts legislature. That document portrayed a community whose inhabitants were so widely separated "one from another, some a mile, some further" that even "six or eight watches will not serve."[32]

One of the villagers opposed to Parris, Peter Cloyce, was a former inhabitant of York whose wife, Sarah, would eventually be hanged as a witch in August of 1692. Every Indian war had brought refugees to Essex County towns from the "eastward." These persons generally returned to their homes when hostilities ceased, but some stayed. Two victims of the 1692 witch hunt, Abigail Hobbs of Topsfield and Anne Pudeator of Salem Town, had originally lived in Casco or Falmouth,

30. Boyer and Nissenbaum, *Salem Possessed*, pp. 55–57, 65–66.
31. Thomas Hutchinson, *The History of the Colony and Province of Massachusetts Bay*, ed. Lawrence Shaw Mayo, vol. 1 (Cambridge: Harvard University Press, 1936), p. 343; Petition from Wells, 27 January 1692, Massachusetts Archives 37:259.
32. Massachusetts Archives 112:175–77.

Maine, until the Indians forced their migration south. In her confession Hobbs said that she had first seen the devil in the Maine woods. Goody Pudeator, who was hanged, still had children living at Casco at the time of her death.[33]

Among the small group of the accusing "afflicted girls" who lived in Salem Village was Susanah Sheldon, the daughter of yet another refugee family from Black Point, Maine. Not only had the family of this seventeen-year-old been driven from Maine in 1675 during King Philip's War and again in William's War, but her twenty-four-year-old brother, Godfrey, had been killed at the "eastward" in early July of 1691.[34]

Though Susanah Sheldon may have justly harbored a deep hatred or fear of the Indians as a result of her experiences, almost every one of the girls at one time or another during the witch hunt also revealed a dread of the heathen. Mary Walcott, the "afflicted" stepdaughter of the village's militia captain, accused Capt. John Alden of witchcraft because he "[sold] powder and shot to the Indians and French, and [lay] with Indian squaws and had Indian papooses." This abuse of Alden might well have been engendered by his having negotiated a truce with the Indians that led indirectly to the attack upon York when the French sought to revive their alliance with the northern tribes. Alden's association with the York massacre took another form as well, for he had been responsible for securing the redemption of the captives.[35]

Eleven-year-old Ann Putnam, another of the "afflicted" children, accused George Burroughs, the village's former minister and the survivor of two Indian massacres in Maine, of having murdered the son of Deodat Lawson while young Lawson was a chaplain in the service of Sir Edmund Andros, saying that the chaplain had "preached soe to the

33. Examination of Abigail Hobbs, 19 April 1692, "Salem Witchcraft, 1692. In three volumes. Verbatim Transcripts of Salem Witchcraft Papers, Compiled Under the Supervision of Archie N. Frost, Clerk of Courts" (Salem: 1938), vol. 2, unpaginated.

34. See entry on the family of William Sheldon in James Savage, *A Genealogical Dictionary of the First Settlers of New England, showing three generations of those who came before May, 1692 on the basis of Farmer's Register*, vol. 4 (Boston: Little, Brown, 1862), pp. 70–71; "Reverend Samuel Parris's Record of Deaths at Salem Village During his Ministry," *New England Historical and Genealogical Register*, 36 (1882), p. 188 (hereafter referred to as *NEHGR*).

35. Robert Calef, *More Wonders of the Invisible World: Or, The Wonders of the Invisible World Display'd in Five Parts*, in *Narratives of the Witchcraft Cases, 1648–1706*, ed. George Lincoln Burr, (1914; reprint ed., New York: Barnes and Noble, 1972), pp. 353–55.

souldiers." She also claimed that Burroughs had "bewicthed [sic] a grate many souldiers to death at the eastword."[36]

It was, though, Mercy Lewis, the Putnam family's seventeen-year-old servant, who uttered the most direct denunciation of the Indians or heathen, and she did so in a manner characteristic of the New England Puritans when she derived her language directly from the Bible. The Reverend Lawson witnessed the unusual display, as Mercy "sang the song in the fifth of Revelation, and the 110 Psalm, and the 149 Psalm." In both of these Psalms, the word *heathen* occurs:

> He shall judge among the heathen, he shall fill the places with the dead bodies: he shall wound the heads over many countries.
>
> Psalm 110:6

> Let the high praises of God be in their mouth, and a twoedged sword in their hand;
>
> To execute vengeance upon the heathen, *and* punishments upon the people.[37]
>
> Psalm 149: 6-7

Mercy Lewis's confusion over the identities of Indians and witches was as much a product of Puritan influences upon her as these Biblical quotations. During the most discouraging moments of her captivity, Mrs. Rowlandson similarly found security in the Psalms. On one occasion it was to alleviate her anxiety over the welfare of her ill son and missing daughter:

> I repaired under these thoughts to my Bible (my great comfort in that time) and that scripture came to my hand, "Cast thy burden upon the Lord, and he shall sustain thee," Psalm 55:22.[38]

According to Samuel Parris, the New England Puritans belonged to the family of man, but were distinct from all other peoples because God had created them for a special mission. This was as much a convention

---

36. Testimony of the younger Ann Putnam against the Reverend George Burroughs, in *The Salem Witchcraft Papers*, ed. Boyer and Nissenbaum vol. 1, p. 164.

37. Deodat Lawson, *A Brief and True Narrative of Some Remarkable Passages Relating to Sundry Persons Afflicted by Witchcraft, at Salem Village Which Happened from the Nineteenth of March, to the Fifth of April 1692*, in *Narratives of the Witchcraft*, ed. Burr, p. 161.

38. Mary Rowlandson, "The Sovereignty and Goodness of God," in *Puritans Among the Indians*, ed. Vaughan and Clark, p. 49.

of Puritan thought as was the reliance upon the Bible. But Parris had an unusual way of introducing the idea which stressed kinship of Puritan and pagans; "we are all one by nature," he once informed the Salem Village congregation, "with Egyptians, Turks, Pagans, Indians and Ethiopians."[39]

IV

During the first year of King William's War, Cotton Mather exhorted readers to:

> tell mankind that there are Devils and Witches: and that those night-birds least appear where the Day-light of the Gospel comes, yet New England has had examples of their existence and operation: and that not only the wigwams of Indians, where the pagan powaws often raise their masters, in the shapes of bears and snakes and fires but also in the homes of white English men and women.[40]

That same year, 1699, the captive John Gyles was warned by "an old squaw" to whom he had confided his desire to observe an Indian powow in progress, "that if they knew of my being there, they would kill me. . . . When she was a girl she had known young persons to be taken away by a hairy man." Gyles was in danger of being carried off by the "hairy man" also if the wizards had discovered him.[41]

The near encounter with the "hairy man" reflected a consensus opinion of seventeenth-century New England; the Elect perceived themselves as having been encroached upon by unregenerates who acted as the instruments of Satan to obstruct or destroy their labors for God in the wilderness of the New World, and they believed as well that the devil had inspired the Indians to go to war, and to perpetrate massacres. Each story of atrocity or torture served to reinforce these simple ideas and helped to make the affinities all the more apparent. Increase Mather observed that the "barbarous Indians (like their Father the Devil. . .delighted in crueltyes)."[42]

39. Larry D. Gragg, "Samuel Parris," *EIHC* 119(1983):225.

40. Cotton Mather, *Memorable Providences Relating to Witchcraft and Possessions*, in *Narratives of the Witchcraft*, ed. Burr, p. 99.

41. John Gyles, "Memoirs of Odd Adventures," in *Puritans Among the Indians*, ed. Vaughan and Clark, pp. 114–15.

42. Peter N. Carroll, *Puritanism and the Wilderness: The Intellectual Significance of the New England Frontier, 1629–1700* (New York: Columbia University Press, 1969), p. 78.

For the inhabitants of Essex County in 1692 this belief had important consequences. Witchcraft appears to have been generally regarded as a preliminary weakening of a community's moral strength or resistance, so that the inhabitants might eventually fall victim to the Indians and French. This can be inferred from Cotton Mather's revelation learned from:

> one who was executed at Salem for witchcraft who confessed that at their cheef witch-meetings, there had been present some French Canadiens, and some Indian sagamores to concert the methods of ruining New England.[43]

Essex County had already displayed signs of what social psychologists refer to as "invasion neurosis," the extreme tension of anticipating an attack which does not materialize. The tendency of the county's population to react to rumour and to sense imminent danger was exemplified by two incidents which occurred during King William's War. In the first case, there was just cause for fear; an escaped slave revealed details of a conspiracy which a fanatic French sympathizer named Isaac Morril had organized in the autumn of 1690. Morril not only planned to overwhelm northern Essex County with 500 Indians and 300 French soldiers, he also hoped to incite servants to murder their masters and to fight beside him as allies (fig. 2). Morril's preparations had included an alarmingly thorough reconnaisance of the region's garrisons, which, according to witnesses Robert and Elizabeth Long, he had inspected while carrying a concealed weapon on his person.[44]

A much stranger example of war hysteria occurred at the town of Gloucester in the summer of 1692, but this episode seems largely to have been the fault of that town's excitable minister, the Reverend John Emerson. A potential source of trouble for the town had surfaced two years earlier, when in July of 1690, Emerson had implored Maj. Wait Winthrop to release forty-seven members of the village's militia company who had been impressed into the army which was then being as-

---

43. Cotton Mather, *A Brand Pluck'd out of the Burning*, in *Narratives of the Witchcraft*, ed. Burr, pp. 281–82.

44. David T. Konig, "A New Look at the Essex 'French': Ethnic Frictions and Community Tensions in Seventeenth Century Essex County Massachusetts", *EIHC* 110 (1974): pp. 178–79.

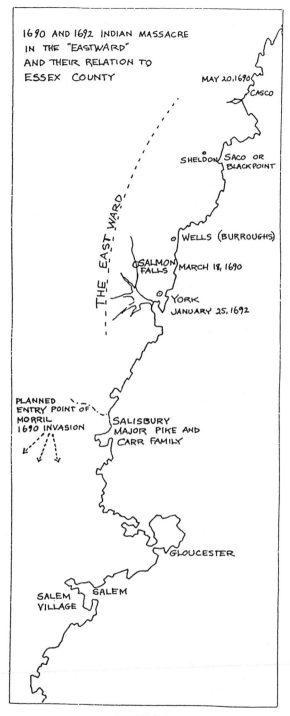

FIGURE 2

sembled for the attack upon Quebec. Otherwise, Emerson complained, "wee must all be forced to leave the towne for we are not able to stay any longer after they are gone." The extraordinary levy, if enacted, would have divested the town of two-thirds of its men, and the group of fifteen soldiers that would be retained to defend Gloucester would have been easily overwhelmed by a French raiding party which tried "to breake in upon" the town.[45]

Emerson's anxiety over possible attack appears to have been contagious, for in late June of 1692 Ebenezer Babson reported to him of the occurrence of furtive activity in the vicinity of his house. Babson had seen, or so he told the minister, "men which looked like Frenchmen" moving stealthily through the swamps. Upon hearing this rumour, several persons abandoned their farms and fled to the garrisons to evade what by that time Emerson thought to be the "Devil and his agents." In a letter written to Cotton Mather after the panic had subsided, Emerson described some of the strange happenings witnessed by the town that summer which included an account of Babson's encounter with the nebulous enemy:

> Bapson . . . saw three men walk softly out of the swamp . . . being within two or three rod[s] of them he shot, and as soon as his gun went off they all fell down. Bapson then running to his supposed prey, cried out unto his companion. . ."he had killed three!" "he had killed three!" But coming about unto them they all rose up.[46]

At Gloucester, the rapid shift in interpretation of the menace as first an actual enemy, and then to one of supernatural origin, was due in part to the memory of the 1653 and 1657 witchcraft outbreaks in the town, and also to the mind-set of Essex County in 1692. The critics of the witchcraft trials who have condemned the Puritans for callousness and lack of sophistication have largely ignored the evidence in the confessions, of "witch militias" and nests of witches at garrisons, such as Chandler's garrison in Andover—the kind of information which only helped to further aggravate "invasion neurosis." The Reverend Deodat Lawson recorded many examples of these admissions in his *Brief and True*

45. Rev. John Emerson to Maj. Wait Winthrop, 26 July 1690, The Winthrop Papers, *Collections of the Massachusetts Historical Society*, fifth series, 1:438.

46. Cotton Mather, *Magnalia Christi Americana or the Ecclesiastical History of New England, 1629–1698*, vol. 2(1702; reprint ed., Hartford: Silas Andrus and Sons, 1853), p. 621.

Narrative, and he shows—through an aggressive confrontation between the "afflicted" girls and Martha Cory—that the witch militia appeared as real as that which Jonathan Walcott captained in Salem Village; "the afflicted persons asked Cory why she did not go to the Company of Witches which were before the Meeting house mustering? Did she not hear the drum beat?" The "company," as Lawson later explained, was composed of "about 23 or 24" individuals.[47]

Boyer and Nissenbaum argue that the witchcraft accusations were influenced by the conscious and even subconscious resentments among the faction that supported the church in response to gestures of disloyalty by its enemies. Such a gesture seems implicit in a June 1690 notice from the colonial government to the officers of the Beverly troop. Those officers were assured that if they could "make up a number of forty able Troopers. . . with the addition of those of Salem Village now listed with them they may continue" as a troop.[48]

Eligibility for the troop of horse—one of the most prestigious branches of the colonial service—was determined by wealth, as the trooper was expected to purchase his own costly accoutrements: a horse, saddle and equippage, carbine, pistols, and a sword or cutlass. These acquisitions were beyond the means of the majority of Parris's supporters, who lived too far west of Beverly to have frequented the town. The men, whoever they might have been, probably lived on the Ipswich Road, close to the taverns and shops alien to the less wordly farmers.[49]

It is possible that wartime disloyalty was the nucleus of discontent that resulted in the spread of accusations of witchcraft to the town of Andover, which soon rivaled Salem Village in the number of arrests. The source of trouble in Andover was exposed when the government attempted to reorganize the Upper Regiment, the regiment of militia in northwestern Essex County, by transferring the Boxford militia from that unit to another regiment in the county. A group of men from

47. Deodat Lawson, *A Brief and True Narrative*, in *Narratives of the Witchcraft*, ed. Burr, pp. 156, 163.

48. Boyer and Nissenbaum, *Salem Possessed*, pp. 186–88; Massachusetts Archives 36:112a.

49. Requirements for the troop of horse, "An Act for Regulating of the Militia," 1693, Chap. 7, section 6, *The Charter Granted by their Majesties King William and Queen Mary, to the Inhabitants of Massachusetts Bay in New England* (Boston: S. Kneeland, 1761), pp. 38–39; Boyer and Nissenbaum, *Salem Possessed*, pp. 96–97.

Andover promptly sent a petition to Boston to protest the action because the two towns:

> [lay] soe neare to each other & ready upon all occasions of ye enemy's approach to releive each other, which if disjoyned wee cannot doe, & for many other reasons we humbly pray . . . that Boxford might still continue as part of ye upper Regiment.[50]

The "many other reasons" alluded to in this petition signed by Capt. John Osgood, John Barker, and Stephen Johnson, who were to be in 1692 the husbands and fathers of ten Andover witches, suggest that these families may have begun to gravitate toward Boxford. There is no direct evidence of any ambitions to secede from Andover, as it was never formally asserted; there are, however, occasional expressions of close association, such as the extensive land holdings of the Barker family in Boxford.[51]

After having witnessed Rowley's experience with secession, the Andover selectmen would have been especially alert to prevent any attempted move, and this inchoate faction, if any factionalism actually existed, may have been on their minds during the summer of 1692, when Joseph Ballard "sent horse and man" to Salem Village to fetch little Ann Putnam so that she might discover the cause of his wife's illness—an action that resulted in an epidemic of witchcraft accusations in Andover. Ballard's ailing wife, Elizabeth (Phelps) Ballard was related to Thomas Chandler, the keeper of the infested garrison house, through the marriage of two of his children, daughter Sarah and son William, to members of the Phelps family in 1682 and 1687.[52]

Two possible exhibitions of disloyalty at Salem Village and an adjacent town symbolized the disintegration of the communal covenant that was so important to the Puritans. As Boyer and Nissenbaum have shown, Samuel Parris espoused this particular theme obsessively from 1689 until 1692. In January of 1690, Parris informed his congregation, "there is no trust to a rotten hearted person, whatever friendship may

50. Petition from Andover, 11 March 1690, Massachusetts Archives 35:296.

51. On Andover witchcraft accusations see, Marion L. Starkey, *The Devil in Massachusetts: A Modern Inquiry into the Salem Witch Trials* (New York: Alfred A. Knopf, 1949), chap. 15.

52. "Andover Marriages," *Vital Records of the Town of Andover, Massachusetts to the end of the year 1849*, vol. 2 (Topsfield: Topsfield Historical Society, 1912), p. 81.

be pretended." Parris also tended to portray the church as a fortress—and in a real sense a garrison house—and its communicants as soldiers obligated to defend it:

> Christ furnisheth the believer with skill, strength, courage, weapons and all military accomplishments for victory . . . the Lord Jesus sets them forth, furnisheth them with all necessaries for battle. The Lord Jesus is the true believer's magazine. [19 July 1691][53]

Cotton Mather reported after his detailed discussions with the "afflicted" Mercy Short about her spectral visions:

> that at such times the spectres went away to ther witch-meetings: but that when they returned the whole crew, besides her daily troublers look'd in upon her, to see how the work was carried on: that there were French Canadiens and Indian sagamores among them, diverse of whom shee knew.

Her familiarity with the enemy resulted from Mercy's experiences as a survivor of an Indian massacre and as a redeemed captive. She was the daughter of Clement Short, a farmer from the small southern New Hampshire coastal community of Salmon Falls.[54]

Mercy's ordeal had begun on 18 March 1690 when a war party led by the French-Canadian, Hertel, simultaneously assaulted the settlement's three garrison houses. Surprised and defenseless, Salmon Falls was destroyed; thirty-four people were killed and another fifty-four were captured. On that day the Indians and French "horribly butchered Mercy's father, her mother, her brother, her sister and others of her kindred." Three other brothers and two sisters were carried off to Canada. Mercy Short had in common with the "afflicted" of Salem Village her age and lack of family, as well as the severe form of dislocation that she had suffered as a result of the Indian attack.[55]

Six of the eight "afflicted" girls in Salem Village were not living in their parent's households in 1692. Some of them worked as servants,

---

53. Boyer and Nissenbaum, *Salem Possessed*, pp. 168–71.

54. Cotton Mather, *A Brand Pluck'd out of the Burning*, in *Narratives of the Witchcraft*, ed. Burr, p. 282.

55. Douglas Leach, *Arms for Empire*, p. 88; Mather, *A Brand Pluck'd out of the Burning*, p. 259.

and others lived in the homes of relatives. The deliberate separation of teen-aged children from their parents was a fundamental idea of the social or family ethic of New England Puritanism. Edmund S. Morgan maintains that this practice of "putting children out" as apprentices or to live with other families was often done for the purpose of establishing a "necessary distance between parent and child." A recent contrasting view accounts for the behavior as an intuitive response by parents concerned with "insulating themselves to some extent against the shock that the death of a child might bring."[56]

Separation from parents was also a frequent theme of Puritan ministers in their dialogues with children. Cotton Mather explained gravely to youthful listeners, "That which will exceedingly Aggravate [the] *Torments* of your *Damnation*, will be the Encounter which you shall have with your Godly Parents," for on that Day of Judgement such children will see their parents concur in their condemnation and will hear them say, "We now know them no more, Let them depart among the Workers of Iniquitie."[57]

The Reverend Michael Wigglesworth employed the imagery of separation in his poem "The Day of Doom," composed in the 1660s:

> The tender Mother will own no other
> of all her num'rous brood,
> But such as stand at Christ's right hand,
> acquitted through his Blood.[58]

A grim specter seen by the "afflicted" girls Mary Walcott and Susanah Sheldon during the witchcraft episode seems the embodiment of the Puritan Father. This specter, which the girls called the "shining man," had once interceded to rescue Susanah Sheldon from the witchspectre of John Willard. The shining man then commanded her to tell what:

> I had heard and seen to Mr. Hathorn this Willard being there present tould mee if I did hee would cutt my throate. At this

---

56. Boyer and Nissenbaum, *Salem Possessed*, p. 35fn.; David E. Stannard, *The Puritan Way of Death: A Study in Religion, Culture, and Social Change* (New York: Oxford University Press, 1977), p. 58.

57. Cotton Mather as quoted in Stannard, *The Puritan Way of Death*, p. 64.

58. Michael Wigglesworth, *The Day of Doom; or a Poetical Description of the Great and Last Judgement* (1715; reprint ed., New York: American News Company, 1867), verse 199, p. 78.

same time and place this Shining Man told mee that if I did goe to tell this to Mr. Hathorn that I should be well goeing and coming but I should be afflicted there, then said I to the Shining Man hunt Willa[r]d away and I would beleeve what he said that he might not chock mee with that the Shining Man held up his hand and Willard vaneshed away.[59]

Children who were denied genuine closeness to their parents through emotional or physical distance were sometimes brought closer together as an artificial family; but such an intimate unit can work only as long as conditions are not too demanding. False families of "disaster" children tended only to cultivate their fears.

Regarding the above, it was not the January 1692 York massacre alone which forced the children to behave this way, but rather the earlier massacres at Salmon Falls and Falmouth, Maine, in March and May of 1690 respectively, which the girls still remembered two years later when York fell.

The critical factor in the children's response to the 1690s massacres could have been Mrs. Ann Putnam, whose eleven-year-old daughter and namesake had accused the Reverend Burroughs of murder. Prior to her 1678 marriage to Lt. Thomas Putnam, Jr., immediately after King Philip's War, Ann Carr had lived in Salisbury, in the extreme northern part of Essex County. Her father (George Carr) had owned, in addition to a large estate, a shipworks and ferry, and upon his death in 1682, his widow and one of his sons took control of the entire enterprise, not only causing enmity between them and Ann, but even producing litigation.[60]

In August of 1672, through the marriage of her brother William Carr to Elizabeth Pike, Ann (Carr) Putnam became a relation of Maj. Robert Pike, the individual who in May of 1690 was appointed commander in chief of all Massachusetts militia forces in New Hampshire and Maine. A year before her own marriage, while she still lived in Salisbury, Ann Putnam had witnessed a violent argument between Major Pike and the Reverend John Wheelright during which the town of Salisbury divided itself into factions around the two men. Wheel-

59. Testimony of Susanah Sheldon against John Willard, in *The Salem Witchcraft Papers*, ed. Boyer and Nissenbaum vol. 3, p. 837.

60. Boyer and Nissenbaum, *Salem Possessed*, p. 135.

right had succeeded one morning in having Pike excommunicated when during an Indian alarm he took advantage of the absence of the soldier's supporters from the meeting house.[61]

On 13 September 1677 the Massachusetts government severely reprimanded both individuals: Major Pike for having:

> . . . shewed himselfe too litigious in impeaching him [Wheelright] with soe many articles under his hand, thereby creating great disturbance to the church & place, & alsoe much contempt of sd. Wheelright's person & office. . . . But neither can wee excuse Mr. Wheel- of too much precipitancy in pronouncing a sentance of excommunication against sd. Pike without further triall for repentance according to the vote of the church if he repent.[62]

Ann Carr's brother William was one of Pike's supporters who signed a complaint against Wheelright in May of 1677. The Massachusetts officials castigated these men for having contributed greatly to the disruption of the town:

> Wee cannot but condemne that evill practice of those of the church & towne that did endeavour in their petition to the Generall Court to eject off Mr. Wheelright from his ministry.[63]

In 1685 another scandal engulfed the Carr family, and again Major Robert Pike was involved, as revealed in a reference from the diary of Samuel Sewall:

> Mr. Stoughton also told me of George Car's wife being with child by another man, tells the father, Major Pike sends her down to prison. Is the Governour's grandchild by his daughter Cotton.[64]

Mrs. Putnam's perception of these negative events might have had a direct bearing on her reaction to the 1690 massacres; being herself a

---

61. "Salisbury Marriages," *Vital Records of the Town of Salisbury, Massachusetts to the end of the year 1849* (Topsfield: Topsfield Historical Society, 1915), p. 299; notice of Pike commission, 30 May 1690, Massachusetts Archives 36:101a.

62. Remonstrance of 13 September 1677, Massachusetts Archives 10:63.

63. Massachusetts Archives 10:63.

64. Samuel Sewall, *The Diary of Samuel Sewall*, ed. M. Halsey Thomas, vol. 1, 1674–1708 (New York: Farrar, Straus and Giroux, 1973), p. 70. The husband of the imprisoned woman was Ann Putnam's brother, George Carr, Jr.

victim of early parental separation and an individual who probably felt considerable ambivalence toward her family, the fragmentary reports of an Indian massacre at Salmon Falls, only fifteen miles from where she had spent her childhood, might well have revived these feelings in the adult Ann Putnam, and made her anxious for the safety of relatives or family friends, and she could have manifested that anxiety to her daughter. The evidence in a preponderance of recent studies concerning the effects of war and natural catastrophe upon children suggests that the most vulnerable children in such situations are those whose mothers are easily agitated and whose fathers react angrily or aggressively. There is no evidence of isolated children being particularly disturbed; rather, "each problem proved to be that of a disturbed family."[65]

A striking modern example of a "vulnerable" child's hallucinating devils and witches can be found in an early 1970s report of an eleven-year-old Catholic girl from Northern Ireland who, after having been subjected to a gas attack and to contact with a bloodied body, had the first of her hallucinations. She said that the figure she saw was "a tall man with a big hat, brightly colored coat and frightening eyes. He was, he said, a Protestant, because he was 'evil' and was trying to kill her."[66]

Normally, following a disaster or some other frightening experience, children attempt to comprehend what has happened to them through play-acting, or by constantly talking about the episode—a means of "ventilating" those aspects of the event that most trouble them. Attentive parents recognize the signs and respond, but if the parents are not alert to the signs or remain too anxious in the aftermath, the signs are not perceived, and the child shows nervous symptoms instead. In 1692, in Salem Village, the girls described sensations of biting, strangulation, convulsions, and hallucinations. The combination of the parental distance endemic to New England Puritanism and the tensions of factional conflict doubtless prevented the Salem parents from recognizing what was wrong with their children.[67]

Further, the quality of communication in 1690 probably resulted in the children's learning about the massacres in successive waves of rumor and misinformation as messengers, soldiers, and other witnesses

65. Morris Fraser, *Children in Conflict: Growing up in Northern Ireland* (New York: Basic Books, 1973), p. 75.

66. Fraser, *Children in Conflict*, pp. 66–67.

67. On mastering of anxiety through ventilation see, Fraser, *Children in Conflict*, p. 84.

traveled south to Boston with inflated reports of casualties and destruction. In addition, many of the girls were approaching marriageable age and were powerless to stop the departures of eligible men in their early twenties to the "eastward" and the war. As many as seven men ranging in age from sixteen years to their mid twenties perished in King William's War:

1690
April 17, John Bishop(18 years) killed with ye Indians.
September 21, Nicholas Reed(18 years) Edward Putnam's
    man killed with ye Indians.

1691
July 3, Godfrey Sheldon(24 years) killed by ye Indians.
July 4, Thomas   (18 years) killed at Casko.
July 5, Edward Crocker(19 years) killed at Casko.
July 6, George Bogwell(16 years) killed at Casko.

1693
June, William Tarbell, soldier at ye Eastward.[68]

If the girls' different anxieties relating to Indian massacre had remained unresolved from the spring of 1690 to the time of the York massacre in January 1692, that incident would have revived all of the old fears and uncertainties surrounding Salmon Falls and Falmouth in March and May 1690, perhaps accounting for the apparent concentration of afflictions and arrests on specific days and weeks in the spring of 1692.

This was not the first example in New England of witchcraft accusations being generated by Indian war. At the town of Scituate in Plymouth Colony in March of 1677, Mary Ingham was accused by Mehittable Woodworth of being the cause of her violent fits (fig. 3). While at the time of Ingham's accusation the town was entirely free of an Indian menace, exactly one year earlier, in March of 1676, the town of Scituate remained under constant threat of Indian attack for two months.[69]

68. List of village men who were killed in the war, from "Reverend Samuel Parris's Record of Deaths at Salem Village During his Ministry," *NEHGR* 36 (1882): 188.
69. Mehittable Woodworth was born 15 August 1662, "Scituate Births," *Vital Records of the Town of Scituate to the end of the year 1849*, vol. 1 (Boston: Stanhope Press, 1909),

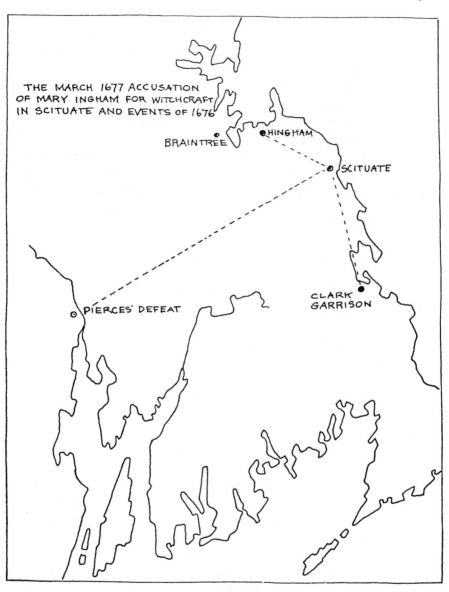

THE MARCH 1677 ACCUSATION
OF MARY INGHAM FOR WITCHCRAFT
IN SCITUATE AND EVENTS OF 1676

BRAINTREE

HINGHAM

SCITUATE

PIERCES' DEFEAT

CLARK
GARRISON

FIGURE 3

p. 418; Ingham case, 6 March 1677, in *Records of the Colony of New Plymouth*, ed. Nathaniel B. Shurtleff, vol. 5, 1668–1678, Court Orders, (Boston: William B. White, 1856), p. 223.

From late February of 1676 Indian raids had occurred within a ten-mile radius of Scituate on the average of once a week with assaults upon Weymouth, Braintree, Bridgewater, and Attleborough. Then, on Sunday, 12 March 1676, the Indians penetrated to the center of Plymouth and massacred eleven persons at Clark garrison house. Less than two weeks later, Capt. Michael Peirse of Scituate and forty-two soldiers—fourteen of them Scituate men—were massacred by the Indians five miles north of Providence.[70]

On 19 April 1676 the destruction of the war reached the immediate environs of Scituate when John Jacob was killed by the Indians at the adjacent town of Hingham. The following day the Indians burned five houses at Hingham and then advanced south to Scituate and burned nineteen houses in the town; exactly one month later on 20 May 1676 the Indians attacked again and destroyed the mill of Cornet Robert Stetson, father to Robert Stetson, Jr., whose house had been burned in April. Plymouth Court records of July 1676 reveal a controversy between the Stetson and Woodworth families involving the birth of an illegitimate child to Elizabeth Woodworth that was apparently fathered by Stetson, Jr.[71]

Mehittable Woodworth was probably a "vulnerable" child long before February 1676, and the progress her phobia took can be easily traced from the moment of the first attack near her town and her correct anticipation of a second, a third, and fourth visitation. The embarrassment of a local scandal and the targeting of the Stetsons by the Indians might also have frightened her.

Hysterical behavior triggered by the first or second anniversaries of critical events was the common element in both the Scituate and Salem Village episodes. In late February of 1692 Tituba (Samuel Parris's Carib Indian slave), Sarah Osborne, and Sarah Good were the first women to be arrested for witchcraft. Three more women were accused in March. On 18 March 1692—the second anniversary of Salmon Falls—Ann (Carr) Putnam claimed to have been afflicted by the specter of Martha Cory, stating that Cory had "tortured me so as I cannot express, ready to tear me all to pieces." Goody Cory was summarily arrested as was

---

70. Douglas Edward Leach, *Flintlock and Tomahawk*, pp. 166–67; Samuel Deane, *History of the Town of Scituate* (Boston: James Loring, 1831), pp. 123, 126.

71. Stetson-Woodworth controversy, 22 July 1676, in *Plymouth Colony Records*, ed. Nathaniel Shurtleff, vol. 5, Court Orders.

Rebecca Nurse, also largely as a result of "severe spectral afflictions which befell the elder Ann Putnam between March 19 and 24."[72]

The cluster of arrests for witchcraft in late May 1692—the anniversary of Falmouth or Casco—was quite large; thirty arrests were made in a twenty-day period. Of those, ten arrests occurred on 28 May and were the result of spectral afflictions experienced by Mary Walcott. Among those arrested that day were Capt. John Alden, Martha Carrier, and Martha Toothaker—the Billerica woman who had dreamed of fighting Indians. A fourth arrestee, Capt. John Floyd of Rumney Marsh, had, like Alden, associations with the York massacre, having been in command of the militia (including Salem men) which had found the town in ruins. On 27 January 1692 he had written to his superiors, "The 25 of this instant I having information that York was destroyed made the greatest hast that I could w^t my Company for their reliefe if there were any left w^e I did hardly expect."[73]

The "afflicted" may have accused men who had been prominently involved in the prosecution of the Indian because of the simple conviction that persons who had been in close contact with the Indians and survived were in fact witches; those who had died, like Godfrey Sheldon, were true Christians. This assumption would have been consistent with the Puritan belief that Indians and witches were synonymous, and may even have been responsible for the process of affliction itself. The "afflicteds' " perception of Indian war had always been a distorted one, especially for the three seventeen-year-olds, Mary Walcott, Mercy Lewis, and Susanah Sheldon, who were infants in 1675 and 1676. In the early 1680s, when these girls were between five and six years of age, King Philip's War was still a vivid memory—the ruins, the wounded, and the widowed women were very likely all around them. And the Puritans produced a considerable war literature: histories, captivity narratives, and memorial sermons, which further contributed to the symbolization of the war. Just how much the "afflicted" knew about Philip's War from this literature is impossible to determine. It does, however, seem plausible that at some time while they were growing up, the girls became familiar with the "cenotaphic" hills in

72. Boyer and Nissenbaum, *Salem Possessed*, pp. 146–48.

73. Massachusetts Archives 37:257; petition of Charles Mackarly of Salem for compensation for injuries sustained while a corporal in Captain Floyd's company, 1692? Massachusetts Archives 37:318.

the village which, although bearing the names of earlier owners of the properties (Davenport, Leach, Smith, Thorndike, and Whipple) also seemed to memorialize their direct descendants who fought or were killed by Indians in King Philip's War. The map shown in figure 4 shows the location of the hills and the properties of individuals (called "accusers" and "defenders" by Boyer and Nissenbaum) who represented opposing factions in the witchcraft dispute.

By 1692 the village girls' fear of the Indian had advanced to such an irrational state that they were unable to think directly about him; instead, they used the witch as his symbolic substitute—and a witch was any person who distressed either the girls or their parents. As previously noted, the "afflicted" would also have held such people responsible for the failure of their parents to supply needed emotional support.

The charging of the Reverend George Burroughs, "the little black minister from Casco Bay," is the best illustration of how actively the girls sought agents of the war at a symbolic level. Burroughs was regarded as the source—even the mastermind—of the spectral assault which emerged from his "eastward" domain, and the "afflicted" girls had been inclined to perceive the world typologically—especially in light of Samuel Parris's encouragement to reduce complex disagreements to distinctions of good and evil. The influence of Parris and their ingrained fear of the Indian made it easy for the girls to see the "eastward" as an allegorical hell, and even to interpret the events of the war as signs that the end of the world was approaching.

Evidence for a too-literal misreading of Revelations in 1692 comes from two sources—Deodat Lawson, who heard the possessed Mercy Lewis sing:

> Thou art worthy to take the book and to open the seals therof:
> for thou wast slain and has redeemed us to God by thy blood.
>
> Revelations 5: 9

and from occasional reference to the existence of a seal on the forehead of a specter of the witch's victim—possibly traceable to Revelations 9, which is most suggestive as a plan for the infestation of the region by witches, in that it describes an assault by locusts following the opening of a "bottomless pit."[74]

---

74. Lawson, *A Brief and True Narrative*, in *Narratives of the Witchcraft*, ed. Burr, p. 161.

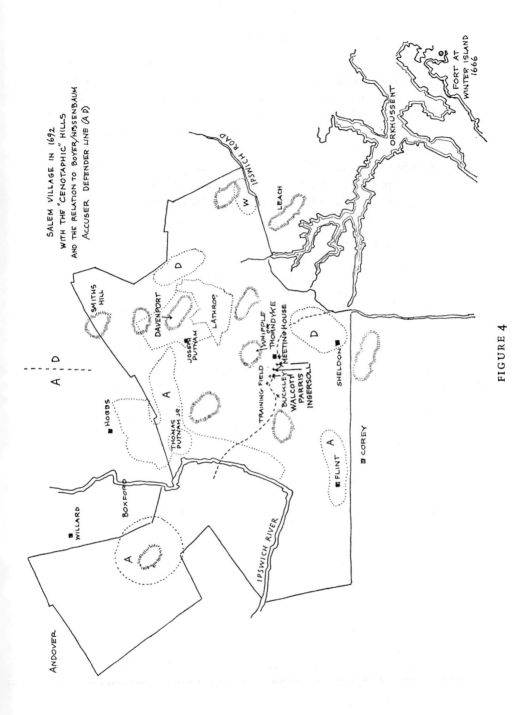

SALEM VILLAGE IN 1692
WITH THE "CENOTAPHIC" HILLS
AND THE RELATION TO BOYER/NISSENBAUM
ACCUSER DEFENDER LINE (A D)

FIGURE 4

189

The act of opening the pit was represented by "the smoke of a great furnace [which darkened] the sun and the air," an image of which the York massacre could be a symbolic equivalent. The locusts which appeared had been "commanded [not to] hurt the grass of the earth, neither any green thing, neither any tree, but only those men which have not the seal of God in their forehead," and the pain which they were to inflict was to cause "the torment of a scorpion when he striketh a man." The parallel between the Biblical locusts and the Essex County witches is evident even in the description of their appearance:

> And they had hair as the hair of women, and their teeth were as the teeth of lions.
> And they had breastplates, as it were breastplates of iron: and the sound of their wings was as the sound of chariots of many horses running to battle.
> And they had a king over them which is the angel of the bottomless pit.
>
> Revelations 9: 8,9,10

Abigail Williams, who lived in the Reverend Parris's home was, with the minister's daughter, one of the first to have been afflicted, displaying behavior imitative of these locusts in the presence of Deodat Lawson. The incident occurred on 19 March 1692, and Lawson noted that she was "hurryed with violence to and fro in the room, sometimes making as if she would fly, stretching up her arms as high as she could, and crying 'Whish, Whish, Whish' several times." Abigail next debated with a specter, and then retreated from it "to the fire and begin to throw fire brands about the house, and run up against the back, as if she would run up chimney."[75]

In this compact allegorical drama, Abigail Williams seems to have performed the parts of both the locust and its victim. Mercy Lewis had attempted to inform Lawson in the same indirect way with recitations against the heathen, but Lawson and his colleagues never understood the New Testament allusion, and the frustrated girls soon advanced from play-acting to "fits."

In February of 1692 Abigail Williams developed an illness and suffered with "pains in her head and other parts" throughout that month. This illness, which was coincident with Tituba's first supposed contact with the devil, is significant because the devil had constantly advised

75. Lawson, *A Brief and True Narrative*, in *Narratives of the Witchcraft*, ed. Burr, p. 153.

Tituba to "doe hurt" to the children "and pinch them." Tituba attempted to resist the devil and to ignore his orders, but said she was coerced into obedience:

> they hall me [away] and make me pinch Betty, and the next Abigaill, and then quickly went away altogether.[76]

Like the children, Tituba was also hallucinating, but for different reasons. The emphasis upon physical injury in her fantasies—particularly acts against Elizabeth Parris—seems derived from a psychological conflict made worse by her frequent dislocation from a familiar place. Tituba's impulse to pinch seemed to Abigail Williams like the torments of the Biblical locusts, and as further reinforcement, Tituba as an Indian could be linked at a symbolic level to the fiendish Indians of the "eastward."

VI

The more accurate historical understandings of the witch hunts have during the last few decades resulted largely from an effort to comprehend the event more as a social phenomenon than as a crime. Practically all of the agents involved in the events of 1692—witches, judges, and ministers—have been perceived as having behaved as the culture expected they should; but this objectivity has not been extended to the "afflicted" girls. While they are no longer accused of fraud, it has become easier to dismiss them as being insignificant. The spectrum of analysis regarding the cause of the afflictions has embraced ergot poisoning, hysterical symptoms owing to fear of magic, and antecedents of the revivalism of the eighteenth century. The Indian war and the complex of fears which it might have generated would, in contrast with these other conjectures, help to make the girls' behavior comprehensible as a contemporary and appropriate response under very real emotional stress.[77]

The 1692 witch hunt was very much a product of King William's War, which seemed not only to have exacerbated village factionalism, but to have promoted the further alienation of Salem Village from Salem Town. For two and a half years, Samuel Parris had—on a weekly basis—impressed upon his congregation the fact that they might be

76. Examination of Tituba, in Samuel G. Drake, ed., *The Witchcraft Delusion in New England: Its Origins, Progress and Development*, vol. 3 (1866; reprint ed., New York: Burt Franklin, 1970), pp. 187–94.

77. Boyer and Nissenbaum, *Salem Possessed*, pp. 23–30.

betrayed, and that they would have to be vigilant to survive. Less so-phisticated persons might have easily confused his rhetoric with admonitions about the war in the "eastward"; and among these less-sophisticated individuals were the female children who were deprived of an active role in the war and were thus forced to stand helplessly by as spectators to the massacres. The magnitude of the witch hunts increased, because these same girls influenced the spread of accusations into the frontier towns of Andover and Billerica, where massacres had taken place and where the people were uneasy.

New England Puritanism transformed the anxieties of children in wartime into a witch panic, because Puritans regarded the relationship of Indian and witch as fundamental to a perception of Indian war; nor was theirs a religion which could accommodate itself to the needs of children or be sympathetic in dealing with their fears. Finally, Puritanism was oriented toward Biblical symbolism, which greatly affected the colonists' outlook upon the present. Indian wars and captivities were described in epic language, and the Indian's power was exaggerated so that his defeat would appear more meaningful and heroic. The mundane and the accidental aspects of Indian war should have helped the girls to see the Indians more realistically, but the Puritan emphasis was on the heathen's devil-inspired omniscience and omnipotence; it is thus not difficult to see how fear of Indians evolved into a deep-rooted belief that they were creatures of the devil. It is somewhat ironic that this dark vision of the Indian is clearly apparent even in an official directive to one of the men who would himself later be accused of witchcraft. The instructions that were delivered to Capt. John Alden following his assignment to redeem the York captives from the Indians reminded him that:

> it will be necessary that you represent unto them their baseness, treachery and barbarities practised in carrying on of this warr. . . haveing alwaies declined a fair pitch battle acting [instead] like bears and wolves.[78]

This grisly analogy shows how much the Indian's diabolic nature seemed to be an established reality in 1692, not only to the "afflicted" of Salem Village, but to the authorities of law and order as well.

78. Instructions to Captain John Alden, 5 February 1692, Massachusetts Archives 37:305.

NOTES ON THE HISTORY OF WITCHCRAFT IN MASSACHUSETTS;

WITH ILLUSTRATIVE DOCUMENTS.

By George H. Moore.

I DESIRE to call attention to certain errors in the current history of Witchcraft in Massachusetts, and must ask your indulgence for my inability to make these dry bones live in more pleasing forms.

The first errors I note are in the statements—that there was no colonial or provincial law against witchcraft in force at the time of the witchcraft proceedings in 1692, in Massachusetts—that the prosecutions took place entirely under English law, that law being the statute of James I.— and that witchcraft was not a criminal offence at common law. It is probable that these errors may be traced mainly to Hutchinson, whose statements I quote. It should be remembered that Hutchinson was not originally bred to the profession of the law.

He says (vol. ii., page 52) : "At the first trial there was no colony or provincial law against witchcraft in force. The statute of James the first must therefore have been considered in force in the provinces, witchcraft not being an offence at common law. Before the adjournment the old colony law, which makes witchcraft a capital offence, was revived, with the other local laws, as they were called, and made a law of the province." Again (p. 59), "The general court also showed their zeal against witchcraft by a law passed in the words of the statute of James the first, * * * * If the court was of opinion that the statute extended here, I see no necessity of a provincial act exactly in the same words; if the statute did not extend here, I know not by what law the first that was tried could be sentenced to death."

With reference to the same period, and the same proceedings, George Chalmers said: "What reflects disgrace on the province, it was then doubtful, but is now certain, that there existed no law in Massachusetts for putting supposed witches to death." *Cont. Polit. Ann. : Coll. N. Y. Hist. Soc.* 1868 : p. 111.

Hutchinson was a loyal son of Massachusetts, but Chalmers felt pleasure in this severe and unjust reflection upon the people of that province. From the earliest period there had never been any lack of law against witchcraft in England. Blackstone found the "antient books " of the law full of this "offence against God and religion." He adds " the civil law punishes with death not only the sorcerers themselves, but also those who consult them, imitating in the former the express law of God, ' thou shalt not suffer a witch to live.' And our own laws, both before and since the conquest, have been equally penal; ranking this crime in the same class with heresy, and condemning both to the flames." *Comm.* iv., 60.

I suppose Hutchinson's error arose in part from the following passage in Hale's History of the Pleas of the Crown: "If a man either by working upon the fancy of another, or possibly by harsh or unkind usage puts another into such a passion of grief or fear, that the party either dies suddenly, or contracts some disease, whereof he dies, tho' as the circumstances of the case may be, this may be murder or manslaughter in the sight of God, yet *in foro humano* it cannot come under the judgment of Felony, because no external act of violence was offered whereof the common law can take notice, and secret things belong to God; and hence it was, that before the statute of 1 *Jac. Cap.* 12, witchcraft or fascination was not felony, because it wanted a trial, though some constitutions of the civil law make it penal." *Hist. P. C., Cap.* 33, I. 429.

See Barrington's reference to this: *Observations on the Statutes*, p. 528, "Hist. P. C., iv., 429," in which he explains that the proof of allegations of witchcraft is "attended with infinite difficulty. Lord C. J. Hale for this reason informs us that 1 James I., Cap. 12 (which makes it felony to kill any person by the invocation of an evil spirit), was occasioned by there being no external appearance of violence which might make it criminal by the common law, though the offence was punished with death by the Romans."

"Plato saith well the strongest of all authorities is, if a man can allege the authority of his adversary against himself." Bacon: *Case of the Post Nati.* We have the authority of Lord Chief Justice Coke and Chief Justice Hale himself for the statement that witchcraft, as a capital offence immediately against the Divine Majesty, at common law, was punished with death, as heresy. Coke: 3 *Inst.*, Cap. vi. Hale: *P. C.*, pp. 3, 6.

The declaration of heresy, and likewise the proceedings and judgment upon hereticks, were by the common law of the realm referred to the ecclesiastical jurisdiction, and the secular arm was reached to them by the common law, and not by any statute for the execution of them which was by the King's writ *de haeretico comburendo.* *Bacon's Cases of Treason:* Chap. xiii. *Harl. Misc.* v. 20.

Before the statute 2 Henry IV., Cap. 15, no person could be convicted of heresy, but by the archbishop, and all the clergy of the province; but, by that statute, any particular bishop might in his diocese convict of heresy, and issue forth his precept to the sheriff, to burn the person he had convicted, a law whereby the clergy gained a dominion over the lives of the subjects, independent upon the crown. It was repealed by the statute 25 Henry VIII., Cap. 14. . But so as particular bishops might still convict; though without the king's writ *de haeretico comburendo*, first obtained, no person convicted could be put to death, and so the law stood until   .   .   .   [1677.]   *Harleian Misc.* viii. 70.

" Under the general name of *heresy* there hath been in ordinary speech comprehended three sorts of crimes: 1. *Apostacy.* . . . . 2. *Witchcraft, Sortilegium*, was by the antient laws of England of ecclesiastical cognizance and upon conviction thereof without abjuration, or relapse without abjuration, was punishable with death by writ *de haeretico comburendo, vide Co. P. C.*, Cap. 6, *et libros ibi, Extr' de haereticis* Cap. 8, § 5, *n.* 6. 3. *Formal heresy* . . ." Hale: P. C. i. 383. *Hawkins, P. C. Cap. III.* 2. All these [including those guilty of witchcraft] were anciently punished in the same manner as hereticks, by the writ *de haeretico comburendo*, after a sentence in the ecclesiastical court and a relapse. And it is said also that they might be condemned to the pillory, &c., upon an indictment at common law. 3 *Inst.* 44, *F. N. B.* 269. *S. P. C.* 38. *Croke, Eliz.* 571.

Fitzherbert, in his *Natura Brevium*, says in a note: " It appeareth by *Britton* in his book, that those persons shall be burnt who feloniously burn other's corn, or other's houses, and *also those who are sorcerers or sorceresses;* and sodomites and heretics shall be burnt; and it appeared by that book, lib. I., cap. 17, that *such was the common law.*" *Natura Brevium*, 269.

A reference to Britton amply sustains this ancient oracle of the common law: "Let inquiry also be made of those who feloniously in time of peace have burnt others' corn or houses, and those who are attainted thereof shall be burnt, so that they may be punished in like manner as they have offended. *The same sentence shall be passed upon sorcerers, sorceresses*, renegades, sodomites, and heretics publicly convicted." *Britton:* Lib. I., Cap. X.

The learned editor of Britton says: "It seems as to these offences, though the King's court was in general ancillary to the ecclesiastical tribunal, it sometimes acted independently." And he cites a contemporary MS. that "if the King by inquest find any person guilty of such horrible sin, he may put them to death, as a good marshall of Christendom." Compare also *Britton, lib.* 1, *cap.* xvi   sect. 6, and chap. xxx. sect. 3.

I am well aware that the King's Writ did never run in Massachusetts; but Law and History alike will sustain the assertion that the Fathers of Massachusetts never failed in their duty, if they knew it, " as good marshalls of Christendom."

Four years before it was abolished by the Statute of 29 Ch. II., there was a debate in the House of Lords concerning taking away the Writ *De haeretico comburendo.* The discussion plainly shows that it was well known as a writ in the Register, and before 2 Henry V., in which time the Statute against *Lollards* was made, and put in execution against them and that the *writ was, before that time, a Writ at Common Law.*[1] The Bishop and Ecclesiastical Power were Judges of Heresy, who, upon condemnation of the party, delivered him up to the secular Power; and the Writ *De haeretico comburendo* was thereupon issued out. It was declared in Parliament that the writ was still in force at Common Law, and the same power in the Clergy, notwithstanding the Statute of Queen Elizabeth of the thirty-nine Articles, and the Statute of Heresy, so that if they fell into the misfortune of Catholic Governors and Clergy, as in the *Marian* days, that writ was still in force, and might be put in execution.

The Act for taking away this writ was passed four years afterwards, 29 Charles II., 1677, declaring " that the writt commonly called *Breve de heretico comburendo*, with all Processe and Proceedings thereupon in order to the executeing such writt or following or depending thereupon and all punishment by death in pursuance of any Ecclesiastical Censures be from henceforth utterly taken away and abolished."

But the abolition of the law and process for burning heretics did not finish or do away with the legal penalties for witchcraft.

It was declared felony by Statute 33, H. VIII. c. 8. [1541–2] which was repealed by the operation of the Statute 1 Edward VI., c. 12. Again declared felony by Statute 5 Elizabeth, c. 16, it was only more accurately defined by the Statute Jac. I., c. 12, by which the previous statute was also repealed. This law, which was " enacted (as Mr. Bancroft says) by a House of Commons in which Coke and Bacon were the guiding minds," continued to disgrace the English statute book until 1736. By it the Invoking or Consulting with Evil Spirits, taking up Dead Bodies, &c., for purposes of witchcraft, &c., or practising Witchcraft, &c., to the harm of others, was declared Felony without Clergy. It also imposed penalties on declaring by Witchcraft where Treasure, &c., is hidden; procuring unlawful love; or attempting to hurt Cattle or Persons: for the first offence a year's Imprisonment and Pillory; for the second, that of Felony, without Clergy.

The original Body of Liberties of the Massachusetts Colony in New England made Witchcraft a capital offence. This article follows immediately after the provision for the punishment of idolatry, which is the first article of the capital code.

" 2. If any man or woman be a witch (that is hath or consulteth with a familiar spirit)[2] they shall be put to death."

It is fortified by scriptural authorities in the margin—viz: by references to Exodus 22: 18; Leviticus 20: 27; Deuteronomy 18: 10;

---

[1] Barrington says (p. 126) there is no legal argument which hath such force, in our courts of law, as those which are drawn from ancient writs; and the Registrum Brevium is therefore looked upon to be the very foundation of the common law. St. 13 Edw. I. Statute of Westminster the Second.

[2] This legal definition of a witch seems to have been adhered to throughout the examinations and proceedings at Salem in 1692.

18

and continued without modification through the whole period of the government under the first charter, appearing in all the editions of the laws which have been preserved.

The contemporary code, drawn up by John Cotton, printed in London in 1641, and long supposed to have been the actual "laws of New England as established," gives the same prominence to witchcraft in the chapter of crimes. After blasphemy and idolatry, comes

"3. Witchcraft which is fellowship by covenant with a familiar spirit, to be punished with death.

"4. Consulters with Witches not to be tolerated, but either to be cut off by death, or by banishment."

His authorities from Scripture are Exodus 22: 18; Leviticus 20: 27, and 19: 31.

This alternative penalty of banishment, "the consulters with witches" shared with "scandalous livers" and "revilers of religion." Those who reviled the church establishment of Massachusetts came under the latter description.

The laws of the colony of New Plymouth, in 1636, enumerated among "capitall offences lyable to death," as the third in order after treason or rebellion, and murder, "solemn compaction or conversing with the divell by way of witchcraft, conjuration or the like."

By the revision of 1671, this law appears to have been modified. The eighth section of chapter II., Capital Laws, provides that "if any *Christian (so called)* be a Witch, that is, hath, or consulteth with a familiar Spirit; he or they shall be put to death." This qualification of "Christianity" (so called) "was probably a saving clause for the Indian inhabitants of the territory within the jurisdiction of the colony. The Indians had been always regarded as worshippers of the Devil, and their Powwows as wizards.

From the date of the judgment in the King's Bench, by which the Colonial Charter was cancelled, Massachusetts was governed by a Royal Commission until, in 1689, the news of the English revolution produced an insurrection at Boston, in which the Royal Governor was deposed, and the "antient Charter" and its constitutions *de facto* resumed. During this period, the Royal Commission and Instructions established the government "according to such reasonable laws and statutes as are *now in force* or such others as shall hereafter be made and established within our territory and dominion aforesaid." And the King declared his royal will and pleasure to be "that all lawes, statutes and ordinances [therein] * * * shall continue and be in full force and vigor," excepting such as might be in conflict with the Governor's Commission and Instructions, &c.

On the 22d June, 1689, after the deposition of Andros, "at the Convention of the Governor and Council and Representatives of the Massachusetts Colony, it was declared that all the laws made by the Governor and Company of said colony that were in force on the 12th day of May, 1686 (except any that are repugnant to the laws of England) are the laws of this colony, and continue in force till farther settlement, to which all inhabitants and residents here are to give due obedience." 3 : *Hutch. Papers*, 372, in M. H. S. Lib., quoted by Gray in *Reports IX.* 517.

Under this temporary settlement of the laws, the authorities in Massachusetts did not hesitate to exercise the highest judicial powers and even to inflict capital punishment; taking the highest steps in the administration of government, by trying, condemning, and executing some notorious criminals found guilty of piracies and murder. Bradstreet to Increase Mather, 29 January, 1689. *Hutch. Papers*, 576.

Chief Justice Shaw stated very clearly the doctrine which has always prevailed : " We take it to be a well settled principle, acknowledged by all civilized states governed by law, that by means of a political revolution, by which the political organization is changed, the municipal laws, regulating their social relations, duties and rights, are not necessarily abrogated." *Commonwealth v. Chapman*, 13 *Metcalf*, 71.

Nor should it be forgotten here that the validity of the judgment against the Charter in 1684, which was decided by the House of Commons, and " questioned by very great authority in England," was never admitted in Massachusetts. 9 *Gray*, 517. As there was nothing in the repeal of the Colony Charter to affect the private rights of the colonists, 9 *Gray*, 518, so generally the rights of the inhabitants, as well as the penalties to which they might be subjected, continued to be determined by the effect and according to the form of the colonial and provincial legislation, *i. e.* the common law of Massachusetts, rather than by the ancient common law of England. 5 *Pickering*, 203. 7 *Cushing*, 76–77. 13 *Pickering*, 208. 13 *Metcalf*, 68–72.

I may be permitted also, at this point, to state a fact which (so far as I know) has escaped attention entirely in all the later discussions of this topic : that it was deemed necessary by the Legislature of this Commonwealth, to pass an act as late as the year 1824, for the repeal of a law of the Colony passed in 1660 ![1]

Thus far legislation under the Colony Charter. On the arrival of Phips with the Province Charter, the change which was made was scarcely perceptible, almost the same men continued in power, the

---

[1]CHAP. CLXIII.

An Act to repeal an Act, entitled " An Act Against Self-Murder."

BE *it enacted by the Senate and House of Representatives in General Court assembled, and by the authority of the same*, That an Act entitled "an Act against self-murder," passed in the year of our Lord one thousand six hundred and sixty, and providing that the bodies of persons who shall be guilty of self-murder shall be buried in some public highway, be, and the same is hereby repealed.

[Approved by the Governor, February 21st, 1824.]

laws and customs of former times remained, and the spirit of the people had undergone little alteration.

The provincial legislature met for the first time on the 8th of June, 1692. Proceedings and examinations upon charges of witchcraft had been going on for several months before; the special court of Oyer and Terminer had been organized on the 27th of May, and sat, on the 2d of June, for the trial of its first victim, whose death warrant, signed on the very day the legislature came together, was executed two days afterwards.

One of the first acts of the Great and General Court, passed on the 15th of June, 1692, was to continue all the local laws of the former governments of Massachusetts Bay and New Plymouth, being not repugnant to the laws of England, nor inconsistent with the new constitution and settlement by the Province Charter—to stand in force till November 10th, in the same year.

This was that "Greatest General Court that ever was in New England," in the early part of whose session (June 9th), Increase Mather appeared and gave an account of his doings as Agent of the Colony at London.

On the 29th of October they passed an act for the punishing of capital offenders, in which Witchcraft maintains its old position in the list of Capital Crimes, being declared to be felony, of which persons legally convicted were to be "adjudged to suffer the Pains of Death." The text is the same as that of the former law, but the scriptural authorities are omitted. The description of what constitutes a witch, furnished a legal definition of the crime. This law was subsequently disallowed in England by reason of the Articles relating to Witchcraft, Blasphemy, Incest. and slaying by Devilish Practice, which were declared by the Privy Council to be "conceived in very uncertain and doubtful terms," etc. *Letter from the Privy Council*, 26 Dec. 1695.

Before the end of the same session, on the 14th December, 1692, the General Court of Massachusetts reinforced their own local law by the substantial re-enactment of the English Statute.

This "Act against Conjuration, Witchcraft, and dealing with Evil and Wicked Spirits," is expressly declared in the preamble to be "for more particular *direction in the Execution of* the Law against Witchcraft." The original Bill is preserved among the Archives in the State House at Boston, with such changes by way of correction as indicate the design of its promoters still more clearly. "For Explanation [or Explication] of the Law against Witchcraft, and more particular direction therein, the execution thereof, and for the better restraining the said offences, and more severely punishing the same," etc. *Mass. Archives.* This phraseology shows conclusively that they had previously been proceeding upon their own or the common law, for if they had been guided by the statute of James I., they needed not to re-enact it, for particular direction, or to increase the severity of punishment.

The fac-simile given in the *Memorial History of Boston*, Vol II., 153, does not indicate this important feature in the original, and the error to which I call attention is reiterated there in the statement that "the witches had been tried without any Colony or Province Law on the subject, and presumably under the English statute of James I." *Ibid.* 154.

Mr. Bancroft, in his exhaustive and most able discussion of this topic, states that the General Court adopted the English law, "*word for word as it stood in the English Statute Book*," but the differences between the original statute and that of Massachusetts are considerable, and characteristic, even when not very important, which some of them certainly are.[1]

In the enacting clause, "the Governor, Council, and Representatives in General Court assembled" take the place of "the King our Sovereign Lord, the Lords Spiritual and Temporal, and the Commons in parliament assembled."

The denial of "the privilege and benefit of Cleargie and Sanctuarie" to persons convicted, which is a conspicuous feature in the English law is omitted in that of Massachusetts.

"The Markett Town, upon the Market Day, or at such tyme as any Faire shall be kept there," as the place of exposure and confession upon the pillory four times during the year's imprisonment, finds its substitute in "some Shire town" of Massachusetts, where it was also required in addition, that the "offence shall be written in Capital Letters, and placed upon the Breast of the Offender."

A much more important omission was that which excluded the provisions for saving of Dower, Inheritance, Succession, &c., as well as the proviso that "Peers shall be tried by Peers." The want of agreement with the English statute, "whereby the Dower was saved to ye Widow and ye Inheritance to ye heir of ye party convicted" is expressly mentioned in the letter of the Privy Council to the Governor, &c., of the Province, 26th December, 1695, as the reason for its repeal.

The rights of heirs had also been saved in the previous statute of the same session—"*An Act setting forth General Priviledges*"—which provided that they should not be defeated by any forfeitures for crime, except in cases of high treason. This saving applied only to "lands and heritages," so that goods and chattels might be forfeited in cases of felony. This act met a similar fate at the hands of the Privy Council, as being repugnant to the laws of England.

Yet the laws of Massachusetts from the beginning had preserved the

---

Mr. Bancroft was evidently misled by Hutchinson, as quoted *ante*, p. 162. The passage in the first edition of the History of the United States, is as follows: "The General Court adopted what King William rejected— the English law. word for word as it stood in the English Statute Book." Edition 1840, iii., 95. As subsequently revised for the centenary edition, it stands "the English law, word for word, as it was enacted by a House of Commons, in which Coke and Bacon were the guiding minds." Edition 1876, ii., 265.

rights of heirs by the entire exemption of lands and heritages from
" forfeitures, upon the deaths of parents or Ancestors, be they naturall,
casuall or Juditiall." *Body of Liberties*, Art. 10.   Under this law of the
colony, traitors as well as other felons might dispose of their estates,
real and personal, by will, after sentence, and if they died intestate, distribution was made, as in other cases.   In 1678, the Attorney General
of England objected to this feature of the colonial law as repugnant to
the laws of England, to which the General Court replied that they conceived it to be according to their patent; and "its originall, vizᵗ that of
East Greenwitch, according unto which, as we conceive, notwithstanding
the father's crime, yet the children are to possesse the estate." *Mass.
Rec.*, v., 199.

I have thus shown that, whatever may be the estimate placed upon the
proceedings of the authorities against alleged witches, the disgrace does
not attach to them of having acted without warrant of law.   In point
of fact a popular devotion to law that was fanatical, was an influence
second only to their fidelity to religious conviction, among the moving
causes of the witch delusion.   *Palfrey*, iv., 130.

Another error has been constantly repeated in the statement that no
lawyer was engaged in the proceedings. Gov. Washburn said there was
not a lawyer concerned in the proceedings of the court.   *Judicial Hist.*,
p. 145.   And Mr. Chandler in his Criminal Trials followed the Governor
somewhat literally.   He says—"it was a popular tribunal; there was
not a lawyer concerned in its proceedings." *Am. Crim. Trials*, i., 92.
And again—"Neither is the common law, nor are its professors responsible
for their mistaken proceedings.   The special court of Oyer and Terminer
was essentially a popular tribunal.   There was not a regular lawyer
concerned in its proceedings." *Ib.*, 137.   Mr. Palfrey confirms this
statement of the case :   " there were no trained lawyers in the province."
Hist. N. E., iv., 120.   And the statement has been generally accepted.
But it is not true.   In the original constitution of the court—on Friday,
the 27th May, 1692, Mr. Thomas Newton was appointed to officiate as attorney for and on behalf of their Majesties at the special court of Oyer
and Terminer.   He took the oath before Stoughton, June 2, in open
court at Salem, and continued to act until 26th July, when he was succeeded in that service by Anthony Checkley, who had been previously
employed in that office, and who continued in the same position for
several years after the witchcraft trials had passed by.

Newton was an Englishman by birth, bred a lawyer, and appears to
have come to Boston in 1688, when he is noticed in a contemporary
diary as a new-comer and sworn an attorney.   Edward Randolph had
represented to Mr. Povey of the English Board of Trade a year or two
before "the want of two or three honest attorneys, if [there be] any
such thing in nature," and Newton probably came under that encouragement.   He was Attorney General in New York in 1691, and prosecuted
Leisler, Milborne and others in the trials for high treason in that year—

returning to Boston, however, very soon after those trials were over. It is a curious fact never before noticed which thus connects the judicial murders of Leisler and Milborne in New York, with those of the alleged witches at Salem.

It is hardly less remarkable that a brother of the same Milborne, an Anabaptist minister who had been conspicuous in the proceedings against Andros and Randolph, and evidently one of the leaders of the popular party, was arrested and held to bail by the government of Phips, apparently because he had appealed to the Assembly against these very proceedings in the witchcraft cases.[1]

I have not time in this place to give details of the career of Newton as

---

[1] " June 25, 1692. There being laid before his Excellency and Council two papers directed unto the Assembly one of them subscribed by William Milborne of Boston, and several others, containing very high reflections upon the administration of public justice within this their Majesty's Province, the said William Milborne was sent for, and upon examination owned that the said papers were of his writing, and that he subscribed his name to one of them.

"*Ordered* to be committed to prison or give bond of £200 with two sureties to appear at next Superior Court to answer for framing, contriving, writing and publishing the said seditious and scandalous papers' or writings, and in the mean time to be of good behaviour." *Council Records.*

The following document is evidently a part of the same proceedings:

"To the Sheriff of the County of Suffolke.
" By his Excellency the Govern.

" These are in their Maties name to will and require you forthwith to take into yor custody the Body of William Milborne of Boston, and to cause him to make his appearance before myselfe and Council to answer what shall bee objected against him on their Maties behalf for writing, framing, contriving and Exhibiting under his hand, with the names of several others, a scandalous and seditious paper containing very high reflections upon their Maties Government of this their Maties Province of the Massachusetts Bay in New England. Inscribed to the Grave and Judicious Members of the General Court for the said Province. Hereof fail not and make Return of this Precept with your doings therein. Given under my hand and seal at Boston the 25th of June, 1692.
WILLIAM PHIPS."

Mass. Archives, cvi., 372.

Edward Randolph, writing from the " Common Gaole" in Boston the 29th of May, 1689, says : " Five Ministers of Boston, vizt. Moode, Allen, Young, Mather, Willard and *Milborne, an Anabaptist Minister,* were in the Council Chamber on the eighteenth of Aprill when the Govern^r [Andros] and myselfe were brought out of the Fort before them, writeing orders, and were authors of some of their printed papers." *N. Y. Coll. MSS.,* iii., 582. And a letter of Colonel Bayard, from Albany, 23d September, 1689, speaks of Jacob Milborne as a "brother to *Milburn the Anabaptist preacher,*" etc. *Ib.,* 621. See also Bullivant's Diary in *Proc. M. H. S.,* March, 1878. " The Northend men, headed by Sir William Phips, *Milbourne* and Way, apply to the Deputies for the discharge of Turell and White in execution for a just debt," etc.   18 March, 1689-90.

a lawyer, but his obituary in the "Boston News Letter" of June, 1721, speaks of him as "having been for many years one of the chief lawyers of Boston."

And here I may remark in passing that notwithstanding the extreme sensitiveness of Massachusetts writers of history on this subject—if English law, English judges or English lawyers are to be taken as standards of comparison, I can see no necessity to apologize for those of Massachusetts in that day and generation. "SIMEON AND LEVI ARE BRETHREN; INSTRUMENTS OF CRUELY ARE IN THEIR HABITATIONS." *Gen.* 49 : 5.

The first conspicuous sign of recovery from this awful delusion and earliest public demonstration of the strong and certain reaction which had slowly set in, was the Fast of 1696-7. A proposition for a Fast and Convocation of Ministers had been made as early as October, 1692, but it did not receive the sanction of the Council.

[Mass. Archives,] xi., 70.

" WHEREAS it hath pleased the MOST HIGH out of Sovereign and holy will, in this Day of Tryall and Adversity, to Exercise his people with sore trouble and Affliction in divers Respects; more Especially in permitting the Grand Enemy of Mankind to prevaile so far, with great Rage, and Serpentine Subtilty; whereby severall persons have been Seduced, and drawn away into that horrid and most Detestable sin of Witchcraft; to the great vexation, and Amazeing affliction of many persons wch is Notoriously known beyond Expression; And That for the Due derserved punishment of the Nocent, clearing the Reputation, & persons of the Inocent, and by Divine Assistance in the use of meanes to prevent the farther progress and prevailence of those SATANICALL Delutions; a Speciall Comission hath been granted to Certaine Gentlemen of the Council, and thereby a Court Errected by those persons of known Integrity, faithfullness and (according to man) Sufficiency who have Strenuously Endeavored to Discharge their Duty to the utmost of their Power for the finding out and Exterpation of that Diabollicall Evill : so much prevaileing amongst us, But finding (Notwithstanding the Indefatigable Endeavors of those Worthy Gentlemen with others to Suppress that Crying Enormity) the most Astonishing Augmentation and Increase of the Number of Persons Accused, by those Afflicted : many of whom (according to the Judgment of Charity) being persons of good Conversation Godliness and honiesty; And on the Other hand severall persons have Come and Accused themselves before Authority, and by many Circumances, confessed themselves Guilty of that most abominable Wickedness; with divers Other Strang & Unaccountable Occurrances of this Nature through the Rage and malice of Sathan. greatly threatening the utter Ruine and Distruction of this poor Country; if the Lord in his Tender Mercy, doth not Wonderfully Appear for ye Salvation of his People : by Expelling those Dismall Clouds of Darkness, and Discovering the wiles of the Devil, and that mistry of Iniquity that doth so much abound; and by his Gracious guidance, and Divine assistance; Direct his people in the Right way, that those That are guilty may be found out, and brought to Condigne punishment, the Inocent may be Cleared, and our feares and troubles Removed.

"To wch End, it is humbly PROPOSED by the Representatives now Assembled, That a Generall Day of Humilliation may be Appointed, Sollemnly to Seek the LORD and to Implore his Ayd. That he would be graciously pleased to Shew unto his people What they Ought to doe at such a time as this; And that A Convocation of the Elders may be called who with the Honble Council and Other persons, (whom they in their wisdoms shall deem meet) may Seriously Consider the Premisses; and make Inspection into these Intricacies humbly Enquiring that they may Know the mind of God in this Difficult Case; That so if it be his Blessed Will, all dissatisfaction may be Removed, peace, love, and Unity may be increased and Continued amongst us, and that ye Gracious Presence of Our Blessed God may Remaine with us.

"Octob^r : 26 : 92 : This Bill read a first second & third time in ye house of Representatives & voted passed in ye Affirmative & Sent to his Excellency the Gouerno^r & Councill, for Consent.

WILLIAM BOND, *Speaker.*

"Endorsed.   Read once since returned by ye Committe.   Motion for a Convocation 1692."

Chief Justice Sewall's entry in his diary of this date throws some light on this Bill:

"Oct. 26, 1692.   A Bill is sent in about calling a Fast, and Convocation of Ministers, that may be led in the right way as to the Witchcrafts. The reason and mañer of doing it, is such, that the Court of Oyer and Terminer count themselves thereby dismissed.   29 Nos and 33 yeas to the Bill.   Capt. Bradstreet and Lieut. True, Wm. Huchins and several other interested persons there, in the affirmative."

Hutchinson tells us that:—"The winter of 1696 was as cold as had been known from the first arrival of the English; slays and loaded sleds passing great part of the time upon the ice from Boston as far as Nantasket.   Greater losses in the trade had never been known than what were met with in this year; nor was there, at any time after the first year, so great a scarcity of food; nor was grain ever at a higher price." *History of Mass.*, II., 104, note.

The province had long languished under a war with the French and Indians, by which the estates of the people were much exhausted and many led into captivity or slain.   Their trade had decayed and their population diminished by emigration to other colonies less exposed to the calamities of war and the burdens of taxation which it imposes. Information of all these disastrous events was the burden of letters to England towards the end of the year 1696.

Under these circumstances a Committee of Religion was chosen by the House of Representatives of Massachusetts in which some of the clergy of the neighborhood were joined with the deputies, who prepared a Declaration enumerating Sundry Evills to be confessed on a Publick Day of Humiliation therein proposed.   This is "the Declaration as drawn by the Deputies, with the assistance of the Ministers. but received a Non concurrence," referred to by Robert Calef in his "More Wonders," in his letter to the Ministers, Jan. 12, 1696.

The document is still extant, though unpublished, in the handwriting of Cotton Mather—and is eminently characteristic of the man and the times. I will read from it only the passage which refers directly to the Salem tragedies:

[From Mass. Archives, xi., 120.]

"Inasmuch as the Holy God, hath been, by Terrible and Various Dispensations of His Providence for many sevens of Years Together, most Evidently Testifying His Displeasure against us; and these Humbling Dispensations of Heaven have proceeded from One Degree of Calamity upon us to another, Wherein God hath vexed us with all Adversity, until at last the Symptoms of an Extreme Desolation Threaten us: A More than Ordinary *Humiliation* of this whole people, accompanied with fervent *Supplications*, and thorough *Reformations*, must bee acknowledged Necessary, to prepare us for o^r Deliverance, from o^r most unhappy circumstances.

"Tis to bee Confessed, and it hath been often Confessed, That the people of this land in a long Increasing *Apostasy* from that Religious Disposition, that signalized the first planting of these Colonies, and from y^r very *Errand unto this wilderness*, have with multiplied provocations to the Almighty, *sinned exceedingly*.

"The Spirit of *This World* hath brought almost an Epidemicall Death upon y^r spirit of serious, and powerful Religion.

"The Glorious *Gospel* of the Lord Jesus Christ, here enjoy'd with much plenty as well as purity, hath not been Thankfully, and Fruitfully, Entertained, by those who have been Blessed with the *Joyful Sound*.

"The *Covenant of Grace*, recognized in o^r Churches hath been by multitudes not submitted unto; and of them that have made a *profession* of *submission* unto it, very many have not walked according to the sacred obligations thereby laid upon them.

"A Flood of *Excessive Drinking*, wth Incentives thereto hath begun to overwhelm Good Order, in some Townes & Even to Drown civilitie itself.

"Some *English*, by selling of *Strong Drink* unto *Indians*, have not only prejudiced the Designs of Christianitie, but also been the faulty and Bloody occasions of *Death* among them.

"The most unreasonable Impieties of Rash and vain *Swearing*, with Hellish *Cursing*, on the mouths of some, have rendered them *Guilty Sinners.*

"A Vanity in Apparrel, hath been affected by many, whose *Glory hath bin their Shame.*

"The *Lords-Day*, hath been disturbed, with so many profanations, that wee may not wonder, if the land see *no Rest.*

"The Woful Decay of all Good *Family Discipline* hath opened the Flood-gates for evils Innumerable, & almost Irremediable.

"*Wicked* SORCERIES *have been practised in the land; and, in the late inexplicable storms from the Invisible world thereby brought upon us, wee were left, by the Just Hand of Heaven unto those Errors whereby Great Hardships were brought upon Innocent persons, and (wee feare) Guilt incurr'd, which wee have all cause to Bewayl, with much confusion of o^r Face before the Lord.*

"It is commonly and credibly Reported, That some, who have belonged unto this country, have committed very Detestable *Pyracies* in other parts of this world.

"The Sins of Uncleanness in many, & y^r Grossest Instances, have *Defiled* the land.

"The Joy of Harvest hath too much forgotten y^r Glad Service of God, when Hee hath given us, an *Abundance of all Things.*

" Much *Fraud* hath been used in the Dealings of many, and mutual and multiplied *Oppressions*, have made a cry.

"*Magistrates, Ministers,* and others that have served the publick have been great Sufferers by their services, and mett with Unrighteous Discouragements.[1]

[Y' Irreverence to Superiors in age & authority & disobedience to parents is too frequent among us.   Parents not keeping up their authority in their families, Neglects in the Administration of Justice impartially and duly in Courts of Justice is too Obvious in this Land. Voted, 10th Dec'.][2]

"*Falsehood* and *Slander*, hath been continually carrying of *Darts* thro' y' Land.

"And the successive and Amazing Judgments of God, which have come upon us for such things as these, have not Reclaimed us, but wee have gone on still in o' Iniquities.

" For these Causes this whole people is Admonished now to Humble themselves before the Lord with Repeted Acts of Repentance; and particularly, To this purpose, It is *Ordered*, That Thursday   be kept as a Day of *HUMILIATION*, by prayer with *FASTING*, before the God of Heaven, in the several Congregations throughout this province; and all Servile labor on y' Day is hereby Inhibited : That so wee may obtain, thro' the Blood of the Lord *JESUS CHRIST*, the Pardon, both of these Iniquities and of whatever other *secret sins the Lord may have sett in the Light of His Countenance.*   And, that wee may Implore y' Effusions of y' Spirit of Grace from on High, upon all ranks of men, and especially upon the Rising Generation, whereby o' Turn to God, y' Fire of whose wrath is dreadfully consuming o' young men, may bee accomplished.

"And it is hereby further signified, That it is hoped, the pastors of the churches, will, in their several charges, by private as well as public Applications, Endeavour to prevent all *Growth of Sin*, as they may discern it, in their Vicinities : and y' churches join with their pastors in sharpening the *Ecclesiastical Discipline* against the *Scandals* that may arise among them.

"And all *Civil Officers* are hereby likewise called upon Vigorously to pursue y' execution of y' lawes, from Time to Time, Enacted against all Immoralities; and in their several places, as well to make *Diligent Enquiries* and *Impartial presentments* of all offences against y' said lawes as to *Dispense Justice equally, for no cause forbearing to do their office,* according to the *Oath of God*, w'' is upon them, and unto this end, frequently to have their consultations in their several precincts, *what may bee done by them to suppress any common evils.*

"Finally, All persons are hereby advised seriously to pursue the Designs of a general Conversion unto God, as y' best expedient for y' encouragement of o' Hopes, That Hee who hath shown us great & sore Troubles may Revive us; and not leave us to perish in the convulsions which are now shaking a miserable World.

"In the House of Representatives.   Read 10th December. 1696—a first and second time.   Voted, and sent up for Concurrance.

PENN TOWNSEND *Speaker.*

" Voted.   That the aforesaid Declaration be published in the respec-

---

[1]Compare Calef: *More Wonders of the Invisible World*, p. 92.

[2]This passage in brackets was the " Streamer," etc. referred to by Chief Justice Sewall in his Diary, as having been added to the original " Bill "—not the passage quoted in *Sewall Papers*, I., 439 note.

tive Congregations within the province by the Ministers therein, and further That a proclamation issue from this Court requiring all Justices Constables Grand jury men Tythingmen, and all other civil officers to be faithful in the Execution of their respective offices; And That the Laws setting forth the dutys of the Respective officers afores⁴ be collected and inserted in the body of s⁴ proclamation. And that five hundred of s⁴ Laws and of the s⁴ Declarations be printed.

PENN TOWNSEND *Speaker.*

Dec*. 11. 1696.   Read in Council and Voted a non-concurrance.

Iˢᵃ ADDINGTON *Sec'ry.*

This Bill, as it was called, on being sent to the Council, met with a prompt negative—the latter body decidedly resenting the movement by the House as an invasion of their prerogative. But after a sharp controversy between the two houses—another document much shorter, originating with the Council, and drawn up by Samuel Sewall, who had been one of the Judges in the Witch Trials—was duly passed—in which a solemn Fast was appointed for the 14th January, 1697.[1]

This paper has been printed and is doubtless familiar to you all. I will not read it here—but I will not hesitate to repeat my humble tribute of admiration for the character of its author. It was at this Fast that Chief Justice Sewall made his public confession of fault and repentance for his part in that bloody Assize of Witches at Salem—a signal example of the genuine old Puritan—a brilliant instance of that magnanimity which submits to just reproof without resentment, and that higher grace which is at once the sign and the blessing of repentance—that real Christian courage which could humiliate itself by confession.

Samuel Sewall's voluntary confession before God and men of his sin in that thing, ought to be cherished as one of the most precious memorials of the history of Massachusetts. That solemn sad figure, handing the confession to his minister "as he passed by" in the meeting-house, "and standing up at the reading of it, and bowing when finished; in the afternoon" of that winter's day, is to me personally more beautiful and glorious than all the heroes of the Magnalia.

[Mass. Archives, XI., 122.]

"By the Honᵇˡʳ the Lᵗ. Govʳ. Council & Assembly of his Majᵗʸˢ Province of yᵉ Massachusetts Bay in General Court Assembled.

---

[1]Dec. 11. 1696. A Declaration containing Several Articles of Confession and Appointment of a Day of Publick Fast sent up from the House of Representatives with their vote thereon, and that a Proclamation be issued to excite officers to their duty, was read, and Voted in the negative.

A Bill for appointing a Public Fast upon Thursday the 14th of January next, was Drawn up and voted and sent down. *Council Records,* p. 499.

Whereas the Anger of God is not yet turned away, but his Hand is still stretched out against his people, in manifold Judgments; particularly in drawing out to such a length the Troubles of Europe, by a perplexing War. And more especially, respecting ourselves in this Province, in that God is pleased still, to go on in diminishing our Substance, cutting short our Harvest; blasting our most promising Undertakings; more ways than one, Unsettling of us; and by his more immediate Hand, snatching away many out of our Embraces by suddain & violent deaths; even at this time, when the Sword is devouring so many; both at home and abroad; and that after many Days of publick and Solemn addressing of Him. And althô, considering the many sins prevailing in the midst of us, we cannot but wonder at the Patience and Mercy moderating these REBUKES; yet we canot but also fear, that there's something still wanting to accompany our Suplications. And doubtless, there are some particular Sins, which God is angry with our Israel for, that have not been duely seen and resented by us, about which God expects to be sought, if ever He turn again our Captivity.

"Wherefore its comand^d & Apoi't^d that Thursday the Fourteenth of January next be observed as a Day of Prayer with Fasting throughout this Province; strictly forbidding all Servile Labour thereon. That so all God's people may offer up fervent Supplications unto him for y^r preservation and prosperity of his Maj^ty Royal person and Governm^t and success to attend his Affaires both at home & abroad That all Iniquity may be taken away, which hath stirred God's holy Jealousie against this Land; that he would shew us what we know not, and help us wherein we have done amiss, to doe so no more: And especially, that whatever Mistakes, on either hand, have been fallen into, either by the body of this People, or any Orders of Men, referring to the late Tragedie raised amongst us by Satan and his Instruments, through the awfull Judgment of God; He would humble us therefore, and pardon all the Errors of his Servants and People that desire to Love his Name, and be attoned to His Land. That he would remove the Rod of the Wicked from off the Lot of the Righteous; That He Would bring the American Heathen, and cause them to hear and obey his voice.

Dec. 11° 1696.   Voted in Council and sent down for Concurrance.

Is^a. ADDINGTON, *Sec'ry.*

Decemb^r 17th 1696.   Voted a Concurrance,

PENN TOWNSEND, *Speaker.*

I Consent.

W^m. STOUGHTON.

Endorsed: Bill for a Fast Vot^d Decr 11° 1696.

When this Bill was first sent down to the House, on the 11th December, 1696, a non-concurrence was promptly voted. The Diary of Chief Justice Sewall throws some light upon the details of the business, in which he says: "I doe not know that ever I saw the Council run upon with such a height of Rage before." *Sewall Papers,* I., 441. The following document belongs to this controversy between the two houses to which allusion has been made.

'[Mass. Archives, XI., 122.]

Decr 1696, In the House of Representatives. *Resolved,* "That ye freedom of speech to debate, so to resolve & vote upon a free debate of any matters for the publick good of the Province without Consulting, advising or asking direction from the Honble Board Above is the Undoubted Right & Priviledge of this House.

Voted, That seeing the Minits of Council are from time to time to be laid before his Majesty and Council at home, for the preventing any Inconveniency to the Honble Board above, This house shall not be Unwilling (always saving the priviledge of this House) to propose and concert by Message such things as shall be thought necessary in Prudence by this house, before they are brought to a vote.

That in ye late choice of a Comittee of Religion by this house ye receiving their Report in ye Bill conteining an Enumeration of Sundry Evills to be Confessed on a Publick day of humiliation therein pposed to be ordered & appointed, & voting said Bill in this house and sending it up to ye Honble Council for their concurr^. This House *Protests,* That these things were not transacted wth any designe to derogate from ye Preheminence of that hon^rble Board, or to cast any disrespect thereon.

That in voting a non-concurrence to ye Bill for a fast sent down to this house from ye Council, This house did not out of any hum^r of Vyeing wth that hon^ble Board vote a non-concurrance.

Proposed. That Both Bills for a fast, upon wch the late debates have been, may be comited to ye Reverend Elders of this Town, and that out of both they be desired to draw a Bill for a fast and lay the same before the Court.

Decemb^r : 15th 1696.   Read a first and Second time.

(Endorsed)   Resolve Vote, &^r.

A careful scrutiny of the original manuscript of the bill adopted revealed its history.   When first sent down from the Council, it was immediately underwritten "Decemb^r 11th Voted a Non Concurrance. Penn Townsend, *Speaker*."   After the matter was composed, the "11th" was altered to "17th" and the "Non" stricken out.

I have still one more error to point out in the history of Witchcraft in Massachusetts.   The statement has been constantly repeated, hitherto without correction, that some years after these melancholy trials, the General Court of Massachusetts passed an act reversing "the several convictions, judgments and attainders against the persons executed and several who were condemned, but not executed."   An act of this sort has actually been printed and has found place and authority among recognized materials of history : but no such act ever became a law.[1]   A

---

[1] The act referred to has not only been quoted as authority (UPHAM, II., 465, 479), but published at large in the *Records of Salem Witchcraft,* vol. ii., pp. 216–18. Mr. CHANDLER says : "a law was made reversing the attainders of those convicted, and making a grant for and in consideration of the losses sustained." *Am. Crim. Trials,* i., 135. Mr. POOLE says : "October 17, 1711, the General Court passed an act reversing 'the several convictions, judgments and attainders against the' persons executed, and several who were condemned but not executed, and declaring that [them] to be null and void." *Witchcraft Delusion,* etc. page 43, note 57, and again, in *Memorial History of*

private act of a similar character *was* passed in 1703, with reference to three of the surviving sufferers; and a few years later—sundry appropriations were made from the public treasury in aid of families who had been ruined by this storm; but none were adequate to the occasion—all were scanty and insufficient: and although the subject was revived from time to time during the next half-century, nothing else was done.[1]

It has not been my purpose, in the small collection of historical notes which I have thus had the honor to submit to you, to repeat the often told story of the Salem Witchcraft, or to recall any of the gloomy scenes of suspicion, persecution, prosecution, imprisonment, torture and death: which still glare out from the history of that period like flames from the pit. The main facts are familiar and they will never be forgotten.

Nothing could be more dramatic, full of interest, marked characters and striking situations. Strong as the impression of those scenes must have been on those who lived at the time, no events of American Colonial History have more earnestly engaged the attention of men in later years: and while the events themselves can hardly be said to have been viewed in opposite lights, the characters of those who were actors in them have furnished themes of lasting controversy.

Permit me to introduce here an illustration of this—in extracts from two writers both eminent and both belonging to Massachusetts.

"Next to the fugitives whom Moses led out of Egypt, the little shipload of outcasts who landed at Plymouth two centuries and a half ago are destined to influence the future of the world." This statement is the key-note of a comparatively recent and sympathetic essay on "New England two Centuries ago," by James Russell Lowell. I quote it here simply as an introduction to the same writer's summary of affairs in the latter part of the seventeenth century, when the Witchcraft Delusions of that generation culminated in the Salem tragedies. Mr. LOWELL says: "Till 1660 the Colony was ruled and mostly inhabited by Englishmen closely connected with the party dominant in the mother country, and with their minds broadened by having to deal with questions of state and European policy. After that time they sank rapidly into provincials, narrow in thought, in culture, in creed. Such a pedantic portent as Cotton Mather, would have been impossible in the first generation; he was the natural growth of the third,—the manifest judg-

---

Boston, ii., 172: "Twenty years afterwards, when the General Court reversed the attainders of the persons executed in 1692," etc. Mr. PALFREY says: "Twenty years after, the General Court annulled the convictions and attainders, etc." *Hist. N. E.*, iv., 117. And in another place: "All the attainders, twenty-two in number, were reversed, etc." Mr. SIBLEY says: "The General Court, 17 October, 1710, passed an act that 'the several convictions, judgments and attainders be, and hereby are, reversed and declared to be null and void.'" *Harv. Grad.*, ii., 433. (Printed Dec. 17, 1880, and published since 30 May, 1881.) Other eminent authorities might be cited, but perhaps these will suffice.

[1] See Appendix—*post*.

ment of God on a generation who thought "Words a saving substitute for Things."

From this picture of the younger Mather, turn to that of the elder, drawn by another hand, but not less true to the traditions in which it was trained.

Prof. ENOCH POND, in the "Lives of the Chief Fathers of New England," writing of the Father of Cotton Mather, says:

"Among the stars in the right hand of the great Head of the Church, which glittered upon the Golden Candlesticks of primitive New England, none have shone with a brighter and more attractive lustre than Increase Mather."

These views of the personal character of the Mathers, to whom history has assigned so conspicuous a place in the picture of Witchcraft in Massachusetts, furnish an illustration of the differences which still pervade the discussions of scholars concerning the period of which I have spoken.

The extreme facility of belief that was displayed by these eminent men even in matters that were not deemed supernatural, can only be realized by those who have an intimate acquaintance with their works.[1] Of this, as well the general historical question whether the tendencies of the age, the general spiritual movement and agitation of opinion in Massachusetts, had produced an exceptional amount of credulity during the half century or more before the occurrences at Salem in 1692—it is no part of my present purpose to enter into discussion.

Out of differences such as those to which I have alluded and the collision of critical judgments respecting men and events, the truth of history is ultimately to be developed.

But as it is the essence of history to be true, the judicious student of its records will always be justified in every faithful attempt to correct errors, and to apply the strict principles of historical criticism to every doubtful passage. Doubtless there may be some to whose minds (as Lord Bacon happily expressed it) "the mixture of a lie doth ever add pleasure." "It is not only the difficulty and labour which men take in finding out of truth; nor again that when it is found, it imposeth upon men's thoughts, that doth bring lies in favour; but a naturall, though corrupt love of the lie itself." But such as these do not belong to the School of History in our day. "There is nothing more modern than the critical spirit which dwells upon the difference between the minds of

---

[1] Both the Mathers were ambitious of distinction as authorities on the subject of witchcraft, and proud of the recognition of Baxter and others. See the letter of Cradock to Increase Mather in the postcript to *Cases of Conscience*, London: 1690. I have myself read in the handwriting of Cotton Mather his own record of an interview with an angel of God. It was written in Latin in one of his Diaries with the following remarkable marginal note, giving the reason for his veiling it in the obscurity of a learned language—"*Hæc scribo Latiné, ne chara mea conjux, has chartas aliquando inspiciens, intelligat*"!

men in one age and another; which endeavours to make each age its own interpreter, and judge what it did or produced by a relative standard."

Many are the errors produced by the want of this historical feeling and leading to an entire misunderstanding of the nature of events. We may be keenly sensible of the strange contrasts in human nature, as we endeavor to scrutinize the motives of the chief actors, the natural leaders of the people and councillors of the government; and it is easy for us who read the history of that day in the light of those which have followed it, to perceive that these men erred: but we should hesitate before judging the actors of 1692 as we would judge our contemporaries.

19

The Case of Giles Cory

By DAVID C. BROWN*

THE case of Giles Corey, who was pressed to death in Salem in 1692, is one of the most intriguing cases of the Salem witchcraft trials. It is also one of the most remarkable episodes in the entire history of American jurisprudence, yet historians since the nineteenth century have consistently distorted the facts of his case. The prevailing view holds that he resolutely refused to plead to the indictments brought against him, and endured the *peine forte et dure* rather than risk the forfeiture of his estate that would have resulted from his conviction.[1] That view has prevailed in no small part because historians have failed to understand the legal complexities that bear on Corey's case. It is totally incorrect.

This article will attempt to set the record straight. It will conclusively show first, that Giles Corey pleaded "not guilty" to his indictment, but was pressed to death because he would not "put himself on the country," that is, submit to trial by jury; second, that whatever Corey's motive for

---

*David C. Brown of Drexel Hill, Pennsylvania, is the author of a recently published book on the Salem witchcraft phenomena titled *A Guide to the Salem Witchcraft Hysteria of 1692*.

1. The major histories of the Salem witchcraft give inaccurate accounts of why Giles Corey was pressed to death. Charles W. Upham, in his *Salem Witchcraft*, 2 vols. (Boston: Wiggins and Lunt, 1867; reprint ed., New York: Frederick Ungar, 1978), 2:337, states that Corey "did not plead 'Guilty,' or 'Not guilty,' but stood mute" because he feared that his conviction "might invalidate all attempts of his to convey his property." Marion Starkey, in *The Devil in Massachusetts* (New York: Alfred Knopf, 1949; reprint ed., Garden City, N.Y.: Anchor Books, Doubleday & Company, Inc., 1969), 206, adds drama but no greater accuracy to the case. Corey, she notes, "stood speechless before the judges. He would not plead" because "without conviction his property could not be confiscated." Recent scholarship has only continued the error. Boyer and Nissenbaum in *Salem Possessed* (Cambridge, Mass.: Harvard University Press, 1974), 8, state that Corey "stood mute before the authorities, his refusal to plead to the charges constituting an implicit denial of the court's right to try him." Only Chadwick Hansen, in *Witchcraft at Salem* (New York: George Braziller, 1969), 153–54, comes close to giving a true account of what happened to Giles Corey in 1692. But his account is based primarily on secondary sources and indicates that he did not understand the legal basis of Corey's case.

282

"standing mute," fear of forfeiture was not a part of it because forfeiture of one's estate upon conviction for witchcraft was illegal both in Massachusetts and in England; and third, that the *peine forte et dure*, to which Corey was subjected in 1692, was not only illegal in Massachusetts, but was only one of a number of illegal acts performed by the Massachusetts authorities during the Salem witchcraft trials.

Giles Corey was eighty-one years old in 1692 and lived on a farm of over one hundred acres located off what is now Pine Street in West Peabody.[2] His wife, Martha, had been arrested, examined, and imprisoned on suspicion of witchcraft in March 1692. In April it was Giles's turn. On 18 April, a warrant was sworn out for his arrest together with the arrests of Mary Warren, Abigail Hobbs, and Bridget Bishop:

> for high Suspition of Sundry acts of Witchcraft donne or Committed by them, upon the Bodys of: Ann putnam. Marcy Lewis, and Abig'l Williams and Mary Walcot and Eliz. Hubert—of Salem village—whereby great hurt and damage hath benne donne to the Bodys of Said persons above named.[3]

The following day, Corey was examined by John Hathorne and Jonathan Corwin in Salem Village. The girls accused him of grievously afflicting them; but Corey maintained his innocence. He protested that "I never had no hand in [witchcraft], in my life."[4] After his examination he was imprisoned first in Salem and later in Ipswich gaol awaiting trial.

While in prison in Ipswich, Corey drew up a deed conveying his property to two of his sons-in-law, William Cleeves of Beverly and John Moulton of Salem. In it Corey wrote that he lay "under great trouble and affliction" and knew "not how soon I may depart this life."[5] He had good reason to be afraid. Between June and August 1692,

---

2. John A. Wells, *The Peabody Story: Events in Peabody's History 1626–1972* (Salem, Mass.: Essex Institute, 1972), facing 183.

3. Quoted from the warrant for Corey's arrest, from Paul Boyer and Stephen Nissenbaum, eds., *The Salem Witchcraft Papers*, 3 vols. (New York: Da Capo Press, 1977), 1:239 (hereafter cited as *Witchcraft Papers*).

4. From the examination of Giles Corey, appended to the 1823 Salem edition of Robert Calef's *More Wonders of the Invisible World* (Salem, Mass.: printed for Cushing and Appleton, 1823).

5. From Giles Corey's will, as excerpted in Upham, *Salem Witchcraft* 2:336.

the infamous Court of Oyer and Terminer[6] sat three separate times in Salem. At these sittings, twelve people were tried for witchcraft and condemned, of which all save one, Elizabeth Proctor, had been executed.

On 8 June 1692, the first General Court under the new charter met in Boston. Seven days later they passed an act to continue all the laws of the former governments of Massachusetts Bay and New Plymouth that were neither repugnant to the laws of England nor contrary to the provisions of the new charter:

> That all the local laws respectively ordered and made by the late governour and company of the Massachusetts Bay and the late government of New Plymouth, being not repugnant to the laws of England nor inconsistent with the present constitution and settlement by their majesties' royal charter, do remain and continue in full force in the respective places for which they were made and used until the tenth day of November next . . . .[7]

6. Even by its contemporaries, the 1692 Court of Oyer and Terminer was considered a *special* Court of Oyer and Terminer. Calef, in his *More Wonders of the Invisible World* (as excerpted in George L. Burr, ed., *Narratives of the Witchcraft Cases: 1648–1706* [New York: Charles Scribner's Sons, 1914; reprint ed., New York: Barnes & Noble, 1975], 289–393), writes that on 2 June "special Commission of Oyer and Terminer" was issued (355) and later, at the court's dissolution, records that "the Special Commission of Oyer and Terminer comes to a period" (373). However, under English law, commissions of Oyer and Terminer could be either general or special: "general when they were issued to commissioners whose duty it was to hear and determine all matters of a criminal nature within certain local limits, special when the commission was confined to particular cases." (From Sir James Stephen, *A History of the Criminal Law of England*, 3 vols. [London: MacMillan & Co., 1883], 1:106). The Salem Court of Oyer and Terminer, as originally constituted on 27 May 1692, was commissioned "To enquire of hear and determine for this time, . . . *all and all manner of crimes and offences* [author's italics] had, made, done or perpetrated within the counties of Suffolk, Essex, Middlesex, and of either of them." (As quoted by Abner C. Goodell, "Trials of the Witches in Massachusetts," *Proceedings of the Massachusetts Historical Society*, 1st ser., 20 [June 1883]: 324). Moreover, Justice Samuel Sewall wrote in his diary on 10 October 1692: "The Court of Oyer and Terminer is opened at Boston to trie a French Malatta for shooting dead an English youth." (See Samuel Sewall, *The Diary of Samuel Sewall*, ed. M. Halsey Thomas, 2 vols. [New York: Farrar, Straus, and Giroux, 1973], 1:298). The court's jurisdiction was thus not confined to cases of witchcraft. Legally, therefore, the witchcraft court should be considered a general court and not a special court of Oyer and Terminer.

7. Commonwealth of Massachusetts, *The Acts and Resolves, Public and Private, of the Province of the Massachusetts Bay* (Boston: Wright & Potter, 1874), vol. 1, 27 (hereafter cited as *Acts of the Province*).

In reaffirming the old Massachusetts laws, this act rejuvenated not only the colony's earlier statutes against witchcraft, but also confirmed its laws prohibiting both forfeiture and the use of barbarous punishments on criminal offenders. It therefore has great relevance to the case of Giles Corey.

The Court of Oyer and Terminer sat by adjournment in Salem on 9 September 1692 and tried six women for witchcraft. On the same day the jury of inquest[8] heard evidence against Giles Corey. The testimony centered primarily on the horrible torments Corey's spectral shape had inflicted on the afflicted girls on the day of his examination. Elizabeth Woodwell and Mary Walcott testified for good measure that Corey's apparition had attended the lecture day church service in Salem prior to Bridget Bishop's execution in June. His specter, they said, had come "in & sat in the middlemost seat: of the mens seats: by the post."[9] Based on such testimony, Giles Corey was indicted.

Sometime after 9 September (the records do not indicate exactly when), Corey was brought to trial before the petty jury of the Court of Oyer and Terminer. According to Robert Calef, who gives the most detailed account of the event:

> Giles Cory pleaded not Guilty to his Indictment, but would not put himself upon Tryal by the Jury (they having cleared none upon Tryal) and knowing there would be the same Witnesses against him, rather chose to undergo what Death they would put him to.[10]

Other contemporaries give the story somewhat differently. Nicholas Noyes and Cotton Mather wrote that Corey refused to plead; whereas Thomas Brattle and Samuel Sewall both wrote that Corey stood "mute"

---

8. In English law, the jury of inquest (or grand jury) brought the indictment against the defendant, whereas the trial itself occurred before a petit jury, also known as the jury of trial. The commissions given to courts of Oyer and Terminer instructed the commissioners "to enquire of hear and determine." The inquiry was held by means of the jury of inquest while the charge to "hear and determine" refers to the actual trial before the petit jury. (See Sir William Blackstone, *Commentaries on the Laws of England, in Four Books*, ed. William D. Lewis, 4 vols. (Philadelphia: Rees Welsh & Co., 1897), 4:270 (hereafter cited as Blackstone, *Commentaries*; the page numbers refer to those of the original).

9. Boyer and Nissenbaum, eds., *Witchcraft Papers* 1:243.

10. Calef, as excerpted in Burr. *Narratives of the Witchcraft Cases*, 367.

before the court.[11] The weight of available evidence supports Calef's account. Both Sewall's and Brattle's accounts, as we will see, are entirely compatible with Calef's version; and the accounts given by Noyes and Mather are sketchy and most likely represent a simplification of what actually occurred.

Legal procedures have changed considerably since the seventeenth century. Under seventeenth-century English law, a defendant could not be tried for any crime unless he pleaded to his indictment,[12] and if he pleaded "not guilty," submitted himself to trial by the petit jury. After pleading "not guilty," the court would ask the defendant, "Culprit, how will you be tried?" to which he was required to answer "By God and my country." The phrase "by God and my country" was sacrosanct, and had to be said in its entirety—answering either "by God" or "by my country" alone did not suffice—before the defendant could be tried.[13] Saying this phrase was known legally as "putting oneself on the country"; and it is this phrase that Giles Corey refused to say.

The history of the phrase "by God and my country," is itself very interesting. In the early middle ages, English trials were based on the ordeal, in which the defendant was required to perform a miraculous feat to prove his innocence. This was grounded in the belief that God would always intervene to acquit an innocent man and grant him the power to perform the required feat. Trial by a jury of one's peers came later and was, at first, an exceptional privilege; so exceptional, in fact, that initially the defendant paid money to the king in order to exercise it. At some point in the history of English law, the defendant no doubt answered the question "Culprit, how will you be tried?" by saying "by God" if he intended to undergo the ordeal or "by my country" if he chose a trial by jury. After 1215, when the ordeal was abolished, its

11. Mather's and Brattle's remarks are to be found in Burr, *Narratives of the Witchcraft Cases*, 250 and 185 respectively. Noyes's comment is recorded in the records of the First Church in Salem for 18 September 1692 and can be found quoted in Upham, *Salem Witchcraft* 2:344. Sewall's remark is recorded in his diary for 19 September 1692 (Sewall, Diary 1:295).

12. A defendant could plead not guilty, guilty, *autrefois acquit*, or *autrefois convict*. The last two pleas were used by defendants maintaining that they had previously been tried and either acquitted or convicted for the same offense with which they now were charged (see Stephen, *A History of the Criminal Law of England* 1:297).

13. The history of "putting oneself on the country" is presented in Stephen, *A History of the Criminal Law of England* 1:297–301.

vestiges nevertheless persisted in the inclusive phrase "by God and my country." And because defendants had historically requested jury trial, they could not be tried until they requested it from the authorities by "putting themselves on the country."

There is no doubt that the requirement that the defendant "put himself on the country" was strictly adhered to by the Court of Oyer and Terminer in Salem in 1692. Although the records of the proceedings of that infamous court have disappeared, accessory documents shed light on the manner in which its victims placed themselves on trial. Bridget Bishop's death warrant, for example, which was signed by Chief Justice William Stoughton himself on 8 June, states that she "pleaded not guilty and for Tryall thereof put her selfe upon God and her Country."[14] Similar words are to be found in the death warrant for the five women hanged on 19 July[15] and in the records of the witchcraft cases tried before the Superior Court of Judicature in 1693.[16]

Giles Corey's refusal to "put himself on the country" was known as "standing mute" in the seventeenth century. According to Blackstone:

> . . . a prisoner is said to stand mute when, being arraigned for treason or felony, he either, 1. Makes no answer at all; 2. Answers foreign to the purpose, or with such matter as is not allowable; and will not answer otherwise; or, 3. Upon having pleaded not guilty refuses to put himself upon the country.[17]

Clearly, Corey "stood mute" because he violated Blackstone's third tenet. But modern historians, who apparently have been unable to reconcile the fact that Corey pleaded "Not guilty" and still "stood mute," have invented the fiction that Corey remained absolutely silent when he was brought to trial. Note that, in light of Blackstone's definition, Brattle's and Sewall's statements that Corey "stood mute" agree entirely with Calef's account.

Had Corey, indeed, refused to answer to his indictment, as one might infer from the statements of Mather and Noyes, one would hope that documentary proof might have survived to the present day. Unlike cases in which the defendant refused to "put himself on the country,"

14. Boyer and Nissenbaum, eds., *Witchcraft Papers* 1:109.
15. Boyer and Nissenbaum, eds., *Witchcraft Papers* 2:378.
16. Boyer and Nissenbaum, eds., *Witchcraft Papers* 3:903–44.
17. Blackstone, *Commentaries* 4:324.

when a prisoner refused to answer his indictment, the court would im-
panel a jury to determine if the prisoner "stood mute" of malice or
ex visitatione Dei (by the visitation of God], that is, that God had intervened and struck the prisoner dumb. If the jury decided that the prisoner
"stood mute" of malice, he was treated like the prisoner who refused to
"put himself on the country." If the prisoner was instead found to
"stand mute" *ex visitatione Dei*, his trial would proceed as if he had
pleaded "not guilty." In Giles Corey's case, there is not one scrap of
evidence to suggest that any jury was impaneled to determine why he
"stood mute." The reason is obvious: Corey answered his indictment
but refused to "put himself on the country."

The nature of the offense with which the defendant was charged
determined how the court dealt with prisoners who either "stood mute"
of malice or refused to "put themselves on the country." If the prisoner
was charged with high treason, petty larceny, or a misdemeanor, standing mute was equivalent to conviction. But in cases of petty treason[18]
or felony (and under English law, witchcraft was considered a felony),
the ancient laws of England did not equate standing mute with conviction; and since the defendant could not be tried if he "stood mute" of
malice or refused to "put himself on the country," these prisoners instead received the dread sentence of the *peine forte et dure*.[19]

Before this sentence was passed, however, "the prisoner had not only
trina admonitio,[20] but also a respite of a few hours, and the sentence was
distinctly read to him, that he might know his danger."[21] If he persisted
in standing mute after these warnings, however, the sentence was pronounced. According to Blackstone, the prisoner was then:

> ... remanded to the prison from whence he came, and put into a
> low, dark chamber, and thereby laid on his back on the bare
> floor, naked, unless where decency forbids; that there be placed
> upon his body as great a weight of iron as he could bear, and
> more; that he have no sustenance, save only, on the first day,
> three morsels of the worst bread; and, on the second day, three
> draughts of standing water, that should be nearest to the prison-

18. Petty treason included crimes such as a wife bewitching her husband to death or a
servant murdering his master.
19. Meaning literally, "hard and severe punishment."
20. "A third warning."
21. Blackstone, *Commentaries* 4:325.

door; and in this situation this should be alternately his daily diet
till he died, or (as anciently the judgment ran) *till he answered.*[22]

Barrington adds that, on occasion, a sharp stone was placed beneath the
victim's back, and that the prisoner would often be staked to the
ground with ropes extending his limbs "as far as they could be stretched."[23]

The history of the *peine forte et dure* provides another example of the
evolution of English law. Originally, the law provided that prisoners
charged with felony or petty treason who "stood mute" were to be
subjected to *prisone forte et dure*[24] which consisted of "a very strait confinement in prison, with hardly any degree of sustenance."[25] The prisoner was thus confined until he either pleaded (or, depending on the
circumstances, "put himself on the country") or died. The English laws
do not mention pressing at all, initially. Rather it appears that pressing
was a later innovation. The itinerant justices of Eyre and justices of gaol-
delivery, who traveled around the country and tried the cases brought
before them in each town, could afford to remain in each town for only
a few days. A prisoner who "stood mute," however, could endure the
prisone forte et dure for weeks and delay the justices' work indetermi-
nately. So pressing was gradually introduced between the statutes of 31
Edw. III. and 8 Hen. IV., at which point it finally became law. No
prisoner could survive the *peine forte et dure* for days on end; and the
justices could again go about their work on schedule.

Felonies, under seventeenth-century English law, were crimes punishable with death, with corruption of blood, with forfeiture of goods,
and with the escheat of the criminal's lands to his superior lord. This
definition derived from the feudal principle that vassals held their estates
of a superior lord provided that they fulfilled certain feudal conditions.
Commission of a felony violated those conditions and abrogated the
felon's right to his land; hence it reverted back into the possession of his
superior lord. The culprit's goods were likewise forfeited. Conviction
for felony also made the felon's blood "attainted or corrupted. He could
not own any property himself, nor could any heir born before or after

22. Blackstone, *Commentaries* 4:327.
23. Daines Barrington, *Observations Upon the Statutes, Chiefly the More Ancient, From Magna Charta to the Twenty-first of James the First*, Ch. 27., 2d ed. (London: Bowyer and Nichols, 1766), 64.
24. "Hard and severe imprisonment."
25. Blackstone, *Commentaries* 4:328.

the felony claim through him."[26] A felon was thus stripped of his possessions and could not pass them on to his descendants.

By "standing mute," however, prisoners indicted for felony or petty treason could not be tried and so could escape conviction, the corruption of their blood, and the forfeiture of their lands, although by law their goods were still forfeited. For "standing mute" these defendants were sentenced to the *peine forte et dure* and died a horrible death but retained the right to bequeath their lands to their heirs. Almost every historian of the Salem witchcraft has incorrectly cited this fear of forfeiture as Corey's chief motive for "standing mute." Although witchcraft was a felony, it was a special felony, and the laws of both England and Massachusetts in 1692 prohibited the forfeiture of the criminal's estate after conviction for witchcraft.

No one will ever know exactly what happened to Giles Corey in September 1692. It appears that the court gave him the required three warnings, for in a letter written by Thomas Putnam to Samuel Sewall on 19 September, Putnam wrote that Corey was "often before the Court."[27] If the English laws were strictly followed, after the sentence was passed, Corey would have been taken to the Salem gaol and pressed there. Tradition has it, however, that he was executed in an open field near the gaol and that, seeking to hasten his death, he pleaded for "more weight" from the authorities. Calef describes his last moments: "In pressing his Tongue being prest out of his Mouth, the Sheriff with his Cane forced it in again, when he was dying."[28]

No one is even sure how long Corey was subjected to the *peine forte et dure*. Calef wrote that Corey was pressed to death on 16 September; but Judge Sewall, under his diary entry for 19 September 1692, has written:

> About noon, at Salem, Giles Corey was press'd to death for standing Mute; much pains was used with him two days, one after another, by the Court and Capt. Gardner of Nantucket who had been of his acquaintance: but all in vain.[29]

26. W. S. Holdsworth, *A History of English Law* (London: Methuen & Co., 1909), 3:62.

27. Boyer and Nissenbaum, eds., *Witchcraft Papers* 1:246.

28. Calef, as excerpted in Burr, ed., *Narratives of the Witchcraft Cases*, 367.

29. Sewall, *Diary* 1:295.

Perhaps Calef's date of 16 September is a printer's error—or perhaps it represents the date that Corey's ordeal actually began. It is almost certain that it took more than one day for Giles Corey to be pressed to death. Putnam's letter to Sewall states that on the night of 18 September, his "Daughter Ann was grievously Tormented by Witches, Threatning that she should be Pressed to Death, before Giles Cory."[30] This clearly implies that Corey's pressing began as early as 18 September. Furthermore, he was excommunicated by the Salem church on the very same day. The church gave as its reason that "he refused to plead, and so incurred the sentence and penalty of *pain fort dure*."[31] It is apparent, then, that the court sentenced Corey sometime on or before 18 September; and since it is doubtful that the sheriff waited long to begin his execution, the Salem church, unwilling to let him die a member, hurriedly passed and pronounced to him the dread sentence of excommunication.

It is also possible that Corey's punishment commenced even earlier than 18 September. As noted earlier, Calef gives 16 September as the date of Corey's death, but Calef may refer here to the date that Corey's pressing began. Because Judge Sewall wrote that "much pains was used with him two days, one after another," some historians, most notably Chadwick Hansen, have concluded that it took two days for Corey to die. While that view may be correct, Sewall's reference to "much pains" is too ambiguous to justify such a conclusion; it is not clear whether it refers to the punishment itself or to the complex legal proceedings (the *trina admonitio*, etc.) which the court was obliged to follow before sentence could be pronounced. Therefore, the most we can say with any certainty is that Corey's punishment began on or before 18 September.

No historian of the Salem witchcraft, to my knowledge, has ever taken any notice of the mysterious "Capt. Gardner of Nantucket" that Sewall refers to in his account of Corey's death; and although Captain Gardner figures prominently in the early history of the Nantucket settlement, both the histories of Nantucket and a recent Gardner biog-

---

30. Boyer and Nissenbaum, eds., *Witchcraft Papers* 1:246.
31. Upham, *Salem Witchcraft* 2:344.

raphy[32] fail to mention that he played a role in the most famous case of the Salem witchcraft trials.

Captain John Gardner of Nantucket was born at Cape Ann in 1624, the son of Thomas Gardner, who had come to Massachusetts from England. The son lived for many years in Salem, and removed to Nantucket in the early 1670s to escape harassment from the Puritan authorities. Giles Corey also lived in Salem Town in those early years, and it is probable that prior to 1659, when Corey sold his Salem house and completed his transferal to Salem Farms, the two men became close friends. Gardner is variously described during his Salem years as a captain, a mariner, and a surveyor. Like Corey, Gardner had frequent brushes with the law. If the two men's characters were at all similar, then John Gardner's life sheds some light on Giles Corey's motives for so obstinately "standing mute" in September 1692.

John Gardner left Salem for Nantucket prior to April 1674, joining his brother, Richard, and friend, Peter Folger. Upon his arrival he was commissioned the "Chiefe Military Officer" of the island.[33] By 1677, however, John Gardner's fortunes had changed for the worse. He was hauled before the Nantucket General Court to answer charges of stirring up trouble among the Indians. The court record on that occasion notes that when Gardner:

> ... came to the Court, [he] demeaned himself most irreverently, sitting down with his Hat on, taking no Notice of the Court, behaveing himself so both in Words and Gestures, as declared great Contempt of Authoritie of this Court, tending to the great dishonour of his Majesties Court Authoritie the Incouragement of others, and espetially the Heathen who being before by some evil Spiritt persuaded that there was no Authoritie, were hardly diswaded from using Violence.[34]

The court disenfranchised him and fined him £10 for his insolent behavior. Evidently John Gardner had little respect for the law and on this occasion did not refrain from manifesting his contempt. We shall

---

32. William E. Gardner, *The Triumphant Captain John and Gardners and Gardiners* (Nantucket, Mass.: Whaling Museum Publications, 1958).

33. As quoted by Alexander Starbuck, *The History of Nantucket* (Rutland, Vermont: Charles E. Tuttle Co., 1969), 38.

34. As quoted in Starbuck, *The History of Nantucket*, 62.

never know the advice that he gave Giles Corey in 1692. He probably counseled his old friend to "put himself on the country" and save himself from the terrible *peine forte et dure*. But if Giles Corey was at all like John Gardner, then Corey's refusal to submit to a trial by jury in Salem in 1692 reflected his utter contempt for the Court of Oyer and Terminer. It is an ironic footnote to Corey's case that John Gardner later served on two separate Courts of Oyer and Terminer at Nantucket, for the trials of Indians accused of murder.[35]

As previously mentioned, almost every historian of the Salem witchcraft has attributed Corey's refusal to stand trial to his fear that, upon conviction of the felony of witchcraft, his entire estate would be forfeited.[36] The laws of both Massachusetts and England in 1692, however, forbade forfeitures after conviction for witchcraft. Unless someone cruelly deceived Giles Corey into believing that, contrary to law, his property would be forfeited upon his conviction, the preceding historical myth is completely untenable.

In 1641 the famous Body of Liberties, which protected the rights of the colony's inhabitants, was drawn up by Nathaniel Ward of Ipswich and was adopted by the General Court. Two of its articles are relevant to the question of forfeiture:

> 1. ...no mans goods or estaite shall be taken away from him, nor any way indammaged under coulor of law or Countenance of Authoritie, unlesse it be by vertue or equitie of some expresse law of the Country waranting the same, established by a generall Court and sufficiently published, or in case of the defect of a law in any parteculer case by the word of god.
>
> 10. All our lands and heritages shall be free from all fines and licences upon Alienations, and from all hariotts, wardships, Liveries, Primer-seisins, yeare day and wast, Escheates, and forfeitures, upon the deaths of parents or Ancestors, be they naturall, casuall or Juditiall.[37]

35. Goodell, "Trials of the Witches in Massachusetts," 325.

36. This fiction in the historical accounts of Corey's case first appears in Emory Washburn, *Sketches of the Judicial History of Massachusetts* (Boston: Little and Brown, 1840), 142.

37. *The Laws and Liberties of Massachusetts 1641–1691*, comp. John D. Cushing, 3 vols. (Wilmington, Delaware: Scholarly Resources, Inc., 1976), 3:690 and 3:691 (hereafter cited as *Laws and Liberties*, comp. Cushing).

With one sweeping judicial measure, Massachusetts abolished the long-standing English precedent of forfeiture in cases of treason and felony. Notice that Article 10 expressly forbids forfeiture of "lands and heritages," that is, real property, under all circumstances. Article 1, on the other hand, allows for forfeiture of goods (moveable property), but only when expressly permitted by a law either enacted by the colony's General Court or contained within the word of God. These articles were faithfully followed. Hutchinson, in his *History of the Colony of Massachusetts Bay*, wrote that in 1656, when Ann Hibbins was executed for witchcraft (the same crime for which Giles Corey was accused), her lands were not only inherited by her heirs, but "there was no forfeiture of goods for felony."[38]

In 1692 there were no provisions under Massachusetts law which would have permitted forfeiture of estates upon conviction for witchcraft. An express law permitting forfeiture in cases of witchcraft would have been required and there was, in fact, no such statute on the books. That an express law was required to permit any such forfeiture can be seen from the 1652 act against arson which provided that anyone convicted of arson would:

> be putt to death, and to forfeit so much of his lands, goods or chattels, as shall make full satisfaction, to the party or parties damnifyed.[39]

Note that this act provides for forfeiture of as much of the arsonist's estate as would be needed to compensate the victim's losses in the fire; it is very different from the English laws of forfeiture in cases of treason and felony, which permitted *total* forfeiture of the criminal's estate. Under the English legal tradition, forfeiture resulted directly from the criminal's violation of the feudal obligations which entitled him to his estate; it was not designed as a means of compensating the victim of his crime.

On 15 June 1692 the General Court passed the act continuing all the Massachusetts laws passed under the colony governments that were "not repugnant to the laws of England."[40] In this manner, the Body of

38. Thomas Hutchinson, *The History of the Colony of Massachusetts Bay*, 2d ed. (London: M. Richardson, 1760), 188 footnote.

39. *Laws and Liberties*, comp. Cushing, 1:102.

40. Commonwealth of Massachusetts, *Acts of the Province* 1:27.

Liberties of 1641 continued as recognized law of the land; and the forfeiture of goods, chattels, lands, or heritages upon conviction for witchcraft was illegal. These provisions were not tampered with until 13 October 1692, almost a month after Corey's death, when the General Court passed "An Act Setting Forth General Privileges" which provided in part that:

> All lands and heritages within this province shall be free from year, day and wast, escheats and forfeitures, upon the death of parents or ancestors, natural, casual or judicial, and that for ever, except in cases of high treason.[41]

This provision is essentially identical to Article 10 of the 1641 Body of Liberties except that forfeiture was now permitted in cases of high treason (but not felony).

Although the Massachusetts laws prohibiting forfeiture for felonies were, indeed, "repugnant to the laws of England," their prohibition of forfeiture in cases of witchcraft was completely consistent with English law in 1692. The statute of 1 Jac. I, c.12, enacted in 1604 and in effect throughout the entire seventeenth century, provided that the heirs of persons convicted of witchcraft were entitled to "his or their titles of inheritance, succession and other rights, as though no such attainder of the ancestor or predecessor had been made."[42] Witchcraft, then, was a special felony under English law. Conviction for witchcraft did not "corrupt" the felon's blood and his heirs inherited his estate without any fear of forfeiture. There was, therefore, no provision for forfeiture in cases of witchcraft under Massachusetts law; and under English law, forfeiture had been expressly forbidden by the statute of 1 Jac. I, c. 12. It therefore seems unlikely that Giles Corey refused to "put himself on the country" to avoid the forfeiture of his estate, unless he was deceived by the authorities.

The history of the Salem trials is replete with the illegal seizures of the property of persons condemned or accused. The authorities seized John Proctor's estate while he was awaiting trial in prison.[43] This constituted

---

41. Commonwealth of Massachusetts, *Acts of the Province* 1:41.

42. Statute quoted in Barbara Rosen, ed., *Witchcraft*, The Stratford-Upon-Avon Library, vol. 6 (London: Edward Arnold, 1969), 57–8.

43. The seizure of Proctor's estate is told by Calef, as excerpted in Burr, ed., *Narratives of the Witchcraft Cases*, 361.

a gross violation of English law, which permitted forfeiture only after conviction for felony or treason, and prohibited forfeiture *before* conviction. The actions taken against Proctor's estate, then, were clearly illegal, and were nothing less than outright robbery. Similarly the estate of George Jacobs, Sr., was confiscated after he was condemned in August 1692. Calef relates that Jacobs's wife even "had her Wedding Ring taken from her, but with great difficulty obtained it again."[44]

One of the authorities' most grossly illegal acts in 1692 was their attempt to seize not only the estate of a condemned witch, but also the estates of totally innocent parties. Joseph and John Parker, sons of Mary Parker of Andover who was hanged for witchcraft on 22 September, wrote in a petition to the governor and council on 7 November 1692 that after their mother's death:

> the sherriff of Essex sent an officer to seise on her estate. The said officer required us in their majestyes name to give him an Account of our mothers estate, pretending it was forfeited to the King; we told him that our mother left no estate; (which we are able to make appear) notwithstanding which, he seised upon our cattell, Corn & hay, to a considerable value; . . . Now if our Mother had left any Estate, we know not of any Law in force in this Province, by which it should be forfeited upon her condemnation; much less can we understand that there is any Justice or reason, for the Sherriff to seise upon our Estate.[45]

Note that the Parker sons explicitly state that they knew of no laws permitting the forfeiture of their mother's estate, let alone laws permitting the sheriff to confiscate their own property. There is good reason for their seeming ignorance. There were no laws whatsoever to countenance these outrageous and illegal confiscations. The authorities, in their zeal to obliterate witchcraft, themselves violated the law; and history should never refute how disgracefully they acted.

On 14 December 1692 the General Court passed "A Bill Against Conjurations, Witchcraft, and Dealing with Evil and Wicked Spirits." The legislators enacted the bill ostensibly "For more particular direction in the Execution of the Law against Witchcraft."[46] It is essentially

44. Calef, as excerpted in Burr, ed., *Narratives of the Witchcraft Cases*, 364.
45. Boyer and Nissenbaum, eds., *Witchcraft Papers* 2:636–37.
46. Boyer and Nissenbaum, eds., *Witchcraft Papers* 3:885.

a copy of the statute of 1 Jac. I, c. 12 that was referred to earlier. There is, however, one very important difference between the Stuart statute and its Massachusetts copy, and it is a difference that bears directly on the question of forfeiture. The Massachusetts bill omitted, in its entirety, the English provision that the heirs inherited the estates of any ancestor convicted of witchcraft. In fact, in 1695, the Privy Council specifically disallowed this Massachusetts law because it was:

> not found to agree with ye Statute of King James ye First where-
> by the Dower is saved to ye Widow and ye Inheritance to ye heir
> of ye party convicted.[47]

Massachusetts had laws prohibiting forfeiture in 1692 and the laws of England expressly forbade forfeiture in cases of witchcraft. Why then, in December 1692, did the General Court pass a bill that, in not expressly prohibiting forfeiture in cases of witchcraft, violated not only the laws of England but the very legal tradition in Massachusetts that had existed since 1641? There is, in my opinion, only one purpose for which this December bill against witchcraft was enacted. The authorities finally realized that the confiscations of the previous summer were illegal; and by bringing in this bill which sanctioned those confiscations with the force of law, the authorities sought to prevent legal retribution from overtaking them.

Unless someone deceived Giles Corey and told him that his estate would be forfeited if he were convicted of witchcraft, fear of forfeiture could not have prompted his "standing mute" in September 1692. In 1710 Corey's son-in-law, John Moulton, wrote that "after our fathers death the sh'rife thretened to Size [seize] our fathers Estate."[48] So it is possible that someone told Giles Corey that his estate would be forfeited after his conviction. But I find it hard to believe that such a counselor could have been both so ignorant of the laws as to suggest to Corey that his estate would be forfeited upon conviction (which was clearly illegal) and at the same time so knowledgeable of the laws of England as to advise him that, by "standing mute," his lands would not be forfeited (and even then goods and chattels were still forfeited when the defendant "stood mute"). Such a counselor could only have desired Corey's death by the *peine forte et dure*, and nothing else. Clearly this was

47. Commonwealth of Massachusetts, *Acts of the Province* 1:91.
48. Boyer and Nissenbaum, eds., *Witchcraft Papers* 3:985.

not the court's intent; the justices wanted Corey to "put himself on the country" so that his trial could proceed. "Much pains was used with him two days, one after another," Judge Sewall wrote. If the court wanted to avoid pressing Giles Corey, and knew that fear of forfeiture was his sole reason for refusing to submit to a jury trial, it would have only required one more illegal act on the authorities' part to inform Corey, incorrectly, that his estate was forfeit even if he were pressed to death and not convicted.

The history of Massachusetts records only one other case in which a prisoner was threatened with the *peine forte et dure*. In the winter of 1638–39, Dorothy Talbye, a onetime member of the Salem church, was indicted for murdering her three-year-old daughter; and although she confessed to the crime at her arrest, Gov. John Winthrop recorded in his *History* that "at her arraignment, she stood mute a good space, till the governour [Winthrop himself] told her she should be pressed to death, and then she confessed the indictment" and was later hanged.[49]

Two years later, cruel and unusual punishment was abolished by the Body of Liberties: "For bodilie punishments we allow amongst us none that are inhumane Barbarous or cruel."[50] In 1692 this abolition was confirmed, when on 15 June the General Court passed the bill continuing all the colony laws that were not repugnant to the laws of England. Thus the *peine forte et dure* was illegal in Massachusetts for two reasons: first, there was no express law of the province permitting pressing; and second, because it violated the provisions of the Body of Liberties regarding barbarous punishments. Pressing was one of the cruelest punishments ever devised and it is a stark testimony to its cruelty that so few felons "stood mute" and chose to endure the horrible *peine forte et dure* rather than stand trial. By Massachusetts law, Corey's punishment was illegal. It was borrowed from the English legal tradition to coerce this poor but obstinate prisoner to put himself on the country." Calef, who noted the strange use of this English punishment, wrote that "the Executions seemed mixt, in pressing to death for not pleading, which most agrees with the Laws of England."[51]

Why then did Giles Corey "stand mute" in September 1692 when he

49. John Winthrop, *The History of New England from 1630 to 1649*, ed. James Savage (Boston: Phelps and Farnham, 1825), 279.
50. *Laws and Liberties*, comp. Cushing, 3:695.
51. Calef, as excerpted in Burr, ed., *Narratives of the Witchcraft Cases*, 374.

was brought to trial before the Court of Oyer and Terminer? Calef, who gives the fullest account of the event, relates that Corey:

> . . . would not put himself upon Tryal by the Jury (they having cleared none upon Tryal) and knowing there would be the same Witnesses against him, rather chose to undergo what Death they would put him to.[52]

The Court of Oyer and Terminer that summer had failed to acquit anyone accused of witchcraft; and the magistrates at Corey's examination in April and the jury of inquest that considered his case on 9 September had willingly believed the same witnesses who were to appear at his trial. No doubt Corey felt that if he were tried, his conviction was a foregone conclusion. When he was brought before the court, he pleaded "Not guilty" to his indictment and thus maintained his innocence; but to the question, "Culprit, how will you be tried?" he "stood mute" and would not answer "by God and my country." He thus refused to submit himself to the jurisdiction of a court which had predetermined his guilt, and he showed his contempt for that court by suffering the *peine forte et dure* rather than by standing trial.

Giles Corey has the dubious distinction of being the only person ever pressed to death in the history of this country. But his case has been consistently distorted by historians of the Salem witchcraft who, having failed to understand the prevailing laws governing trials in England and Massachusetts, invented the fictions that Corey refused to plead and that he refused because he feared the forfeiture of his estate. His case has finally been presented in accordance with the known facts: that Giles Corey pleaded "not guilty" and refused to "put himself on the country" not out of fear of the forfeiture of his estate (which, as has been said, was illegal in cases of witchcraft in both England and Massachusetts) but out of contempt for the court that was to try him. The spirit of Giles Corey at last can rest in peace.

---

52. Calef, as excerpted in Burr, ed., *Narratives of the Witchcraft Cases*, 367.

$\mathcal{N}$otes and Documents

"Reformation Is Our Only Preservation": Cotton Mather and Salem Witchcraft

Richard H. Werking*

A CCOUNTS of Cotton Mather's connection with the Salem witch-craft episode are hardly new. From Robert Calef's denunciations of the younger Mather in the 1690s to Chadwick Hansen's efforts in the 1960s to vindicate him, historians have expended considerable effort either attacking or defending his behavior in the Salem affair.[1] Charles W. Upham, politician and Unitarian minister at Salem in the mid-nineteenth century, was particularly vociferous in his attacks on the Puritan clergy in general and Cotton Mather in particular. He accused Mather of "getting up" the Salem tragedy by publicizing a case of witch-craft that occurred in Boston in 1688; attempting to revive the matter after the Salem trials had ended by zealously and credulously attempting to cure persons allegedly victimized by witches; urging the magistrates to continue the prosecution of witches when he drafted the advice of the clergy to the judges; and failing to put forth effort to stop the witch trials, instead writing an exoneration of the judges in October 1692. Other historians, among them George Bancroft, George L. Burr, Justin Winsor, George Moore, and James Truslow Adams, have been sympathetic to Upham's charges.[2]

As Chadwick Hansen has recently pointed out, such has remained

* Mr. Werking is a graduate student at the University of Wisconsin, Madison. He would like to thank Stanley N. Katz for his assistance.

[1] Robert Calef, *More Wonders of the Invisible World* . . . (1700), in Samuel G. Drake, comp., *The Witchcraft Delusion in New England* . . . (Roxbury, Mass., 1866), II and III, *passim;* Chadwick Hansen, *Witchcraft at Salem* (New York, 1969), esp. ix-xiv, 95-102, 171-172, 194-195.

[2] Charles W. Upham, *Lectures on Witchcraft,* . . . (Boston, 1831), 103, 106-115, 184; Upham, *Salem Witchcraft; With An Account of Salem Village* . . . , II (Boston, 1867), 366-369, 487, 503; Upham, "Salem Witchcraft and Cotton Mather," *Historical Magazine,* 2d Ser., VI (Sept. 1869), 129-219; George Bancroft, *History of the United States of America* . . . , rev. ed., II (New York, 1891), 53-54, 62; George L. Burr, ed., *Narratives of the Witchcraft Cases, 1648-1706* (New York,

the popular view of Mather's place in the history of Salem witchcraft, due largely to the influence of Bancroft's work.[3] This view has persisted in the face of repeated attempts by historians to place Mather in a more favorable light. W. F. Poole challenged Upham's accounts on more than one occasion in the nineteenth century, and others have followed him, among them Josiah Quincy, Barrett Wendell, Kenneth B. Murdock, Samuel Eliot Morison, and, of course, Hansen himself.[4] Hansen in particular successfully defends Mather against the greater number of the accusations, showing that witchcraft was frightfully real to virtually all the residents of New England and not just to Cotton Mather, that Mather was not responsible for the outbreak of the witchcraft incidents in the first place, that he advised the judges to be extremely cautious in the use of the all-important "spectral evidence," and that he used considerable caution in his own dealings with persons whom he was attempting to cure of witchcraft's effects.[5]

Despite the considerable heat generated by debate over the degree of Cotton Mather's "guilt" or "innocence," something remains less than fully clarified.[6] We still do not know just what Mather intended his connection with the witchcraft episode to be, or why it was what it was. In

---

1914), 141n, 379n; Justin Winsor, "The Literature of Witchcraft in New England," *American Antiquarian Society, Proceedings,* N. S., X (1895), 351-373; George H. Moore, "Notes on the Bibliography of Witchcraft in Massachusetts, *ibid.,* V (1887-1888), 262-267; James Truslow Adams, *The Founding of New England* (Boston, 1921), 454-455.

[3] Hansen gives a good general outline of the evolution of the anti-Mather line. *Witchcraft at Salem,* xi-xiv.

[4] W. F. Poole, "Cotton Mather and Salem Witchcraft," *North American Review,* CVIII (Apr. 1869), 337-397; Poole, "Witchcraft at Boston," in Justin Winsor, ed., *The Memorial History of Boston . . . ,* II (Boston, 1886), 131-172; Josiah P. Quincy, "Cotton Mather and the Supernormal in New England History," *Massachusetts Historical Society, Proceedings,* 2d Ser., XX (1906-1907), 439-453; Barrett Wendell, *Cotton Mather, The Puritan Priest* (New York, 1891), Chap. 6; Kenneth B. Murdock, *Increase Mather: The Foremost American Puritan* (Cambridge, Mass., 1925), Chap. 17; Samuel Eliot Morison, *The Intellectual Life of Colonial New England* (New York, 1956; publ. in 1936 as *The Puritan Pronaos: Studies in the Intellectual Life of New England in the Seventeenth Century*), 258-259, 263-264. Perry Miller's analysis, whose conclusions correspond with many of my own, falls between the two "schools." See *The New England Mind: From Colony to Province* (Cambridge, Mass., 1953), Chaps. 10, 11, 13.

[5] More than once Mather received the names of suspected witches, but he kept such information to himself. Hansen, *Witchcraft at Salem,* 23-24, 179.

[6] As John Demos has observed recently, the historiography of Salem has been devoted principally to judging the participants and affixing blame. "Underlying Themes in the Witchcraft of Seventeenth-Century New England," *American Historical Review,* LXXV (1969-1970), 1311-1312.

other words, why did this Boston minister, who managed not to attend a single witch trial at Salem, insinuate himself so actively into the affair in the manner that he did?[7] An explanation lies in his experience with the Boston witchcraft case of 1688 and in the way he viewed his role within the context of the Puritan mission in late seventeenth-century Massachusetts.

In the eyes of the Puritan clergy, the latter decades of the century were a troubled time for the colony of Massachusetts Bay. Perry Miller has demonstrated very well the anxiety of the ministers and their increasing reliance upon the jeremiad to steer the straying colonists onto God's path.[8] King Philip's War in 1675-1676 and the crown's attacks upon the colony's charter appeared as examples of divine wrath turned upon a spiritually declining people. "The countrey is Distress'd in many points," wrote Cotton Mather in 1686. "Wee are in great Hazard of losing our Colledge. . . . The Charters of our Colonies are in Extreme Danger also to be lost."[9]

According to the clergy, the great danger—and the cause for divine displeasure—was increasing secularization in the life of the colony and the consequent loss of religious zeal.[10] In order to reverse this trend a number of the clergy stressed the necessity of continually reminding the people of the existence of the spiritual world and of its close connection with the material world. Joseph Glanvill and other English writers had been calling for the collection of remarkable occurrences in order to confound the secularists. "Modern relations" of such events, Glanvill wrote in 1661, "being fresh, and near, . . . it may be expected they should have more success upon the obstinacy of Unbelievers."[11] At a conference of the ministers in Cambridge, Massachusetts, in 1681, Increase Mather and others repeated Glanvill's plea. Three years later, Increase published his *An Essay for the Recording of Illustrious Providences* . . . (better known

[7] Although he was not in attendance at the trials, some historians have speculated that he may have attended one or more of the pretrial examinations. Upham, "Salem Witchcraft," *Hist. Mag.*, 2d Ser., VI (Sept. 1869), 162; Burr, ed., *Narratives*, 214n.

[8] Miller, *New England Mind*, Chap. 2.

[9] *The Mather Papers* (Massachusetts Historical Society, *Collections*, 4th Ser., VIII [Boston, 1868]), 389. Hereafter cited as *Mather Papers*. An editorial note gives 1686 as the "probable" date of this paper.

[10] Miller, *New England Mind*, 49; Worthington C. Ford, ed., *Diary of Cotton Mather, 1681-1708* (Mass. Hist. Soc., *Collections*, 7th Ser., VII [Boston, 1911]), xviii. Hereafter cited as Mather, *Diary*.

[11] Burr, ed., *Narratives*, 5. English writers engaged in this activity included Richard Baxter, Henry More, and Matthew Poole. See also George L. Burr, "New England's Place in the History of Witchcraft," *Amer. Antiquarian Soc., Proceedings*, N. S., XXI (1911), 185-217.

as *Remarkable Providences*), in which he recorded, among other things, miraculous sea rescues, "strange apparitions," "witchcrafts," [and] "diabolical possessions."[12] He intended it to be only the first in a succession of similar projects, for he explained: "In this essay I design no more than a specimen; and having (by the good hand of God upon me) set this wheel a going, I shall leave it unto others, whom God has fitted and shall incline thereto, to go on with the undertaking."[13]

Although the story thus far is familiar to anyone acquainted with the Salem episode, the activity that had occurred is important in explaining Cotton Mather's interest in and behavior toward the witchcraft cases, for the younger Mather would be most industrious in keeping the "wheel a going." In March 1681 he had already recorded in his diary his five most important daily duties which involved not only prayer and meditation but also the duty "to be diligent in *observing* and *recording* of *illustrious Providences*."[14] Then, in 1688, he became prominent in the handling of the Boston witchcraft case, another well-known story. Briefly, Mather and several other ministers prayed with and for the children of John Goodwin, who had become subject to hysterical fits. When Goodwin swore out a complaint against an old woman in the neighborhood, Goody Glover, the authorities searched her house and found small images made of rags and goat hair, which in their eyes furnished evidence that she was a practicing witch.[15] She confessed her guilt and received a sentence of death after being declared *compos mentis* by several doctors. Cotton Mather attempted to pray with her, but she refused to repent and embrace the covenant.[16]

[12] (Boston, 1684; reprinted London, 1856, as *Remarkable Providences Illustrative of the Earlier Days of American Colonisation*), Preface, n.p. See also Robert Middlekauff, *The Mathers: Three Generations of Puritan Intellectuals* (New York, 1971), 143-148.

[13] *Ibid.*

[14] Mather, *Diary*, 4-5. Hansen in particular tends to see Cotton as more the dispassionate observer than the Puritan minister investigating for a vital purpose. While he is certainly correct in pointing out that Mather was not "a witch hunter" and that he was "a witchcraft scholar," a more precise term would be "witchcraft hunter." *Witchcraft at Salem*, 172. As Perry Miller wrote some time ago, to call Mather's work an "inductive investigation . . . allows us to suppose the incredible: that, at the moment Mather and his colleagues were engaged in a struggle for existence, they idly embarked upon a collection of curiosa!" *New England Mind*, 143.

[15] One of Hansen's chief points is that there were at least several women in the colony actually practicing witchcraft through image-magic. He argues that, like voodoo, this often worked, since the target of the witch's ill will believed that it did. *Witchcraft at Salem*, x, xiv-xv, 10-11, 22-23, 70, 81-86, 219, 226.

[16] As Mather related, "I Sett before her the Necessity and Equity of her breaking her Covenant with Hell, and giving her self to the Lord Jesus Christ, by an everlasting Covenant; To which her Answer was, that I spoke a very Reasonable

Glover's execution did not halt the afflictions of the Goodwin children —an important point. They continued to suffer for some time, while Mather diligently prayed and fasted with them. He did not feel it necessary to seek out possible suspects, since he thought "we should be tender in such Relations, lest we wrong the Reputation of the Innocent by stories not enough enquired into."[17] Eventually the fits left the children, and Mather gave the credit to particular techniques. "Prayer and Faith," he concluded, "was the thing which drove the Divils from the Children."[18]

Mather's account of the case, entitled *Memorable Providences,* consciously followed the work of other recorders of the spirit world's manifestations, including his father and Joseph Glanvill:

I can with a Contentment beyond meer Patience give these . . . Sheets unto the Stationer, when I see what pains Mr. Baxter, Mr. Glanvill, Dr. More, and several other Great Names have taken to publish Histories of Witchcrafts and Possessions unto the world. I said, Let me also run after them; and this with the more Alacrity because, I have tidings ready. Go then, my little Book, as a Lackey to the more elaborate Essayes of those learned men. Go tell Mankind, that there are Devils and Witches. . . . Go tell the world, What Prayers can do beyond all Devils and Witches. . . .[19]

Seemingly his propensity to witness and record evidence of witchcraft made Mather more zealous than the other ministers in his efforts to help the Goodwin children.[20]

This twin desire to seek out and register examples of witchcraft while at the same time using the techniques of prayer, fasting, and caution also motivated Cotton Mather during the witchcraft outbreak at Salem in 1692. As he had done in the Goodwin case, he asked that he might take some of the afflicted children into his own home.[21] This time

---

thing, but she could not do it." Mather, *Memorable Providences, Relating to Witchcrafts and Possessions* . . . (1689), in Burr, ed., *Narratives,* 106.

[17] *Ibid.,* 107.

[18] *Ibid.,* 126.

[19] *Ibid.,* 98-99.

[20] John Goodwin related how "Mr. Mather particularly . . . not only pray's with us, and for us, but he taketh one of my Children home to his own house; . . . a troublesome guest, for such an one that had so much work lying upon his hands and heart." Goodwin went on, in the classic pattern of the jeremiad, to thank God for the affliction which had cleansed him of sin and had effected a renewal of the covenant. The lesson was plain: "The Lord help us to see by this Visitation, what need we have to get shelter under the wing of Christ, to hast to the Rock, where we may be safe." *Ibid.,* 129-131.

[21] Mather, *Diary,* 151-152.

he was not permitted to handle matters as he wished, and after October 1692, when he wrote the defense of a court which had tried the accused witches, his reputation suffered a blow from which it has not yet recovered.

Historians have since debated Mather's responsibility for the Salem tragedy without emphasizing the dual nature of his conduct. Defenders have continually pointed to Mather's frequent advice for caution, especially regarding the crucial question of spectral evidence. Accusers have denounced what they consider to have been his credulity in believing in witches, his zeal in seeking them out (including two communications to the judges urging them to be zealous), and his defense of the court. That both interpretations are possible suggests an ambiguity that has often gone unnoticed.[22] If people were to renew the covenant, they had to be reminded of the nearness of the spiritual world, and no opportunity should be lost in doing so.[23] But at the same time, a good deal of caution had to be used toward those accused of witchcraft. Here was a delicate balance, which Mather was able to maintain when he himself was investigating presumed witchcrafts, but which disintegrated when he was not. His obsession with this balance is evident in a number of his writings connected with the witch trials.

Cotton Mather's letter to his friend Judge John Richards on May 31, just before the trials began, is a most revealing document. As historians have repeatedly shown, he urged Richards to be very cautious regarding spectral evidence. At the same time, he told the judge that "the indefatigable paines that are used for the tracing [of] this Witchcraft are to be thankfully accepted, and applauded among all this people of God." The most direct proof of guilt for Mather was a confession, and toward the end of the letter he suggested:

It is worth considering, whether there be a necessity alwayes by Extirpations by Halter or fagott, [ ] every wretched creature, that shall be hooked into some degrees of Witchcraft. What if some of the lesser Criminalls, be onely scourged with lesser punishments, and also put upon some solemn, open, Publike and Explicitt renunciation of the Divil? I am apt to thinke that the Divels would then cease afflicting the neighbor-hood. . . . Or what if the death of some of the offenders were either diverted or inflicted, according to the successe of such their renunciation.

But I find my free thoughts, thus freely layd before your Honour,

---

[22] Perry Miller's account of Mather's activity is the one which most successfully pinpoints his agonizingly ambiguous situation. *New England Mind*, Chap. 13.

[23] Cotton observed in his diary for early 1692 that a great "Lethargy" lay on the land, and that the churches needed to be awakened. Mather, *Diary*, 144-146.

begin to have too much freedome in them. I shall now therefore adde no more. . . .[24]

It was evidently more important to Mather that the reality of witches be made apparent and the covenant renewed than that witches be executed. He later returned to this theme.

In mid-June *The Return of Several Ministers . . .* was delivered to the court, which had paused to ask the advice of the clergy. One accused witch had been tried and executed, and the court was recessed temporarily. The *Return,* written by Cotton Mather,[25] is probably the best-known document dealing with the Salem episode and has been reprinted frequently. Yet virtually every historian who has commented on it has ignored the subtlety of some key paragraphs in it.[26] After discussing the suffering of the afflicted in the first paragraph, Mather wrote:

We cannot but with all Thankfulness acknowledge, the Success which the merciful God has given unto the sedulous and assiduous Endeavours of our honourable Rulers, to detect the abominable Witchcrafts which have been committed in the Country; humbly praying that the discovery of these mysterious and mischievous Wickednesses may be perfected.

We judge that in the prosecution of these, and all such Witchcrafts, there is need of a very critical and exquisite Caution, lest by too much Credulity for things received only upon the Devil's Authority, there be a Door opened for a long Train of miserable Consequences, and Satan get an advantage over us, for we should not be ignorant of his Devices.

Paragraphs four through seven continued the emphasis on caution, but Mather concluded:

Nevertheless, We cannot but humbly recommend unto the Government, the speedy and vigorous Prosecution of such as have rendred themselves obnoxious, according to the Direction given in the Laws of God, and the wholesome Statutes of the *English* Nation, for the Detection of Witchcrafts.

[24] Cotton Mather to John Richards, May 31, 1692, *Mather Papers,* 392, 393, 396-397. Cf. Mather's opinion some three years earlier: "That the Grace of God may be admired, and that the worst of Sinners may be encouraged, Behold, Witchcraft also has found a Pardon. . . . From the Hell of Witchcraft our merciful Jesus can fetch a guilty Creature to the Glory of Heaven. Our Lord hath sometimes Recovered those who have in the most horrid manner given themselves away to the Destroyer of their souls." *Memorable Providences,* in Burr, ed., *Narratives,* 135. Burr himself quoted a portion of the above passage of the letter to Richards, remarking that the failure to execute a single confessing witch was "the most striking feature of the Salem trials." *Ibid.,* 374n.

[25] Mather, *Diary,* 151.

[26] Kenneth B. Murdock was an exception. *Increase Mather,* 295n. The text of the *Return* is taken from David Levin, ed., *What Happened in Salem? Documents Pertaining to the 17th-Century Witchcraft Trials* (New York, 1952), 160-162.

It is apparently the second and final paragraphs which have been the basis of the charge that Mather and the other clergymen "approved, applauded, and stimulated the prosecutions."[27] But the second paragraph did no such thing. What Mather praised was the effort to "detect" and "discover" witchcrafts. The third paragraph began the discussion of prosecution, which was something else again, and the language was that of extreme caution. The final paragraph did urge the prosecution of persons, but only "such as have rendred themselves obnoxious," i.e., "liable to punishment or censure; guilty, blameworthy."[28] Cotton Mather was praising the zealous investigation of the spiritual world in order to confound atheists and inject religious zeal, but he was simultaneously urging great caution in the handling of suspected witches encountered in the course of such activity.[29]

A letter in August to John Foster, member of the governor's council, demonstrates the same pattern. Cotton Mather, although more complimentary toward the judges than the language in his two communications to them might indicate, offered a way out of the increasingly bloody business at Salem.[30] He suggested that perhaps "a famous divine or two" might be appointed to the court, as had occurred during an outbreak of witchcraft in England in 1645. One of the ministers, Mather told Foster, "did preach two sermons to the court before his first sitting on the bench, wherein having first proved the existence of witches he afterwards showed the evil of endeavoring the conviction of any upon defective evidence. The sermon had the effect that none were condemned who could be saved without an express breach of the law. And then, though 'twas possible some guilty did escape, yet the troubles of those places

[27] Upham, *Salem Witchcraft*, II, 368. Barrett Wendell felt that it was this document more than anything else which had prompted historians to burden Mather with the charge of urging "judicial murder." *Cotton Mather*, 98-99.

[28] *Oxford English Dictionary*.

[29] For obvious reasons, I cannot agree with Hansen when he says that paragraphs three through seven constituted "the heart of this document." *Witchcraft at Salem*, 125. This communication was considerably more cautious than the author's letter to Richards. In that document Mather had allowed several methods of inquiry that were specifically rejected in the *Return*, as well as the infamous water test for witches. Hansen contends that it was the presence of Increase at the meeting of the clergy (which authorized the document) that made for the yet more cautionary tone. *Ibid.* He may be correct, but another explanation suggests itself as well. By mid-June, a witch trial had been held and the accused executed without a confession forthcoming. Perhaps the younger Mather now had less confidence in the judges' ability and wisdom than he had possessed previously and thus sought to limit the methods he had then sanctioned more freely.

[30] When addressing themselves solely to the judges, the clergy were more outspoken in their advice for caution than they were when addressing others. As Mather recorded in his diary, "Tho' I could not allow the *Principles*, that some

were, I think, extinguished."[31] As when he had offered to take some of the afflicted children into his home, Mather was very anxious to keep his own hand on affairs.

Nevertheless, the desire for caution did not slow Mather's own quest for evidence of the diabolical. The next year he went to Salem to collect as much information as he could on the witchcrafts, because such an account "might in a while bee a singular Benefit unto the Church, and unto the World."[32] By this time he had already been investigating similar phenomena in Boston. First Mercy Short, and later Margaret Rule, seemed to be victims of witchcraft. Circumstances allowed Mather to repeat the procedure he had followed with the Goodwin children: praying and fasting with the young women, suppressing as unfounded the accusations against various persons, and writing accounts of both cases. He himself published neither account but merely circulated them among his friends.[33] Toward the conclusion of the Margaret Rule narrative, Mather spelled out what he viewed as the result of his activity: "The Devil got just nothing; but God got praises, Christ got subjects, the Holy Spirit got *Temples,* the Church got *Addition,* and the Souls of Men got everlasting *Benefits;* I am not so vain as to say that any *Wisdome* or *Vertue* of mine did contribute unto this good order of things: But I am so just, as to say I did not hinder this Good."[34]

This essentially was Mather's goal, and it was not necessary that witches be apprehended and executed in order to carry it out. Glover's execution did not end the Goodwin children's torment, but it seemed that prayer and fasting did. If witches happened to be apprehended, Mather hoped they would confess. Indeed, he wrote Richards that it was not so great a crime for these "wretched creatures" to be "hooked

---

of the Judges had espoused, yett I could not but speak honourably of their *Persons,* on all Occasions." Mather, *Diary,* 151. Similarly, in early August the ministers appeared to be backing away from their stronger stand of June, again in a message meant for persons other than the judges. As Hansen very perceptively observes, the pursuit of consensus by the ministers and magistrates was all-important. Real differences had to be glossed over, for if such dissension broke out, it would be an admission that "the Massachusetts way of life was . . . a failure." *Witchcraft at Salem,* 137.

[31] Hansen, *Witchcraft at Salem,* 143. Cf. Mather's account of a sermon he had delivered the previous May concerning religious dissenters, in which he had cautioned against "the *Persecution* of erroneous and conscientious Dissenters, by the *civil Magistrate,*" because he "feared, that the *Zeal* of my Countrey had formerly had in it more *Fire* than should have been." Mather, *Diary,* 149.

[32] Mather, *Diary,* 171.

[33] *A Brand Pluck'd Out of the Burning* (1693), in Burr, ed., *Narratives,* 253-287; *Another Brand Plucked Out of the Burning* . . . (1693), in Drake, comp., *Witchcraft Delusion,* II, 23-48.

[34] Mather, *Another Brand,* in Drake, comp., *Witchcraft Delusion,* II, 47.

in" by the Devil as it was to fail to confess.[35] If the accused were to confess and renounce the Devil "openly and publicly," perhaps the people would be made aware of their reliance upon God, the churches, and the ministers. Mather outlined the procedure in *The Wonders of the Invisible World:*

> With a *Great Zeal,* we should lay hold on the *Covenant* of God, that we may secure *Us* and *Ours,* from the *Great Wrath,* with which the Devil Rages. Let us come into the *Covenant of Grace,* and then we shall not be hook'd into a *Covenant with the Devil,* nor be altogether unfurnished with *Armour,* against the Witches that are in that *Covenant.* . . . While others have had their Names Entred in the *Devils Book;* let our Names be found in the *Church Book.* . . . So many of the *Rising Generation,* utterly forgetting the Errand of our Fathers to build Churches in this Wilderness, . . . 'tis as likely as any one thing to procure the swarmings of *Witch Crafts* among us.[36]

Such a renewal of the covenant was presumably the colony's only hope. As Mather put it more succinctly a few pages earlier, *"Reformation* is . . . our only *Preservation."*[37]

We can, then, understand Cotton Mather's role at Salem only within the context of the temper of Massachusetts in the late seventeenth century and of Mather's own feeling that the spirit of the people was in decline. Not only did he feel constrained to protect the judges' reputations, but he also tried to keep the spiritual world a reality by reporting instances of witchcraft at the same time that he sought to protect persons accused in the process. Others were either less interested or less successful in maintaining that balance.

[35] George L. Haskins has emphasized that confession and repentance were an important part of legal theory in 17th-century Massachusetts. He argues that the most important and striking influence of the Puritans upon the law can be found in their emphasis on "moral persuasion in order to reform the offender" rather than on retribution. *Law and Authority in Early Massachusetts, A Study in Tradition and Design* (New York, 1960), 204. See also 91-92, 121, 209-212; Hansen, *Witchcraft at Salem,* 123; Miller, *New England Mind,* 180, 197, 199. One critical observer of the witch trials noted, too, that the judges were upset when the accused showed no tears of remorse. Thomas Brattle to ———, Oct. 8, 1692, Mass. Hist. Soc., *Collections,* 1st Ser., V (Boston, 1798), 67. But the importance of a confession of guilt and a reaffirmation of established values has not been confined solely to residents of colonial Massachusetts. Witness the amount of praise that has been heaped on Samuel Sewall, one of the trial judges, for his public confession in 1697. Bancroft, *History of the U. S.,* II, 66; Morison, *Intellectual Life,* 164-165; Marion Starkey, *The Devil in Massachusetts, A Modern Inquiry into the Salem Witch Trials* (New York, 1949), 272-274; Charles A. and Mary R. Beard, *The Rise of American Civilization,* I (New York, 1927), 150.

[36] Cotton Mather, *The Wonders of the Invisible World* . . . (London, 1862), 101-102; Middlekauff, *The Mathers,* 160.

[37] Mather, *Wonders of the Invisible World,* 95.

MUTATIONS OF THE SUPERNATURAL: WITCHCRAFT, REMARKABLE PROVIDENCES, AND THE POWER OF PURITAN MEN

ANN KIBBEY

Yale University

ON APRIL 19, 1962, MARY WARREN APPEARED BEFORE THE COURT CONVENED to try suspected witches at Salem. Having testified initially as a victim of witchcraft, the twenty-year-old woman now stood accused of it herself. After altering her plea several times over a period of several weeks, she finally confessed she had signed the "Devil's Book." Strangely, this yielding to Satan did not damage Warren's credibility as a star witness for the court. Self-confessed witch though she was, the court continued to take depositions from her and she continued to be "afflicted," paradoxically performing the legal roles of accuser and accused simultaneously. Warren's capacity to be at once both agent and victim of the devil's power was only a particular instance of her capacity to offer contradictory views of witchcraft, for she was just as inconsistent when she ventured into non-religious explanations. When it was deposed that she had accused her peers of fraud, that "she the Said Mary said that the afflicted girls did but dissemble," Warren paradoxically responded by falling into a "fit" herself. She continued to experience numerous other seizures during her testimony, despite her own assessment of fraud. Warren also resorted to the belief that the afflicted were merely insane, that "the Majestrates Might as well Examine Keysars Daughter that has Bin Distracted Many Yeares And Take Noatice of what Shee said: as well as any of the Afflicted pe'sons." Presumably she included herself in this repudiation, for some of her fellow prisoners testified that Mary was well aware of her own self-contradiction, that she had explained to them in the jail:

> When I was Afflicted I thought I saw the Apparission of A hundred persons: for Shee said hir Head was Distempered [so] that Shee Could not tell what Shee Said, And the Said Mary tould us that when Shee was well Againe Shee Could not Say that Shee saw any of [the] Apparissions at the time Aforesaid.

Nonetheless, Warren was never so self-disparaging or skeptical in court.

Before the judges, she agreeably testified at length of "apparissions" who had appeared to her and threatened her.[1]

More than any other witness, Mary Warren appears to be a totally unreliable source on the Salem witchcraft trials, someone who did not even understand herself, much less anyone else. Yet her case record is unusually interesting because, ironically, in her mental wanderings she managed to delineate the whole range of interpretations that historians have since offered to explain the Salem afflicted. From the earliest, Robert Calef's charge of fraud in 1697, through Chadwick Hansen's 1969 analysis of hysteria (coupled with his belief in "real witches"), to Paul Boyer and Stephen Nissenbaum's recent assertion that the behavior of the "afflicted girls" is interpretively insignificant—Mary Warren had already suggested these conflicting possibilities, albeit not in such finished form.[2] Pleading both innocence and guilt, both insane hallucinations and belief in witches and, as it were, both fraud and fits, Warren was admirably comprehensive in her incoherence. Perhaps, then, this servant woman's nonsense was also unwitting insight.

Although Warren seems nearly unintelligible as an individual subject, she makes much more sense from a cultural perspective. Her sense of interchangeable, opposing views was tacitly corroborated by the reversal of legal opinion in 1711, when the legislature formally exonerated most of those who had been convicted in 1692. Declaring these defendants innocent, official authority then changed sides itself, blaming "the Influence and Energy of the Evil Spirits so great at that time *acting in and upon those who were the principal accusers and Witnesses* proceeding so far as to cause a Prosecution to be had of persons of known and good reputation."[3] The dualist opposition between divine power and witchcraft seems to have been much more fragile, much more vulnerable to reversal, than the occurrence of the trials and executions might otherwise suggest. Even before 1692, there was obvious evidence of deep confusion about the nature of supernatural influence in Increase Mather's *Essay for the Recording of*

---

[1]Paul Boyer and Stephen Nissenbaum, eds., *The Salem Witchcraft Papers: Verbatim Transcripts of the Legal Documents of the Salem Witchcraft Outbreak of 1692*, 3 vols. (New York: DaCapo Press, 1977), 793, 802–03, 795. See also 103, 680 for descriptions of Warren.

[2]Robert Calef, *More Wonders of the Invisible World* (London, 1700). Marion L. Starkey, *The Devil in Massachusetts* (New York: Knopf, 1949), tends to follow Calef. Modern historians share Warren's credulity as well as her incredulity. Chadwick Hansen, *Witchcraft at Salem* (New York: Braziller, 1969), analyzes the "afflicted" in terms of Freud's studies of hysteria and anthropological studies of voodoo, concluding that "at least two of the persons still attainted as witches under Massachusetts law—Bridget Bishop and Mammy Redd—actually were witches" (219). In the most recent study of Salem, Paul Boyer and Stephen Nissenbaum, *Salem Possessed: The Social Origins of Witchcraft* (1974; rpt. Cambridge: Harvard Univ. Press, 1977), the authors explain, "Oddly enough, it has been through our sense of 'collaborating' with [the Salem minister] Parris and [the main family of accusers] the Putnams in their effort to delineate the larger contours of their world, and our sympathy, at least on the level of metaphor, with certain of their perceptions, that we have come to feel a curious bond with the 'witch hunters' of 1692" (180).

[3]"Reversal of Attainder, October 17, 1711," in Boyer and Nissenbaum, *Witchcraft Papers*, 1015–156 (italics added). A few attainders were not reversed.

Illustrious Providences (1684). Mather, a Boston minister and politician, had collected narratives from his fellow colonists to demonstrate that, despite the Indian wars and loss of the colony's original charter, the deity had consistently singled out New Englanders for special benevolence. However, this collection of "remarkable and very memorable events" in New England included not only the narratives of providences, but also numerous accounts of sorcery, apparitions, demonic possession, magic, and witchcraft—many of them culled from English collections. In short, Mather included every form of supernatural power he knew of, good or evil, and inexplicably offered them all under one cover as the "illustrious providences" of the Puritan deity. Moreover, many providences of the divinity were more bizarre and horrifying than clearly benevolent: among the more impressive close calls, people survived being captured by Indians, burned by gunpowder, shot in the head, struck by lightning, and having houses fall down on them. Even in the 1690s Mather's book was viewed by some as an irresponsible incitement to the Salem tragedy, mainly because he had introduced a wealth of occult tales to the American Puritan imagination and lent his prestige to their circulation. In retrospect, however, it seems equally significant that Mather implicitly attributed occult power and apparently hostile acts to the Puritan deity as well as to the witch. Mather's editing seems just as fickle as Warren's testimony, and from a close perspective, just as idiosyncratic.

Warren's testimony, Mather's book, the reversal of legal opinion— taken singly, each appears to be an atypical moment of emotional indulgence. Taken together, they begin to imply that a confusing similarity between divine and occult power was actually characteristic of Puritan thought. Indeed, if we step back from the immediacy of the Salem witchcraft decade, and take a secular view of Puritan beliefs about supernatural power as they developed in the seventeenth century, the confusion surrounding Salem looks very different. From this broader perspective, the stark, dualist opposition between divine power and witchcraft appears to have been superimposed over a chronic similarity in the acts attributed to the deity and the witch. As I will show, the Puritan concept of divine power, particularly among American Puritans, developed in part by appropriating the powers attributed to sorcerers and witches in pre-Reformation Europe. Beginning in the late 1500s the Puritan deity steadily acquired these powers, so much so that the power of the medieval *wicche* came to characterize divine power.

The startling resemblance between the Puritan deity and the witch has been obscured by considerable misunderstanding in our own century about the history of witchcraft beliefs. Although the diabolic image of the witch has long been presumed to be as old as Christianity itself, historians have recently proved this to be false. Actually, belief in the diabolic witch developed on the Continent sometime in the fifteenth century, when the Church's attack on magicians and heretics was expanded to include witches *per se*. Christian society concomitantly began to believe that most witches were women, despite the fact that it continued to accuse and convict significant numbers of men. (At Salem, about one-third of the accused, and one-third of those tried and convicted, were men.) Adapting already existing beliefs about magicians and heretical sects, and further incorporating symbolic images of women and reports of pagan religious practices among women, Continental clerics and lawyers of early modern Europe produced a synthetic nightmare of powerful, dangerous, numerous, and distinctly female witches who paid homage to Satan and threatened all of society. At the height of prosecution in Europe, roughly 1550–1650, this new diabolic, sexualized image of the witch was a staple of Continental trials. People were convicted as much—or more—for spiritual and sexual relations with the devil as for any particular harm to their neighbors.[4]

The typical emphasis placed on the symbolic female witch has done more than just distort the chronology of witchcraft beliefs. It has also made it easy to overlook the significance of the most obvious fact of witchcraft prosecution: that men were responsible for the public articulation of the concept of the symbolic witch and for the social fact of widespread prosecution and execution. While many women also believed in witches, the court authorities who initiated and conducted the prosecutions were men; they were sanctioned by laws created by men, defended in tracts written by men, and their court convictions led to executions conducted by men. Nonetheless, men have been a neglected subject in analyses of witchcraft prosecutions, hidden from history (as perhaps they wished to be) by the impressive diabolic witch. Even Boyer and Nissenbaum, whose study of Salem has done much to correct the imbalance, fall back at crucial points on conventional symbolic images of female witches to explain the dynamics of specific charges.[5] Furthermore, while they describe at length the jealous-

---

[4]Severe problems with chronology were first noted by Charles Edward Hopkin, *The Share of Thomas Aquinas in the Growth of the Witchcraft Delusion* (Philadelphia: Univ. of Pennsylvania Press, 1940), 174–84, but the forgeries were not exposed until Norman Cohn, *Europe's Inner Demons: An Enquiry Inspired by the Great Witch-hunt* (New York: Basic Books, 1975). Cf. Richard Keickhefer, *European Witch Trials: Their Foundation in Popular and Learned Culture, 1300–1500* (Berkeley: Univ. of California Press, 1976), who independently confirms Cohn; and Edward Peters, *The Magician, the Witch, and the Law* (Philadelphia: Univ. of Pennsylvania Press, 1978). Cohn, Keickhefer, and Peters agree that pre-Reformation trials were overwhelmingly concerned with magic and heresy, not witchcraft, and that massive witch-hunts were a phenomenon of early modern Europe. For basic statistics on Salem, see John Demos, "Underlying Themes in the Witchcraft of Seventeenth Century New England," *American Historical Review*, 75 (1970), 1311–26. Clarke Garrett, "Women and Witches: Patterns of Analysis," *Signs*, 3 (1977), 461–70, greatly oversimplifies available European data. See instead H. C. Erik Midelfort, *Witch-hunting in Southwestern Germany, 1562–1684: The Social and Intellectual Foundations* (Stanford: Stanford Univ. Press, 1972), 179–81; and E. William Monter, *Witchcraft in France and Switzerland: The Borderlands During the Reformation* (Ithaca: Cornell Univ. Press, 1976), 119–23.

[5]Boyer and Nissenbaum, *Salem Possessed*, 147–51. The highly speculative descriptions of two wealthy women, Elizabeth Carr and Mary Veren, 135–44, markedly resemble fairy-tale portraits of evil stepmothers, as the authors admit, 144. The description of Sarah Good, 203–06, accepts at face value the stereotypic image of the symbolic witch in forming accusations against her, offering no alternative interpretation of Good's behavior. These are only a few examples from a book marred throughout by recourse to symbolic images of women.

ies, hatreds, and rivalries that fueled the Salem trials, they never explain why these hostile emotions took the particular form of *witchcraft* accusations. The purpose of this essay is to explore the social as well as the religious significance of the concept of witchcraft in the thought of Puritan men.

As Alan MacFarlane and Keith Thomas have shown, witchcraft accusations in the courts of Elizabethan and Stuart England differed significantly from the accusations of diabolism that inundated Continental courts in early modern Europe. Although Englishmen shared the new Continental predilection for prosecuting women, they were preoccupied with witchcraft as a material, much more than a spiritual crime. Despite the warnings of a few English authors (such as William Perkins) who shared the Continental terror of diabolic compacts and devil-worship, English judges and accusers rarely gave their attention to Sabbats, covens, or pacts with the devil. According to MacFarlane's analysis of Essex prosecutions, ninety-two percent of witchcraft charges in Assize Court indictments were for injuring or killing people or livestock, or damaging property. While Continental indictments included these crimes, they were typically interwoven with the more volatile charge of heretical devil-worship. By contrast, English courts prosecuted witches in small numbers and principally for deeds that intervened in the material world of the ordinary person's life in a direct and obvious way. How the witch acquired her power was not very important to the magistrates. Instead, they sought proof of malice and tangible harm. The relation between the individual witch's own hostility and the victim's material misfortune was the focus of the trial.[6]

By concentrating almost exclusively on material crimes and the motive of malice, the English courts clearly maintained an older image of the witch's powers, one found in European sources antedating the concept of the diabolic witch. Medieval authors indentified the witch by his or her capacity and desire to perform *maleficia*. *Maleficium* originally meant "an evil deed or mischief," but from the fourth century on, it appeared in official documents meaning "harm-doing by occult means." *Maleficia* were ascribed to witches and sorcerers alike, and authors writing in English or French similarly made no distinction between witchcraft and sorcery. The Old English *wicca*, the etymological root of "witch," simply meant a man who practiced magic and divination. The Old French equivalent was *sorcier*. Not all harm-doing was ascribed to magic, and certainly magic had a broad range of common uses, many of them benevolent. *Maleficium* denoted only one kind of deed within a wide range of occult possibilities, and certain adversities were believed to be especially typical *maleficia*: natural disasters such as storms and fires that damaged grain, livestock, or

[6]American historiography assumes, erroneously, that Perkins was representative of English thought. See Alan MacFarlane, *Witchcraft in Tudor and Stuart England: A Regional and Comparative Study* (New York: Harper and Row, 1970), 23–25, 134–39, 189; Keith Thomas, *Religion and the Decline of Magic* (New York: Scribner's, 1971), chs. 5–6, 9, 15; John L. Teall, "Witchcraft and Calvinism in Elizabethan England: Divine Power and Human Agency," *Journal of the History of Ideas,* 23 (1962), 21–36.

household, or killed or injured people; and diseases in human beings or animals, particularly if they resulted in death. Unlike the later image of the diabolic witch, the concept of *maleficium* drew attention to a concrete event and its effect (harmful), the supposed means (preternatural, but not diabolic), and the implied motive (malice), but it did not stereotype the characteristics of the person who did it. Anyone with malicious intent and occult knowledge was capable of *maleficium*, and terminology suggests that both men and women were believed to be culpable. The agents of these evil deeds were called, in Latin, *maleficus/malefica;* in Old English, *wicca/wicce;* and in Old French, *sorcier/sorcière.* The Middle English *wicche* was used for both men and women and so, initially, was the modern English "witch."[7]

It was the medieval sorcerer-witch, not the later diabolic witch, that the Puritan deity came to resemble. Drawing on the general credence of *maleficia,* Puritans imagined a deity who performed the same deeds as the medieval *wicche,* intervening in the natural course of events in the same ways. Of course the Puritans gave these supernatural acts a different name and a different motive, variously calling them "afflictions," "remarkable providences," and "memorable deliverances." However adverse events seemed to be, when Puritans believed them to be special acts of their divinity, they reinterpreted the motive as the correcting hand of divine love, the deity's edifying intervention meant to instruct erring souls and provoke repentance. In retrospect, what really seems remarkable about "remarkable providences" was the capacity of Puritan imaginations to transform bad fortune into good fortune. Mather indirectly conceded as much in his *Essay,* concluding his "philosophical meditations" with an anecdote in which "a prophane man" contrasts his own, non-Puritan view of misfortune with the Puritan belief in divine benevolence. A faithless man who "greatly trembled" when it "thundered very dreadfully," the "prophane man" was astonished when his pious wife was "not at all afraid." Impressed by her fearlessness, he inquired why she was so calm and was "amazed" at her reply: "I know it is the voice of my Heavenly Father: and should a child be afraid to hear his fathers voice?" The husband concluded, "these Puritans have a divine principle in them, which the world seeth not, that they should have peace and security in their souls when others are filled with dismal fears and horrors."[8]

The thunderstorm that occasioned this man's insight into Puritan religion was also one of the oldest and most common *maleficia* in the repertoire of medieval witches and sorcerers, even something of a specialty. Norman

---

[7]On *maleficia* and their agents, see Cohn, *Europe's Inner Demons,* 147–224; Peters, *Magicians, the Witch, and the Law,* xvii, 17, 139, 145, 154, 160–61, 165, 168–69; The *Oxford English Dictionary; Stratmann's Middle-English Dictionary.* On magic, see Thomas, *Religion and the Decline of Magic,* chs. 7–9; Peters, *Magicians, the Witch, and the Law,* chs. 1–3; MacFarlane, *Witchcraft in Tudor and Stuart England,* 67, 128; D.P. Walker, *Spritual and Demonic Magic: Ficino to Campanella* (London: Warburg Institute, 1958).

[8]Increase Mather, *Remarkable Providences* (originally published as *Essay for the Recording of Illustrious Providences*) (1684; rpt. London: John Russell Smith, 1856) 94–95.

Cohn has described at length the evidence for widespread belief in the powers of medieval *"tempestarii"* to conjure storms. According to Cohn, legal records imply that sorcerers regularly threatened people with the ruination of their crops by storms, and the writings of a ninth-century bishop of Lyons indicate that "almost everybody—nobleman and commoner, town dweller and peasant—believed in the supernatural power of storm-makers." Among his examples, Cohn describes a sorceress arraigned in London in 1493, who "freely boasted that she could make it rain at will."[9] As Mather's tale suggests, among his adherents the Puritan deity was also a noted *tempestarius*, and New England narrators seem to have been especially impressed with their deity's capacity and inclination to "make it rain at will." They praised their deity's weather-magic, believing such afflictions expressed divine approval of the colonists' immigration. For example, Edward Johnson saw the power of the divinity in a storm of 1634 which nearly capsized an embarking ship with two noted preachers on board, John Norton and Thomas Shepard. Barely escaping arrest in Yarmouth, they had set sail only to find the ship driven back to the English coast by a storm causing "the losse of the Ships upper worke." This adversity might easily have been construed as divine *dis*approval of their journey, but Johnson nevertheless interpreted the event as a show of benevolence: "The Lord Christ intending to make his *New England* souldiers the very wonder of this Age, brought them into greater straites, that this *Wonder-working Providence* might the more appeare in their deliverance." Johnson's narration, like Mather's, shows he was well aware of the possible confusion of *maleficia* and remarkable providences. As Johnson tells it, the ship captain and the sailors had their own ideas about who caused the storm, believing it to be the malice of witchcraft: "The Master, and other Sea men made a strange construction of the sore storme they met withall, saying, their Ship was bewitched." But Johnson was certain the sailors were wrong, that "assuredly it was the *Lord Christ*, who hath command both of Winds and Seas" who had caused the storm to "have his people know he hath delivered, and will deliver [them] from so great a death."[10]

Shepard and Norton finally succeeded in their intentions, but other Puritans experienced more convoluted and painful forms of divine caring. Anthony Thacher recounted a "remarkable sea deliverance" occurring in 1635 on a voyage from Ipswich to Marblehead. On this short but disastrous trip, Thacher, his cousin, Peter Avery, and their families also experienced the power of the Puritan deity as storm-maker: "Before daylight it pleased the Lord to send so mighty a storm, as the like was never known in New England since the English came, nor in the memory of any Indians." Despite the fact that the families were making the trip for a holy purpose (Peter had been called to the ministry at Marblehead), the boat capsized in

[9]Cohn, *Europe's Inner Demons*, 152–53.
[10]Edward Johnson, *Wonder-Working Providence of Sions Saviour in New England* (London, 1654), ch. 29.

the storm. Floundering in the sea, the sinking Thacher prayed to the divine storm-maker and found himself enabled to walk in, if not on, water: "I lifted up both my heart and hands to the God of heaven. For note, I had my senses remaining perfect with me all the time that I was under and in water, who at that instant lifted up my head above the top of the water, that so I might breathe without any hindrance by the waters. I stood bolt upright as if I had stood upon my feet, but I felt no bottom, nor had any footing to stand upon, but the waters." The deity was benevolent, but not very—only Thacher and his wife survived this remarkable providence. After watching Avery's entire family and his own five children drown, himself unable to rescue any of them, Thacher was finally cast up on a "desolate island" where "I and my wife were almost naked both of us, and wet and cold even unto death." Grostesquely, he emphasized that the deity did not fail to provide for them in their grief and deprivation, for Thacher found his dead son's coat washed up on the beach, along with some water-logged supplies: "Going further I found a drowned goat, then I found a hat, and my son William's coat, both which I put on . . . . Thus the Lord sent us some clothes to put on, and food to sustain our new lives which we had lately given to us." For a devout Puritan, even the most anguished misfortunes were construed as acts of divine benevolence. When Mather reprinted this narrative in *Illustrious Providences,* he tried to smooth away the incongruity of benevolent disaster by not mentioning who had died, introducing the story as "Mr. Anthony Thacher's relation concerning his and his wife's being marvellously preserved alive, when all the ship's company perished." Unlike Johnson, neither Thacher nor Mather mentioned any possibility of sorcery. For them, perhaps, the deity was fully credible as benevolent only if there were no alternatives broached.[11]

Unlike the medieval *tempestarii,* the Puritan deity was rarely accused of damage to crops, at least not in the annals of early historians and journalists. Nevertheless, the old notion was still influential, for in 1646 Winthrop recorded that a supernatural power had contrived a "thunder shower" of caterpillars to destroy their crops:

> Great harm was done in corn (especially wheat and barley) in this month by a caterpillar, like a black worm about an inch and a half long. . . . It was believed by divers good observers, that they fell in a great thunder shower, for divers yards and other bare places, where not one of them was to be seen an hour before, were presently after the shower almost covered with them.[12]

The analogy of a biblical plague might have been more ready-to-hand, but Winthrop and his fellow Puritans were probably inspired instead by the

---

[11]"Thacher's Narrative of His Shipwreck," in Alexander Young, ed., *Chronicles of the First Planters of the Colony of Massachussets Bay, From 1623 to 1636* (Boston: Little and Brown, 1846), 483–95; Increase Mather, *An Essay for the Recording of Illustrious Providences,* (Boston, 1684), 1.
[12]"Journal," July 1646, quoted in Perry Miller and Thomas E. Johnson, eds., *The Puritans* (New York: Harper and Row, 1963), I, 141.

tradition of storm-makers' sorcery. The Puritans counteracted with their prayers to the deity, and the caterpillars departed. Witches were also believed to kill livestock as well as crops. Cohn cites an eleventh-century source referring to people "who actually boasted that they could remove or kill chickens, young peacocks, whole litters of piglets, by a word or glance."[13] Less prominent in Puritan thought, this *maleficium* nevertheless hovered in the background of Puritan sermons and narratives, as in Thacher's unwitting rhyme of "drowned goat" and "William's coat," associating the deaths of children and livestock, or John Cotton's sermon describing the effects of the deity's curse: "A man that doth despise the patience and bounty of God, hee doth pro-cure to himselfe speciall, rare, choyse, and extraordinary wrath and judgement, not onely one or two, but variety, choise and store, upon body, soule, and conscience, upon children and estate left behinde."[14] Personal harm sounds more foreboding here, but the destruction of livestock as a portion of the targeted estate was well within the domain of providential "variety" that a sinner could expect. The witch or sorcerer might also destroy property by fire, as Richard Rosse of Little Clapton, Essex, knew. In 1582, when his barn mysteriously caught fire, he accused Henry Celles of witchcraft.[15] Similarly, the divinity was an occasional incendiary. Although the deity did not often indulge in this *maleficium*, the insightful Increase Mather readily recognized the divine power behind the great Boston fire of 1711, rushing into print with *Burnings Bewailed . . . In which the Sins which Provoke the Lord to Kindle Fires are Enquired into*. When Samuel Sewall's house caught fire in 1709, he also discerned the hand of Providence, although he claimed he was too slow-witted to understand the divinity's edifying message about his sins: "The good Lord sanctify this Threatening; and his Parental Pity in improving ourselves for the Discovery of the fire, and Quenching it. The Lord teach me what I know not; and wherein I have done amiss help me to do so no more!"[16]

Although theologically the divinity was not limited to any particular means or ends, in their daily lives the Puritans applied the criteria of *maleficia* to identify the special providences of their deity. Colonial narratives yield many more examples like the illustrations I have given above. They are equally numerous in the writings of clerics and laymen, and indeed it is difficult to find a colonial narrative that does not employ this concept of the deity. Strange as it seems, what for centuries had been the evil deeds of witches and sorcerers became, for American Puritans, the benevolent signs of divine love. Whether this was also true for other Protestant sects is difficult to assess, since studies of European witchcraft

[13]Cohn, *Europe's Inner Demons*, 152.
[14]John Cotton, *God's Mercie Mixed With His Justice* (London, 1641), 17–18.
[15]Thomas, *Religion and the Decline of Magic*, 559.
[16]*The Diary of Samuel Sewall, 1674–1729*, 2 vols., ed. M. Halsey Thomas (New York: Farrer, Straus, and Giroux, 1973), 621–22.

do not address this question. What evidence can be gleaned from existing interpretations strongly suggests, however, that the Puritans were by no means unique. In Thomas's study of beliefs about supernatural power in early modern England, the chapter on providences and the chapter on witchcraft describe very similar kinds of events. In his detailed study of Essex for the same period, MacFarlane concludes in perplexity, "Yet, as a method of explaining misfortune and evil, witchcraft beliefs to some extent overlapped with religious explanations," and adds further that "the difference between the Puritans and those they castigated was merely in the details." MacFarlane makes nothing of this, but his own evidence indicates that the "details" were crucial to contemporary writers because the "overlap" was very substantial. The minister George Gifford complained that his congregation constantly confused the deity with the witch: "They can by no means see, that God is provoked by their sinnes to give the devill such instruments to work withall, but rage against the witch." Reginald Scot likewise viewed witchcraft accusations as mere delusions of impious souls who could not bear to see divine power for what it really was:

> The fables of witchcraft have taken so fast hold and deepe root in the heart of man, that fewe or none can (nowadaies) with patience indure the hand and correction of God. For if any adversitie, greefe, sicknesse, losse of children, corne, cattell, or libertie happen to them; by & by they exclaime uppon witches. As though there were no God in Israel that ordereth all things according to his will.

Neither a Puritan nor a cleric, Scot nevertheless derided those Englishmen who did not yet understand Reformation religion, who mistook the Protestant deity's providences for *maleficia*.[17]

In general, European authors and judges consistently suggested a significant resemblance between the power of the new Protestant deity and the traditional powers of the sorcerer-witch. Sometimes the resemblance was expressed unwittingly, as in the English account of Elizabeth Jackson's "prophesying threatenings, ever taking effect, which Judge Anderson observed as a notable property of a witch."[18] The charwoman's curses were described in the same terms used for the Old Testament prophecy of Jeremiah. Moreover, Puritan ministers called their own conventicles "prophesyings." In the writings of the French political theorist, Jean Bodin, the similarity between his concepts of the deity and the witch made his argument for witchcraft prosecution nearly unintelligible. Believing that witchcraft was an "insult" to the "majesty of God," Bodin contended that witches should be executed not so much to punish malicious harmdo-

---

[17]Thomas, *Religion and the Decline of Magic*, chs. 4, 14; MacFarlane, *Witchcraft in Tudor and Stuart England*, 189, 194, cites Gifford, 194, and Scot, 192.

[18]On the Jackson case, see Thomas, *Religion and the Decline of Magic*, 511. On prophesying, see Irvonwy Morgan, *The Godly Preachers of the Elizabethan Church* (London: Epworth Press, 1965).

ing as to appease the deity's wrath. He confusedly warned that those "who let the witches escape, or who do not punish them with the utmost rigor, may rest assured that they will be abandoned by God to the mercy of the witches. And the country which shall tolerate this will be scourged with pestilences, famines, and wars."[19] But who would cause all this harm? The escaped witches, or the enraged and "insulted" deity? To judge from Bodin's reasoning, the deity and the witch were equally capable of such vengeful attacks. German Protestant theologians at Württemberg, far more aware of the possible confusion between the powers of the deity and the witch, argued that such confusion was itself the work of the devil. In 1613 Johann Sigwart, a Professor of Scripture at Tübingen and a follower of the Württemberg school, explained that the hailstorm near his city of Tübingen was not witchcraft, but that the devil had tried to make it seem so: "For when Satan . . . notices that according to nature a storm may arise, he suggests to his witches . . . to work their magic, and to cook and stir this or that together in their hail pot." But the apparent power of *maleficia* was the devil's delusion, for "at the same time it thunders and hails, not because they [the witches] caused it, but because it was already about to happen without them, either by nature or at God's decree."[20] Only deluded witches, Sigwart argued, could fail to see that the hailstorm was the work of an all-powerful deity.

For Sigwart, as for Scot and Gifford in England, the concept of divine power as the author of disaster had become important enough to make it an act of bad faith if one believed in the witch's power to perform *maleficia* at all. Regardless of whether they supported or opposed the prosecution of witches, European authors searched urgently for ways to distinguish their deity as the sole perpetrator of misfortune. The ideological threat of resemblance, not misfortune itself, was what they feared. Historians have speculated that the Protestant lack of techniques for combating witchcraft may have weakened their struggle against Catholicism, that pious prayers and counsels to endure must have seemed dangerously inadequate when compared to the battery of Catholic ritual.[21] However, this hypothesis altogether misses the nature of the major threat presented by witchcraft beliefs: the Protestant deity was communicating his presence in the same way that sorcerers and witches had traditionally communicated theirs. And it misses, as well, the Protestants' real "defense" against Catholicism. We are accustomed to interpreting the Reformation as an effort to eradicate traditional beliefs in Europe, but when we consider the growth of Protestantism in light of traditional beliefs about witches and sorcerers, the influence seems rather to have gone the other way. Far from eliminating these older beliefs, Protestantism appropriated them for its own cause.

[19]Jean Bodin, *De la Démonomanie des Sorciers* (Paris, 1850), quoted in Alan C. Kors and Edward Peters, eds., *Witchcraft in Europe 1100–1700: A Documentary History* (Philadelphia: Univ. of Pennsylvania Press, 1972), 215.
[20]Midelfort, *Witch-hunting in Southwestern Germany*, 44.
[21]For a recent statement of this view, see Thomas, *Religion and the Decline of Magic*, chs. 1–9.

The Puritan injunction to endure any affliction, any harm or misery, as a just punishment meted out by the deity was not theologically innovative. What was new was the significance afflictions received from the Puritan theory of history. Sacvan Bercovitch has shown how English Protestantism assigned religious significance to contemporary events by discovering, they believed, parallels between Israel's history and English history. As he explains, American Puritans tipped the balance of the analogy decisively in favor of contemporary events, producing a "wholesale inversion of traditional hermeneutics" that "transferred the source of meaning from Scripture to secular history."[22] Restricting the relevance of Israel's history to themselves alone, American Puritans treated the events of their own lives as types prophecying the millenial, definitive revelation that would vindicate their interpretation of their own importance in the world. It was not that pre-Reformation Christians had never read the book of nature, but they had never read it in this way. While typological interpretation had been applied to the history of the Catholic Church, and while any medieval theologian would readily have agreed that history was providential, they did not read the ordinary, material events of their own lives as a divine prophecy with an unprecedented message to convey to the rest of the world. The Puritans, well aware of the novelty of their perspective (that was exactly the point), advertised it with such phrases as "remarkable providences," "wonder-working providences," and "remarkable deliverances" to announce the deity's interventions in the world on their behalf.

Puritan hermeneutic theory claimed that significant events in Puritan lives had clear biblical equivalents, but in practice the analogy with Israel's history was difficult to discern beyond the initial emigration/exodus from England/Egypt and the crossing of the Atlantic/Red Sea. For the most part, the hermeneutics intended to reveal their own history instead tended to conceal it in suggestive biblical symbolism. Puritans made this biblical analogy credible to themselves not so much through parallels to Scriptural chronicles, but by appropriating the Old Testament prophetic jeremiad, the anxious warning of Jeremiah that an elect people must expect warning chastisements from the deity whenever they lost their sense of spiritual purpose. Unlike specific events of Israel's history, the "prophesying threatenings" of Jeremiah were extremely versatile, for the general logic maintained an abstract connection with Israel's history, while the indefiniteness of the threat freed interpretation from the necessity to argue any particular parallels between Puritans and Israelites. Short of the whole society being utterly "consumed out of the land," any adverse events were an oblique confirmation of their elect status.[23] Thus affliction became a convoluted divine sanction, however much it might appear to the uninitiated to be a sign of rejecting wrath. Since the deity's blessing could take

[22]Sacvan Bercovitch, *The Puritan Origins of the American Self* (New Haven: Yale Univ. Press, 1975.) See esp. 109, 113.
[23]On the jeremiad in American thought, see Sacvan Bercovitch, *The American Jeremiad* (Madison: Univ. of Wisconsin Press, 1978).

apparently hostile forms, the gracious blows of the correcting hand of affliction, "remarkable providences" could be anything as long as the event was considered extraordinary, an intrusion of supernatural power into their otherwise ordinary lives. What made an event a sign of election was the perceptible disruption *per se*, not the consequences of it. Destruction, disease, and death, if they seemed unusual, could be just as persuasive as health and prosperity.

Preternatural events, disrupting ordinary life, and expressing a personal, vengeful anger, causing harm and promising the possibility of more harm—for the Puritans these events proved to be, not surprisingly, the same ones European culture had recognized as such for centuries. Under the aegis of the jeremiad, however, the whole range of *maleficia* acquired a new importance and a new meaning as the Puritans' means of religious self-identification. In between the biblical metaphors and public histories, and tucked away in the privacy of journals and diaries, Puritan narrators had their moments of "remarkable" clarity in which they detailed the particular storms, fires, diseases, premature deaths, and destruction of property that marked their lives—not now as *maleficia*, but as the crucial signs of the Puritan deity's loving displeasure. Conversely, the tradition of *maleficia* lent credence to Puritanism, for Puritan narrators felt no need to prove, to themselves or to others, that these events were preternatural, or even that they were expressions of a personally directed anger: *maleficia* bore the sanction of centuries of custom declaring them to be just that. And because these misfortunes had long been interpreted as the expression of someone's displeasure at someone else, they resembled biblical types as purposeful communications carrying semantic value. When the English witches performed *maleficia*, they acted out of anger, seeking vengeance against those who had denied or offended them. And so did the deity of the jeremiads, promising the vengeance of destruction for the sins that offended and denied him.

Because the Puritan deity's "signs" were also the witch's *maleficia*, and because both were motivated by angry vengeance, the Puritans were threatened by belief in witchcraft as they never were by official religions such as Catholicism and Anglicanism. Arguments with these latter opponents were always concerned with what constituted a proper religious practice, an efficacious invocation of supernatural power—the Catholic Mass or the Puritan Lord's Supper? The Anglican Prayer Book or the Puritan sermon? Dismissing these official religious opponents as frauds, the Puritans saved their credulity for the witch. Since Puritanism and witchcraft came to focus on the same set of events, in effect agreeing on what constituted a spiritual intervention in the natural world, the contention with respect to the witch was not what constituted a properly supernatural event, but rather, who was producing it? From this perspective, the image of the deity as the author of remarkable providences, and the image of the witch as the author of *maleficia*, were positive and negative forms of a single idea about supernatural power.

That the image of a deity is a projected image of power in human society is a long-standing, if not very well-understood, argument. What I would like to consider here instead is the way in which the negative form, the image of the witch, is similarly a projection. (The psychological phenomenon of projection is the location in another person of qualities or feelings which the subject does not recognize in the self.[24] As a social relation, projection paradoxically permits the subject to enact prohibited behavior while still treating it as prohibited, for the projected qualities in turn become the rationale for the subject's own acts.) There is, of course, an important difference in the displacement: where the projected image of the deity is displaced on an imagined anthropomorphic being, the image of the witch is, in the act of accusation, displaced on a real human being. MacFarlane has shown how projection describes the actions of accusers in English courts: when someone accused another person of angry and hostile acts of witchcraft, that is, *maleficia*, the accusation was an expression of hostility that was in turn justified by the projected hostility. Moreover, the accuser's hostility was easy to discern, for it had already surfaced in some previous altercation. Accusers regularly produced explanations for why witchcraft had been practiced against them in particular, and their explanations followed a consistent pattern. Prior to the occurrence of some *maleficium*, the accused witch had asked for some trivial act of charity, or simply begged outright, and the accuser had refused them. Angry at this refusal, the accused witch sought reprisal through acts of witchcraft.[25] The case against the accused witch, then, was not that the accused had acted with complete illogicality, without any provocation. Rather, the crime of the accused witch was that he or she had retaliated with grossly disproportionate anger and hostility. Sarah Good, the first person accused at Salem, fits the archetype of English cases, for she was an indigent villager who, according to the many witnesses testifying against her, was a chronic beggar in the town and was easily angered by refusals. According to MacFarlane's model, the Salem Villagers, angry at her continual begging because they were guilt-ridden by their own uncharitable refusals, expressed that anger in accusations of witchcraft. MacFarlane's interpretation is viable as far as it goes, but he neglects to show the importance of the specific accusation of witchcraft itself. The accused witch was not accused of hostile anger in the abstract, but of hostile anger expressed through particular *maleficia*. For example, when Sarah Gadge testified against Sarah Good, she first recounted Good's entreaty, her own refusal, and Good's subsequent anger at being refused, all as MacFarlane's model predicts. But Gadge then went on to couple this sequence with another story of the sudden death of the Gadge cow, which the Gadges believed (and the court agreed) had been killed by

---

[24]See J. Laplanche and J.-B. Pontalis, *The Language of Psychoanalysis*, trans. Donald Nicholson-Smith (New York: W. W. Norton, 1973), 349 (def. II).
[25]MacFarlane, *Witchcraft in Tudor and Stuart England*, 158–64, 192–209. Demos and Boyer and Nissenbaum use MacFarlane's model.

Good's retaliatory witchcraft.[26] The projection offered by the witness and acted upon by the court was not just a general image of unjustified or disproportionate anger, but the image of Sarah Good as author of *maleficium*. How, then, can we interpret the attribution of *maleficia* as a projection?

We can begin to answer this question by considering the one *maleficium* of medieval tradition we have not yet considered with respect to Puritanism: mysterious illnesses that often resulted in death. Over the course of the seventeenth century, this *maleficium* became an increasingly important indictment and seems to have focused on dependent family members as victims. As greater numbers of witches were accused of it, greater numbers of dependents appeared in court as afflicted accusers, like the "afflicted girls" of Salem. The murder of children was a relatively frequent accusation at Salem. In the precedent-setting case against Bridget Bishop, the first person tried and executed at Salem, witnesses related numerous stories of local children's deaths, many occurring before 1692 but all attributed to her supposed witchcraft. For instance, one married man testified he did "verily believe that the said Bridget Bishop was instrumental to his daughter Precilla's death about two years ago. The child was a likely, thriving child, and suddenly screeched out and so continued in an unusual manner for about a fortnight, and so died in that lamentable manner." Samuel Gray also believed that his child had died of witchcraft, recounting how he had seen the apparition of Bishop in his house at night, "standing between the cradle and the bedside." The apparition vanished, and then returned,

> and the child in the cradle gave a screech out, as if it was greatly hurt, and she disappeared. . . . From which time, the child, that before was a very likely, thriving child, did pine away and was never well, although it lived some months after, yet in a sad condition, and so died.

Samuel Shattoch, a middle-aged father like Samuel Gray, blamed his child's insanity on Bishop, whose frequent visits to his house seemed to him to coincide with his son's mental deterioration. As these narratives suggest, Salem residents saw the fits of the "afflicted girls" in the same light. They were, contemporaries observed, very like the fits and strange experiences other children had had before dying or becoming insane.[27]

The Puritan deity shared this *maleficium*, too, for deaths of dependents were among the most frequent of his remarkable providences. Although the doctrine of affliction has usually been understood as punishment of the *self* for the self's own sins, the deaths of Puritan children show that the idea was more complicated—and more painful—than this. Thomas recounts the Puritan Ralph Josselin's grief and anguish over Josselin's son's death:

---

[26]Paul Boyer and Stephen Nissenbaum, eds., *Salem-Village Witchcraft; A Documentary Record of Local Conflict in Colonial New England* (Belmont, Calif.: Wadsworth, 1972), 14.
[27]On Continental cases, see Monter, *Witchcraft in France and Switzerland*, 100, 198. On Salem cases, see Boyer and Nissenbaum, *Salem-Village Witchcraft*, 42-43, 30.

When the infant son of Ralph Josselin, vicar of Earl's Colne, Essex, died of diphtheria in 1648, his bereaved father sought to know which of his faults God was punishing, and concluded that the judgment must have partly been provoked by his vain thoughts and unseasonable playing at chess.[28]

The ambiguity in Thomas's pronouns arises from the social ambiguity in Josselin's head concerning who had died for what. Only when we realize that the infant son could not himself have played the chess games that killed him do we then understand that the *father's* sins caused the *son's* death— or so Josselin believed. The son's death was supposed to be "edifying" to the father, a mode of instruction that would reveal to Josselin the gravity of his, the father's, sins, and encourage him, the father, to repent. Thus the Puritan father was meant to "profit from affliction." Thomas Shepard, a minister in Cambridge, Massachusetts, arrived at the same explanation for John Shepard's death: "My son John, after sixteen weeks departed on the Sabbath-day morning, a day of rest, to the bosom of rest to him who gave it, which was no small affliction and heartbreaking to me that *I should provoke the Lord to strike at my innocent children for my sake.*" Shepard similarly explained his wife's death:

But the Lord hath not been wont to let me live long without some affliction or other . . . he took away my dear, precious, meek and loving wife in childbed. . . . This affliction was very heavy to me, for in it the Lord seemed to withdraw his tender care for me and mine which he graciously manifested by my dear wife. . . . And I saw that if I had profited by former afflictions of this nature I should not have had this scourge.[29]

Men like Shepard interpreted their personal histories in the same way they understood the history of the Puritan community as a whole. Unusual events disrupting their personal lives were similarly interpreted as signs of the Puritan deity's disposition toward them as individuals. Thus, in the context of events in a Puritan man's individual life, the death of his wife or child became one more index to the state of his soul. Shepard, writing his autobiography, described his son as "innocent" and his wife as far more saintly than himself, but as he tells it, their grace did not outweigh the importance of his sin in the eyes of the Puritan deity. Both these dependents died, according to Shepard, for the instruction of their father's and husband's soul. These narratives imply there were limits to the concept of the

[28]Thomas, *Religion and the Decline of Magic*, 83.
[29]Thomas Shepard, "Autobiography," in Michael McGiffert, ed., *God's Plot* (Amherst: Univ. of Massachusetts Press, 1972), 69, 70 (italics added).

Puritan father's power, that each father was held responsible only for deaths of dependents in his immediate family. Anthony Thacher's story of his disastrous voyage to Marblehead bears this out. He blamed himself for the deaths of his own children, but not for the deaths in his cousin Avery's family. In commemorating the tragedy, he named each of the fathers on the voyage and, of course, only them: "In a boat that came that way, we went off the desolate island, which I named after my name, Thacher's Woe; and the rock, Avery his Fall: to the end that their fall and loss, and mine own, might be had in perpetual remembrance."[30] To be an unnamed dependent, in this story as in others, meant that the wife's or child's very life was only a function of the husband's or father's moral condition in the eyes of the deity, a sacrifice toward the education of someone else's soul. When Thomas Shepard himself died in 1649, just a few years after his son and first wife, no one related *his* death to the sins of his surviving sons or second wife. He was thought to have died autonomously, just as Avery had died in his own right in the storm.

Insofar as the deaths of wives and children were believed to be the result of the husband's or father's sins, the Puritan adult male, if he married, acquired a power commensurate with the witch's. Within this religious framework the nature of his relationship to his dependents was in effect the same as the witch's relationship to other members of the community. This likeness is particularly important because it suggests a perspective for the whole pattern of resemblance between the acts of the deity and the witch. The *maleficium* that resulted in personal injury or death emphasizes an aspect of Puritan thought that is less obvious, but still present, in other accounts of remarkable providences: the belief in the indirect power of the Puritan adult male's own moral acts to literally destroy the lives of people around him.

Ironically, despite a man's theological guilt before the deity, the Puritan father and husband whose sins supposedly caused the destruction of property, or worse, the deaths of his wife and children, received no blame from society; his grief and guilt were his double testimony of his social innocence and his spiritual grace. As for his dependents, their grace consisted in their willingness to be sacrificed. As Thomas Shepard observed of his wife, "She was a woman of incomparable meekness of spirit, toward myself especially," and "she was fit to die long before she did die."[31] Despite the power Puritan men assigned to themselves, such as Shepard believed he held over his wife, it would be erroneous to presume that a Puritan man was enjoined by his religion to feel guilt for the death of a dependent *per se.* These deaths were the consequences of the soul's sin, of his offense against the deity, and in order to "profit from affliction" the Puritan father or husband had to repent to the deity for the sin that had led the deity to punish

---

[30]"Thacher's Narrative," 494.
[31]Shepard, "Autobiography," 70–71.

him by the death of his wife or child. The sin, not the death, was the theological source of guilt.

Personal narratives imply that this displacement could be a very painful experience, that the theological shift of focus from the death to the sin that 'caused' it left a reservoir of unresolved grief and guilt. Shepard, after advancing the doctrine of affliction to explain his wife's death, then protested, "but this loss was very great." He continued praising her and finally balked at the whole self-conception demanded of him by Puritan religion: "Thus God hath visited and scourged me for my sins and sought to wean me from this world, but I have ever found it a difficult thing to profit even but a little by the sorest and sharpest affliction." His autobiography stops abruptly here, just short of total disbelief, as if he were too horrified and pained by the deaths he believed he had inscribed with the sins of his soul to continue to narrate his life. Anthony Thacher also implied that he could not fully accept the doctrine of affliction, expressing his grief at one point by attempting to attribute his children's deaths more directly to his own acts. He remarked at one point, "Then it came to mind how I had occasioned the death of my children, who caused them to leave their native land, who might have left them there, yea, and might have sent some of them back again and cost me nothing; these and such like thoughts do press down my heavy heart very much. But I must let this pass." The deity of remarkable providences notwithstanding, Thacher momentarily expressed more direct guilt, and more direct responsibility, for his children's deaths.[32]

The concept of the deity that assigned the power of *maleficia* to Puritan men also prohibited the recognition of that power for clerics such as Shepard, concealing it in the necessity for repentance to divine power and attributing remarkable providences to the deity of the jeremiads. But to the extent that Puritan fathers such as Thacher claimed a personal responsibility for the deaths of family dependents, the locus of the power to enact remarkable providences/*maleficia* overtly shifted from the deity to the Puritan adult male. Of course, Thacher could not have known in England that two years after his immigration his children would die in a storm while traveling from Ipswich to Marblehead, but he nevertheless implies that he could and should have been omniscient—more like the deity. Such shifts as occur in the Thacher narrative invite us to consider that the persistent resemblance between the Puritan deity and the witch was itself a displacement, mirroring a more fundamental tension in Puritan social thought: the resemblance between the Puritan concept of the father and husband and the concept of the witch as the author of *maleficia*. Puritan sermons also suggest a displacement, for the most frequent description of the deity was the metaphor of the father, and the convert's relation to the deity was described in terms of the metaphor of marriage to this figured father/husband. What Puritan fathers confronted in the Puritan concept of the

[32]Ibid., 71; "Thacher's Narrative," 493.

deity, then, was a projected figure of their own social role. The conflicting interpretations of remarkable providences/*maleficia* in personal narratives of dependents' deaths reflected the conflict engendered in individual Puritan fathers by this contradictory system of religious language: while the use of the metaphor of the father greatly enhanced the power of literal fathers by associating them closely but ambiguously with divine power, it contradictorily demanded that an adult male see himself figuratively and theologically as a powerless "child of God."

The resemblance between witchcraft beliefs and remarkable providences, between the power of the traditional European sorcerer-witch and the power of Puritan husbands and fathers, shows that traditional cultural beliefs about witchcraft strongly influenced the concept of the deity and the concept of the adult male social role in seventeenth-century Puritan culture. It suggests as well that some of our previous assumptions about the history of witchcraft beliefs have diverted us from asking major interpretive questions about witchcraft prosecutions. While I cannot here offer a comprehensive model for interpreting the Salem prosecutions, let me suggest some of the possible implications of this essay and give some examples of what sort of inquiries we might make in constructing such a model.

First, that the concept of *maleficia* continued to inform the concept of the Puritan father's power, but that this concept had become intolerable for many people, is implied in at least two important ways in the Salem trials. When Thomas Putnam journeyed with three other men into Salem town to enter the first charge of witchcraft in February, 1692, setting in motion the infamous trials, in effect he turned his back on the conventional doctrine of affliction as a way to explain the strange, disturbing behavior of his daughter, Ann Putnam, his servant, Mercy Lewis, and his niece who lived with him, Mary Walcott. His wife, Ann Carr Putnam, would soon become "afflicted" too. In effect, his accusation of witchcraft meant that their fits and seizures were not the result of his own sins. They were, rather, caused by someone else—a witch. From the broader perspective of Puritan cultural assumptions, the point is not that there was no explanation for the behavior of the "afflicted girls." Indeed, this way of describing them refers us to it. Nonetheless, that Putnam made the accusations suggests that important changes had occurred in the cultural experience of Puritan fathers and husbands in the late seventeenth century, changes that made the doctrine of affliction so undesirable or implausible that Putnam refused the self-interpretation it offered him, and reverted instead to the older explanation of such events as the *maleficia* of witchcraft. In the assertion that his family members were "afflicted" by witchcraft was the oblique confession of Putnam's own *lack* of power as a Puritan father, and perhaps this aspect of his accusation had something to do with the positive response he received from legal authority. Boyer and Nissenbaum have documented the numerous occasions before 1692 on which Putnam men had made appeals to legal authority and lost, emphasizing the seeming irony of

Thomas Putnam's immense success in 1692 from this perspective. But insofar as Putnam was asserting his own *lack* of power, a lack that successful prosecution would only validate, the positive response of legal authority was quite consistent with its earlier refusals to help Putnam either acquire or recover political and economic power.[33]

That Putnam's individual dilemma and his choice of a solution evoked widely shared attitudes is suggested not only by the large public response in favor of the trials and concern for the "afflicted girls," but also by elements of subsequent accusations. For example, the accusations against George Burroughs, the first Puritan man accused at Salem, are a mirror image in negative form of the powers of Puritan fathers and husbands. In the initial deposition, Ann Putnam's, Burroughs was accused of killing his first two wives. Other "witnesses" corroborated her testimony, Susanna Sheldon elaborating that "He appeared to me at the house of Nathanniel Ingolson and told me he had been the death of three children at the eastward and had killed two of his wives, the first he smothered and the second he choked, and killed two of his own children." Burroughs, like other defendants, was also accused of causing the fits of the "afflicted girls," but more severely in his case, "almost choking them to death." The "witchcraft" Burroughs practiced, however, was none other than a diabolic version of Puritanism itself. His case record contains the first deposition on Black Sabbaths at Salem, a staid parody of a Congregational service that the Salem judges construed as witchcraft. Burroughs, a former minister of Salem village, was accused of returning to hold illicit diabolic services at night—in the pasture *next to* the parish house of the current minister, an appropriate metaphor for displacement. A minister as well as a husband and father who had suffered the deaths of spouses and children, Burroughs was a particularly apt "place" to project the power attributed to adult men by the deity of remarkable providences. Boyer and Nissenbaum show that the accusations against Burroughs were an important turning point in the development of the Salem trials, that after these charges were made accusations increased rapidly and the Salem trials assumed major proportions. It is also true that, relative to preceeding accusations, this watershed case focused with unusual clarity on the power of adult men in relation to the deaths of family dependents, and associated that power with an organized sect and formal religious thought that is easily recognizable as a parodic inversion of Puritan church ordinances.[34]

A second dimension of relevance concerns the power of figurative "father," how the Puritan concept of a literal father's power influenced concepts of public authority. In a colony where the public authority of men was explicitly justified by analogy with the structure and character of

---

[33]On Thomas Putnam and the Putnam family, see Boyer and Nissenbaum, *Salem Possessed*, 5–6, 110–52.

[34]Boyer and Nissenbaum, *Salem-Village Witchcraft*, 68–69, 73–74, 77, 79, 70, 82.

power in the literal family, how far did the concept of *maleficia*/remarkable providences also define the power of public "patriarchs?" Historians have long argued that the effects of the Glorious Revolution on the colony government were an important influence on the Salem prosecutions, that it was not sheer coincidence that prosecutions occurred at a time of instability and confusion about the character of legal authority in the colony. Since the Salem court was convened for the sole purpose of trying witchcraft cases, it seems plausible that its contribution to changing concepts of legal power would especially reflect the importance of *maleficia*. That is, what the figurative "fathers" of the court borrowed through the analogy of the family was not just a general notion of partriarchy, but rather the more specific concept of the Puritan father's power over his dependents as it resembled *maleficia*. Since the case records repeatedly show that the judges were hardly impartial observers and frequently adopted an accusatory stance themselves, we could well begin to explore this question by extending MacFarlane's model to the court itself. Did the capacity to intentionally cause sudden death as an act of revenge, an expression of disproportionate anger, describe the social character of the Salem court's power? If we set aside the concept of the deity/witch as the cause of events, the concept that overtly justified the prosecutions, then the projection becomes apparent: although the defendants were the ones accused of exacting revenge, it was the court—and the witnesses through the power of the court—who actually got it. Without the concealment of supernatural intervention, the discernable social facts in the Salem testimony show only the occurrence of petty offenses to which the court responded by sanctioning legal murder. In Sarah Good's case, for example, her acts of begging were punished with execution, surely a grossly disproportionate response to such trivial social offenses. In short, what legal authority condemned in the accused it also enacted in the very process of condemnation.

What the legal process seems to have offered witnesses was the vicarious satisfaction of a new mutation of *maleficia* in a systematically "true" projection produced at the will of the court but guided by the "requests" for specific targets named in witnesses' accusations: the gratuitous execution (sudden death) of "witches" and the confiscation (destruction) of their property. Indeed, the court delivered with unerring accuracy, for the conviction rate at Salem was astonishingly high, even by Continental standards—one hundred percent.[35] Unlike literal fathers, the figurative fathers of judicial authority possessed a real social power to intentionally cause death and destruction by secular means. However much Puritan fathers such as Shepard may have believed that the deaths of their dependents were the intentional punitive consequences of their own sins, from a

---

[35]On European conviction rates, see Midelfort, *Witch-hunting in Southwestern Germany*, 179–81; Monter, *Witchcraft in France and Switzerland*, 119–23.

secular point of view this is no more plausible than the capacity of accused witches to actually accomplish *maleficia*. From a secular point of view, the court's version of themselves as the cause of death and destruction is much more persuasive. Moreover, the court claimed a conscious intention: it did not simply offer retroactive explanations for unwitting death and destruction, but intentionally produced such events through the purportedly rational mechanism of the legal process. In this sense, the judicial authority of the Salem court freed itself from the accidents of remarkable providences as the unpredictable occasions for the expression of its "fatherly" power, and consequently freed itself in a crucial way from the power of the Puritan deity.[36]

Extending MacFarlane's model in this way shifts the primary point of tension away from the relation between witnesses and the accused and toward the relation between court authority and the accused. This is exactly where the history of witchcraft beliefs indicates the focus really was, however, for the century of great persecution was marked first and foremost by the widespread execution of people for witchcraft *through the mechanism of the legal process of the state*. After all, people had believed in witches for centuries, and private citizens had made informal accusations of witchcraft and punished witches for just as long. What was new in early modern Europe, and what distinguished Salem in the New England history of witchcraft beliefs, was the massive intervention of state authority to prosecute witchcraft—and the subsequent epidemic of accusations and executions that intervention produced.

The Salem trials may also have been an expression of new conflicts among men about different versions of figurative fatherly power. Did the court in effect assert a new superiority of the figurative "fathers" of state power, attacking men who refused to be obedient "sons" in the new patriarchy of the new charter? That the figurative dimension of fatherly power was important in the Salem trials is suggested by the fact that the figurative "fathers" of the court found very cooperative witnesses in women and girls who, as servants or slaves, knew well how to live by this analogy: Mary Warren, servant of John Proctor; Mercy Lewis, servant of Thomas Putnam; Sarah Churchill, servant of George Jacobs; Tituba, slave of Samuel Parris; and Elizabeth Hubbard, servant of William Griggs. Two more major witnesses, Abigail Williams and Mary Walcott, were living in the households of their uncles at the time of the trials. Of all the "afflicted" who were consistently the center of attention and the main source of testimony, only two, Ann Putnam and Elizabeth Parris, were living in the households of their literal fathers—and both these fathers were among the

---

[36]No wonder, then, that the clergy for the most part opposed the trials. On ministerial opposition, see Hansen, *Witchcraft at Salem*, passim; and Perry Miller, *The New England Mind: From Colony to Province* (1953; rpt. Boston: Beacon Press, 1961), 191–208.

most ardent public supporters of the court. The depositions of female servants include complaints of mistreatment by their employers, suggesting that young women like Mary Warren and Sarah Churchill exploited the power of one father-figure to retaliate against another. The court in turn exploited the grievances of the "afflicted" servants to punish men like Proctor and Jacobs who expressed disdain for the court's power. Whatever the individual antagonisms here, the struggle between the figurative "fathers" of the court and the figurative "fathers" of private households seems to have been an important dimension of the Salem trials.[37]

Finally, understanding the importance of *maleficia* for the Puritan concept of adult male power enables us to ask different kinds of questions about the accusations made against women at Salem. Since the power of *maleficia*/remarkable providences had been attributed throughout the seventeenth century to a deity invariably described as male, or to adult men by means of their sins, how can we explain the accusations against *women* at Salem? That women should be prone to accusations of witchcraft has always been taken for granted, but since Puritan culture so strongly associated the power of *maleficia* with adult males, we need to ask seriously why and how were women accused of witchcraft at Salem at all? The research of Boyer and Nissenbaum is an instructive point of departure insofar as it interprets the wider social context of conflicts between women expressed in court depositions. Boyer and Nissenbaum, analyzing economic conditions in Salem Village, argue that traditionalist agrarians such as Thomas Putnam, whose status was declining, were extremely jealous of arrived, newly successful men like Daniel Andrew and Philip English, who were accused of witchcraft. What Boyer and Nissenbaum ignore is the relevance of these same economic tensions to accusations among married women. For example, their lengthy discussion of Thomas Putnam, the leading male accuser, culminates very oddly—in speculation about his *wife's* grievances with other wives in order to explain her accusations against such women as Rebecca Nurse. What their own evidence most clearly suggests, however, is that Thomas Putnam, through his wife, attacked Francis Nurse, through his wife. Francis Nurse was an economically successful late arrival in Salem Village, just the sort of enterprising upstart who, Boyer and Nissenbaum argue, was vulnerable to accusation.[38] In a society where the experiences of wives and children, indeed their very lives, were mere signs of an adult male's own personal success or failure, where the identity of family dependents was a mere extension of

---

[37]Boyer and Nissenbaum, *Salem Possessed*, 5–6, 35n. The "girls" are also identified in arrest warrants in Boyer and Nissenbaum, *Salem Witchcraft Papers*, passim. Further information appears in depositions against their employers, among which see esp. the George Jacobs and John Proctor case records.

[38]Boyer and Nissenbaum, *Salem Possessed*, 80–109, 120–22, 131–32, 147, 181–82, 192, 210; and *Salem-Village Witchcraft*, 148–54. Nurse may have symbolized a new style of agrarianism in buying his farm on a mortgage.

their father/husband, conflicts between women could easily be exploited to express conflicts between the men with/by whom they were identified. That Puritan culture still very strongly associated the power of witchcraft with the power of adult men, to the point that Puritan men were actually hesitant to ascribe *maleficia* to women alone—despite centuries of custom that would have supported such accusations—is suggested by the impact of the accusations against Burroughs. Reportedly, the Black Sabbaths of the diabolical Burroughs were initially attended by the women who had already been accused of witchcraft, and only when these already accused women were further accused of having acquired their power of *maleficia* from an adult male did the Salem trials begin to take on major proportions. Conceivably, the crime of which women were accused at Salem was really two-fold: not only that they were engaging in *maleficia*, but that they were *women* engaging in *maleficia*, attempting to take for themselves a power that Puritan culture had come to associate with adult male sexual identity.

HISTORICAL COLLECTIONS

OF THE

ESSEX INSTITUTE.

VOL. XXIX. JULY, AUG., SEPT., 1892. NOS. 7, 8, 9.

WERE THE SALEM WITCHES GUILTLESS?

A PAPER READ BEFORE THE ESSEX INSTITUTE, FEBRUARY 29, 1892.

BY BARRETT WENDELL

Assistant Professor of English at Harvard College.

WITHIN the past few years, I have happened, at the suggestion of friends interested in psychic research, to observe three different phases of occult phemonena. The first
is materialization, a process by which professional mediums
pretend to call up the visible and tangible bodies of the
dead. The second is trance-mediumship : the medium, in
this case also professional, pretends to be controlled by some
departed spirit who uses the tongue of the medium, rather
unskilfully, as a means of communication with living beings. The third is automatic writing : in this, acting as a
medium myself, I have held a pencil and allowed my hand
to run unwatched and uncontrolled by any conscious act
of will. I have thus written a great many distinct words,
and a few articulate sentences.

10 (129)

Remote as this statement may appear from a confession of capital crime, and far from conclusive as my limited observation and experiment must be, I found that when, in studying the life of Cotton Mather, I was compelled to examine the history of Salem witchcraft, my own occult experiences had induced in me a state of mind that led to some speculative conclusions widely different from those commonly accepted. These I shall venture to state, wholly aware that I have neither the scientific nor the historical learning necessary to give them even a semblance of authority, but hoping that they may perhaps prove suggestive of a line of study which, in more competent hands than mine, might lead to interesting results; for I am disposed to believe not only that in 1692 there was existent in New England, under the name of witchcraft, a state of things quite as dangerous as any epidemic of crime, but also that there is perhaps reason to surmise that not all the victims of the witch trials were innocent.

To explain what I mean, I may, best, perhaps, begin by briefly recounting my own observations and experiments, and then turn to some of the evidence in the witch trials. By comparing this with my experience and with a few facts admitted nowadays—such as the phenomena of hypnotism —I may indicate why I am disposed so heartily to dissent from that rationalistic view of the tragedy of two centuries ago, which has been so admirably and honestly set forth by standard historians.

My own observations of modern occultism were made in the order in which I have named them. I saw the materialized spirits first; later I visited a trance-medium; and not till some time later did I try my hand at automatic writing.

Materialization impressed me as indubitable fraud from beginning to end. You went into a room which was subsequently so darkened that you could not discern the hands of your watch. In this dim light, a small company, mostly ardent believers, were wrought up into such emotional excitement as could be awakened by hymn tunes played on a common parlor organ, and presently uncanny shapes began to flit about. Sometimes these emerged from a cabinet in which the medium had professed to go into the trance state, sometimes they apparently rose through the floor; at least once,—to all appearances—they took shape on top of an ordinary three-legged table. These figures would talk with you, would shake hands with you, would sometimes be unpleasantly affectionate in demeanor, and would often end by "dematerializing"—that is, by suddenly flopping down into nothing, much as figures in the pantomime disappear through trap-doors. You could not see how the trick was done, but the trick was essentially like what any number of travelling magicians perform. Before long, however, you remarked that the habitual frequenters of these unedifying exercises seemed fervently to believe in them. I remember once finding at my side an elderly man who passionately embraced a male spirit that appeared, and returning to his seat whispered to me in agitated tones that it was his son, who had lately killed himself. The son had been a friend of mine; and when I told the father so, he begged the medium to recall him, that I might speak to him myself and be convinced. But the medium professed inability to recall that particular spirit at the moment, so I was forced to remain sceptical of everything but the fervent belief of the heart-broken father. Next you remarked that, knaves and charlatans as the mediums seemed, they seemed knaves and charlatans of a specific kind. There was no doubt in your mind that they lied to you and tricked you, but I for one could never feel satisfied as to how thoroughly they were aware of the

exact extent of their falsehood,—as to whether beneath all
this nonsense and rascality there were not lurking some
mysterious subjective experience that had to them a semblance of fact. Finally, you felt a growing sense of debasement in such surroundings. The uncanny insincerity of the
mediums, the crass superstition of the believers who formed
the circle, the meaningless words and conduct of the
materialized spirits—never indecent, but always petty,
trivial, low—led me by and by heartily to agree with a
friend who declared that while he did not for a moment
believe these were spirits at all, he had no shadow of doubt
that if they were spirits they were devils.

The chief trance-medium I visited was a woman of high
respectability, and of great apparent sincerity of character.
In her normal condition she professed complete ignorance
of what occurred when she was in the trance state. Into
this state she could throw herself at will. Once in this
state she assumed a voice and manner totally unlike
her own, and professing to be controlled by a spirit, she
gave you any number of messages from departed friends,
whom she sometimes described and sometimes named. In
a sitting with her of some two hours I remarked that, in a
vague kind of way, she seemed to follow my line of thought.
For example, she made a queer noise that reminded me of
the death agony of a friend some time before. This recalled him and the circumstances of his death to my mind.
By and by, she named him, and described him with some
approach to verisimilitude. The correspondence between
what I knew and what she told me was never exact enough
to convince me of anything remarkable, but it seemed close
enough to warrant me, if I had believed in mind reading,
in classing her conduct as mind reading, once for all.
When the time came for her to emerge from this trance,
she had a startling fit. Amid the contortions which ac-

companied what she asserted to be the departure of the spirit which had controlled her, she fell on her knees with a cry of terror, and clutching me begged me not to let *it* take her away; and she looked with every appearance of agonized alarm, at an empty corner of the room from which she shrank away; you would have said she saw the devil himself waiting for her. In a very short time she resumed her natural condition, at first rather dazed, and declared that she had no idea whatever of anything that had happened since she first went into the trance-state two hours before. The most remarkable thing to me about her was that in her normal condition she was the sort of person whom you instinctively believe to speak the truth. It was perfectly easy to assert that she was a common trickster; but to my mind, at all events, the assertion was by no means convincing. My own impression was strongly that she was an honest person, in a very abnormal state, honestly self-deceived; and in this abnormal display and in this self-deception was a quality of debasement, more subtile, less tangible, than I had found in materialization, but, if you granted the supernatural hypothesis at all, equally diabolical.

A year or two after this I found that if, pencil in hand, I left my hand free to run as it would, and occupied my eyes and thoughts with other matters, my hand would clumsily scrawl first queer tremulous lines, then letters, then words. This experience was in no wise peculiar. The friend who first directed my attention to these experiments had made a considerable collection of automatic writings from various people; and these had in common a trait that mine shared with them. The avowedly unguided hand would make for a while—sometimes day after day—apparently meaningless lines that constantly repeated themselves. In time, these lines would grow more definite.

Finally a word would be written; and by comparing a number of the writings you could trace what looked like a long series of almost impotent experiments, finally resulting in this distinct achievement. The first word my hand thus wrote was "sherry."

That it was going to write "sherry" I had no idea. To this point I had been incredulous that it would actually write anything at all. "Sherry" once written, I began to feel more interest in what it might write next. And then soon followed an experience that determined me to give the matter up. In the first place, I found that experiments in automatic writing left me in an irritable nervous condition for which I can find no better name than demoralized. The whole fibre of character seemed for the moment weakened; will, intelligence, self-control, temper, were alike inferior things after the experiments to what they had been before. In the second place, I found that very soon I could not be quite sure whether I actually let my hand run unguided, or whether I slyly helped it write. And whenever that doubt arose in my mind, there always came with it so strong an impulse to deny its existence, to assert that I had no idea what I was about, that I found myself for the moment a completely untrustworthy witness. In other words, the further I got in my very slight excursion into occult experiment, the further I was from intelligence, veracity and honesty. The definite result of these experiments for me was a conviction that no man's word about automatic writing, at any rate, is worth the breath that utters it. The thing is not all fraud,—there is something very queer about it; but not the least phase of the queerness is that it is constantly, increasingly credulous, tricky and mendacious.

In reflecting on these three experiences, I found them by and by grouping themselves as three stages of what

I may call a specific mental or moral disorder. The first and simplest was the automatic writing, whose ill effects induced me to abandon the whole thing. The second was the mediumistic trance, in which a woman whom I believe honest in her natural character hypnotized herself, and in the hypnotic state became perhaps abnormally perspicacious, and almost certainly a dangerous charlatan. The third was the elaborately dishonest mummery of materialization, where the fraud was so palpable that it seemed almost indubitably deliberate from beginning to end. But comparing this deliberate fraud with the simpler phases of occultism that I had observed, I found myself more and more disposed to believe it a kind of deliberate fraud, in all respects debasing, into which I could easily conceive an originally honest person to be unwittingly led.

All this time my impressions of Salem witchcraft had been derived from two absorbing days that I had passed with Mr. Upham's book some years ago. It had never occurred to me to question his conclusions ; nor would it have occurred to me had I not been called on to make a careful study of the life and character of Cotton Mather, whom I found on intimate acquaintance by no means the deliberate villain I had been led to believe him. In making that study, I had occasion to read the original evidence in the witch-trials.[1] And what most impressed me in that evidence was its startling familiarity. The surroundings were in all respects different from anything I had known. In a century and a society far more remote from us in condition than they are in time, certain unhappy people were bringing against others more unhappy still charges that involved their lives. But the controlling spirit, the atmosphere of this grotesque tragedy was something I had known in the flesh. Whoever has frequented materialization

---

[1] Woodward, W. E. Records of Salem Witchcraft, 1691-2, copied from the original documents. Roxbury, 1864-65, 2v., 4to. (Woodward's Hist. ser., v. 1, 2).

séances, and who then reads with sympathetic imagination the broken records of the witch trials, can hardly help admitting, I think, that these things are of the same kind. There is fraud in both—horribly tragic fraud then, grotesquely comic fraud now,— but in both the fraud is of the same horrible vaporous kind; and in both there is room for a growing doubt whether there be not in all this more than fraud and worse. If there be, that mysterious thing is subtly evil beyond words; if there be an incarnate spirit of evil, then that mysterious thing is the direct work of that spirit. The nineteenth century has discarded the devil; to the seventeenth century, at least in New England, he was just as real as God. And the sin that transcended all other sin that could be done by the fallen children of Adam was the sin of those who, despairing of Heaven, leagued themselves before their time with Hell.

This is not the moment to analyze in detail the tremendous force of the doctrine of election that lay at the base of the creed which for seventy years dominated New England. But whoever would understand the society from which sprang the witches and the witch-judges of 1692 must never forget the grim creed which, declaring that no man could be saved but by the special grace of God, and that the only test of salvation was ability to exert the will in accordance with His, bred in the devout, and in whoever was affected by their counsels, an habitual introspection, and an habitual straining for mystical intercourse with the spiritual world, to-day almost inconceivable. In a world dominated by a creed at once so despairing and so mystic, it would not have been strange if now and then wretched men, finding in their endless introspection no sign of the divine marks of grace, and stimulated in their mysticism beyond modern conception by the churches that claimed and imposed an authority almost unsurpassed in history, had been tempted to seek, in premature alliance with the powers of evil, at least some semblance of the freedom that their inexorable God had denied them. It was such an alliance with which the Salem witches were charged. It is just such miserable debasement of humanity as should follow such an alliance that pervades the evidence of the witch-trials, just as to-day it pervades the purlieus of those who give themselves up to occultism in its lower forms.

The question I asked myself, when this view of the matter became clear to me, was whether in this evidence I could find traces of the other stages of occultism to which I have already called your attention. To answer this question to anybody's satisfaction would need longer and more careful study than I have been able to give the documents; but what little study I have had time for has suggested to me, more and more strongly, that prolonged study might yield surprising results. I will try very briefly to analyze the evidence, to show what I mean.

It is not generally remembered, in spite of Mr. Upham's admirable work, that the great bulk of this evidence is what was called spectral. A girl, for example, was bewitched, and testified that the physical torture she was apparently undergoing was caused by the conduct of the apparition of one of the accused—an apparition providentially invisible to whoever was not bewitched. It was the acceptance by the court of this obviously worthless evidence that hanged the witches; it was the throwing out of such evidence that brought the witch trials to a close. It was his momentary faith in such evidence—not in the horrible reality of witchcraft itself—that Samuel Sewall publicly repented in the Old South Church. And in analyzing the records of these old trials, we must put aside, once for all, every particle of this evidence, save as it tells against the witnesses themselves.

In a way, however, this evidence tells against the wit-

11

nesses themselves rather startlingly. It was often accompanied in full court, by conduct that went far to make judges and attendants believe it. I cite almost at random, a single example of what I mean. In the examination of Rebecca Nurse is this passage :[1]

"Why should not you also be guilty for your apparition doth hurt also.

"Would you have me bely myself.

"*She held her neck on one side, and accordingly so were the afflicted taken.*"

A moment later[2]—"Nurse held her neck on one side and Eliz. Hubbard (one of the sufferers) had her neck set in that posture whereupon another patient Abigail Williams, cryed out, set up Goody Nurse's head, the maid's neck will be broke, and when some set up Nurse's head Aaron Wey. observed y[t] Betty Hubbards was immediately righted."

This tells nothing whatever against Rebecca Nurse. What it tells against Betty Hubbard would have seemed a few years ago merely that she was a deliberate and unprincipled trickster. To-day, I think, it goes far to suggest a much less simple state of things : namely, that Betty Hubbard was a hypnotic subject, so far gone as to be instantly affected by the slightest suggestion from a person on whom her diseased attention was concentrated. And it is typical of things that occurred throughout the sessions of the witch-courts. I am no expert in hypnotism, but what little I have read and seen of it so exactly corresponds with so much that is in this witch-evidence that I should be gravely surprised if experts who examined the evidence did not find the evidence going far to suggest that almost all the bewitched were probably victims of hypnotic excesses.

---

[1] I: 86-7. [2] I: 87.

It is only in recent times, I believe, that careful study of the still mysterious and dangerous phenomena of hypnotism has tended to show that it depends far more on the subject than on the operator, and that a good subject, by careful concentration of attention, can hypnotize himself. That the bewitched sufferers at Salem often hypnotized themselves is highly probable. Here is another extract from the evidence—this time from one of those unaccountable confessions which have so baffled cool critics.[1]

"Now Mary Warren fell into a fit, and some of the afflicted cryed out that she was going to confess, but Goody Korey and Procter and his wife came in their apparition and struck her down and said she should tell nothing.

"Mary Warren continued a good space in a fit, that she did neither see, nor hear, nor speak.

"Afterwards she started up, and said I will speak and cryed out, Oh! I am sorry for it, I am sorry for it, and wringed her hands and fell a little while into a fit again and then came to speak, but immediately her teeth were set, and then she fell into a violent fit and cryed out, Oh Lord help me! Oh Good Lord save me!

"And then afterwards cryed again, I will tell, I will tell and then fell into a dead fit again"—which continued until " she was ordered to be had out."

A little later she was "called in afterwards in private before magistrates and ministers.

"She said I shall not speak a word; but I will I will speak Satan.—She saith she will kill me. Oh! she says she owes me a spite and will claw me off.

"Avoid Satan, for the name of God Avoid and then fell into fits again; and cryed will ye, I will prevent ye in the name of God."—

---

[1] I: 120.

But in spite of her will, her fits persisted and "her lips were bit so that she could not speak so she was sent away."

Within two days she made an elaborate, and apparently mendacious confession of all sorts of occult absurdity, beginning with the assertion that her master and mistress had forced her into witchcraft, making her sign a book, and that they had made her stick a pin into a puppet, and so on.

Without putting the least credence in this testimony against her employers, I am nevertheless very much struck by the likeness between this poor creature's conduct before the Salem magistrates and ministers, and the conduct of the trance-medium in Boston, who, as she was emerging from her trance, begged me to save her from the horrible creature she thought she saw in the corner. This medium was undoubtedly given to hypnotizing herself. How she had learned to do so I do not know. Is there not reason to guess that Mary Warren may have been given to hypnotizing herself, too; and that very possibly she may have been taught to do so?

In the midst of all this horrible confusion, then, there are glimpses of two of the stages of occultism to which I bore personal testimony. Is there any of the third, such as I dabbled in myself? Of automatic writing, I have found no trace: that experiment I conceive to be a very modern one. But here is what poor Giles Corey testified against his wife.[1]—

"Last Satturday in the Evening Sitting by the fire my wife asked me to go to bed. I told her I would go to prayer and when I went to prayer I could not utter my desires w^h any sense, *not open my mouth to speake*,[2] my wife did perceive itt and came towards me and said she was coming to me. After this in a little space I did according

---

[1] I: 55–6. [2] These italics are mine.

TO MY MEASURE attend the duty . . . My wife hath ben
wont to sett up after I went to bed and I have perceived
her to kneel doun on the harth as if she were at prayer but
heard nothing."

A mere question of temper, if you please; but if he had
set about to describe an elementary hypnotic experiment,
could he have said much otherwise? And is that kneeling
figure at the hearth, in the flickering firelight of two centuries ago, quite godly in aspect?

Again[1]: "John Blye Senior agett about 57 yeers and
William Blye aged about 15 years both of Salem Testifieth
and sayth yt being Imployed by Bridgitt Boshop Alies Oli-
uer of Salem to helpe take doune ye Cellar wall of The
Owld house she formerly Lived in wee ye sd Deponents in
holes in ye sd owld wall belonging to ye sd Cellar found
seuerall popitts made up of Raggs And hoggs Brussells
wth headles pins in Them. wth ye points outward and
this was about Seauen years Last past."

Children's toys, to a nineteenth century mind. But all
through the records of mediæval witchcraft and magic lie
just such children's toys which the world believed very fatal
engines of death. I spoke of that testimony the other day
to a friend who happens to be—what I am far from being—
an ardent believer in that prevalent mysticism called Christian Science. To me, I said, the evidence went a good
way to show that somebody had actually been trying in
Salem to see whether by sticking pins into a doll you could
not torture the enemy that the doll represented: the practice certainly had existed in Europe, absurd as it must seem
to us. To my surprise, my friend replied that to her it
did not seem absurd at all: any believer in Christian Science, she went on, knew that by concentrating your mind
on an absent person you could affect that person for good

---

[1]: 163.

or for ill ; and that while the actual sticking of pins into dolls could never directly hurt anything but the dolls, it could help a malevolent mind so to concentrate itself on the person a doll represented as to injure him with far less effort than when there was no doll to aid it ;—which view, she added, was the view of Paracelsus.

I mention that case just to remind you how curiously some of the educated minds of our own time are recurring to kinds of mysticism that have so long seemed purely superstitious ; how much more credible witchcraft is than it used to be, now that we see these honest, intelligent mystics all about us.

For only change the impulse of these very people from the pure one it generally is, to the base one that was held to actuate the witches, and you have at your very firesides not a few examples of what witches were. And do not the silenced husband of Martha Corey, and the pin-riddled dolls hidden in Bridget Bishop's cellar wall go at least a little way to suggest that perhaps they had made unholy experiments ?

Only a little way, I hasten to add. No one can be better aware than I that such evidence as I have offered here is very slight—at best not more than suggestive. Nor can any one know better than I what I cannot too earnestly repeat, that I have neither the scientific nor the historical learning that would be necessary to make anything I should say more than suggestive to better and wiser students. But this evidence, typical of much more that can be dug out of those bewildering old documents, will show you the sort of thing that has led me both to believe that there was abroad in 1692 an evil quite as dangerous as any still recognized crime, and to wonder whether some of the witches may not after all, in spite of the weakness and falsity of the evidence that hanged them, have deserved their hanging.

It remains for me to show why I believe this evil so

serious and the crime of whoever committed it in the seventeenth century so gross. I cannot do so better than by repeating some words I published a few months ago[1]:— If, as modern science tends to show, human beings are the result of a process of evolution from lower forms of life, there must have been in our ancestral history a period when the intelligence of our progenitors was as different from the modern human mind as were their remote aquatic bodies from the human form we know to-day. It seems wholly conceivable, then, that in the remote psychologic past of our race there may have been in our ancestors certain powers of perception which countless centuries of disuse have made so rudimentary that in our normal condition we are not conscious of them. But if such there were, it would not be strange that, in abnormal states, the rudimentary vestiges of these disused powers of perception might sometimes be revived. If this were the case, we might naturally expect two phenomena to accompany such a revival :   in the first place, as such powers of perception belong normally to a period in the development of our race when human society and moral law have not yet appeared, we should expect them to be intimately connected with a state of emotion that ignores the moral sense, and so to be accompanied by various forms of misconduct ; in the second place, as our chief modern means of communication—articulate language—belongs to a period when human intelligence has assumed its present form, we should expect to find it inadequate for the expression of facts which it never professed to cover, and so we should expect such phenomena as we are considering to be accompanied by an erratic, impotent inaccuracy of statement, which would soon shade into something indistinguishable from

---

[1] In my Life of Cotton Mather, pp. 95–6.

deliberate falsehood. In other words, such phenomena
would naturally involve, in whoever abandons himself to
them, a mental and moral degeneracy which any one who
believes in a personal devil would not hesitate to ascribe to
the direct intervention of Satan.

Now what disposes me, scientifically a layman I cannot
too earnestly repeat, to put faith in this speculation concerning occultism is that mental and moral degeneracy,—
credulity and fraud,—seem almost invariably so to entan-
gle themselves with occult phenomena that many cool-
headed persons are disposed to assert the whole thing a
lie. To me it does not seem so simple. I incline more
and more to think that necromancers, witches, mediums
—call them what you will—actually do perceive in the
infinite realities about us things imperceptible to normal
human beings; but that they perceive them only at a sacrifice of their higher faculties—mental and moral—not
inaptly symbolized in the old tales of those who sell their
souls.

If this be true, such an epidemic of witchcraft as came
to New England in 1692 is as diabolical a fact as human
beings can know: unchecked, it can really work mischief
unspeakable. For unchecked it would mean that more and
more human beings would give themselves up to deliberate, or perhaps instinctive, effort to retrace the steps by
which human intelligence, in countless centuries, has slowly
risen from the primitive consciousness of the brute creation.

To my mind, then, the fatally tragic phase of the witch
trials is not that there was no evil to condemn, but that the
unhappy victims of the trials were condemned literally on
clairvoyant evidence. And what I have already said shows
that in all probability those really guilty of the nameless
crime I have tried to indicate were, in my opinion, not so
often the witches as the bewitched.

But let us look at the matter a little more closely again. These wretched bewitched girls were in all probability victims of hypnotic excess. In all probability they had learned, willingly or unwillingly, to hypnotize themselves. But is there not a likelihood that first of all they may have been hypnotized by others? And is there not, in the records of those terrible days, some faint suggestion that among those who first dragged the wretched girls down may have been some of the accused? The actual charges are sometimes manifestly false, almost always utterly incredible,— lying, contradictory, vaporous,— but beneath them all there remains a something which would make me guess that not all of the accused believed themselves innocent.

Put yourself for a moment in the place of those petty New England Calvinists, born and bred under an iron creed that forbade all hope of salvation to any but the elect of a capricious God. Fancy yourself toiling for years in vain to make your human will agree with His, to find in yourself the divine marks of grace. Then, in a moment of despair, fancy yourself toying with occult experiment— not as a scientific observer of the nineteenth century, but as a creed-ridden zealot of the seventeenth, bound to believe that mysterious phenomena are the direct handiwork of either God or Satan. Fancy yourself finding that you could exercise over other and weaker wills than yours that power which, under the name of hypnotism, scientific folks are studying to-day, and not a few of them denouncing as terribly dangerous. Fancy yourself finding that the more you exercised this power the more your victims yielded to it. Remember the debasement and the fraud that come as a hardly resistible temptation to dabblers in occultism to-day. And then ask yourselves if any one, who yielded himself up in old Salem to

HIST. COLL.   XXIX   12

such temptations as these, could have doubted that, in the devil's mysterious way, he was doing the devil's chosen work.

I cannot assert a single one of the dead witches to have been such a figure as I have asked you to fancy. But I can assert that if any of them were by chance such a figure,—and it seems to me that careful study might go far to show that more than one of them may have been,—then the dreadful fate that came to him, though it came through evidence hopelessly weak and false, was his moral due.

I have said enough to suggest to you the view of Salem Witchcraft that has forced itself on me. From personal observation I have seen enough of modern occultism, of the lower kind, to believe it unholy. From the evidence of the witch-trials I have gathered hints enough to make me believe that beneath its horrible vaporous confusion lurks just such unholiness as I have seen in the flesh. And no one who knows a bit of the inner history of New England Puritanism can doubt that if this be true, then there were in old Salem men and women who had deliberately sinned against God. I have told all this in a manner that may well have seemed too personal, too assertive of myself. I have chosen to tell it thus deliberately. No one can be better aware than I that to be proved, such views as I have suggested need the full authority that should come from years of scientific and of historical research. No one can know better than I how far I am from such learning as should give my words authority. But sometimes, I think, a frank statement of how an old matter looks to a fresh eye that glances at it never so superficially, may suggest to eyes familiar with it, views that their very familiarity would have prevented them from seeing for themselves. Such a service as this is among the best that men of letters can do for men of learning. And it is only as one who has tried to make himself a man of letters that I have earned the privilege of telling here not what is known of old Salem, but what seems to me perhaps knowable.

NOTE: It is interesting to reflect that if the views presented in this paper are valid, the witch trials, far from being abortive, may have accomplished a result of lasting importance in the history of New England. There was no more playing with occultism here, I think, until modern spiritualism arose, to be followed by the excessive interest in occult matters so notable within the last ten years. Is it not possible that the witch trials, surrounding the whole subject with horror, may actually have checked for more than a century the growth of a tendency which un- checked might gravely have demoralized our national character?

Progress in Pediatrics

PEDIATRIC ASPECTS OF THE SALEM WITCHCRAFT TRAGEDY

A LESSON IN MENTAL HEALTH

ERNEST CAULFIELD, M.D.

HARTFORD, CONN.

I

From the innermost recesses of his Puritan heart and soul, the Rev. Samuel Parris hated Sin. He hated all the Evil Angels, the Devil, Venomous Pilot of Hell; above all, he hated Shee-Witches and the whole Damned and Detestable Art of Witchcraft. Fate was indeed unkind to Parris, for when the terrible stench of witchcraft first became discernible in his little, secluded, backwoods parish of Salem Village, his own daughter Elizabeth and his niece Abigail were the very first to be afflicted. Though the real facts are rather obscure, according to all historical accounts it was actually Tituba, his West Indian servant girl, who initiated the events that culminated in the Salem tragedy, when, during some unexciting winter days and nights, she told weird tales and taught tricks of magic or sorcery to a group of imaginative girls who came to play in the Parris home. At any rate, in January 1692 some of these children became afflicted with a strange, unknown distemper. They crawled into holes, crept under benches and chairs, assumed "sundry odd Postures and [made] Antick Gestures, uttered foolish, ridiculous Speeches, which neither they themselves nor any others could make sense of." After many of the ministers from neighboring towns had met on a day of solemn fast and prayer and especially after Dr. Griggs, whose niece was also among the afflicted, had been unable to find any physical cause for this unusual behavior, it was decided that the children were certainly bewitched. In response to searching questions, the children alleged that they had been tormented by three women: Tituba, the servant; Goody Osburn, a sickly old creature who later in her trial admitted that she had suffered from vivid dreams, had heard voices and had not regularly attended church, and old Sarah Good, a pipe-smoking, disorderly and somewhat demented beggar. The trials got off to a dramatic start when Tituba confessed that she had often ridden through the air on a pole to witch meetings and that the very Devil himself, appearing before her sometimes as a black dog, a yellow bird or a red rat, had compelled her to torment the children on many occasions and in numerous ways. She also claimed that others were involved, and later, when some other women confessed that they too were pawns of the Devil, the witch hunt was on in earnest. At the preliminary hearings and subsequent trials, the children fell into extraordinary fits whenever Good or Osburn gazed on them. In witchcraft lore, it was a common belief that when a witch cast her evil eye on an innocent person some occult substance, called an "Apperishion," entered the body and mind of the victim but when the witch subsequently touched that person this substance was immediately released. On evidence of this sort, old Goody Osburn and Goody Good were promptly condemned to death.

An after-dinner talk at the annual meeting of the Society for Pediatric Research, Skytop, Pa., May 1, 1940.

788

Panic rapidly spread throughout the neighboring countryside. Numerous others claiming to be afflicted heedlessly accused their imaginary tormentors until about 250 persons, mostly women, were arrested. The jails at Ipswich, Boston and Salem were packed beyond their capacities, and, though many escaped, two or three died in custody. Thirteen women and six men, many of them 60 to 80 years of age, were hanged, and one old man was slowly pressed to death with heavy stones for refusing to plead. Also among the victims were two dogs. The affair reached its climax when the afflicted persons began to accuse some of their prominent neighbors. A magistrate in Andover, after signing many warrants for the arrest of others, had to flee for his own life when he was accused of being an accomplice of the witches merely because he had refused to indict an obviously innocent person. The governor's wife and the wife of a minister who had been active in ferreting out witches were also incriminated. Finally, in May 1693, when the whole affair was obviously getting out of hand and was rapidly making itself ridiculous to thoughtful persons, the governor dissolved the special court and released all the suspects still in jail. According to a contemporary account: "The Lord then so chained up Satan, that the afflicted grew presently well."

II

Even while some of the "Fire Brands of Hell" were still dangling by their necks on Gallows Hill, the more conscientious of the bewildered spectators, suddenly realizing that something had gone awry, began to cry pitifully to Heaven for forgiveness; and soon thereafter the first of the numerous historians began to offer explanations or apologies for this horrible tragedy. This black page of American history certainly needed explanation, but the explanations are nearly as numerous as the historians themselves. In the volumes devoted to witchcraft in Salem appear some theories to explain how such a catastrophe could happen in this little colonial town of a few hundred God-fearing inhabitants. It has been shown that from the fourteenth to the seventeenth century there was a widespread belief in witchcraft throughout the Christian world, with the result that in Europe between 200,000 and 500,000 persons were burned at the stake or put to death in other ways for witchcraft. Though a few brave men had previously risked their fortunes and their very lives by denying the existence of "secret, black, and midnight hags," by 1692 the vast majority of persons here and abroad, including the greatest theologians, scientists, lawyers and physicians, indeed nearly every one except the "learned witlings of the Coffee House," sincerely believed that witches and their male counterparts, wizards, were made of real flesh and blood, could really evaporate into fog and filthy air and, being in league with the Devil, were always intent on harming ordinary mortals. Because this belief in witchcraft was so widespread, some attempt has been made to minimize the Salem tragedy as only a brief and transitory scene in a worldwide drama. But even though it is true that there were only about 30 victims of witchcraft in all the North American colonies and that the only horrible episode lasted little more than a year, in contrast to the centuries of persecution for witchcraft abroad, the Salem tragedy, nevertheless, still stands as one of the outstanding events of American history and still arouses curiosity, because it involved man's deepest emotions and had many aspects difficult to explain.

Though occasional cases of witchcraft cropped out in nearly all of the colonies during the last half of the seventeenth century, the reason it reached its climax in Massachusetts and not in Virginia, for instance, is usually attributed to the Puritan belief, as expressed by the Rev. Cotton Mather and the Rev. Samuel Parris, that a real, personal, revengeful Devil, previously in full possession of the heathen Indians and their lands, was then concentrating his attention on New England in a brazen attempt to regain his lost possessions by the destruction of all churches and all religion. In short, the Kingdom of God in New England was in imminent jeopardy. From their reading of foreign books on witchcraft, the leaders of New England, many of them able, educated men, were well informed on how to detect and try a witch; and, since any alliance with the Devil was a heinous sin, they considered it

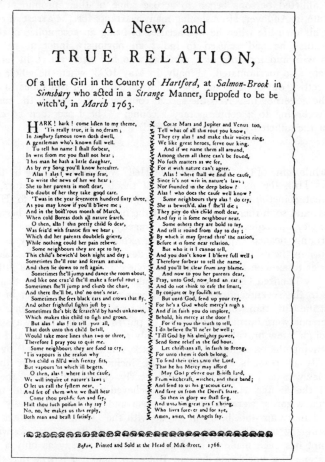

Fig. 1.—A broadside of 1766 from Boston, dealing with a belated case of witchcraft. (Published by courtesy of the American Antiquarian Society.)

their first duty to caution their people to watch for any evidence of diabolic possession. It was no fairy tale that the wily and deceitful Devil would first attempt to get possession of human souls, even pious ones if possible; and, should he succeed, these contemptible, treacherous cohorts would, in turn, possess the power to torment other innocent persons in order to make them sign the Devil's book, willingly or no. All this may sound pretty foolish today, but it should be remembered, first of all, that the Puritans were in dead earnest, constantly striving to uplift the pitiful state of man even in the face of vehement criticism. Cotton

Mather clearly expressed it when he said: "Flashy people may burlesque these things, but . . . hundreds of the most sober people of a country, where they have as much mother-wit certainly as the rest of mankind, know them to be true. . . ."

So, when the Devil in a "vehement and terrible Rage" attempted to set up his own kingdom in or near Salem, which, after all, was the very birthplace of Puritanism in America, it was tantamount to a declaration of war—not an ordinary colonial war for the possession of lands against an ordinary enemy like the Indians or the French, but an intense, emotional religious war that was to determine, once and for all, whether righteousness, truth and honor should eternally prevail over injustice, wickedness and depravity. Emblazoned on the Puritan standard was the biblical injunction "Thou shalt not suffer a witch to live."

The more immediate causes of the "Witchcraft Delusion" have been frequently disputed by many able historians. It used to be customary to fasten all the blame on Cotton Mather, the most representative member of the clergy, for his misguided zeal in spreading all this so-called superstition and thereby indirectly causing all the subsequent trouble. This is not the place to discuss Mather's relation to the legal aspects of the trials, whether or not he influenced the governor to appoint a special court or the judges to admit the spectral testimony. Suffice it to say that Cotton Mather with his soul-terrifying sermons and pamphlets no doubt vigorously fanned the flame of witchcraft; but if he went off to war as the self-appointed "Ambassador of the Lord," it was only because he, like his father and grandfather before him, was one of the most respected leaders of the people and, having devoted nearly his whole life to the spreading of the Gospel in New England, he considered that to put down this "rebellion against the sovereignty of God" was not only his sacred privilege but his bounden duty. He was eminently sincere, and, besides, as I hope to show later in more detail, he himself had discovered some incontrovertible evidence of witchcraft.

But no one man could have possibly influenced a people to hang some of the most upright members of their church unless, deep in their emotional life, lurked something which might have prepared them to commit so horrible a blunder. I believe that fundamentally there existed a problem involving the mental health of the Puritan children. To show this it is necessary to reexamine some of the contemporary records; but, since it would be too tedious to discuss all aspects of the case, I propose to limit the discussion to those aspects which help to explain the peculiar behavior of the "afflicted children."

III

From a medical standpoint, the most interesting part of the witchcraft trials concerns the behavior and testimony of the girls. Of the ten, four were servants 17 to 20 years of age; one of them at least had apparently been frequently overworked and beaten, so doubtless had a reason to testify that her master was a wizard. As the trials progressed, more and more persons became "afflicted," until there were about 50 who claimed to be bewitched; but concerning most of these, particularly the young and middle-aged men and women, there is only meager information. Nor can much be said about Elizabeth Parris, the 9 year old daughter of the minister, for, although she is said to have been one of the chief accusers, she appeared in only one trial and had only a few fits. But among the ringleaders appeared the truly remarkable Ann Putnam, 12 years old, who testified in nineteen trials; the 11 year old niece of of the minister, Abigail Williams, who testified in eight trials, and Elizabeth Hubbard, 17 years old, who testified in twenty trials. Though there were many adult witnesses in most of the trials, nearly all of the victims were condemned chiefly on the testimony and behavior of the girls.

As has been stated, the usually accepted version is that the children had been led astray by the weird tricks and stories of Tituba, the servant in the Parris home. There is a little doubt about this, however, for Robert Calef, who was one of the first to question the validity of the witchcraft trials and on whose writings a good deal of the Salem story depends, said that Tituba had been beaten by her master until she was very willing to confess that she had ridden through the air and had partaken of the Devil's sacraments. Nevertheless, the belief still persists, especially among popular authors, that the children began, innocently at first, to practice their magic tricks, which to them was only sport but which of course was intolerable under the roof of any good New England minister's home, and, having been caught, rather than suffer the punishment that was sure to befall them they began to act even more strangely and to pretend that their actions were far beyond their control. Once having ventured to name the actual witches who were tormenting them, they continued in their nefarious schemes regardless of consequences. In other words, it

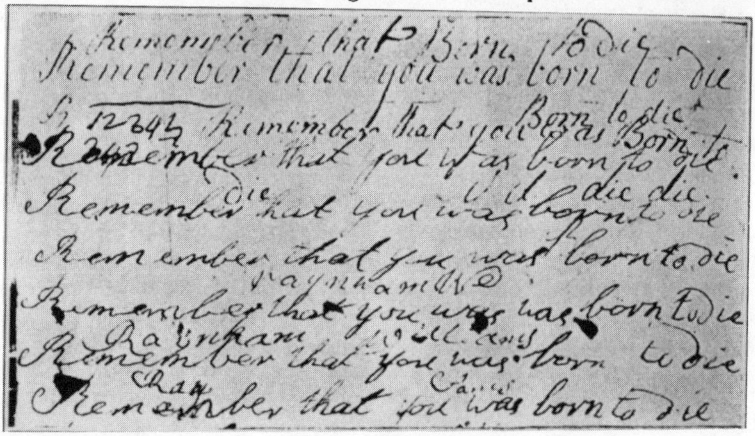

Fig. 2.—"Remember that you was born to die." A lesson in penmanship. (Reproduced from Edmund Williams' copy of Nathaniel Ames's "Astronomical Diary or an Almanack for 1753" and published by permission of the American Antiquarian Society.)

is the common belief that they were exceedingly bad, dishonest children who did not realize the seriousness of their tricks or games, who derived considerable personal gratification from being the center of the excitement or were, perhaps from spite, deliberately deceitful from the very beginning and continued so in all their acts and testimony.

The array of historians who have thought that the children were primarily to blame for the whole witchcraft imbroglio is a notable one. Calef, writing in 1697, was among the first to express suspicion of the motives of the children, when he pointed out that in one of the trials they complained of being bitten and displayed the bites on their arms even when the accused "had not a tooth in his head wherewith to bite." Hutchinson, an early historian who talked with many of the courtroom spectators, thought that the judges and jury were altogether too credulous in believing such "fraud and imposture" on the part of the children. Upham, the most thorough of the witchcraft students, devoted almost the whole of his two volumes to proving his discovery of a horrible conspiracy on the part of Parris and particularly of the children, who with fiendlike satisfaction descended to the very depths of wickedness and depravity in their testimony, which was nothing short of "wicked perjury and wilful malice." Professor Kittredge mentioned the children's "pranks." Even in the last few years the popular Kenneth Roberts, in his "Trending into Maine" (1938), described the witchcraft children as "a group of the coldest blooded and most malignant brats ever spawned," and the entertaining Eleanor Early, in her "New England Sampler" (1940), took particular delight in referring to them as "The Puritan Song and Dance Girls . . . eight of the nastiest brats on record." Nothing is to be gained by citing numerous other authorities who have accepted this interpretation; it should be mentioned, though, that a few of them have asserted flatly that the whole sorrowful performance could easily have been averted by a good stiff birch rod frequently and liberally applied.

The basis for this harsh opinion of the children is that they frequently told the most deliberate lies. They actually seemed eager to testify against any poor old crone brought into court, saying that they had been long tormented by the accused, when it was plainly apparent that they had never seen or heard of the supposed witch until that very day. They would swear with the utmost sincerity that they had seen the defendant at a witch assembly on a particular day when, as even the judges and jury must have known, the accused was in another town or chained in jail. They told the most fantastic atrocity stories of what happened at those meetings but asserted that not by tempting promises, horrible tortures or even threats of death had they been made to jeopardize their own little innocent souls by signing the Devil's book. With gory details they excitedly related the confessions to murders which they claimed to have extracted from the defendants or their "apparitions" and thus explained many deaths in the neighborhood which up to that time had been most mysterious.

There were many other peculiar complaints not altogether unrelated to their lies. Nearly all of the children swore repeatedly that they had been pinched, choked and bitten, occasionally exhibiting marks of the bites or pinches on their arms. Screaming hideously, they would claim that pins and knives were being stuck into their bodies. There were times when many apparently could not talk or walk; some appeared suddenly struck deaf, dumb and blind all at once. Others complained of a mist before their eyes or of stomach sickness or of breathlessness. Over and over again the "apparitions" appeared to them, sometimes as a yellow bird, a cat with ears like a man, a little turtle, a streaked snake or a hairless pig. The Devil appeared to Susannah Sheldon on at least three different occasions and always in the form of a little black man in a high-crowned hat.

Regardless of what the children said, the evidence most convincing to the judges, jury and spectators came when the judges ordered the afflicted children to look on the captured witches, whereupon they promptly went off into fits but, as a general rule, recovered as soon as the accused were made to touch them. This sort of evidence appears with monotonous regularity throughout the court records, and the apparent ease with which the children threw and recovered from their fits has been considered absolute proof that they were merely acting. The more one reads between the lines, however, the more it becomes evident that it was generally those "hideous clamours and screechings" that made their stories seem true, and it is also apparent that the dramatic and "violent fits of torture" were ample proof to nearly all who saw them that the children were actually bewitched. Herein lies the crux of the whole Salem episode. Whether or not to blame the children for the executions depends almost entirely on the true nature of the fits; and it is a curious fact in the history of witchcraft in New England that the judges, jury and spectators who actually saw those fits had not the slightest doubt that the children were being

291

tormented, while most the historians, who based their conclusions on the cold, disconnected and imperfect transcriptions of the court records, believed that the children were only putting on a show. Unfortunately, in the Salem records the fits are not described in any connected fashion, and one has to piece together many stray bits of testimony to get a clear conception of their nature; yet so palpably convincing was this evidence of bewitchment that the help of 12 year old Ann Putnam and her friends was sometimes sought by persons in distant towns when they suspected witchcraft in their households. In one instance, a man brought his sick infant from Boston to Salem merely for these girls to name the persons who had bewitched his child and two women of Boston were actually named, though the girls had never seen them. At another time, the afflicted Ann, so richly endowed with extrasensory perception, was taken to Andover to see a sick old woman, and before long fifty of the inhabitants of that town were under arrest for witchcraft. The conclusion seems inescapable that if these children were merely putting on a show they displayed consummate skill in acting in an extraordinary show indeed.

IV

Fortunately, because it is helpful in the diagnosis, there still exists a record of one case of witchcraft in which the fits of some bewitched children are described in great detail. This is called "Memorable Providences, Relating to Witchcraft and Possessions," and chiefly because of its detailed descriptions it is a most valuable contribution to early American medicine, though not hitherto so regarded. This case history of the Goodwin children was written a few years before the Salem tragedy. On the surface, it may seem illogical to use a Boston witchcraft case of 1688 to help explain the Salem cases of 1692, but all historians agree on the almost perfect similarity [1] in the cases and my only reason for citing these earlier cases from Boston is that here one finds a connected story limited almost exclusively to a description of the fits. Another objection to using the "Memorable Providences" is that the author, Cotton Mather, is known to have been prejudiced in favor of witchcraft. But strange as it may seem to some, the Puritans, and particularly Cotton Mather, did not oppose, but indeed advanced, the growth of science. It was this same Cotton Mather, member of the Royal Society, who wrote the first American description of measles (which, incidentally, is an American classic), and it was he who, in spite of tremendous opposition from the medical profession, influenced Zabdiel Boylston to try inoculation against smallpox, the first step toward the prevention of diseases. Mather steadfastly maintained in his "Memorable Providences" that he was recording actual facts, and, though considerable allowance should be made for his superstition, gullibility and firm belief in witchcraft, it is clear that the descriptions must have been founded mostly on observations, not only because of the similarity to the Salem court records, with which he had nothing to do, but chiefly because, even after these two hundred and fifty years, one can recognize the sickness that afflicted the Goodwin children as easily as though they had had the smallpox.

---

1. This similarity is so striking that any explanation of Salem witchcraft should be applicable to the Goodwin cases. This automatically eliminates the role of Tituba, the Salem Village jealousies and dissensions, the mob hysteria in the Salem courtroom and numerous other theories of students of witchcraft. These students generally dismiss the Goodwin cases on the supposition that the children of Salem had read Mather's account and had decided to imitate the Goodwin children. Totally ignored is the more plausible theory that the adults of Salem Village had read Mather's account and were thus able to recognize witchcraft when they saw it.

The "Memorable Providences" concerns John Goodwin, a mason, and his wife, who with their six children, Nathaniel 15, Martha 13, John 11, Mercy 7 and Benjamin 5 years and Hannah 6 months old, comprised an extremely religious family. Indeed, from some of his devout letters still extant it appears that John Goodwin was the kind of mason who would have said a prayer every time he laid a brick. One day Martha Goodwin accused the family washerwoman of stealing some of the family linen, whereupon the washerwoman's "wild Irish" mother, old Goody Glover, "bestow'd very bad Language upon the Girl . . . immediately upon which, the poor child became variously indisposed in her health, and visited with strange Fits, beyond those that attend an Epilepsy, or a Catalepsy, or those they call The Diseases of Astonishment." Shortly after, John, Mercy and Benjamin began to behave in a strange manner too, though "the godly father and the suckling Infant, were not afflicted" nor was Nathaniel except in slight degree. The most skilful Boston physicians, unable to find any physical cause, concluded that the children were afflicted with "an Hellish Witchcraft," and, needless to say, poor Goody Glover was therefore put to death. Later, Cotton Mather took the afflicted Martha Goodwin into his own home and after many months of observation wrote his account, from which the following passage is taken:

The variety of their tortures increased continually; and tho about Nine or Ten at Night they alwaies had a Release from their miseries, and ate, and slept all night for the most part indifferently well, yet in the day time they were handled with so many sorts of Ails, that it would require of us almost as much time to Relate them all, as it did of them to Endure them. Sometimes they would be Deaf, sometimes Dumb, and sometimes Blind, and often, all this at once. One while their Tongues would be drawn down their Throats; another-while they would be pull'd out upon their Chins, to a prodigious length. They would have their Mouths opened unto such a Wideness, that their Jaws went out of joint; and anon they would clap together again with the Force like that of a strong Spring-Lock. The same would happen to their Shoulder-Blades, and their Elbows, and Hand-wrists, and several of their joints. They would at times ly in a benummed condition; and be drawn together as those that are ty'd Neck and Heels; and presently be stretched out, yea, drawn Backwards, to such a degree that it was fear'd the very skin of their Bellies would have crack'd. They would make most pitteous out-cries, that they were cut with Knives, and struck with Blows that they could not bear. Their necks would be broken, so that their Neck-bone would seem dissolved unto them that felt after it; and yet on the sudden, it would become again so stiff that there was no stirring of their Heads; yea, their Heads would be twisted almost round; and if main force at any time obstructed a dangerous motion which they seem'd to be upon, they would roar exceedingly . . .

The Fits of the Children yet more arriv'd unto such Motions as were beyond the Efficacy of any natural Distemper in the World. They would bark at one another like Dogs, and again purr like so many Cats. They would sometimes complain, that they were in a Red-hot Oven, sweating and panting at the same time unreasonably: Anon they would say, Cold water was thrown upon them, at which they would shiver very much. They would cry out of dismal Blowes with great Cudgels laid upon them; and tho' we saw no cudgels nor blowes, yet we could see the Marks left by them in Red Streaks upon their bodies afterward. And one of them [John, 11 years old] would be roasted on an invisible Spit, run into his Mouth, and out at his Foot, he lying, and rolling, and groaning as if it had been so in the most sensible manner in the world; and then he would shriek, that Knives were cutting of him. Sometimes also he would have his head so forcibly, tho not visibly, nail'd unto the Floor, that it was as much as a strong man could do to pull it up. One while they would all be so limber, that it was judg'd every Bone of them could be bent. Another while they would be so stiff, that not a joint of them could be stir'd. . . .

Many wayes did the Devils take to make the children do mischief both to themselves and others; but thro the singular Providence of God, they always fail'd in the attempts. For they could never essay the doing of any harm, unless there were some-body at hand that might prevent it; and seldome without first shrieking out, "They say, I must do such a thing!" Diverse times they went to strike furious Blowes at their tenderest and dearest friends, or to fling them down staires when they had them at the top, but the warnings from the mouths of the children themselves, would still anticipate what the Devils did intend. They diverse times were very near Burning or Drowning of themselves, but the Children themselves by their own pittiful and seasonable cries for help, still procured their Deliverance. . . . But if any small Mischief happen'd to be done where they were; as the Tearing or Dirtying of a Garment, the Falling of a Cup, the breaking of a Glass or the like; they would rejoice extremely, and fall into a pleasure and Laughter very extraordinary . . .

Variety of Tortures now seiz'd upon the Girl [Martha, 13 years old]; in which besides the forementioned Ails returning upon her, she often would cough up a Ball as big as a small Egg, into the side of her Wind-pipe, that would near choak her, till by Stroking and by Drinking it was carried down again . . .

The Last Fit that the young woman had, was very peculiar. The Dæmons having once again seiz'd her, they made her pretend to be Dying, and Dying truly we fear'd at last she was: She lay, she tossed, she pull'd just like one Dying, and urged hard for some to dy with her, seeming loth to dy alone. She argued concerning Death, in strains that quite amazed us; and concluded, That though she was loth to dy, yet if God said she must, she must: adding something about the state of the Country, which we wondered at. Anon, the Fit went over; and as I guessed it would be, it was the last Fit she had at our House.

V

Inasmuch as old men and women were condemned to death as wizards and witches on this sort of evidence, it is easy to understand the unbridled scorn of the historians; and yet it is important to emphasize that there is enough here, to say nothing of other passages not cited, for an absolute diagnosis. It is also easy to show that the Salem children suffered from hysteria too, for there is hardly a sign or symptom manifested by Martha Goodwin that did not have its counterpart in one or another of the Salem children during their bewitchment. They too made "great noises" during their "lamentable fits and agonies"; they too were "dreadfully tortured" and "struck dumb and senseless for a season"; according to the Rev. Mr. Hale, "Sometimes they were taken dumb, their mouths stopped, their throats choked, their limbs wracked and tormented so as might move an heart of stone." Samuel Sewall, of all the Puritans the most generally successful in keeping his feet on the ground, meant exactly what he said when he wrote in his diary: "It was awful to see the tortures of the afflicted." During the trial of that "rampant hag" Martha Carrier, the afflicted were "so tortured that every one expected their death upon the very spot."

By patching together the sworn testimony of numerous witnesses during the trial of Mary Easty and by making a few minor alterations for the sake of continuity, one can obtain a fairly connected first-hand description of the fits of the Salem children on one occasion at least. At the preliminary hearing in Salem Village during April 1692, five of the afflicted children were "choked in such a most grievous maner" that the examination had to be interrupted, and in spite of the prayers of the Rev. Mr. Hale they remained "almost choked to death." For some now unknown reason Mary Easty was released on May 18. On May 20, Mercy Lewis, a 17 year old servant girl, had a fit in the home of her master, Constable John Putnam.

One man testified:

I went to that house about 9 a clock in the morning and when I came there Mercy Lewis lay on the bed in a sad condition and continued speechless for about an hour. [He then left for a while but came back.] She continued in a sad condition the greatest part of the day being in such tortures as no tongue can express; but not able to speak. But at last she said "Deare Lord Receive my soule" and again said "Lord let them not kill me yett" but at last she came to herself for a little while and was very sensible and then she said that Goody Easty said she would kill her before midnight. . . . Then again presently she felt very bad and cried out "Pray for the salvation of my soule for they will kill me."

Four other men who were in that house between 8 and 11 o'clock that night testified that Elizabeth Hubbard, another 17 year old girl, was brought in while they were there. They found Mercy Lewis "in such a case as if death would have quickly followed . . . being unable to speak most of the day." The two girls then "fell into fits by turns, the one being well whilst the other was ill . . . and [the apparition] vexed and tortured them both by choking and seemingly breathless fits and other fits, threatening Mercy Lewis with a winding sheet & afterwards with a Coffin if said Mercy would not signe the Devil'ʒ book. Abundance more of vexations they both received from her [the apparition]."

Still two other men had been at the house that day and found Mercy Lewis in a very Dreadful and Solemn Condition so that Shee could not continue long in this world without a mitigation of those Torments. [They left the house for a while but] Returning the same night aboute midnight, wee found Mercy Lewis in a Dreadful fitt but. her reason then Returned Again. She said "What, have you brought me the winding sheet, Goody Easty? Well, I had rather go into the winding sheet than Sett my hand to the Devil's book" but after that her fitts was weaker and weaker but still complaining that Shee was very sick of her stomake. About break of Day She fell asleep but still Continues extreem sick and was taken with a Dreadful fitt just as we left her so that we perceived life in her and that was all.

Another man testified that she was "grievously afflicted and tortured . . . choked allmost to death . . . and we looked for nothing else but present death." Her fit continued well into the next day.

During most of the fit the girl was in a stupor and could not speak; so Ann Putnam (12 years), Abigail Williams (11 years) and Elizabeth Hubbard (17 years) were summoned to the bedside to attempt to identify the apparition that was tormenting Mercy Lewis. The three said that it was the apparition of Goody Easty. Near midnight, when the fit was extra severe, two men rushed out of that haunted house, hastened to Salem for a warrant and then went to Topsfield and dragged Goody Easty out of bed. She was 58 years old and the mother of seven children, yet they took her back to Salem jail and chained her in a cell. She was brought to trial, and, chiefly because of Mercy Lewis' fit and similar evidence, she was convicted and subsequently hanged.

Because of the similarity in the two instances, one could expect that the same historians who have considered the Salem children as "frauds" should have also condemned the Goodwin children as deceitful "pests," they apparently having overlooked the fact that Cotton Mather, like the Salem judges, did consider the possibility of sham but quickly rejected it. Just because some passages in the "Memorable Providences" make it appear as though Martha Goodwin may have had her tongue in her cheek while she was being observed, one can hardly conclude that Cotton Mather's whole account was ludicrous, written in a "style of blind and absurd credulity that cannot be surpassed." That the children's afflictions were attributed to the capital crime of witchcraft is deplorable enough, to say the least, but that is not the point at issue. It is essential to remember that lying was only a symptom and that primarily the children were afflicted with a mental illness. Having studied medicine and probably knowing as much about sickness as any New England physician, Mather deserves a little credit for recognizing that there was at least something unusual about this girl. "But I am resolved after this" he wrote after observing her for many months, "never to use but one grain of patience with any man that shall go to impose upon me a Denial of Devils, or of Witches. I shall count that man Ignorant who shall suspect, but I shall count him down-right Impudent, if he Assert the Non-Existence of things *which we have had such palpable convictions of.*" (The italics are mine).

It therefore seems reasonable to conclude that not the apparent lying but the "extreme agony of all the afflicted" accounts for the decided convictions of the judges, jury and spectators, many of them educated and reasonable men. In some cases "the tortures and lamentations of the afflicted" convinced even the relatives of the accused, and in the trials of Rebecca Nurse and a few others even the accused themselves, though vehemently denying their own guilt, nevertheless admitted that the children acted as though bewitched. Not unimportant is the fact that more than one trial had to be postponed because the children could not possibly be relieved of their "agony" by binding the accused, by prayer or by any other means. And when their trials were over, at least two convicted witches were unanimously excommunicated from the church, a horrible punishment in Puritan times, especially to one about to die. The possibility that the judges were unfair being laid aside for the moment, would the men and women of the church willingly and unanimously convict their intimate friends, whom they knew to be otherwise honorable, except for this very, very convincing evidence of "stupendous Witchcraft?"

VI

Far more fundamental to a true understanding of the Salem tragedy than the diagnosis of hysteria are the factors at play which could have caused so much hysteria among the children of those days; hence, by far the most interesting feature of Mather's account of the Goodwin children is that every now and then he allows a glimpse of the underlying cause. The following quotation is not an isolated passage lifted from its context merely to prove a point but is representative of many similar passages, and consequently the cause and effect sequence seems more than accidental:

But nothing in the World would so discompose them as a Religious Exercise. If there were any Discourse of God, or Christ, or any of the things which are not seen and are eternal, they would be cast into intolerable Anguishes. Once, those two Worthy Ministers, Mr. Fisk and Mr. Thatcher, bestowing some gracious Counsils on the Boy, whom they then found at a Neighbours house, he immediately lost his Hearing, so that he heard not one word, but just the last word of all they said. Much more, All Praying to God, and Reading of his Word, would occasion a very terrible Vexation to them: They would then stop their own Ears with their own Hands; and roar, and shriek; and holla, to drown the Voice of Devotion. Yea, if any one in the Room took up a Bible to look into it, tho the Children could see nothing of it, as being in a croud of Spectators, or having their Faces another way, yet would they be in wonderful Miseries, till the Bible were laid aside. In short, No good thing must be endured near those Children, which (while they are themselves) do love every good thing in a measure that proclaims in them the Fear of God. . . .

Devotion was now, as formerly, the terriblest of all the provocations that could be given her [Martha]. I could by no means bring her to own, That she desired the mercies of God, and the prayers of good men. I would have obtained a Sign of such a Desire, by her Lifting up her hand; but she stirr'd it not: I then lifted up her hand my self, and though the standers-by thought a more insignificant thing could not be propounded, I said, "Child, If you desire those things, let your hand fall, when I take mine away:" I took my hand away, and hers continued strangely and stifly stretched out, so that for some time, she could not take it down. During these days we had Prayers oftener in our Family than at other times; and this was her usual Behaviour at them. The man that prayed, usually began with Reading the Word of God; which once as he was going to do, she call'd to him, "Read of Mary Magdalen, out of whom the Lord cast seven Devils." During the time of Reading, she would be laid as one fast asleep; but when Prayer was begun, the Devils would still throw her on the Floor, at the feet of him that prayed. There she would lye and Whistle and sing and roar, to drown the voice of the Prayer; but that being a little too audible for Them, they [the devils] would shut close her Mouth and her ears, and yet make such odd noises in her Throat as that she herself could not hear our Cries to God for her. Shee'd also fetch very terrible Blowes with her Fist, and Kicks with her Foot at the man that pray'd; but still (for he had bid that none should hinder her) her Fist and Foot would alwaies recoil, when they came within a few hairs breadths of him just as if Rebounding against a Wall; so that she touch'd him not, but then would beg hard of other people to strike him, and particularly she entreated them to take the Tongs and smite him; Which not being done, she cryed out of him, "He has wounded me in the Head." But before Prayer was out, she would be laid for Dead, wholly senseless and (unless to a severe Trial) Breathless; with her Belly swelled like

a Drum, and sometimes with croaking noises in it; thus would she
the stiffness and posture of one that had been two Days laid out for D
as he that was praying was alluding to the words of the Canaanites, ar
mercy on a Daughter, vexed with a Devil; there came a big, but low
"There's Two or Three of them" (or us) and the standers-by were u
as that they cannot relate whether her mouth mov'd in speaking of
ended, she would Revive in a minute or two, and continue as Frolicks

VIII

Perhaps I have been bewitched into drawing false conclusions, but it seems
clear to me that Martha Goodwin had resorted to hysteria mainly because of
religious uncertainties and conflicts; and toward a better understanding why
Puritan children felt insecure as they contemplated this world and the world
hereafter it is now necessary to say something of the Puritan religion. It should
go without saying that no sensible man attempts to ridicule any religion so long
as it remains a force for good, but, on the other hand, it is important to examine
the probable results of the impact of the Puritan religion on the minds of growing
children if one wishes to fathom the disastrous events that took place in Salem.

Long before they attained the age of reason, Puritan children were made to
learn the contents of John Cotton's catechism, called "Spiritual Milk for Babes,
Drawn out of the Breasts of both Testaments, for their Souls Nourishment."
Among the first things they learned were the dreadful consequences of Original
Sin. All wickedness, all sufferings and diseases, all catastrophes were only manifestations of God's "Holy Anger" and "Holy Jealousy" because of the fall of Adam
and Eve. This doctrine (the sixth question and answer in the catechism) that all
children were "conceived in sin and born in iniquity" was later carried to its logical
conclusion by the preachers of the early eighteenth century. When the Rev. Jabez
Fitch found that over 90 per cent of all the deaths from "throat distemper"
occurred among children, that to him was mathematical proof of the "woful Effects
of Original Sin." The brilliant theologian Jonathan Edwards stoutly maintained
that sinful children were more hateful than vipers because vipers had no souls.
Whitfield literally screamed at his audiences that children were worse than rattle-
snakes and alligators, which, he said, were also beautiful when small; and Benjamin
Wadsworth said that "They're Children of Wrath by Nature, liable to Eternal
Vengeance, the Unquenchable Flames of Hell. . . . Truly it behooves them
most seriously to consider how filthy, guilty, odious, and abominable they are both
by Nature and Practice."

There is an illustrative passage in the *Diary of Cotton Mather* dated Nov. 7,
1697:

> I took my little [5 year old] daughter, Katy, into my Study, and there I told my child
> That I am to Dy Shortly and Shee must, when I am Dead, Remember every Thing, that I
> now said unto her. I sett before her, the sinful . . . condition of her Nature, and I charged
> her to *pray in secret places* every day, . . . I gave her to understand that when I am taken
> from her, shee must look to meet with more Humbling Afflictions, than she does.

The literature of colonial times abounds in examples of early piety, instances
of "joyful deaths" of children who had learned every word of the catechism, for
the Puritans were eager to preserve these instances of holiness in order to impress
their remaining children. Cotton Mather has left an account of the precocious
Elizabeth Butcher, 2½ years old. "As she lay in the Cradle, she would ask herself
that Question, What is my corrupt Nature? and would make Answer to herself,
It is empty of Grace, bent into Sin, and only to Sin, and that continually." Many
more examples of early piety are related by the Rev. John Brown in his account

297

remarkable deaths" during the great diphtheria epidemic in Haverhill.)idemics, catastrophes or deaths of playmates seemed to be opportune occasions to impress on children that they were born under the wrath and curse of God. Here is an interview with a dying 7 year old child:

> Being ask'd if she was willing to die, and go to Christ; she said, Yes: But Child you know you are a Sinner; she said Yes: And you know where the Wicked go when they die; she said, Yes they are cast into Hell. And Being asked, if she was not afraid of going thither: she said No, for Christ is an all sufficient Savior, and He is able to save me I hope he will: Tho' I have not yet seen Christ, yet I hope I shall see him. . . .
>
> A while after she said, I am weary of this World, and long to be gone!

The most pitiful, yet most significant, aspect of this gruesome theology was that the children, once convinced that they were dreadful sinners by birth, could do absolutely nothing about it. There was no use in begging for mercy or forgiveness, because every good Puritan firmly believed in predestination. God, even before the creation of the earth, the sun, the moon and the stars, had already determined who were to be saved and who were to be damned, and no one on earth could be certain whether or not he was among the elect. If God was willing, the adults, by constant prayer and good works, might experience a salvation or a flooding of the soul with an irresistible grace, and with this came the joyful feeling that they were among the elect. But this involved a complex mental process that no child could experience, much less enjoy. And so, with the avenue to mental peace left open only to adults, thoughtful children became terribly bewildered. There are no more pitiful passages in all Puritan literature than those in Sewall's diary wherein he related the gloomy religious outlook of his daughter Betty:

> It falls to my [7 year old] daughter Elizabeth's share to read the 24. of Isaiah [which concerns the earth's turning upside down and the inhabitants thereof falling into space] which she doth with many tears not being well and the contents of the chapter and sympathy with her draw tears from me also. . . . .
>
> When I came in, past 7. at night, my wife met me in the Entry and told me Betty [13 years old] had surprised them. I was surprised with the abruptness of the Relation. It seems Betty Sewall had given some signs of dejection and sorrow; but a little after dinner she burst out in an amazing cry, which caus'd all the family to cry too; Her mother ask'd the reason; she gave none; at last she said she was afraid she should goe to Hell, her Sins were not pardon'd. She was first wounded by my reading a Sermon of Mr. Norton's, about the 5th of Jan. Text of Jno. 7. 34. Ye shall seek me and shall not find me. And those words in the Sermon Jno. 8. 21. Ye shall seek me and shall die in your sins, ran in her mind and terrified her greatly.

At the age of 16 Nathaniel Mather wrote in his diary: "When very young I went astray from God, and my mind was altogether taken with vanities and follies; such as the remembrance of them doth greatly abase my soul within me. Of the manifold sins which then I was guilty of, none so sticks upon me, as that being very young, I was whittling on the sabbath-day; and for fear of being seen, I did it behind the door. A great reproach of God! a specimen of that atheism that I brought into the world with me." When 19 years old, he confessed on his deathbed that the most bitter of all his trials on earth were "the horrible conceptions of God, buzzing about [his] mind."

It is needless to say much about Puritan conceptions of hell except that epidemics and earthquakes seemed to offer opportune moments for the publication of broadsides and sermons containing the most lurid descriptions. Children were taken on walks through cemeteries to see where other smaller children were buried, for a child was "never too little to die, and never too young to go to hell." The classic example of all this is Michael Wigglesworth's oft-quoted 224 stanza poem on "The Day of Doom" (1662), a work which went through numerous editions and was familiar to nearly every Puritan child. In it are depicted the terrors of the damned in terms that might even today send shivers up the spine of the most confirmed atheistic pediatrician. Of some interest are Wigglesworth's ideas of the punishment inflicted on the newly born, or, as he expressed it, on those who went "from the womb unto the tomb." On the fateful Day of Doom those little infants, exceedingly reluctant to be cast into hell because of Adam's sin, put up a strenuous argument:

> Not we, but he ate of the tree
>   whose fruit was interdicted:
> Yet on us all of his sad fall,
>   the punishment's inflicted.

But all cases were predetermined, so the sentence was nevertheless pronounced:

> You sinners are, and such a share
>   as sinners may expect,
> Such you shall have; for I do save
>   none but my own elect.
> Yet to compare your sin with their
>   who lived a longer time,
> I do confess yours is much less,
>   though every sin's a crime.
> A crime it is, therefore in bliss
>   you may not hope to dwell,
> But unto you I shall allow
>   the easiest room in hell.

VIII

Enough has been told to show that the average Puritan child, if he paid any attention to the rigid Calvinism of the times, must have had gloomy prospects of life beyond the grave; and there can be little doubt that some of them at least lived in constant, gnawing fear not only of death but of eternal damnation after death. Thus the appearance of hysteria among the children of Salem Village has an adequate explanation, as it has in the numerous other case histories that are known. Preserved in the Puritan literature are many isolated instances of strange diseases among children which sound much like hysteria. Though perhaps not so dramatic, because there were no executions, but just as important are the examples of mass religious hysteria during the frequent revivals, of which the "Great Awakening" in 1740 is the best example. And it is a curious fact that no one ever blames the children for the outbreak of hysteria at Northhampton in 1740, yet the children of Salem are held responsible for what was an essentially similar affair. With a knowledge of the religious background of the Salem children it seems rather unimportant to argue whether Cotton Mather was guilty of the witchcraft hangings by influencing the governor, the judges or the mob on Gallows Hill. He was guilty only insofar as he was a Calvinist; but so, indeed, was nearly everybody else.

The history of the Salem witchcraft should be more concerned with the family background and medical history of the afflicted children, for they were victims as well as the persons who were hanged. It was no coincidence that Martha Goodwin, child of devout parents, acquired her hysteria just at the time when "she was in the dark concerning her Souls estate" and the mere sight of the Bible or the catechism always sent her into "hideous convulsions." Nor was it very strange that the first cases in Salem Village occurred in the very home of that red-hot Devil-chaser, the Rev. Samuel Parris. "Pray for the salvation of my soule for they will kill me," from the mouth of the bewitched Mercy Lewis, was one of the most significant remarks made during the Salem trials. Those children had ample reason to become hysterical when repeatedly told that the monstrous, invisible, venomous, hissing and sooty Devil was right in their neighborhood ready to devour them; and no doubt many of them were positively convinced that they were actually bewitched.

One is not obliged to accept the verdict of the popular historians that the children were deceitful, wicked, malicious and dishonest. History has been unkind to them along enough. They were not imposters or pests or frauds; they were not cold-blooded malignant brats. They were sick children in the worst sort of mental distress—living in fear for their very lives and the welfare of their immortal souls. Hysteria was only the outward manifestation of their feeble attempts to escape from their insecure, cruel, depressive Salem Village world—a world thoroughly saturated with the pungent fumes of burning brimstone.

BIBLIOGRAPHY

The possibility that the children suffered from mental or physical illness was at least suspected by the Puritans themselves when they consulted the physicians before pronouncing a verdict of witchcraft. Cheever[2] also considered this possibility but treated it only in a footnote. Even Upham[3] considered it only long enough to disprove it. The best medical analysis is by Taylor.[4] He attributed some of the hysteria to Tituba. Robbins[5] also discussed some of the medical aspects.

Miller and Johnson[6] provided a bibliography of the Salem witchcraft in general, and Fleming[7] has included a bibliography of the religious background of Puritan children but not in relation to witchcraft. Cotton Mather's "Memorable Providences" has been reprinted by Burr.[8]

683 Asylum Avenue.

2. Cheever, G. F.: Essex Inst. Hist. Coll. 2:196, 1860.
3. Upham, C. W.: Salem Witchcraft, with an Account of Salem Village, Boston, Wiggin and Lunt, 1867, vols. 1 and 2.
4. Taylor, E. W.: Problems of Personality, London, 1925, p. 167.
5. Robbins, F. G.: Essex Inst. Hist. Coll. 65:218, 1929.
6. Miller, P. G. E., and Johnson, T.: The Puritans, New York, American Book Company, 1938, p. 826.
7. Fleming, S.: Children and Puritanism, New Haven, Conn., Yale University Press, 1938.
8. Burr, G. L.: Narratives of the Witchcraft Cases, 1648-1706, New York, Charles Scribner's Sons, 1914.

Article III.—WITCHCRAFT IN CONNECTICUT.

1647–1697.

THE historian, Lecky, has devoted some exceedingly interesting pages of his History of Rationalism to the decadence, nay, to the virtual extinction of the belief in Witchcraft. It may be possible that the change has been one of name and form, rather than of substance. The superstition is no longer crude, except in isolated communities. English soil is no longer blighted by the unholy orgies of a witch's Sabbath. English folk to-day do not generally believe that the Devil may still carry about in his pocket blank formulas for contracts, or that his victims may still shrivel up their foes with glances of the evil eye. Yet, in that little corner of the world which proudly defines itself by the epithet "Enlightened," impostors gain disciples by the pretense of familiarity with the spiritual world, clairvoyant quacks flourish and negro "Voudoo" seers find their best customers among their former masters, or, more properly, mistresses. The wonders of psychology and of muscular action have not become so familiar to us that we can afford to sneer at the Puritan's affright before psychic and physiological mysteries. The age of Darwin and Huxley sees aggressive Spiritualism numbering its adherents by hundreds of thousands in England and the United States, and a leading clergyman of Brooklyn (for the Rev. Mr. Talmage surely merits that title), gravely informs his hearers at a Friday evening lecture that Satan is the prince of the powers of the air, that the atmosphere is full of demonic spirits, and that a recent series of horrible murders along the shores of Long Island Sound must be attributed to their influence.

The panic of 1692 was not an event peculiar to Massachusetts, or to New England, any more than the "Popish Plot" terror of 1741 was necessarily indigenous to the colony of New York. Anywhere in the Christian world the refined cruelties of neighborhood gossip, joined to the manifestations of "nervous force," so inexplicable at that time, produced similar

results. But let it be remembered that the New England
Puritans were the first of Englishmen to disregard accusations
of witchcraft, and that the typical colonies of Puritan New
Haven, Separatist Plymouth, and Independent Rhode Island,
never knew a conviction for witchcraft within their borders.
A bevy of mischievous, wanton girls, and a scheming parson
have brought upon the colony of Massachusetts an ill-report beyond the measure of its deserts. "New England Witches," in
the common parlance, generally means "Salem Witches." It
is yet a fortunate circumstance if the additional reproach of
"burning witches" is not also heaped upon the Puritan scape-
goat, even though the probable truth is that South Carolina
alone condemned suspected wizards to a fiery ordeal. Drake's
words are :* "About this period (1712), in the colony of South
Carolina, some suspected of witchcraft were seized upon by a
sort of ruffianly Vigilance Committee, and condemned to be
burnt, and were actually roasted by fire, although we do not
learn that the injuries thus inflicted proved fatal. The parties
so tortured, or their friends, brought action in the regular
courts for the recovery of damages, but the jury gave them
nothing." This happened nearly a score of years after the last
witch had been suspended from a Massachusetts gallows. The
last execution of a witch in Connecticut preceded it by more
than half a century.

Doubtless a larger number of people suffered in Massachusetts for the fictitious crime of "Familiarity with yᵉ Devill"
than in any other of the thirteen colonies, but the majority of
the victims were sacrificed at one time and place to an uncon-
trollable popular frenzy. Prior to that time it is historic fact
that public instances of this delusion had occurred most frequently in the colony of Connecticut. The colonial records
may be, and probably are, deficient; but, so far as our present
knowledge can go, either eight or nine persons were hung for
witchcraft in Connecticut before 1692, while only six suffered
in Massachusetts. The last witch-trials in Connecticut, which
terminated fatally, were in 1662–3, thirty years before the
Salem Reign of Terror; although that event was accompanied
by a number of accusations in Connecticut also. But little in-

* *Annals of Witchcraft*, p. 215.

formation upon this subject can be derived from the histories of Connecticut. Dr. Trumbull, whose work is the best that we have for the colonial period, speaks of witchcraft in the preface only, in these words:* "It may possibly be thought a great neglect, or matter of partiality, that no account is given of witchcraft in Connecticut. The only reason is that, after the most careful researches, no indictment of any person for that crime, nor any process relative to that affair can be found. The minute in Goff's journal, published by Governor Hutchinson, relative to the execution of Ann Coles, and an obscure tradition that one or two persons were executed at Stratford is all the information that can be found relative to that unhappy affair." Dr. Trumbull, writing in 1799, may be excused for not discovering the traces of witch-trials in Connecticut and New Haven Records, which were then in MSS., but a reference to his copy of the *Magnalia Christi Americana* ought to have taught him more than he apparently ever knew. Where could the "careful researches," of which he speaks, have been expended? Hollister, who is, after Trumbull, the most prominent historian of the State, volunteers some information that is both scanty and spurious. Even so recent and trustworthy a writer as W. F. Poole† is misinformed about the number of executions in New England before 1692, has apparently never heard of several of the Connecticut trials, and is unable to state details accurately. Since histories fail us, recourse must be had to the materials whence histories ought to be made, to the Colonial Records of Connecticut and New Haven. The archives of the latter colony which, upon this topic are devoid of any fatal interest, are found to be as copious as those of Connecticut are scanty. Most important of all these ancient pages is an unprinted volume of Connecticut Records, which was found, in 1861, in the possession of a private family in New York, by the Hon. Chas. J. Hoadly, the Connecticut State Librarian. The book contains the records of the "Perticular Court" from 1649 to 1663, the very court before which a number of the trials took place.‡

* vol. 1, p. viii.　　　　　† *Memorial Hist. of Boston*, ii. 133.

‡ Extracts from this volume have already appeared in a series of contributions by the Hon. Porter C. Bliss to the columns of a New Haven

Witchcraft was of course a capital crime in both New Haven and Connecticut. Among the twelve offences specified in the Connecticut Code of Laws of 1642, as worthy of the extreme penalty, the second was that of " Being a witch, having or consulting a familiar spirit." In 1655 Governor Eaton prepared a code for New Haven, after an examination of the " New booke of lawes in y⁰ Massachusetts Colony," and of a " Small booke of lawes newly come from England, which is said to be Mr. Cottons."* The second of the " Capitall Lawes " read as follows: " If any person be a witch, he or she shall be put to death." The law is sustained by three Scripture quotations, the same ones that are also appended to the aforesaid Connecticut law. They are all excerpts from the Mosaic code. The law itself is a paraphrase of the first text, Exod. xxii. 18: " Thou shalt not suffer a witch to live." The next selection, from Levit. xx. 27, orders that a witch shall be stoned to death. Lastly, the verses of Deut. xviii. 10–11 forbid the children of Israel to entertain any that useth divination, or an observer of times, or an enchanter, or a witch, or a charmer, or a consulter with familiar spirits, or a wizard, or a necromancer. The introduction to Drake's *Annals* (page xxvi.) states that New Haven Colony was the first one to be disturbed by witches. No vestige of real proof of this assertion appears there, or elsewhere, and Dr. Bacon must be justified in the assertion that there never was a condemnation, or an execution for witchcraft within the bounds of the New Haven jurisdiction.† As the reader will perceive, the New Haven Court, in cases of witchcraft, let its moderation be known unto all men. The earliest evidence of the existence of witches in Connecticut is in Winthrop's *Journal.*‡ Under the date of March, 164⅞, he says, " One of Windsor arraigned and executed for a witch."

daily paper, during the summer of 1883. To these articles I wish to acknowledge my indebtedness. Reference will be made as occasion calls for it, to numerous local histories, and especially to the works of those literary Titans, the Mathers.

Thanks are due to Mr. C. J. Hoadly for advice and assistance, and especially to Dr. Gustavus Eliot, of New Haven, for efficient aid in the tedious labor of examining ancient records.

* *Col. Rec.*, ii. 147, 576.   † See *Historical Discourses.*
‡ Vol. ii. 374.

Mr. Savage, the learned editor, subjoins a note, stating that the "One of Windsor" was probably named Johnson. A search in the colonial records brings to light no trace of a trial for witchcraft in 1647. At the General Court for the twenty-first of August, 1646, one Mary Jonson was sentenced to be whipped for "Theuery," once at Hartford and once at Wethersfield. This person was probably the same Mary Jonson against whom, Dec. 7th, 1648, the jury finds the bill of indictment that, "by her owne confession shee is guilty of familiarity with the Devill." The circumstances of her crimes, trial, and execution, Cotton Mather describes in his chapter of horrors.* He thought that her confession was attended "with such convictive circumstances that it could not be slighted." It seemed that she had work laid upon her which moved her to discontent, and she acquired the habit of wishing " the devil to take this and that, and the devil to do that and t'other thing;" whereupon it happened that the devil began to appear and to do whatever she wished. "Her master sending her to drive out the Hogs that sometimes broke into their field, a Devil would scowre the Hogs away, and make her laugh to see how he scared them. She confessed that she had murdered a Child, and had committed uncleanness both with men and with Devils." . . . . "The famous Mr. Stone labored hard to convert her from the devil to God." She became very penitent, and "dy'd in a frame extreamly to the satisfaction" of the spectators. Her execution probably took place in 1649, for not until May 21st, 1650, is there a record of the bill of charges for her imprisonment. It is ordered that Will. Rescew, the jailer, shall be paid out of her estate. It cannot be positively determined whether this Mary Jonson of 1648–9, and Winthrop's "One of Windsor," in 1747, are identical or not. The absence of allusion in the *Connecticut Records*, and Winthrop's carelessness in assigning dates, uphold the opinion that Mary Jonson was really the first sufferer. But Winthrop was sick through the winter of 1648–9, and died in the ensuing spring. The last entries in his Journal were dated only a few weeks after her trial. Would he have known of her execution? Furthermore, his record for March, 1647, is jotted down in his

* *Magnalia*, Bk. VI., p. 456. Hartford ed. of 1853.

usual, brief, straight-forward manner.   But the paragraphs
that he certainly did write in the winter of 1648–9 are prolix,
and entirely devoted to a recital of remarkable Providences,
such as an old man, feeling the hand of death upon him,
might naturally dwell upon, to the exclusion of public affairs.
The question must remain obscure.   In these same years
1649–50, the Mohegan sachem, Uncas, deemed himself in
danger from the bedevilments of hostile Indians, and besought
his English friends " that hee might be righted therein."   The
Commissioners of the United Colonies advised that Connecticut should appoint a committee of examination.   The issue of
the matter is unknown.   Indians were generally supposed to
be on too familiar terms with the Devil, and the Puritans
would probably be loath to scrutinize closely the powowings of
the red men.   It was expedient, of course, for the rulers of
Connecticut to pay some attention, if only of a formal sort, to
the wishes of their wily Mohegan ally.

Close upon the spectacle of Mary Jonson's " satisfactory "
penitence at her execution followed the indictments of John
and Joanna Carrington of Wethersfield.   The indictments of
husband and wife, *mutatis mutandis*, are precisely similar.
" A perticular Court in Hartford uppon the tryall of John
Carrington and his wife. 20th of Feb. 165$\frac{2}{1}$. Magistrates,
Edw. Hopkins, Esqr. Governor, John Haynes, Esqr. Deputy,
Mr. Wells, Mr. Woollcott, Mr. Webster, Mr. Cullick, Mr.
Clarke."   Here follow the names of the jury, headed by Mr.
Phelps and Mr. " Tailcoat."   John Carrington, of Wethersfield,
Carpenter, is accused of having " Intertained ffamiliarity with
Sathan, the Great Enemye of God and Mankinde," by whose
help supernatural works have been done.   " Therefore according to the laws of God, and of this Commonwealth, John Carrington deserves to die."   The jury approved the indictment
on the 6th of March.   Although the official records probably
contain no proof of the Carrington's final fate, it is asserted
that a diary, belonging to the library of the late George Brin-
ley of Hartford, bears witness to the hanging of the two
unfortunates.*

But no sooner was the Old Serpent well-scotched in one
place than he leaped up in another, as vigorous and venomous

* Referred to by Messrs. Bliss and Hoadly.

as ever. The Hartford magistrates from 1649 to 1651 waged a constant warfare with "Sathan the Great Enemye." For the 15th of May, in the latter year, there is the following entry: "The Governor, Mr. Cullick, and Mr. Clarke are desired to goe downe to Stratford to keep Courte uppon the tryall of Goody Bassett for her life, and, if the Governor cannot goe, then Mr. Wells is to goe in his roome." The *Connecticut Records* are not known to contain any further information concerning the result of this notable journey. But that Goody Bassett was convicted of witchcraft is stated in the New Haven records. During the progress of the libel suit of Staples vs. Ludlow, allusions were made to "Goodwife Bassett when she was condemned," and to "the other witch at the other towne who discovered" all whom she knew to be witches, a revelation that would probably be made only by one whose doom had been fixed. Her execution is the reasonable inference. Before 1652, therefore, four, and perhaps five persons had been hung, under the sanction of Connecticut laws, for the "impossible crime." The next disturbance engaged the attention of the New Haven Colony and proved to be a tragi-comedy. If the subject had not once been so serious a matter, the account of Mrs. Elizabeth Godman's various trials would excite nothing but amusement.* It is a rare picture of neighborhood gossip among the "very first families" of New Haven in the middle of the seventeenth century. In the light of to-day, Mrs. Godman appears to better advantage than most of the other participants in the affair. She was an inmate of the family of Dept. Gov. Stephen Goodyear. Her disposition was probably none of the sweetest. She was talkative and quick-tempered, and hence could not fail to create enemies, especially among her own sex. The first known allusion to her is probably the statement that, in 1642, the quarrel between Mrs. Stolyon, the trader, and Mr. Eliz. Godman is referred to the arbitration of Messrs. Goodyear and Gregson. "Mr." is, of course, a clerical error for "Mrs." Mrs. Godman, moreover, had formed the uncanny habit of talking aloud, or muttering to herself, an usage then universally recognized as the invariable practice of witches. She had been independent enough

* *Col. Rec.*, ii. 29-36, 151-2.

to think that the recent executions in Connecticut for witchcraft might not be judicious, and had alarmed the worthy Rev. Mr. Hooke, teacher of the church, by saying openly that witches ought not to be provoked, but should be brought into the Church. Mrs. Godman was evidently a Radical, and destined to get into trouble. Sympathy with witches would surely justify suspicions against herself. The trouble began by a quarrel with her neighbor, Mrs. Atwater, wife of the Colonial Treasurer. Mr. Goodyear lived on Chapel st., midway between Church and College streets; and Mr. Joshua Atwater dwelt diagonally opposite the present New Haven House, on the corner where college boys now love to congregate. Mrs. Atwater was surprised that the intricacies of her pocket could not conceal the presence of " figgs" from Mrs. Godman, and the latter's explanation that she had smelt them was deemed inadequate. Further, on the same evening of the miracle of the " figgs," Mrs. Godman, being at the house " cutt a sopp and put in pann;" Betty Brewster, watching her with fear, and saying to the maid that Mistress Elizabeth was "aboute her workes of darkness" was put that night " in a most misserable case." She heard a dreadful noise and fell into a profuse " sweate," and "in ye morning she looked as one yt had bine allmost dead." In short, it appears that Betty had suffered from an ague. However to Betty and to Betty's friends, it was plain that Mrs. Godman and the Devil were leagued against her. Mrs. Atwater was excited and "forwarned Mrs. Godman of her house." The story started around the little community and lost nothing on the way. Mrs. Godman showed herself a woman of wisdom as well as spirit. She did not wait to be thrust behind bolts and bars, but boldly summoned before the magistrates Mr. and Mrs. Goodyear, Rev. Mr. Hooke and his wife, Mrs. Bishop, wife of the Colonial Secretary, Mrs. Atwater, and several others, some of them no less prominent members of the community, and complained of them all that they suspected her for a witch. The sagacity of her course was evident when it appeared how much alone in the village she stood. The plaintiff was more truly the defendant than the accused persons were. The report of the first hearing of the case, May 21st, 1653, was en-

titled by Secretary Bishop, "The examination of Eliz. Godman."
The most prominent figure among the defendants was the Rev.
Mr. Hooke, afterwards Court Chaplain to Oliver Cromwell.
This learned divine testified at length. He had first suspected
Mrs. Godman when he heard of her doings at Mrs. Atwater's
house. He described her disposition as "mallitious" and in-
stanced her defense of witches elsewhere. He recited some of
her froward speeches. She had said "If they accuse me for a
witch I'll have them to the Governor, I'll trounce them."
Witches are with difficulty thrust away from houses where
they do mischief, and Mrs. Godman could not be kept from
Mr. Hooke's boy when he was sick, "which was in a very
strang manner." Mrs. Hooke pushed her from "ye boye,"
but Mrs. Godman turned again and said that she would look
upon him. Mrs. Godman suggested that Mr. Hooke's son had
"turned his braines with sliding;" but the doctor was at hand
to say that he "had never mett with the like." As a clincher,
Mr. Hooke deposed that, at the time, he had dreamed about
witches. It seemed mysterious to him that Mrs. Godman
knew immediately what was done at church meeting about
Delaware Bay, or about Mr. Cheever, although she herself was
absent; and Jane Hooke, and Time, Mr. Hooke's Indian servant, confirmed the assertion. The reverend gentleman closed
with a choice titbit of scandal. Mrs. Godman, not satisfied
with her probable diabolical connections, had cast favorable
glances upon Secretary James Bishop, and when Mr. Bishop
married one of Mr. Goodyear's daughters, Mrs. Godman was
troubled. No sooner were the parties contracted than Mrs.
Bishop was affected with strange "fitts," "which hath continewed," and none of her children have lived. Who but Mrs.
Godman could have done this? Thus far the whilom chaplain
to the Lord Protector! Both Mr. and Mrs. Goodyear had
accused her to her face of being a witch, and had been horror-
struck when Mrs. Godman met the charge with ridicule. She
had even ventured to assert that these fits were hereditary in
the Lamberton family, and that one who was unwell was not
necessarily bewitched.* Hannah Lamberton and her sister

* The Lamberton girls were Mrs. Goodyear's daughters, by a former
husband.

lived with the Goodyears. One day, the girls, anxious to sub-
serve the cause of public morality, climbed into the garret to a
place where they could overlook Mrs. Godman as she lay in
bed. Both of the damsels were sure that they saw a devilish
apparition in the bed with Mrs Godman, but they were immediately frightened away by the woman's threats. "About two
days after, Hanah's fitts began and one night, especially, she had
a dreadful fitt, and was pinched, and heard a hedious noise,
and was in a strang manner sweating and burning and sometime cold and full of paine so that she shriked out."

Verily, the uses of "malaria" have been numerous and vast.
There was a succession of examinations and depositions through
the summer. To some of them even Mr. Davenport lent his
august presence. If the bubbling mass of gossip and spite
gave signs of cooling, hands to stir the fire were not wanting.
In June, Goodwife Thorpe had a fearsome story to tell. She
had refused to sell Mrs. Godman some chickens. As the witch,
with a jocular remark, walked away, Goody Thorpe had looked
after her fearfully, and had said within herself, "If this woman
is naught as folks suspect, maybe she will smite my chickens."
Sure enough, soon after, a chicken died and was found to be
"consumed in ye gizzard to water and wormes and divers
others of them droped," a sure proof of bedevilment. The
topic so engrossed the public interest, that Mr. Davenport delivered himself from the pulpit upon the subject of witches.
He insinuated his opinion of the actual case by saying that "a
froward, discontented frame of spirit was a subject fitt for
ye Devill to worke upon." At the Court of Magistrates
for the Jurisdiction, August 4th, 1653, all the evidence was
reviewed. After some back-talk from Mrs. Godman, the following story was related to cap the climax of her misdeeds.
"One night Mr. Goodyear said something in the exposition of
a chapter, which she (being present) liked not, but said it was
against her. As soone as Mr. Goodyear had done duties, she
flung out of the roome in a discontented way, and cast a fierce
look upon Mr. Goodyear, as she went out. Immediately Mr.
Goodyear (tho' well before) fell into a swond." After kindly
pointing out to Mrs. Godman that she was a notorious liar, the
Court summed up as follows: The defendants are not guilty,

but "Mrs. Godman's carriage doth render her justly suspitious of witchcraft, which she herself in so many words confesseth, therefore the Court wisheth her to looke to her carriage hereafter, for, if further proofe come, these passages will not be forgotten." She was therefore charged not " to goe in an offensive way to folkes houses in a rayling manner, as it seemes she hath done, but that she keepe her place, and medle with her owne buisnes." It was a mild conclusion after all the ague-stricken girls, enchanted chickens, and "swonding" magistrates, and must have cost the pack of gossips many a wag of the head. The final phrases show that Governor Eaton understood the cause of all the trouble, and was judicious enough to distinguish between a cross-grained temper and possession by a devil. The New Haven Court deserves the more credit for its forbearance, because it was withstanding the force of contemporaneous example.

In the neighboring town of Fairfield, the keen scent of Roger Ludlow had just unearthed a witch, and brought her to the gallows. Nothing is known of the fate of Goody Knapp beyond what was revealed in the suit of Thomas Staples, of Fairfield, against Roger Ludlow for defamation. It was the twenty-ninth of May, 1654, and the dignified magistrates of the colony were assembled at New Haven for their usual spring session. The action was brought before this Court, because Ludlow, a refugee from Connecticut on account of his mutinous acts, had taken shelter in New Haven until he could embark for Virginia. Governor Eaton presided. With him sat Deputy Governor Goodyear, and Magistrates Newman, Fowler, and Leete, of New Haven, Milford, and Guilford, respectively. John Banks, attorney for Thos. Staples, charged Ludlow with slander in reporting to sundry persons, to Mr. and Mrs. Davenport among others, that Goody Staples was a witch and a liar, and that Goody Knapp had disclosed to Ludlow Mrs. Staples' alliance with Satan. It appears that Goody Knapp had been "cast by a jury and godly magistrates," and that the fatal evidence had been the discovery by a female jury of the mysterious witch marks upon her body. She was the victim of a group of malicious, gossiping women, more numerous and less scrupulous than the detractors of Mrs. Godman in

New Haven. Mr. Ludlow stands forth, in unenviable fame, as a stealthy fomenter of the wretched plot.

On the day when Goody Knapp was condemned, seven of these harridans swarmed about her in prison, and tried to induce her to confess her own criminality, and to name her accomplices, or, as Madame Pell expressed it, "to lay open herself and make way for the minister to doe her good." Goody Knapp replied that, if she had any knowledge, she would reveal it to Mr. Ludlow or yᵉ minister, before she went out of the world. "Elizabeth Bruster's" curiosity could not wait so long, and she encouraged the witch by remarking, "The Divill will have you quick if you reveale it not till then." Goody Knapp bluntly explained their innuendoes. "Take heed the devill have not you, for know you not how soone you may be my companions. The truth is you would have me say that Goodwife Staples is a witch, but I have sinns enough to answer for allready, and I hope I shall not add to my condemnation. I know nothing by Goodwife Staples, and I hope she is an honest woman." The coterie cried out that they had named no names, and Goodman Lyon admonished the witch not to breed differences between neighbors. She retorted, "Goodman Lyon, hold your tongue! I have bine fished withal in private, more than you are aware of." After much ingenious urging, Goody Knapp said that an Indian had once offered to Mrs. Staples two Indian Gods, "little things, brighter than the light of day," and with the assurance that they would make the owner "rich, all one God." No evidence more incriminating than that could the female inquisitors obtain, altho' they labored zealously. Goody Knapp did not lack for company in her imprisonment. Criminals, then as now, were a public show; yet she did not receive the sympathy that is lavished on a modern murderer. At one time when Goodwife Gould was impressing upon her the usual moral lesson, Goody Knapp burst forth into weeping, saying, "Never, never was poor creature tempted as I am tempted; pray, pray for me." When Goody Knapp was hung, all Fairfield came to see. As soon as the victim had been cut down, Goodwife Staples went to the body and handled it very much." "Taking ye Lords name in her mouth," she said to Mrs. Lockwood, "These are no witches teates. I have such myself, and so have you, if you search your-self." Madam Lockwood was not disposed to admit the soft impeachment, and answered, " No matter what they are ! She had them, and she confessed she was a witch ; that is sufficient." Goody Staples loudly proclaimed her skepticism, whereupon the whole chorus of goodwives and madams " cryed her down " until she yielded. Her faith finally overcame her rebellious reason. " As they were going to the grave, Goodwife Staples said that it was long before she could believe that this poor woman was a witch, or that there were any witches ; till the word of God convinced her, which saith, ' Thou shalt not suffer a witch to live.' " Such is the mere outline of the amply-recorded story of Goody Knapp's last days. Such were the incidents which Roger Ludlow endeavored to wrest to Goody Staples' destruction. These events were rehearsed to the court, and, in addition, Mr. and Mrs. Davenport testified. They had been told by Ludlow that " Knapp's wife, the witch, at her execution, came down the ladder, and desired to speak with him alone, saying to him that Goodwife Staples was the witch of whom Goody Bassett, of Stratford, had spoken." Mr. Davenport answered that he believed the report to be " utterly untrue, and spoken out of malice." Both Mr. Daven-port and his wife evinced a detestation of Ludlow. Mrs. Davenport accuses him of proneness to gossip. Mr. Daven-port " utterly disliked his speech." Moreover, a dissension had arisen between Ludlow and Davenport, the former taxing the latter with breach of faith in reporting the story. Daven-port affirmed in court that he was careful to make no unlawful promises, and that when he made a lawful promise, he was, thro' Christ's help, careful to keep it. After this Goodwife Staples was reasonably sure of a vindication. Perhaps New Haven's Court loved her for the enemies she had made. Yet Roger Ludlow, when offended, was without doubt, an unpleas-ant customer, and the Court swathed its adverse sentence in thickly-folded phrases. Finally, " seeing no cause to lay any blemish of a witch upon Goodwife Staples," they judge that Mr. Ludlow hath done her wrong; and order him to pay to Thomas Staples, " by way of fine for reparation of his wife's name, tenn pounds," and five pounds costs. The next autumn

Ludlow was mulcted in the sum of ten pounds more for imputing falsehood to Mrs. Staples.

The history of this lawsuit serves a good purpose in displaying the narrowness and vindictiveness of Roger Ludlow. There is nothing to explain why Mrs. Staples had incurred the enmity of her Fairfield gossips, but it is plain that Roger Ludlow persecuted her and tried to compass her ruin, because she would not acknowledge the guilt of Goody Knapp. All these events happened while Roger Ludlow was throwing off the authority of Connecticut, levying an army of his own, and assuming airs of supreme authority. Since he ruled his enemies with such a heavy hand, it is not surprising that he was careful to carry with him into Virginia the Fairfield Town Records. It is not surprising that a man of his abilities and ambitions, whom the latest edition of Bancroft describes as " unsurpassed in the knowledge of the law and of the rights of mankind," should have been forced to quit in disgrace both Massachusetts and Connecticut.*

The closely-crowding circumstances of the Godman, Knapp, and Staples affairs filled New Haven society with suspicion. The goodwives and dames, over their sewing, doubtless discussed the details carefully, and like their modern representatives, unravelled reputations while they closed up seams. The result of their labors was seen on the 3d of July, 1655. "Nicholas Bayly and his wife were told by the Court that sundry reasons (which were read) do render them both, but especially the woman, very suspicious in point of witchcraft; but, for matters of that nature, the Court intends not to proceed at this time."†

The couple appeared several times before the magistrate and were finally encouraged to remove from the colony, apparently not so much on account of witchcraft, as for Goody Bayly's "lying malice and filthy speeches." Even the dignified Court unbent so far as to tell her that she had acted "as one possessed with ye very Devill." Meanwhile the unlucky Mrs. Godman had again become the subject of village scandal and legal complaint. Mr. Goodyear, with whom she lived, had fully joined the hue and cry against her, and, after a "great dis-

* Rec., ii. 77–8, 122.   † Town Rec., ii. 209.

turbance in his family in the night," had warned her to provide another dwelling-place for herself. He did not accord
much respect to Mrs. Godman's excuse. She was hunting for
two grapes which she had dropped and with which she feared
that the mice might play. Even the doors of the neighborhood
prayer-meeting had been closed against her. Goody Thorpe,
whose chickens had formerly been "consumed in ye gisard,"
had been perplexed by Satanic phenomena among her cows.
Those animals had sweated strangely and cast their calves. Having in one case sought God earnestly to resist the evil spirit, she
was gratified by the recovery of the beast. "Aboute a week
after she went by Mr. Goodyear's, and there was Elizabeth
Godman pulling cherries in the streete. She said, 'How doth
Goody Thorp? I am beholden to Goody Thorp; she would
have had me to the gallows for a few chickens.' Also she
gnashed and grinned with her teeth in a strang manner."

To these facial gymnastics, Elizabeth confessed. Allen
Ball's wife deposed that she had refused Mrs. Godman some
buttermilk, and had said, "Begone, I care not for your company." Mrs. Godman rejoined, "What, it will do your Piggs
no good." Soon after, all but one died. Goodman Allen Ball
himself, who was Mr. Davenport's farmer, had tied a calf to a
great post. No sooner did Mrs. Godman turn her evil eyes
upon the animal, than "it rann away with the great post, as if
it had bine a feather, and rann among Indian corne and pulled
up two hills." Upon another similar occasion the unhappy
brute scampered off with a huge rail, "and afterwards dyed."*
Other neighbors added to the heap of grievances. In August
the "Court ordered that she be committed to prison, there to
abide the Court's pleasure, but, because the matter is of weight,
and the crime whereof she is suspected, Capitall, therefore she
is to answer it at the court of Magistrates in October next."
On account of her failing health, she was released from jail in
September, with a warning against offending her neighbors,
and was forbidden to come to the " Contribution," as she had
done. Satan was now let loose again, and many of the too-
credulous villagers trembled. As might be expected, his in-
fernal wrath lighted first upon Parson Hooke. Mrs. Godman

* Town Rec., ii. 213.

went there, strange to say, for a drink of beer, met with some denial, " and went away in a muttering, discontented manner." " Though the beare was good and fresh that night, yet the next morning, it was hott, soure, and ill-tasted ; yea, so hott as the barrell was warme without side, and, when they opened the bung, it steemed forth. They brewed againe, and it was so also, and so continewed foure or five times one after another." It would seem as though the bedeviled beer might have made the cup of her transgressions run over, but the October Court declared that the evidence was not yet sufficient to take away her life, " though the suspitions be cleere and many, and she herself found to be full of lying." She was released with the same injunctions as formerly, " to forbeare from goeing from house to house to give offence," and she pledged fifty pounds of her estate as security for her good behavior. So far as we know, she spent the rest of her days in quiet, though it could hardly have been in happiness. Death released her five years afterwards, October 9th, 1660.

If New Haven had retained trial by jury, its history might have been stained with witches' blood, but Magistrate Eaton was cool-headed and too good a lawyer to over-estimate " the verdict of the vicinage." One remarkable circumstance must have dictated the necessity of unusual caution and forbearance. The Common Law was not paramount in New Haven. The Mosaic Code, which was embodied in her Book of Laws, prescribed death by stoning, as the penalty for witchcraft. Let us hope that other considerations than that of the undoubted dearth of stones in the Quinnipiac's alluvial valley, would have deterred New Haven's Magistracy from the application of the utmost rigors of the law.

There is but one other mention of witchcraft upon the colonial records of New Haven. That one instance was treated in a cavalier manner that demonstrates the damaging effect of a bad reputation, rather than any subsidence of human credulity. Mr. Thomas Moulenor, in 1657, lost several pigs by some curious ailment which excited a suspicion in his mind that they had been bewitched. When the last one sickened, " he cut off its tayle and ear," and threw them upon the fire. He testified in court that this was " a meanes used in

England by some honest people to finde out witches." The
" tayle and ear" not divulging so much as he expected, he put
the " rest of the pigg on the fire until it was dead." After consulting the omens in this wholesale fashion, he sagely observed
that "some of his neighbors were not very good," and made
up his mind that one of them, Wm. Meaker by name, had
practiced the black art upon the beasts.   Wm. Meaker imitated
Mrs. Godman and Thos. Staples by bringing, in June, an action
against Mr. Moulenor for defamation.   Now this same Mr.
Moulenor had been an eye-sore to the saints of New Haven
since the beginning.   He was a man of some rank and property
as his title shows, but his frequent quarrels display a captious
temper, and it is certain that he was not friendly to the peculiar tenets of the New Haven polity.   He was probably the
Thomas Moulenor, who, so early as February, 1640, was accused
of being drunk.   He can be traced through the records by a line
of evil deeds, affronting the Court, quarreling at Totoket, and
refusing to come to the training, or to the watch.   He filled up
the measure of his iniquities by sending his servants to gather
oysters on Sunday.   The only service of a nature befitting his
social position, which he is known to have performed, occurred
in 1647, when he made the "King's Arms," which the town
erected "in the highway by the sea-side," as a witness against
the Dutch.   In 1645, he had been put under bonds of one hundred pounds. to insure his good behavior, and that was kept
hanging over his head as an incentive to subordination.*   His
charge of witchery was scornfully ignored.   He was reminded
of the perilous state in which he lived, and there was a plain
suggestion made that his room would be better than his company in the colony.   Moulenor saw that no attention would be
paid to his allegation of witchcraft, and, shortly after, withdrew the charge.   With his lawsuits. which were continually
recurring, we have no more to do.

   After the treaty of Hartford in 1650, the Connecticut Colony gradually acquired peaceful control over the whole eastern
portion of Long Island, excepting New Haven's possessions at
Southold.   The town of Easthampton, Long Island, introduced
itself into the Connecticut sisterhood with a witch-trial.   Dur.
ing the winter of 1657–58, a quarrel between two women in

* Rec., i. 153, 369.

the household of the famous Lion Gardiner resulted in charges of witchcraft.* One of the women lost a child and accused her fellow servant, Goodwife Garlick, of having killed it by magic spells. Capt. Gardiner testified that the plaintiff had been hired to nurse an Indian baby and, in so doing, had wilfully neglected her own child. Despite Gardiner's influence however, the Magistrates of the town of Easthampton were evidently puzzled by the testimony. At a town meeting, March 19th, 165⅞, it was voted that Thomas Baker and John Hand "should go into Keniticut for to bring us under their Government according to the terms as Southampton is; and also to carry Goodwife Garlick that she may be delivered up unto the authorities there, for the triall of the cause of witchcraft which she is suspected." Her trial was probably the staple of gossip at Hartford in May, 1658, but resulted in her acquittal. The Records say:—"There did not appear sufficient evidence to prove her guilty." With a curious sense of justice it was decided that the costs should be divided between Easthampton, Hartford, and Joseph Garlick, the husband of the accused woman. "Joseph Garlick shall pay her diet and ward at home and her tranceportation both ways. Easthampton shall pay costs of their court, and the transportation of their messengers and witnesses. Connecticut will pay costs of trial at Hartford." The Court understood the principle of the division of labor and its advantages. A letter was written by Governor Winthrop to the authorities at Easthampton wherein he commended their christian care and prudence in making such strict inquiry into cases of possible witchcraft. He gave some excellent advice: "It is expected and desired by this Court that you should carry neighbourly and peaceably to Joseph Garlick and his wife, and that they should doe ye like to you." Such counsel, if followed, would have prevented all the witch-trials that ever took place.

Governor Winthrop was present at a General Court in June, 1659, when Mr. Wyllys was requested to "goe downe to Sea-Brook to assist ye Major in examininge the suspitions about witchery, and to act therein as may be requisite." "Ye Major"

---

* Drake's *Annals of Witchcraft*, p. 110. Prime's *Hist. of Long Island*, p. 89. *Conn. Col. Rec.*, i. 572-3. Wood's *Hist. of Long Island*, p. 24.

VOL. VIII.   23

was the celebrated John Mason. There is no known trace of
the result of Mr. Wyllys' trip down the river, but it is more
than likely that his journey was caused by the wiles of the
Devil with Nicholas and Margaret Jennings. However this
unlucky couple were not indicted until September 5, 1661,
when Nicholas and Margaret Jennings, of Seabrook, were
accused of having caused the death of several."*

On the 9th of October following, the prisoners were given
the benefit of a doubt and were set free by a disagreement of
the jury; "the major part thinking them guilty, and the rest
strongly suspect it that they are guilty." By the 11th of
March, 1663, the General Court of the Colony at Hartford
had grown skeptical about this case. They disallowed the
charges of the "Sea-Brook" constables for witnesses in the
trial of the Jenningses, and furthermore recorded this ungra-
cious comment. "They do not see cause to allow pay to witnesses for time and travaile, nor to any other upon such
accounts for ye future." The Jennings couple probably deserve but little sympathy. They were a rascally pair. There
can be no doubt that they are the Nicholas "Gennings and
Margarett Poore, alias Bedforde" who in 1643 figured in
New Haven as runaway servants, were whipped for lewdness,
theft, and "divers other miscarryages" and were married by
order of the Court.

The machinations of the great adversary at Saybrook were
only a feint to distract attention from his dark devices elsewhere. There had been no fatal termination to a witch-trial
since Goody Knapp's death in 1653. But in 1662, the wretched
mania broke out afresh at Hartford. It ran its course to a fatal
end, and the cause of all was a hystericky maiden, named Ann
Cole. The circumstances of the affair prefigured the Salem
excitement thirty years later. Of Ann Cole's principal victims, there are previous traces, showing some of them at least
to have been persons of the baser sort.

In March, 1650, there is recorded the conviction of Nathaniel
Greensmith for stealing. At a Particular Court in the spring
of 1662,† the same individual sued a neighbor, William Eares

---

* Walker's *History of the First Church in Hartford*, p. 176. *Conn.
Col. Rec.*, i. 338.

† For May 13th.

(Ayres), for damages on account of slander. What the burden of the slanderous reports was, may be inferred from the indictment of Nath'l Greensmith and Rebecca, his wife, on the 30th of the next December, for witchcraft. The immediate impulse to this action was communicated by Ann Cole's ravings. A letter written by the Rev. John Whiting, some time pastor of the church in Hartford, to Dr. Increase Mather, describes the damsel's afflictions.* Twenty years, however, intervened between the description, and the events themselves; for the letter bears the date "December 4, 1682."

It seems that the father of Ann was John Cole, "A carpenter and a godly man." Moreover, he was the next door neighbor to the Greensmiths. Ann Cole, being grown to womanhood, was "taken with strange fitts, wherein she (or rather the Devill, as 'tis judged), made use of her lips, and held a discourse." Her talk appeared to show that a company of devils were debating with each other through her mediation, how they might accomplish their various schemes of mischief upon one and another, but especially upon Ann herself. They planned "to afflict her body, spoile her name, hinder her marriage, etc., wherein the generall answer made among them was 'She runs to her Rock.'" But when her maunderings took the shape of a "Dutch-toned discourse," being expressed sometimes in English, and sometimes in Dutch, and sometimes in a language known only to the devils themselves, her affrighted parents and neighbors ran for the ministers. Clerical power alone could hope to exorcise the satanic influence of the Dutch vocables and gutturals. Parson Haynes hastened in with his pen and paper wherewith he wrote down, no doubt with fear and trembling, her impossible words. Mr. Stone marveled greatly that she should pronounce English words with such a correct Dutch accent, altho' she knew nothing (?) of the latter tongue. But the ministers were able to understand that the devils were reciting various deeds of darkness, and the names of several human participants were divulged. Several persons, including the Greensmiths, were at once arrested. Still Ann Cole's afflictions were no whit lessened. Some of her utterances

---

* *Mass. Hist. Soc. Coll.*, vol. viii., 4th Series. This letter was the source of Cotton Mather's relation in the *Magnalia.*

were very awefull and amazing to the hearers," and she suffered "extremely violent bodily motions." These were the
tricks of modern Spiritist mediums. "Very often, great disturbance was given in the public worship of God by her and
two other women, who had also strange fitts. Once in speciall,
on a day of prayer kept on that account, the motion and noise
of the afflicted was so terrible that a godly person fainted
under the appearance of it." Yet Mr. Whiting did not hesitate to give Mistress Ann a good character, as "a person
esteemed pious, behaving herself, with a pleasant mixture of
humility and faith under her heavy sufferings, professing that
she knew nothing of those things that were spoken by her, but
that her tongue was improved to express what was never in
her mind." The Dutch family, from whose conversation she
imitated her jargon, bore the name of Varleth. A letter is
extant, dated at "Amsterdam, in New Netherlant, the 13th of
X^{br}, 1662, and signed 'P. Stuyvesant.'"* It is addressed to
the "Honorable debuty Governour, and Court of Magistracy
att Hardfort."

Gov. John Winthrop was then tarrying in Europe, after the
successful termination of his suit for a charter, and Dept. Gov.
John Mason was at the helm in Connecticut. With the latter,
therefore, Gov. Stuyvesant pleads in behalf of his "distressed
sister-in-law, Judith Varleth, imprisoned, as we are informed,
uppon pretend accusation of wicherye." The doughty Govern-
or's name was probably powerful enough to secure Judith Varleth's escape, for her name does not appear in the records, but
the English unfortunates were related to no governors. Rebecca
Greensmith, according to Mr. Whiting's testimony, "a lewd,
ignorant, and considerably aged woman," confessed that she
and other persons named, were guilty. She admitted that she
had had "familiarity with the devill," who came to her as a
"deere, or faune, skipping about her." One devil had introduced himself in the form of a crow. She said that she had
promised to go with the devil when he called, but denied making
any covenant with him. "The devill told her that, at the
merry-meeting on the next Christmas, the covenant should be

* Walker's *History of the First Church in Hartford*, p. 176, quoted
from Mr. C. J. Hoadly.

drawn and subscribed." This confession doomed the two Greensmiths. The recovered volume of the Hartford Particular Court records contains the indictments against them, and the adverse verdict of the jury in both cases. But the prevalent excitement involved other victims. One week later, at a " Perticular Court, Jan. 6th, 1662–3," Elizabeth Seager, wife of Richard Seager, and Mary Barnes, of Farmington, were called upon to answer similar accusations. Both submitted themselves to a jury of their peers ; but while the former was acquitted, Mary Barnes was found guilty and was sent to Hartford jail to await, with the two Greensmiths, the impending doom. The only official notice of that fate is the following one :

> " Quarter Court, Held at Hartford, }
>   March 5th, '62–3.   }

" Daniel Garrett is allowed for keeping Goodwife Barnes three weeks, twenty-one shillings besides her fees, which Goodman Barnes is to see discharged. And he is allowed six shillings a week for keeping Nathaniel Greensmith and his wife, besides their fees, which is to be paid out of Greensmith's estate."

Far away in the little village of Milford, Conn., the regicide General Goffe was, at this time, hiding from the royal vengeance. In the diary, with which he beguiled some of the heavy hours, Gov. Hutchinson afterwards read this entry : " Jan. 20, 1662. Three witches were condemned at Hartford. Feb. 24. After one of the witches was hanged, the maid got well." Much relief the execution gave to Ann Cole. As Mr. Whiting testified, " Ann Cole then had some abatement of her sorrows, joined the church, married a good man (Andrew Benton, of Milford), bore children, and lived a godly life."

The same writer says that most of the persons mentioned in her discourse made their escape into another part of the country. But their deliverance was wrought out of much danger, as can be seen by a paragraph in Increase Mather's " Essay for the Recording of Illustrious Providences." " There were some that had a mind to try whether the stories of witches not being able to sink under water were true, and accordingly, a man and woman, mentioned in Ann Cole's Dutch-toned dis-

course, had their hands and feet tied, and so were cast into the
water, and they both apparently swam after the manner of a
buoy, part under, part above the water. A bystander imagin-
ing that any person bound in that posture would be so borne
up, offered himself for trial; but, being in the like manner
gently laid on the water, he immediately sunk right down.
This was no legal evidence against the suspected persons, nor
were they proceeded against on any such account; however,
doubting that an halter would choak them, though the water
would not, they very fairly took their flight, not having been
seen in that part of the world again." Here was a fine picture
of experimental philosophy. The Hartford populace, the
hoodlums of 1662, being desirous of putting a common theory
to the test, treat the unlucky objects of village gossip to a free
bath; and a benevolent Thomas Didymus, looking on with
nervous remonstrance from the bankside, imperils his life in
the unsuccessful effort to vindicate his doubts concerning the
propriety of the operation. The names of the persons who
were thus roughly entreated are not preserved, but it is likely
that Wm. Ayres, whose former lawsuit has been mentioned,
and his wife, were the sufferers. The records reveal that this
couple fled from the colony at this time, and in such haste as
to leave behind them not only their estate and personal effects,
but even their son, who was forthwith apprenticed by the
General Court. Goodwife Seager had escaped death, but she
could not shake off the evil reputation that clung to her. In
1663, she again stood before Deputy Governor, and Major
John Mason, to answer the charges of witchcraft, adultery, and
blasphemy. She was convicted of adultery only, but, two
years after, the indictment for witchcraft was renewed. This
time she was found guilty, but the sentence was respited by
the Governor, Winthrop, who was now at home again. She
probably languished in confinement for a year; not until the
following spring (May 18th, 1666), did the Court "discharge
and set her free from farther suffering or imprisonment," on the
ground of incompatibility between the verdict and the indictment. There was evidently a new spirit among those who
ruled, but the force of popular superstition showed, otherwise,
few signs of abatement. In February, 1665, John Brown, of

New Haven paid dearly for a little joke. He was arrested, and was "very seriously entreated" by the Court because he had frightened some of his weak-minded neighbors with astrological nonsense. He drew on paper a circle with some marks in it; talked about the lords of the fourth and second houses, looked sagely at the stars, chattered gibberish, and asked the awestruck spectators if they would like to see the Divill. He was taught that such jesting is not convenient.* John Brown had not gained a good name with the New Haven Magistrates. Two years before, he and his wife had been reprimanded by the Court for allowing "Dauncing, Cardplaying and unseemly Night-meetings at their house." There was probably some personal spite in the present charges against him. New Haven was, at that time, alive with the amenites of social intercourse. At the same Court Goody Tompson appeared, very much irritated because Hannah Finch had said of her, "If one should rake Hell and skin the Devill, one would not find such a liar." Verily, here was a Western boldness of metaphor! These women did not live in Leadville in 1879, but they were inhabitants of Puritan New Haven, two hundred years earlier. The pristine history of the village of Wethersfield was studded with misfortunes. Its foundation was laid in a quarrel with Hartford. Indian warfare brought sorrow to its homes. Dissensions in its Church twice caused its disruption, the semi-depopulation of the town, and the settlements of Stamford and of Hadley. To crown all, the town was especially cursed by the witchcraft delusion. A special order was issued, in 1670, by the Connecticut General Court, for the trial of Katherine Harrison of Wethersfield on the charge of witchcraft. In May she was convicted by a jury, but the court refused to inflict the sentence of death, and dismissed the supposititious criminal with a recommendation to remove from Wethersfield, "Which is that will tend most to her own safety, and the contentment of the people, who are her neighbors."† However, her judges did not forget thrift, and she was ordered to pay costs. She took refuge at once in Westchester, New York;

---

* Town Rec., iii. 60.

† *Conn. Col. Rec.*, ii. 132. Judd's "Hadley," p. 233. Winthrop, ii. 374. O'Callaghan, *Doc. Hist. of N. Y.*, iv. 136.

but ill-report traveled almost as fast as she did, and, in July, the inhabitants of that town complained to the Court that Captain Wm. Panton was sheltering suspicious persons, one Katherine Harryson, who was recently come from Wethersfield, Connecticut. The Court decreed that she must return to Wethersfield. But that would have been a defiance of death, and she refused to go. In August, the people of Westchester again complained of her baleful presence, and she was summoned to trial in October. The upshot of the judicial investigation was that she was "found to be undeserving of complaint, and had liberty to live where she would." During the temporary occupation of New York by the Dutch in 1673, an accusation was brought against her before Governor Colve but was promptly and contemptuously dismissed. For several years thereafter the godly folk of Hartford and its vicinity rested from the manifestations of satanic subtlety and love for sinful souls. But, in 1683, in the midst of the oft-recurring dread of the coming sway of a Governor General, the wiseacres of the town wagged their heads doubtfully over new supernatural prodigies. The house of Nicholas Desborough was mysteriously stoned from every quarter by an invisible hand. Clods of earth and pieces of Indian corn were thrown through doors, windows and chimneys. A fire was kindled that did some little damage. Plainly, the Prince of the Powers of the air was again active in their midst. But when a chest of cloths that Desborough had detained from a neighbor was returned to its proper owner, the trouble ceased. And it is to be presumed that the wonder ceased also.

It was perhaps inevitable that the contagion of the Salem terror of 1692 should affect the colony of Connecticut, and should either meet or excite there, a similar panic. But the shadow of the grisly fear passed by Hartford and settled upon the town of Fairfield, the town where the infatuation had been most fatal forty years earlier. There the memory of Roger Ludlow was not even yet deprived of venom, and one of the imprisoned wretches was Mrs. Staples, probably the same who in her youth had incurred Ludlow's enmity, and had been shielded therefrom by New Haven justice. A gentleman, whom the records style "Col. Robt. Treat, Esqr., Govr.," himself a resident of the neighboring town of Milford, presided at a "Speciall Generall Court held at Hartford, June 22, 1692."* As in the case of Catherine Harrison, a commission for a special court was issued :

"Whereas, there are at present in the county of Fayrefeild severall persons in durance upon capital crimes which are not soe capeable to be brought to a tryall at the usual Court of Assistants, by reason of the multiplicity of witnesses that may be concerned in the case, etc., this Court doe grant to the Governor, Deputy Governor, and Assistants to the number of seven at the least, a commission of oyer and terminer to keep a speciall court in Fayrefeild, the second Wednesday in December (probably a mistake for September) next, to hear and determine all such capitall cases and complaints, as shall be brought before the sayd Court."

A note in the Connecticut Records says that Mr. William L. Stone, while living in Hartford as the editor of "The Connecticut Mirror," discovered among the documents belonging to the Wyllys family, a manuscript roll, containing the proceedings of this Special Court. It assembled either on the fourteenth or the nineteenth of September. The individuals comprising the court were Gov. Treat, Dept Gov. William Jones, of New Haven, son-in-law of Theophilus Eaton, John Allyn, Secretary of the Colony ; Mr. Andrew Leete, the successor of Gov. William Leete in influence at Guilford ; Capt. John Burr, Mr. Wm. Pitkin, Capt. Moses Mansfield, also of New Haven. Both a petit jury and a grand jury were in attendance, the list of the latter including such names as Samuel Ward and Samuel Sherman. The occasion was evidently felt to be a serious one when such a concourse of dignitaries and chief men was assembled to sit in judgment. "At this court, Mercy Disborough, of Compo, in Fairfield, Goody Miller, Goodwife, alias Elizabeth Clawson, and Mrs. Staples were indicted for familiarity with Satan." The session of the court doubtless made holidays for Fairfield, for nearly the whole town must have taken some personal interest in the trials. The judges listened to the testimony of about two hundred witnesses.†

* *Conn. Col. Rec.*, pp. 76, 77, 79.

† Some of these were published by Mr. Stone in the *New York Commercial Advertiser*, July 14th and 15th, 1820. They were copied into the *New York Spectator*, July 18th, and into the *Hartford Times* and *Weekly Advertiser*, August 8th, 1820.

In the course of the preliminary investigations by the village authorities, the efficacy of the water-ordeal had been tried. Four spectators testified that "Mercy Disborough, being bound hand and foot, and put into the water, swam like a cork, though one labored to press her down." The innocent water also refused to admit Elizabeth Clawson beneath its waves. Yet in spite, or perhaps in consequence, of the two hundred depositions, and in spite of the irrefutable proof of Mercy's, and of Goody Clawson's light specific gravity, the jury were unable to render a complete verdict. That they did practically reject the complaint against Goody Miller, and against Roger Ludlow's ancient foe, Mrs. Staples, appears from the record of "A Generall Court held at Hartford, Oct. 13, 1692. The Govr. haveing given an accot. how far they have proceeded against Elizabeth Clawson and Mercy Disborough, by reason that the jury could not agree to make a verdict, this Court desire the Governor to appoynt time for the sayd Court to meet againe as soone as may be, and that the jury be called together, and that they make a verdict upon the case, and the Court to put a finall issue thereto." In accordance with this vote the Court assembled a fortnight afterwards at Fairfield (Oct. 28, 1692). Additional testimony was taken and there was the usual examination of the bodies of two of the accused by a jury of their sister-gossips.* A formal acquittal was declared for Elizabeth Clawson, Goody Miller, and Mrs. Staples, but Mercy Disborough was found guilty according to the indictment. The jury were sent out to consider their verdict a second time, but reported again the same conclusion. The judges then ratified the finding of the jury and Gov. Robert Treat pronounced the sentence of death. "A memorial to the General Assembly in her behalf was drawn up with some ingenuity and ability, praying for a pardon, and setting forth weighty reasons why it ought to be granted." Unless there were two Mercy Disboroughs in Fairfield, it is likely that the prayer received assent and that the verdict was set aside. "The Probate Records of the town show that Mercy Disborough, widow of Thomas, was appointed with her son, in 1707, to administer upon her husband's estate."

* "A single deposition relating to this can be found in the Record-book of Crimes and Misdemeanors, *Conn. Archives*, vol. i., doc. 187."

Mr. William L. Stone made use of these incidents as the ground work of one of the more pretentious stories in his "Tales and Sketches," published in two volumes in New York in 1834. He depicted a ludicrously absurd plot. The scene was transferred to Guilford, and Mercy herself was transformed into a beautiful young girl, a veritable Priscilla, cruelly pursued with an accusation of witchcraft by a rich and lecherous old deacon, who had been rejected and foiled by the fair one. After the lovely unfortunate had been tied to the stake (*sic*)— and the attendants were kindling the fagots, a sudden attack upon the place was made by a party of Mohegans, led by Owaneco, son of Uncas, and by a young Englishman, Mercy's betrothed lover. The vindictive deacon fell prostrate with Owaneco's tomahawk in his brain, and the young lover cut his affianced bride from the stake and bore her safely away to the remote fastnesses of Litchfield County, where they lived happily ever after. The lamentable list of the unhappy martyrs to human credulity and superstition draws near its close. No lives were sacrificed after 1663. There is only the painful proof of continued suffering and of misguided excitement.

Probably the last indictment in the Connecticut Courts for the impossible crime occurred in Wallingford, in 1697.* A woman and her daughter, a girl of twelve or thirteen years of age, dwellers in that town, were accused of witchcraft by some children who pretended to possess powers of second-sight. As at Salem and Fairfield, the fears of the villagers soon amounted to a panic. Capt. Dan. Clark, as "Attorney in behalf of our Soveraigne Lord the King," arraigned "Winnifrett Denham, Senr." (Fowler writes the name "Benom," Benham), and "Winnifrett Denham, Jun., both of Wallingford, for having familiarity with Sathan, the enemy of God and mankind, and by his aid, doing many preternaturall arts, by misteriously hurting the bodies and Goods of sundry persons, viz: of Jno. Moss, Junr., Joseph Roys and Ebenezer Clark, with divers others, to the great Damage and Disturbance of the public Peace," etc. Mrs. Denham's body was searched for the convicting marks, she was cast into the water, and the Wallingford minister pronounced her excommunicate. Fowler says that the town

* The authorities are Fowler's *Salem Witchcraft*, p. 336 (Boston, 1765), and Davis's *History of Wallingford and Meriden,*" p. 412.

authorities bound the accused persons over to the Superior
Court, and that they were tried and acquitted at Hartford in
August, 1697, but that, when the complaints against them were
renewed, they "fled into the New York Government." The
historian of Wallingford, however, relates the more common
version that the grand jury recorded upon the indictment the
sensible verdict "Ignoramus," but says that there was much
popular commotion and controversy. It is evident that after
the fatal trials of 1662, a disbelief in the wisdom of executing
capital sentences for witchcraft slowly pervaded the minds of
the educated and thoughtful men in the colony, and gradually
filtered down through the inferior strata of society. Hence
would arise the large number of depositions at the great Fairfield trials in 1692, and the increasing discussion of which
there are abundant signs, at each fresh accusation. It has
been seen that official moderation upon the bench and in the
executive seat was able to stave off the three death-sentences
that were incurred during the last third of the seventeenth
century. It may be observed also that this progressive senti-
ment was visible in Connecticut earlier than in Massachusetts,
and was not deprived of effective strength, even in that year of
terrors, 1692. The water ordeal at Wallingford was the last
instance of that torture in Connecticut, perhaps in New England also; but Grace Sherwood was subjected to it in Virginia
in 1712, fifteen years later. The laws against witchcraft stood
in 1715, upon all the colonial statute-books, but so rapid had
been the advance of opinion in New England, even by that
time, those laws were there practically null. After 1697, many
village-societies doubtless often whispered, or openly spoke,
though with bated breath, of the evident presence of Satan in
their midst, and many a friendless old woman crept along the
highway, knowing that the community regarded her broom-
stick as an uncanny chariot, and her ill-fed cat as a demon, but
no more was the majesty of law degraded by the arraignment of a witch before its tribunals. Modern superstitious
belief in spiritual agencies, in changing its name and shape, has
changed its habitat also. It seems inclined to desert the dwelling of the lowly, and to abide in the houses of the prosperous.
It has developed a literature of its own, and can boast of many
notable names, from Swedenborg to Elizabeth Stuart Phelps.

While it has not entirely disappeared from the domain of criminal law, it appears there no longer under the revolting guise of "Familiarity with ye Devil," but as plain, unadorned "Swindling." The popular belief in witchcraft of the ancient and vulgar sort, has been slowly and imperceptibly relegated to that long line of dormant opinions, once dominant, now doubtfully averred, or laughingly denied. Its gruesome horrors serve to daunt unruly boys, or to furnish entertainment for the winter's evening by the crackling fire, from which the fascinated children, reluctantly, with fear-chilled skin, and wide-open eyes, slink away to bed. At the most, the life of some desolate individual is invested thereby with a generally harmless glamour. And the title itself of "Witch" has gradually become a term of semi-endearment, more likely to tint fair faces with the rose-color of pleasure than, as of yore, to blench them with terror.

The following schedule of indictments, verdicts, and executions, shows at a glance not only the progress of the witchcraft delusion in Connecticut, but also how official incredulity in the latter half of the 17th century steadily resisted the clamors of popular fear, even when they were heard from the jury-box.

(1647.	Winthrop's "One of Windsor"	Executed.)*
1648.	Mary Jonson, of Hartford or Wethersfield	Executed.
1651.	Mr. and Mrs. Carrington, of Wethersfield	Executed.
1651.	Goody Bassett, of Stratford	Executed.
1653.	Goody Knapp, of Fairfield	Executed.
1658.	Goody Garlick, of Easthampton, L. I.	Acquitted.
1661.	Mr. and Mrs. Jennings, of Saybrook,	
	Freed by disagreement of jury.	
1662.	Mr. and Mrs. Greensmith, of Hartford	Executed.
1663.	Mary Barnes, of Farmington	Executed.
1663.	Mrs. Elizabeth Seager, of Hartford(?)	Acquitted.
1663.	Mrs. Elizabeth Seager, (2d trial)	Acquitted.
1665.	Mrs. Elizabeth Seager, (3d trial)	Convicted, but freed by the court.
1670.	Katherine Harrison, of Wethersfield,	
	Convicted, the court refused to sentence and dismissed the accused.	
1692.	Mrs. Staples, of Fairfield	Acquitted.
1692.	Goody Miller, of Fairfield	Acquitted.
1692.	Elizabeth Clawson, of Fairfield	Acquitted.
1692.	Mercy Disborough, of Fairfield,	
	Convicted, but probably pardoned by the General Court.	
1697.	Mrs. Denham and daughter, of Wallingford,	
	Acquitted, perhaps accused only before the Grand Jury.	

Summary: eight, possibly nine executions; three more verdicts of "Guilty," that were set aside; indictments, either twenty-one or twenty-two.

* Doubtful.

MARYLAND
HISTORICAL MAGAZINE

| VOL. XXXI. | DECEMBER, 1936. | No. 4. |

WITCHCRAFT IN MARYLAND.*

By Francis Neal Parke.

The first reference in the *Maryland Archives* to the killing of
a witch is found among the Proceedings of the Council of Maryland (1636-1667) where are recorded the depositions of Henry
Corbyn, a young merchant of London, and Francis Darby, a
gentleman, who were passengers on the ship " Charity of London," on her voyage to Saint Mary's city, under command of
John Bosworth, Captain. After making port, these two travelers
appeared before the Governor, William Stone, Thomas Hatton,
Secretary, and Job Chandler, a member of the Council and,
were by them examined under oath on June 23, 1654, with
respect to the hanging of Mary Lee, a witch, by the crew while
on the high seas. These early voyagers gave a graphic description of the tragedy. Their vivid narratives are proof of the
then prevailing belief, as neither the sailors, the captain, a
merchant of a great city, nor the gentlemen present, who represented a cross section of society, entertained a doubt that Mary
Lee was a witch. Their accounts are of things of common
knowledge. *Md. Archives*, v. 3, p. 306.

It is quite likely that the story of the hanging of the witch on

* The substance of a paper read before the Maryland Historical Society,
November 9, 1936. Limitation of space has made it necessary to abridge
the paper as presented.

271

the good ship " Charity " spread among the settlers and, though not preserved, her confession must have been given currency and, so may have loosed the tongue of Peter Godson against whom an action of slander for calling Richard Manship's wife a witch was brought in the Provincial Court, and determined on October 16, 1654. This case, reported in *Md. Archives*, v. 10, p. 399, " was composed and determined before Mr. Richard Preston " . . . " the said Peter Godson and his wife have acknowledged themselves sorry for their speeches and pay charges."

Over two hundred and fifty years after this litigation that was so happily composed by Justice Richard Preston, one Henry Magin came to a lawyer's office in Westminster, and wrathfully demanded that a suit be brought against Alice Carr for defamation of his character. The cause of action was that there had suddenly appeared, nailed high on a number of trees along the roadside leading to the water mill conducted by Magin, new chestnut shingles on which were rudely lettered the accusatory words: " Hen Magin is a Hex." The client was grievously affronted. He explained to the perplexed counsel that " hex " was the German word for witch; solemnly declared the charge was untrue; and asserted that he defied his defamer to prove the statement. The case was declined on various grounds, which left the party much incensed that he could not obtain a vindication at law.

The next execution of which the Maryland Archives bear witness was, also, at sea. John Washington of Westmoreland county, in the province of Virginia, the great grandfather of George Washington, was the complainant, and he charged that in 1658, one Edward Prescott, merchant, had committed a felony by hanging a witch, Elizabeth Richardson, on his ship " The Sarah Artch " as it was bound from England to the colonies. Governor Fendall caused the accused to be arrested, and to be bound for his appearance at court; and, then, Washington was advised of these facts by the Governor, and the following entries in the records of the Provincial Court and the correspondence furnish all that is known of this hanging.

" Whereas John Washington of Westmerland County in Virginia hath made Complaynt agst Edward Prescott mercht, Accusing the sd Prescott of ffelony unto the Gouernor of this Prouince, Alleaging how that hee the sd Prescott hanged a Witch in his ship, as hee was outwards bownd from England hither the last yeare. Vppon wch Complaynt of the sd Washington, the Gour caused the sd Edward Prescott to bee arrested; Taking Bond for his appearance att this Prouinciall Court of 40000l Tob, Gyuing moreouer notice to the sd Washington by letter of his proceedings therein.

Honble Sr

Yors of this 29th instant this day I receved. I am sorry tht my extraordinary occasions will not permitt mee to bee att the next Prouinciall Court, to bee held in Maryland the 4th of this next month, Because then god willing I intend to gett my yowng sonne baptized, All the Company & Gossips being allready inuited, Besides in this short time Wittnesses cannott be gott to come ouer. But if Mr Prescott be bownd to answere it the next Prouinciall Court after this, I shall doe what lyeth in my power to gett them ouer, Sr I shall desyre you for to acquayne mee wither Mr Prescott be bound ouer to the next Court, & when the Court is that I may haue some time for to prouide euidence & soe I rest

Yor ffreind & Serut

30th of Septembr 1659.   John Washington.

To wch Complaynt of John Washington the sd Edward Prescott (submitting himselfe to his tryall) denyeth not, but that there was One Elizabeth Richardson hanged in his ship, as hee was outward Bownd the last yeare from England, & coming for this prouince, neare unto the Westerne Islands, by his Master & Company, (Hee hauing appoynted one John Greene for tht Voyage Master, though himselfe was both mercht & owner of the ship) But further sayth, That he wthstood the proceedings of his sd Master and Company, & protested agst them in that busines. And that thereuppon both the Master & Company were ready to mutiny. And it appearing to the Court by the Printed Custome howse Discharge & Light-howse Bills or acquittances produced & shewen by the s^d Edw: Prescott taken or gyuen in John Greenes name; that the s^d Greene was master for th^t Voyage, & not Edward Prescott. Any noe One comming to prosequute, The s^d Prescott therefore prays that hee may bee acquitted.

Whereuppon (standing uppon his Justificaōn) Proclamaōn was made by the Sheriffe in these very words.

Edward Prescott Prisoner at the Bar uppon suspition of ffelony stand uppon his acquittall. If any person can give evidence against him, lett him come in, for the Prisoner otherwise will be acquitt.

And noe on(e app)earing, The Prisoner is acquitted by the Board." *Md. Archives*, v. 41, pp. 327-329; Brown, *Maryland: The History of a Palatinate*, pp. 83-86; Riley's *Ancient City*, p. 47.

Although the crime charged was a felony, and Washington was notified of the place and time of the meeting of the next court, and was warned that the prisoner must be confronted with the witnesses against him, yet, notwithstanding the passage of the Potomac was quickly made, Washington was unwilling to postpone the baptism of his young son and suggested the trial be deferred to the next term. The right to a speedy hearing could not be postponed for the religious ceremony and the matter was not put off, but Prescott, went to trial, and because it appeared that Prescott, although the owner of the ship and on board, was not her master but that John Greene had been given command and was its master for the voyage, Prescott, the owner and aboard, was acquitted, and, no one appearing against him, was discharged.

The next instance concerns the jeopardy of one Elizabeth Bennett, who was accused of being a witch, and the matter was before the grand jury of the Provincial Court at its October Term, 1665, in Saint Mary's, which had been charged by Philip

Calvert, Chancellor, " concerning witchcraft, Burglary, felony, murther & other Trespases where a Penalty or fine is imposed by the Law of the Province." On October 11 the entry shows that the grand jury " came into court and brought these bills: * * * Elizabeth Bennett for Witch &c. Ret. not prsentable "; and on October 16, 1665, the concluding entry is: " Cleared by Proclamaōn." *Md. Archives,* v. 49, pp. 476, 486, 508.

The first judicial conviction is, apparently, that of John Cowman, who was convicted under the Statute of James I for witchcraft, conjuration, sorcery or enchantment upon the body of Elizabeth Goodale, and sentenced to be hung. He was saved by the intercession of the deputies and delegates of the Lower House of the General Assembly, who petitioned Charles Calvert, the Lieutenant General and the Chief Judge of the Provincial Court for clemency. The Upper House on February 17th, 1674, granted the reprieve, as will be seen from the only records now extant:

" Comes into the house a Petition of the Lower house as followeth Viz^t

To the Honourable Charles Calvert Esqr Lieutenant General and Chief Iudge of the Provincial Court of the Right honourable the Lord Proprietary—

The humble Petition of the Deputies and Delegates of the Lower House of Assembly

Humbly Sheweth to your Excellency

That whereas Iohn Cowman being Arraigned Convicted and Condemned upon the statute of the first of King Iames of England &^c for Witchcraft Conjuration Sorcery or Enchantment used upon the Body of Elizabeth Goodale and now Lying under that Condemnation, and hath humbly Implored and Beseeched Us your Lordships Petitioners to Mediate and Interceede in his behalf with Your Excellency for a Reprieve and Stay of Execution—

Your Excellencies Petitioners do therefore accordingly in

all Humble Manner beseech your Excellency that the Rigour and Severity of the Law to which the said Condemned Malefactor hath Miserably Exposed himself may be Remitted and Relaxed by the Exercise of your Excellencys Mercy & Clemencie upon so wretched and Miserable an Object.

And your Petitioners as in Duty bound will pray &c

Signed by Order of the house Robert Ridgley Cl

Upper house february the 17th

The Lieutenant General hath Considered of the Petition here above and is willing upon the request of the Lower house that the Condemned Malefactor be reprieved and Execution Stayed, Provided that the Sheriff of St Maries County carry him to the Gallows, and that the rope being about his neck it be there made known to him how much he is Beholding to the Lower house of Assemblie for Mediating and Interceeding in his Behalf with the Lieu^t General and that he remain at the City of St Maries to be Employed in Such Service as the Governor and Council shall think fitt during the Pleasure of the Governor."
Md. Archives, v. 2, pp. 425-426.

Although the belief in witchcraft prevailed during the century which followed the foundation of Maryland, the published volumes of the *Archives* do not furnish any additional evidence of judicial prosecutions. However, William Kilty, chancellor of Maryland, in his report to the General Assembly of Maryland of the English Statutes which had been enforced in Maryland before the Revolution, noted that a woman had been hung as a witch and that two others had been tried and acquitted of the crime of witchcraft. Kilty's *English Statutes* (1811), p. 190; Scharf's *History of Maryland,* vol. I, pp. 297-299; Browne's *Maryland,* p. 83.

The belief in witchcraft and its practice has existed among all primitive peoples. The records that remain of Ancient Egypt and Babylonia establish its prevalence. In the Code of Hammurabi, which was promulgated about 2000 B. C. is found in the first two sections of the code: " If a man weave a spell and put a ban upon a man, and has not justified himself, he that wove the spell upon him shall be put to death " (Sec. 1). " If a man has put a spell upon a man and has not justified himself, he upon whom the spell is laid shall go to the holy river; he shall plunge into the holy river and if the holy river overcome him, he who wove the spell upon him shall take to himself his house." " If the holy river makes that man to be innocent, and has saved him, he who laid the spell upon him shall be put to death. He who plunged into the holy river shall take to himself the house of him who wove the spell upon him " (Sec. 2).

The production of effects beyond the natural powers of man by supernatural agencies other than the divine involves in witchcraft the idea of a diabolical pact or an appeal to the intervention of the spirits of evil. The spirits of evil were the devil, under various guises and names, and his demons. According to the Old Testament, the devil was the wisest of all angels, and his virtues were extolled by God, who thus addressed him under the symbolic name of the King of Tyre: " Thou wast perfect in all thy ways from the day thou wast created till unrighteousness was found in thee." Ezekiel, Chapter 28, Verse 12.

The Bible however, enjoined death for merely being a witch in these words: " Wizards thou shalt not suffer to live," " Thou shalt not suffer a witch to live," " A man or a woman in whom there is a pythonical or divining spirit, dying let them die; they shall stone them; their blood be upon them." Deut. XVIII, 11-12; Ex. XXII, 18; Lev. XX, 27. Gal V-20; Apoc. XXI, 8-XXII, 15; Acts VIII, 9; XVIII, 6.

Notwithstanding the penalties prescribed in the Bible, the early church punished witches or sorcerers by excommunication, imprisonment until conversion or expulsion from the diocese. It was not until the thirteenth century that Gregory IX embodied in the Canon Law the mandate that heretics, after condemnation, should be delivered to the secular arm, which burned them at the stake. The Pope's Constitution (1231) was directed against heretics but, although Alexander IV ruled (1258) that the inquisitors should limit their intervention to those cases in which there was some clear presumption of heretical belief, heresy was readily inferred from slight magical practices, and in 1275 at Toulouse, occurred the earliest instance of a witch burned to death after judicial sentence of an inquisitor. Hugues de Baniol, *Cauzons La Magie,* II, 21-7; *Catholic Ency.,* Vol. XV, 675-676. The woman had made a confession of having brought forth a monster after intercourse with an evil spirit and to have nourished it with the flesh of babies which she had procured in her nocturnal expeditions.

By the Constitution *Super illius specula* (1326) Pope John XXII ordained that the penalties of heresy should be imposed upon those "who ally themselves with death and make a pact with hell, who sacrifice to the demons, make or have images, rings, mirrors, phials or other analogous objects, intended to serve as bonds to hold the demons, who ask questions of the demons, obtain answers to them and have recourse to the demons to satisfy their depraved desires."

The prosecution of sorcerers or witches by the church and the secular courts grew and great numbers were punished by death or imprisonment for life or a long term of years. Henry Institoris and James Sprenger, inquisitors, were empowered by Pope Innocent VIII (1484) to deal with persons of every class and every form of crime, and in 1489 published the book Malleus Maleficarum (the hammer of witches), which was divided into three parts. The first two of which contain a dissertation upon the reality of witchcraft and its nature and the manner of dealing with it; and the third part formulates the rules of procedure, whether the trial be had in an ecclesiastical or a secular court. From this handbook the accused were plied with questions and, by a strange perversion, the desired admissions that had been wrung from their victims by rack or thumb-screw were described as voluntary. *Ency. Brittanica,* "Witchcraft." The publication of this book increased the number of prosecutions and became the code of the inquisitors. In 1390 the church in France was deprived of its right to prosecute sorcerers and the trials of the sixteenth and seventeenth centuries were mainly in the secular courts, without, however, any advantage enuring to those prosecuted.

On the continent trials and executions did not cease until the end of the eighteenth century. In Spain a woman was burnt in 1781 at Seville by the Inquisition and the secular courts condemned a girl to decapitation in 1782. In 1783 a girl was executed in the canton of Glarus, Switzerland. An execution took place in Posen in 1793. England and Scotland participated in these prevailing prosecutions, although the witches were not usually burned. An appalling number were unquestionably executed, and many of these occurred after the settlement of Maryland in 1634. The last trial in England for witchcraft was in 1712 when Jane Wenham was convicted but was not executed. In Scotland trials, accompanied by torture, were frequent in the seventeenth century, and the last trial and execution was in 1722. After the law ceased to punish, the mob occasionally did, as is exemplified by the instance Gilbert White gives in The Natural History of Selborne: "no longer than the year 1751 and within twenty miles of the capital, they seized on two superannuated wretches, crazed with age, and overwhelmed with infirmities, on a suspicion of witchcraft, and, by trying of experiments, drowned them in a horse-pond." *Spectator,* vol. 2, pp. 130, 179; vol. 4, pp. 70, 214.

The report of Chancellor Kilty to the General Assembly was in 1810. He classified the English Statutes which had existed at the time of the first emigration of the people of Maryland, and those which had been subsequently passed; and he further designated those which were proper to be introduced and incorporated into the body of the statute law of the State. In the course of this work, the chancellor reviewed the statute law with respect to witchcraft. Witchcraft was by the ancient laws of England of ecclesiastical cognizance, although it is also said that offenders of this kind might be punished at the common law by condemnation to the pillory. Hawkins Pleas of Crown, c. 2; c. 3, s. 2. After a conviction by an ecclesiastical court, and a refusal to abjure, or a relapse into the practice of witchcraft after abjuration, the convict would be turned over to a secular court for punishment with death by burning pursuant to the writ *de heretico comburendo*, which was grantable out of chancery upon a certificate of conviction. The writ was abolished by statute of 29 Charles II, c. 9, 1676, and, after that date the notation on the margin of the court-book of the terse expression of " convicta et combusta," ceased.

A general statute against witchcraft was passed during the reign of Elizabeth which made conjuration and invocation of evil spirits a felony, 5 Eliz. c. 16, and this statute was superseded by an act of parliament known as 1 James I, c. 12, which made it a felony, without benefit of clergy and sanctuary, to use any invocation or conjuration of any evil and wicked spirit, or to consult or covenant with, entertain, employ, feed or reward any evil and wicked spirit, or to take up a dead body or any of its parts to be employed in any manner of witchcraft, inchantment, charm or sorcery whereby any person shall be killed, destroyed, wasted, consumed, pined or lamed in body or its parts. The act of James I was in force until its repeal by 9 George II, c. 5, the effect of which was to prohibit all future prosecutions for conjurations, witchcraft, sorcery or enchantment, but to make it a misdemeanor for a person to pretend to use these arts in the telling of fortunes or the discovery of stolen goods. Blackstone's *Com. Book IV*, Ch. IV, sec. VI, pp. 60-62 (star). This was the state of the law of Great·Britain at the time of the Revolution.

The inquiry made by Kilty convinced him that the statute of James I had been in use in the province. He found and reported that it would appear by the commissions to the judges that they were to determine concerning *witchcraft*, burglary, felony, murder &c. and the charges to the grand juries were to the same effect, until a short period after the making of this statute of 9 George 2 (1736). The commission commanded the justices " to enquire by the oaths of good & lawful men of yor county aforesaid of all manner of felonys, Witchcrafts, Sorceryes, Magic Arts, Tresspasses etc. against the Lawes &

Ordinances of our said Province." Kilty's conclusion to place the statutes among those found applicable but not proper to be incorporated has had universal acceptance. Chancellor Kilty's course was not prompted by his conviction that the residents of the province had displayed any toleration in their attitude toward what Blackstone called "this dubious crime," vol. 2, Part IV, Ch. IV, p. 61. For in classifying the statute of 29 Charles 2, Ch. 9, which did away with the writ *de heretico comburendo*, he wrote: "This statute cannot in strictness be said to have extended to the province, as the writ mentioned in the title was never used therein; but it was one that the courts might have adopted together with 1 Eliz. Ch. 1 (Heresy), if they had been found necessary. See the note on 9 Geo. 2, Ch. 5. And when we consider the violent animosities which prevailed between the different religious sects in the province, it is presumed that the court that would hang a witch, would not scruple to burn a heretic." P. 97.

The record upon which Kilty based the statement that a witch had been hung was believed to be lost. A recent search resulted in the finding of a small, ignored volume among the records of the Court of Appeals. A close inspection of the volume revealed the fact that it was one of the supposedly "lost" records of the Provincial Court, covering the period, 1682-1702. The first 121 pages contain the criminal proceedings of the Provincial Court from March 18, 1683 to August 20, 1686, and the succeeding pages from 122 to 168 are given exclusively to ejectment cases in 1702.

After a century and a quarter of obscurity, a reading of the volumes gives in detail the prosecutions which were indicated by Kilty. The names of the principal actors are preserved in the records and the meetings of the provincial court, the production of the prisoners, the accusations and the judgments are so tersely and vividly stated that it seems best to use in the narrative the text of the original proceedings.

Rebecca Fowler was the first witch tried. The convening of court and her fate are recorded in these words:

" At a provinciall Court held at the City of St. Maries the nine and twentieth day of September in the tenth yeare of the Dominion of the Rt. Hono^{ble} Charles Lord Baron of Baltemore anno Dei 1685 and there continued untill the twelfth day of October following on which said 29th day of September were present.

The hona^{bles}
{
Thomas Tailler, Esqr
Henry Darnall, Esqr
William Digges, Esqr
William Stevens, Esqr
Nicholas Sewall, Esqr
} Justices

Then was the Grand Jury for the body of this province summoned impannelled and sworne whose names are as follows, viz:

Randolph Hinson	John Kirke
Richard Keene	Walter Lane
Hugh Hopewell, jun^r	Wm Blankenstein
John Atkey	Joseph Spernon
Thomas Ford	Richard Holland
Robert Cole	John Hinton
William Ferguson	William Harris
Samuel Wheeler	William Morris

Then was the charge given to the Grand Inquest and they withdrew to consider thereof.

The Sheriff of Somerset County in open Court turned over the body of Thomas Roe and Mary Jones to the Sheriffe of St. Maries County. * * *

The sheriffe of Calvert County turned over in open Court to the said Sheriffe of St. Maries County the bodyies of Richard Vanson, John Edwards, *Rebecca Fowler* and Joseph Tumblinton. This was on September 30, 1685.

The grand inquest presented and indicted Rebecca Fowler and the proceedings are thus recorded:

" Maryland, SS.

The Jurors for the Rt. hono^{ble} Lord prop^{ty} of this province upon their oathes doe present Rebecca Fowler, the wife of John Fowler, late of Callvert County, planter, otherwise called Rebecca Fowler, late of Calvert County, spinster, for that she the said Rebecca Fowler the last day of August in the yeare of our Lord 1685 and at divers other dayes & times as well before & after having not the feare of God before her eyes but being led by the instigation of the Divell certaine evil & dyabolicall artes called witchcrafts, inchantments charmes, & sorceryes then wickedly, divelishly and feloniously at Mount Calvert Hundred & severall other places in Calvert County aforesaid of her malice forethought feloniously did use practice & exercise in upon & against one Francis Sandsbury, late of Calvert County aforesaid, Labourer and severall others psons of the said county whereby the said Francis Sandsbury & several others as aforesaid last day of August in the yeare aforesaid & severall other dayes & times as well before as after at Mount Calvert hundred and several other places in the said County in his & their bodyes were very much the worse, consumed, pined & lamed against the peace & ct. (etcetera) and against the forme of the statute in this case made and provided.

Burford, Attorney Generall.

On the back side of the foregoing presentment was endorsed by the Grand Jury—Billa Vera—Upon which presentment the said Rebecca Fowler was Endicted. Upon her Endictment arraigned and upon her arraignment pleaded not guilty and for her tryall put her selfe upon God & the Country, & Attorny Generall also. Command was therefore given to the Sheriffe of St. Maries County that he cause to come here twelve. & ct.

Now here at this day to-witt the second day of October Annoq Dni 1685 came the said Thomas Burford, Attorney General for the said Lord prop^{ty} and the said Rebecca Fowler was brought to the Barr and the jorors empannelled being called likewise come to-witt Randolph Brandt & Charles Egerton, James Yore,

Michaell Miller, Mathew Lewis, Edward Turner, John Taunt, Andrew Insley, Justinian Tennison, James Neale, Andrew Abbington & Abraham Rhoades, who being elected, tryed and sworne to say the truth in the premises doe say and deliver in writing to the Court the verdict following vizt. Wee find that Rebecca Fowler is guilty of the matters of fact charged in the indictment against her and if the Court find the matters contayned in the Endictment make her Guilty of witchcraft, charmes and sorceries &ct. then they find her guilty. And if the Court find those matters contained in the indictment doe not make her guilty of witchcraft, charmes sorceries & ct then they find her not guilty whereupon judg^{mt} is respited untill the Court further advises themselves upon the premises. Afterwards, to-witt the Third day of October, 1685, aforesaid came againe the said Attorney Generall for the said Lord Prop^{ty} and the said Rebecca Fowler was againe brought to the barr and the Court having advised themselves of & upon the premises It is considered by the Court that the said Rebecca Fowler be hanged by the neck untill she be dead which was performed the ninth day of October afores'd." Judgment Records of Provincial Court, Liber T. G. (2) 1682-1702, pp. 23, 25, 34.

The next case was that of Hannah Edwards. She was tried:

" Att a Provinciall Court held at the Citty of St. Marys the twenty-seventh day of Aprill in the eleventh year of the Dominion of the Right honrble Charles Lord Baron of Baltemore & ct. Annoq Dni 1686; and then continued untill the Tenth day of May then following Att which said seventh day of May were present.

The Honble
$\left\{\begin{array}{l}\text{Vincent Lowe, Esq}^{r}\\\text{Henry Darnall, Esq}^{r}\\\text{William Digges, Esq}^{r}\\\text{William Burges, Esq}^{r}\\\text{Nicholas Sewall, Esq}^{r}\\\text{Clement Hill, Esq}^{r}\end{array}\right\}$
Justices

Then was the Grand Inquest for the body of this Province

Impannelled, sumoned & sworn whose names were as followeth, vizt:

Edward Inglish, foreman	William Turner	Jacob Harriss
	Thomas Smithson	Benjamin Williams
James Phillips	Benjn Priestly	William Yorke
Samuel Cooksey	James Collyer	Thomas Joce
John Watson	Cornelius Comegys	Walter Woolverstone
William Aisquith		Ebenezer Blackiston

Then was the charge given to the Grand Inquest and they withdrew to consider thereof."

The sheriffs of the various counties delivered their prisoners to the sheriff of Saint Mary's County, and the first of the entries in this procedure in reference to Hannah Edwards is thus set forth:

" Sheriffe of Calvert County turned over in open Court to the Sheriffe of St. Marys County the bodyes of *Hannah Edwards* Dorcas Rodgers John Harper & Elizabeth Serjeant." After the court had transacted some of its business, the grand jurors, on April 29th, 1686, brought in an indictment against Hannah Edwards in these words:

" Maryland, SS. The Jurors for the Right hon^{ble} the Lord prop^{ty} of this Province upon their Oathes doe present Hannah Edwards, the wife of Richard Edwards, late of Calvert County, Planter, otherwise Hannah Edwards of Calvert County spinster for that she the said Hannah Edwards the sixth day of February in the year of our Lord 1685 and at divers other days and times as well before and after, having not the fear of God before her eyes but being lead by the instigacon of the Devill certain evil and diabollicall arts called witchcrafts, inchantments, charmes and sorceryes, wickedly, divilishly and felloniously at Mount Calvert Hundred and several other places in Calvert County aforesaid of her malice forethought felloniously did use practice and exercise in, upon and against one Ruth Hutchinson, late of Calvert County aforesaid and severall other persons of the said County whereby the said Ruth and severall others as aforesaid the sayd sixth day of February, in the year aforesaid and several other days and times as well before as after at Mount Calvert hundred, and several other places in the said County in and upon their bodyes were very much the worse consumed, pined and wasted against the peace &c and against the form of the Statute in this case made and provided &c.

On the backside of the aforegoing presentment was endorsed by the Grand Inquest—Billa Vera—Upon which Indictment the aforesaid Hanah Edwards was Indicted upon her Indictment was arraigned and upon her arraignment pleaded not guilty and for her tryall putt herself upon God and the Country and the said Thomas Burford, Attorney Generall for the said Lord, Prop^{ty} also. Therefore it is commanded Sheriff of St. Marye's County that he cause to come here twelve &c.

Now here at this day to witt the Thirtyeth day of Aprill in the Eleaventh year of his Lor's Dominion &c Anno Dni 1686 came Thomas Burford, Attorney Generall aforesaid and the said Hannah Edwards sett to the Barr And the Jurors empannelled likewise came to witt Richard Smith, Andrew Abington, Walter Lane, James Neale, John Atky, Thomas Truxton, John Allin, John Woodward, Moses Jones, Robert Benson, Thomas Price and Thomas Cooke, who being thereto tryed and sworne to say the truth in the premises does say upon their oath that the said Hannah Edwards is not Guilty of the Endictment aforesaid or the witchcraft whereof she standes indicted. Judgment Records of Provincial Court, Liber T. G. (2) 1682-1702, pp. 47, 49, 50.

The third case mentioned by Kilty is that of Virtue Violl. The Provincial Court met at Annapolis, the new capital of the Province, on October 5, 1712, with Thomas Smithson, one of the justices presiding with Thomas Gassaway, Sheriff, in attendance. After the calling of Court, Jo Beale, Robert Bradley and Samuel Young, Justices of same Court, took their seats. Then, quoting the record:

"Foster Turbutt, Sheriff of Talbott County brings into Court the body of *Virtue Violl* and thereupon she is committed into the custody of the Sheriff of Ann Arundel County there to remaine until caled.

Proclamation being made according to Comon forme and the several sheriffs of the respective countys having made return of their severall pannells of the Grand Jurors they are called and appear as follows vizt.

John Bozman, foreman

Jno. Taney	Henry Austin	Thos. Taylor
Notley Maddox	Philemon Armstrong	Patrick Dunkin
Edward Veazey	Ubgate Reeves	Thos. Tolley
Wm. Denton	Joseph Harrison	Thomas Thackstone
Arnold Elzey	Wm. Sweatnam	Wm. Gray
Wm. Willowghby	James Keech	Jon^a Back
Wm. Stevens	Joshua Cecill	Thomas Price
James Monat.	Paul Busey	

who being sworn in common forme and charged and sent out to consider &c in short time after Return and deliver to the Court here the following bills, vizt.

Virtue Violl, Thomas Macnemara, Priscilla Bruin and Negroe Hanniball and Eliz^a Taylor and are content that the Court shall amend forme altering no matter of substance in the afsd bills by them found, and thereupon the said Grand Jurors are Discharged and allowed for their service this Court the sume of three thousand pounds of tobacco to be paid by the publick &c. * * *

Her Majesty
v.
Virtue Violl
} Maryland Ss.
The Jurors for our Sovereigne Lady the Queen that now is of Great Brittain &c To-witt Jno. Bozman, John Taney, Notley Maddox, Edward Veazey, Wm. Denton, Arnold Elzey, Wm. Willoughby, Wm. Stevens, James Monat, Henry Austin, Philemon Armstrong, Ubgate Reeves, Joseph Harrison, Wm.

Sweatnam, James Keech, Joshua Cecill, Paul Bussey, Tho⁸ Taylor, Patrick Dunkin, Thos. Tolly, Thomas Thackstone, Wm. Gray, Jonᵃ Back and Thos. Price, good and lawfull men elected, tryed and sworn to speak the truth upon their oath do present that Virtue Violl of Talbott County spinster otherwise called Virtue Violl of the sd. County of Talbott spinster the nineteenth day of August in the eleventh year of the reigne of our said Lady the Queen that now is of Great Brittaine etc. at Talbot County, afd. the fear of God before her eyes not haveing but being Seduced by the devil most wickedly, & diabollically did use practice & exercise witchcraft whereby & wherewith she did waste, consume and pine the body of a certaine Ellianor Moore of the afd. County spinister then & there in the peace of God and our said Lady the Queen being with such her most wicked and Diabollicall use practice & exercise of witchcraft the Tongue of the said Elinor Moore did then and there and at divers times before within the County lame & render speechless to the great displeasure of Almighty God & agst her majᵗʸˢ peace and the forme of the statute in that case madè and provided. W. Bladen Att Genˡ who followeth for our Lady the Queen.

Wienesses   Elinor Moore, Capt. Jno. Needles, Mrs. Needles,
              Robt. Jadwin, Saml Hatton, Thos. Silvester.

On the back of the foregoing indictment was thus endorst, Vizt.

Billa Vera Jno. Bozman, foreman. Thereupon command was given to the Sherᶠᶠ of Ann Arundˡˡ County to sett the said Virtue Violl, the prisoner at the Barr of the Court who thereupon appeared and being presently demanded how she would acquitt herself of the premises above imposed upon her saith that she is not in anywise guilty thereof and thereof for tryall put herself upon God and her County (and Wm. Bladen her majᵗʸˢ said Attorney Genᵃˡ who for her said majᵗʸ in this behalf prosecuteth says she is guilty & prays it may be inquired into by the country likewise) Thereupon Command is given the Shᶠᶠ of Ann arundˡˡ County that he imediately cause to come here twelve &c by whome &c who unto &c to recognize &c because as well &c of which said precept the said Shff to witt Thomas Gassaway, Gent. makes return that he has here ready twelve &c as by his precept he was commanded, to witt: Daniel Sherwood, Henry Sewall, Wm Veazey, Thomas Cox, Roger Laddemore, Thos. Johnson, Jonn Lanham, Phillip Kersey, Sallandine Eagle, Jno. Houkin, Marmaduke Goodhand and Charles Jones who being duly elected, tryed & sworn to well & truly try and true deliverance make between our Sovereigne Lady the Queen & the said Virtue Violl, prisoner at the barr, according to their evidence upon their oaths do say that the said Virtue Violl is not guilty of the matter whereof she stands indicted whereupon it is considered by the justices here this seventh day of Octob^r Anno Dom. 1712 that the sd. Virtue Violl of the Indictment & premises afd. be acquitt and that she go thereof without day &c and thereupon the sd. Virtue Violl at her prayer was discharged by procl^n made in usual form paying fees. Judgments of Provincial Court, Liber T. P. 1711-1712, pp. 576, 582.

In leaning to mercy's side in their verdict, in this trial, the jury may have held with the conclusion which Addison had expressed a year before in the Spectator: " I believe in general that there is and has been such a thing as Witchcraft; but at the same time can give no Credit to any Particular Instance of it." Vol. 2, No. 117.

While other prosecutions may await discovery, there are but these five instances known to the writer of criminal proceedings in Maryland looking to the punishment of persons charged with witchcraft. The first four of these are within the period from 1665 to 1686, and the fifth was in 1712, after an interval of over a quarter of a century. In the first case, the accused, Elizabeth Bennett, was not presented; and two others, Hannah Edwards and Virtue Violl, were indicted, tried and acquitted. Of the last two named, Hannah Edwards, a married woman, and Virtue Violl, a spinster, were charged with having practised their black arts upon women whose bodies they were said to have caused to be wasted, consumed and pined.

The evil inflicted upon Ruth Hutchinson was alleged to be general in its pernicious effect upon her body but, in the case of Ellianor Moore, the mischief inflicted was that her tongue had been rendered "lame and speechless."

It does not appear in what manner Elizabeth Goodale's body was bewitched by John Cowman. In the indictment against Rebecca Fowler it is alleged that her victim, Francis Sandbury, had been made in his body worse, consumed, pined and lamed. These were the characteristic results of witchcraft or fascination, as it was sometimes anciently called.

The statute of James I imposed the penalty of death when the victim was "Killed, destroyed, wasted, consumed, pined or lamed in his or her body, or any part thereof." The effects of an exercise of the art are stated in the alternative, and the penalty of death is imposed when any one of the named consequences happened. If death followed, it was the practice to allege this result, although in many cases the indictments, after charging the person to have been wasted, consumed and pined in body, added the words "yet still is," in order, probably, to negative the inference of death ensuing. The addition in the Fowler prosecution of the word "lamed," would clearly imply that the laborer had been made lame by the baleful art of the wife of the planter.

Of those accused and tried but one was a man, and he, John Cowman, was found guilty and sentenced, but escaped death by an ignominious reprieve. The others were women and the execution of one of these is apparently the single instance of the infliction of the death penalty in the performance of a judicial sentence. It would seem that not only in England but also in the province the statutes, in the words of Blackstone, continued in force "to the terror of all ancient females in the kingdom." Book IV, ch. IV, p. 61. The Spectator, Vol. II, No. 117 (Addison).

The localities in which the accused lived cannot be given with certainty. The first two, Elizabeth Bennett and John Cowman, were apparently of Saint Mary's County. The charge against Virtue Violl was laid in Talbott County, where the tradition persists that, at a later period, a witch had lived in the neighborhood of Plain dealing Creek, a northern tributary of Tred Avon River. The Land of Legendary Lore (1898), Ingraham, 93.

The names of the victim, and of the witnesses endorsed on the presentment afford some basis for the conjecture that Virtue Violl had lived in the same section of the county.

The indictments against Rebecca Fowler and Hannah Edwards are more definite as to place and fix the scene of the crimes in Mount Calvert Hundred, whose location is definitely known from the circumstance that the origin of the Hundred was in a tract of land containing 1000 acres and called "Mount Calvert" having been granted by patent to Philip Calvert on February 17th, 1658, as a Manor with Court Baron etc. The tract is on the west side of the Patuxent River "in the freshes near the dividing line of the said River" and lies south of Calvert Branch (now Western Branch) at the confluence of the Branch with the River. At this juncture was "Pig Point," which, with a view to the advancement of trade, was made in 1685, a port of entry and export, along with four other ports in Calvert County. In the legislation the port is explicitly stated to be "Att pigg Pointe upon Mount Colverte Mannor in Patuxent River." Proceedings and Acts of the Assembly, Archives, 1678-1683, pp. 540, 541, 1684-1692, pp. 111-120.

The narrator has not been able to find any other proceedings among the records of the provincial court, but, in the search, some other information was obtained which relates more to the civil remedies in force in the county courts. An action for defamation that was founded in an accusation of witchcraft was not rare but, as was remarked by Sir Frederick Pollock, when writing of chancery suits in the 14th and 15 centuries,

"There is, however, one rather curious head of jurisdiction of which I have found no mention in text books. It was not very uncommon to apply to the chancellor for an injunction to restrain the defendant from practising witchcraft against the plaintiff, or, it might be, from making false charges of witchcraft against him." Essays in the Law (1922), p. 191. Holds-worth's History of English Law, vol. V, pp. 289-290.

It would seem that the types of cases mentioned by Pollock and Holdsworth have their counterpart in the proceedings of at least two of the county courts. One instance is found in Charles county and there the alleged witch is seen seeking to prevent others from falsely charging her with witchcraft. The second is an appeal by the victim to the county court of Anne Arundel county for protection against a witch. The earlier proceedings will be first stated.

The writer is indebted to Dr. J. Hall Pleasants, the present accomplished editor of the Archives of Maryland, for the facts, and the opportunity to read the records which are now in the course of printing, in respect of the actions at law brought in 1661 by one Joan Michell, who charged that traducers had called her a witch. From the record of the proceedings of the Court of Charles County, 1658-1662, it will appear that four actions of slander were brought. The first was against Francis Doughty (ie), then the rector of the Church of England parish, who later went to Virginia and became the rector of Rappahannock Parish; the second, against his son, Enoch Doughtie; the third, against James Walker and a fourth against Miss Long. Three of the actions failed because of insufficiency of plaintiff's proof, and the first was not prosecuted.

As a preface to the relation of the law suits, it should be said that Joan Michel had for some while been dreaded because of the belief in her use of the black art. It appeared that several years before the action she had sought to vindicate her character through the effort, it may be inferred, of her husband. For on November 14, 1659, Thomas Michel appeared before a session of the justices of the county court of Charles County. He was indignant and the record is that he " desiereth that Mr. Thomas Lomax and Elizabeth Atwicks might have their oaths given them concerning the abusful reproaches offered unto his wife by M[is] Hatche." The parties named were brought into court and examined severally under oath. Their depositions were so similar that but one will be quoted: " Thomas Lomax sworne & examined in open Court sayeth, that goodie Michel asking Mis Hatche how She did Mis Hatche replied that she thaught she had bewitched her face whereupon goodie Mitchell asked her if She wear in earnest or no and She replied Shee was for shee endureth abundance of Miserie by the soarnes of her mouth and did verilie beleeve that shee was bewitched whearupon thear ware diuers other circumstances past betweene the too parties which this deponent can not at presant call to remembrance onlie goodie michell tould her She woold Arest her to the Court about it; and Mis Hatche Replied that she thaught she durst not but if she durst she woold endeauor to make it appear so or els she woold acknowledge she had wronged her in open Court & bee liable to their censuir & further this deponant at present remembereth not." Infra. pp. 54, 55. The matter then dropped out of the records until almost two years later when the action were begun. A declaration and some testimony will be quoted, since they give a vivid glimpse of the belief and life of the community and of the legal procedure:

" Joan Michell Plantiue Francis Doughtie Minister Defendant	The Plantiue Aresting the Defendant in an Action of Defamation Prefereth her Petition as followeth

To the Worshipfull Commissioner of Charleses Countie

The humble Petition of Joan Michell your Poor Petioner as followeth.

Whereas your Poor Petitioner is most shamfully and her good name taken away from her shee doath desire that shee may bee righted and that shee may bee searched by able woemen whether she bee such a person or no which thos persons say I am and if I bee found to bee such a one I may bee punished by law or els to bee Cleared by Proclamation and that the worshipfull bench would tak it into ther serious Consideration how that I am Abused and my good name taken from mee without disart and I most humbly desire your worships that I may haue the law

against them and I your poore petitioner shall bee bound to pray
for you and yours

I desire th^t Mr Francis Doughty may bring thos Persons to
light that haue raysed this schandalous reports of mee for hee
sayd that I salluted a woman at Church and her teeth fell a
Aking as if shee had bin mad and I desired him to tell mee who
had raysed this report of mee and hee woold not and so from one
to an other my good name is taken away that I Cannot bee at
quiet for them for it is all their delight and table talke how to
doe mee a mischief beeing a poore distressed widow but my trust
is in God that hee will plead my Case for mee and will neuer
suffer the poor and innocent to perish by the hands of their
Enemies for of a sunday as I was going to Church with too of
Capt: Fendalls folks Mr Walkers man hurled stones at mee
as I was going along and so hid himself again which for any
thing that I know his master might set him on to Mischefe mee
and hee himself wrongs mee by word and I your petitioner shal
bee euer bound to pray for you. * * *

" Mis Ane Cage sworne and examined in open Court sayeth
that Mr Enock Doughtie Called unto goodie Michell and sayed
goodie Michel goodie Michell are not you the woman that swom
ouer unto Mr Pillses sometime in June last past and further
sayeth not."

"Richard Tarlin aged 25 years or thearabouts sworne and
examined in open Court sayeth that Mis Long did say that the
hene and Chickings she had of goodie Michell that the Chickings
thearof did die in such a strang manner that she thaught sum old
witch or other had bewitched them and further sayeth not which
was also affirmed and no mor by the sayd Tarlins wife sworn
in open Court."

Francis Ferenla sworne and examined in open Court sayeth
that Richard Tarlin did say that Mis Long did say that goodie
michell did giue her a hen and Chickings but shee thaught shee
had forespoake them and further sayeth not. ("forspoke"
meant here bewitched.)   Advance sheets: *Md. Archives*, Charles

County Court Proceedings, 1658-1662, pp. 139, 142-143, 145, 155-156.

Turning now to the proceedings in Anne Arundel county, it will be learned that a certain Charles Killburn, on January 15, 1702, addressed to the justices of Anne Arundel County Court his petition in which he described himself as being "in a very languishing condition" because of the witchcraft practiced upon him by one Katherine Prout. He represented that oftentimes having been in the way of recovery he had met Katherine and she as frequently had abused and threatened him "wishing withal," as he averred, "that he might languish to death and never recover his health which by your petitioner's unhappy state at present he imagines is the sad effects of her execrable wishes." The petitioner, therefore, prayed that he be examined by the justices concerning his condition and its cause verified; craved "some Tryall may be made on her" as to the justices should seem meet.

Upon a reading of the petition, the court passed an order directing that Capt. Lawrence Draper and Mr. Josiah Towgood take the deposition of the petitioner in writing, and return it immediately for the court's action. The court then sent for Katherine Prout to answer the premises. She appeared in person and proved refractory. After noting her presence, the entry continued: " and, for her misbehaviour in her Saucy Language and abusing this Court, is fined one hundred pounds of Tobbacco."

The two commissioners returned the deposition of Charles Killburn, the petitioner, on the same day they were named. It was in this form:

" The deposition of Charles Killburn aged about fourty years taken this 15th day of Jan^{ry} Anno. 1702.

Your deponent saith ever since the last September he hath not been well and do think that it is occasioned by the within Katherine Prout, and that to the best of his Knowledge he is bewitched by the sd. Katherine and is not well above 3 or 4 days together and further saith not.   Taken before us Lawrence Draper, Josiah Towgood.

The within petitioner prays that Charles Chissell, Jno. Newsam, Mr. Beards Servant Woman, Daniel Camim & wife and Sr. Thomas Laurence's man may be all sumoned to informe the Court what they know." The record then proceeds with this final minute:

" Which evidence being summoned, sworne & examined in open court do declare nothing in respect to the Justification of the petition and deposition of the sd. Charles Kilburne thereupon the said Katherine Prout is discharged from the same, paying her fees."

The matter, however, was not at an end. Two months later Kilburne brought an action for slander against Katherine Prout for calling him " a rogue " and a " foresworn rogue " with the meaning that he had committed perjury. In this second effort, Kilburne won a nominal victory as his damages were but six pence, although the costs were heavy as they were expresssd in terms of 1101 lbs. of tobacco.

Nothing daunted, Katherine, in turn, sued Kate Quillin for slander. The declaration set forth the utterance of two defamatory remarks. The first was that Kate Quillin called the plaintiff " Dame Ye " meaning thereby that she was an old witch. The inversion of the words carried the imputation of witchcraft, since its devotees did or said nothing in its natural order. The second slander was that Katherine Prout had stolen molasses and " New England Capons " from a cellar in Annapolis. The declaration informed the court that " New England capons " were not fowl but mackerel. The plaintiff recovered three pounds damages, and the legal strife of the two Kates was at an end.

The instances brought to light in the records of Charles and Anne Arundel County afford basis for the expectation that the other records before 1736 of these two counties and those which remain of the other counties, Kent (1640), Baltimore (1659),

Talbot (1661), Somerset (1666), Dorchester (1668), Prince George's (1695), Queen Anne (1706), may contain interesting information with reference to litigation growing out of the practice or pretense of witchcraft. The counties of St. Mary's (1638) and Calvert (1654), have had their ancient records unfortunately consumed by fire.

The records extant are, however, sufficient to establish that with reference to witchcraft the law and procedure were directed to the prevention of either the exercise or the imputation of witchcraft; to the compensation of one wronged by its use or by a false accusation of its art; and of the punishment of the crime.

While the belief may not be indulged that this paper has embraced all the prosecutions to be found in the records of the provincial and general courts, it may be said that published volumes of the Archives of Maryland cover the proceedings of the provincial court and general court from 1634 to 1666; of the court of chancery, 1669-1679; of the council, 1636-1770; of the general assembly, 1637-1756; and that there is a general index of the records of the provincial court extending from 1654 to 1778. These have been examined with care but not with that degree of thoroughness which would preclude a mistake. The records of the county courts would probably not furnish a case of a criminal trial under the statute, since witchcraft was a major offence, and its prosecution was within the jurisdiction of the provincial or general court.

A review of the judicial and historical material now available does not indicate that there ever was a period of maniacal prosecution. The only instances which bear any relation in time and place are those against Rebecca Fowler and Hannah Edwards. One of these was convicted and the other was acquitted, although on the jury which freed Hannah Edwards were two of the sixteen grand jurors who had presented Rebecca Fowler, and two of the petit jurors, who had convicted her. It is a hard matter for a man to weigh, reason and decide on the evidence

2

against common opinion. In view of the almost universal belief of the times in witchcraft and its malign consequences, the statute would seem to have been enforced with moderation and restraint. While the record of a single execution is to be deplored, yet the law exacted it. The minutes of the proceedings show an orderly trial and due deliberation in the imposition of the sentence. The single execution of the penalty of death during the century in which the statute was in effect must remain a cherished testimony of tolerance,—a tolerance which, in respect of witches, would " rather have appointed them Helleborum than Hemlocke."

LETTERS OF CHARLES CARROLL, BARRISTER.

Everyone who has read even slightly the history of Maryland during the American Revolution knows that Charles Carroll, Barrister, was one of the most trusted and active leaders of the patriotic party. Indeed his services were scarcely less important than those of Charles Carroll of Carrollton with whom he is now often, as he was then sometimes, confused. But though the public records are full of references indicating his prominence in the patriotic cause little or nothing is known about the man himself. It is now possible not only to supply information about this distinguished Maryland leader but also to cast a flood of light on many aspects of life in Maryland during the period immediately preceding the Revolution.

Some years ago Mr. Alexander Preston first loaned and then presented to the Maryland Historical Society three letter-books in which Dr. Charles Carroll and his son, the Barrister, kept copies of their business correspondence. That of the son occupies a little more than half of the third volume and took place between 1755 and 1769. The letters of Dr. Carroll have already been published in the MARYLAND HISTORICAL MAGAZINE. Beginning with this issue all the letters of Charles Carroll, Barrister, will be printed.

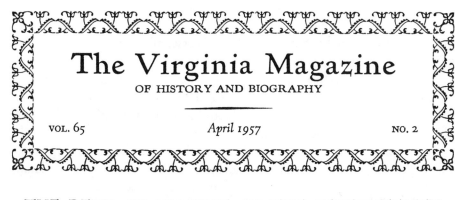

The Virginia Magazine
OF HISTORY AND BIOGRAPHY

VOL. 65   *April 1957*   NO. 2

THE DEVIL IN VIRGINIA IN THE SEVENTEENTH CENTURY

by RICHARD BEALE DAVIS[*]

IN Italy in 1611, George Sandys soberly informed a rustic that "in England we were at defiance with the devill, and that he would do nothing for us." Sandys was evading an appeal that he use the black arts, reputed by Italians to be at the disposal of all Britons, to assist in locating a hidden treasure.[1] Ten years later in the New World as Virginia Treasurer, Sandys was surrounded by aborigines reputed by every European nation to be in league with the Black Man. To the earlier seventeenth-century man, Evil was still incarnate. Particularly was it present in remote and primitive places. King James himself had written in his *Daemonologie* in 1597 that the Devil was present "where [he] finds greatest ignorance and barbaritie," and that the abuses of witchcraft, derived directly from Satan, were "most comon in . . . [the] wild partes of the world."[2] At the same time the King was pointing out that certain of his own subjects might be witches or wizards themselves, and that if they were they should be rooted out. Evidently the Devil was doing something for Britons.

Through the settlement at Jamestown in 1607, James became sovereign over the barbaric as well as the civilized. Both he and his English subjects generally became much interested in the manner and result of the presence of the Black Man among both the red and white Virginians. Much has been written about the presence of the Devil in old and New England in the seventeenth century, but most of us remain in ignorance of the fre-

---

[*]Dr. Davis, professor of English at the University of Tennessee, is author of *George Sandys, Poet-Adventurer* (New York and London, 1955) and other books. The material for this essay was gathered while the author was a Fellow of the Folger Shakespeare Library.
[1]*A Relation of a Journey Begun . . . A. D. 1610* (London, 1615), p. 250.
[2]P. 69.

quency and form of his Satanic Majesty's personal appearance in the Virginia of the period.

Actually the literature of early exploration and settlement is full of allusions to and exemplifications of the Indians as followers of Satan in a quite literal sense. And the court records give us interesting indications of the colonists' attitude towards the presence of the Evil One in witchcraft and other sorts of crime among themselves. As the century goes on, there are fewer references to the Indians as the chief servants of Satan, and more to the evil practices of transplanted Englishmen. Yet even though the belief in black magic apparently persists among some of the educated into the eighteenth century, there never was in Virginia a "darkest page"[3] of history such as the witch persecution in New England. A brief look at Virginians' attitudes toward the *idea* of black magic through the seventeenth century does afford us an interesting and perhaps unusual approach to the southern colonial mind.

I

The mediaeval and renaissance European believed that all infidels or pagans were really direct worshippers of Evil as opposed to Good, or of Satan as opposed to God. As we have noted, Evil was incarnate, and the personalized devil was acknowledged deity in heathen lands. The early Spanish historians of America were careful to point out that the natives of the New World worshipped Satan as sovereign. Englishmen accepted this idea without hesitation. Master George Percy, who stopped in the West Indies on the first voyage to Jamestown, describes the Caribbean "Canibals . . . [who] worship the Devill for their God, and have no other beliefe."[4] Six years later, in dedicating Alexander Whitaker's *Good Newes from Virginia* to a noble lord, good Master William Crashaw assures the reading public that the plantation has been made "to resolve the works of the Divell," for "Satan visibly and palpably raignes there, more then in any other known place of the world."[5] Thus early Virginia was claimed

---

[3]G. L. Kittredge, *Witchcraft in Old and New England* (Cambridge, Mass., 1929), p. 329.

[4]"Observations," in Lyon Gardiner Tyler, ed., *Narratives of Early Virginia, 1606-1625* (New York 1907), p. 6. See also Alexander Roberts (*A Treatise on Witchcraft*, London, 1616, p. 33), who assures us that the "devil in man's form" inhabits the West Indies; and Joseph Glanvill, *Essays on Several Important Subjects in Philosophy and Religion . . .* (London, 1675[6]), pp. 54-56.

[5]London 1613 (also *Scholars Facsimiles and Reprints*), p. C2r. See also Ralph Hamor, *A True Discourse on the Present State of Virginia* (London, 1615), p. 48, *passim* (photostat of the original in the Folger Library); and *A True Declaration of the estate of the Colonie in Virginia . . .*, London 1610 (in Peter Force, *Tracts and Other Papers Relating Principally to the Origin, Settlement and Progress of the Colonies in North America, From the Discovery of the Country to the*

as the favorite dwelling place of Evil, and as a battle ground for the forces of Light and Darkness.

That the Virginia red men were really devils—in their chiefs, their priests, their idols, and their ceremonies—is stated again and again in the literature of the entire century. Even in their fairly ordinary appearance the savages reminded the nervous Englishmen of the dark deity. Percy observed of the first landing at Kecoughtan that the natives were like "so many Wolves or Devils."[6] Captain John Smith alludes to the Indians again and again as devils, and he was certainly thinking as much of their appearance as of their diabolic ways. When he was captured, "They entertained him with most strange and fearful Coniurations;

> As if neare led to hell,
> Amongst the Devills to dwell"

Then, "round about him these fiends danced a pretty while, and then came in three as ugly as the rest, with red eyes, and white stroakes over their black faces."[7] Even Powhatan was "more like a devill then a man, with some two hundred more as blacke as himselfe."[8]

The religion itself, however, was what interested most observers. "In this lamentable ignorance doe these poore soules sacrifice themselves to the Divell, not knowing their Creator."[9] The Indians' chief idol is usually described,—from Smith to Robert Beverley almost a century later,—as being the inanimate representation of the Devil. Smith mentions "their *Okee* (which was an Idoll made of skinnes, stuffed with mosse, all painted and hung with chaines and copper) borne before them," and that that Okee is the devil-witch.[10] In 1612 William Strachey stated flatly that the chief god they worship "is no better then the divell, whom they make presentements of and shadow under the forme of an Idoll which they entitle *Okeus* and whom they worship as the Romaynes did their hurtfull god Veiouis."[11]

Okee's nature may have changed slightly in the second half of the seventeenth century, for later accounts differ in describing his attributes. Actu-

---

Year 1776 [reprinted New York, 1947], III, i, 26; or original in Folger Library), which exhorts, "cast down the altars of Divels, that you may raise up the altar of Christ."

[6]"Observations," p. 12.

[7]Edward Arber and A. C. Bradley, eds., *Travels and Works of Captain John Smith* (Edinburgh, 1910), II, 398-399.

[8]*Ibid.*, II, 400-401.

[9]*Ibid.*, II, 393.

[10]*Ibid.*, II, 393.

[11]L. B. Wright and Virginia Freund, eds., *The Historie of Travell into Virginia Britania* (1612) (Hakluyt Society, London, 1953), p. 88.

ally most later historians mix Smith's descriptions with their own observations or with simple hearsay. In 1670 the Reverend Samuel Clarke gave
an account ultimately based on Smith and other early recorders:

> But their chief God is the Devil whom they call *Oke,* and serve him more for fear
> than love. In their Temples they have his image in an ilfavoured shape, and adorned
> with Chains, Copper, and Beads, and covered with a skin.[12]

In 1672 John Lederer observed that their god was called *Okaee,* or Man-
nith, but that he was a creator who committed the government of mankind
to the "lesser deities, as Quiacosough and Tagkanysough, that is, good and
evil spirits."[13] In 1705 Robert Beverley quotes from Smith the conception
of Okee as Devil who sucks under the left breast in the best witchcraft tradition, but he gives the "Religious Romance" a more rational explanation.[14]
Beverley, an acute observer of Indian customs, distinctly represents a new
era. Okee is now a mere thing of sticks and stones, and the devilish sacri-
fices are merely means by which the priests gather worldly goods unto themselves. Yet the Swiss traveler Francis Louis Michel reported in 1701-1702
that "Regarding their religion I heard from reliable people, who have
much intercourse with them that they fear Satan, who torments them
frequently."[15]

The early narrators relate with some relish stories of diabolic religious
sacrificial ceremonies. Smith and Strachey give accounts of the child sacrifice of the Indians. Referring to these practices in a sermon before the Virginia Company of London, the Reverend Patrick Copland declared that
Opachankano had confessed "that God loved us more then them; and that
he thought the cause of his anger against them, was their custome of making their children Black-boyes, or consecrating them to Satan."[16]

Even less bloody ceremonies reminded the colonist of the devil. Whitaker
earnestly enquired of Master Crashaw in England what he should make

---

[12]*A True, and Faithful Account of the Four Chiefest Plantations of the English in America.
To Wit, of Virginia, New-England, Bermudus, Barbadoes* . . . (London, 1670), p. 10.

[13]Sir William Talbot, Bart., ed., *The Discoveries of John Lederer, In Three Several Marches
from Virginia* . . . (London, 1672, reprinted in C. W. Alvard and Lee Bidgood, eds., *The First
Explorations of the Trans-Allegheny Regions by the Virginians, 1650-1674,* Cleveland, 1912, p.
143).

[14]*The History and Present State of Virginia,* Louis B. Wright, ed. (Chapel Hill, 1947), pp.
198, 206, 208.

[15]This is a modern translation from the German. William J. Hinke, ed. and transl., "Report
of the Journey of Francis Louis Michel from Berne . . . to Virginia," *Virginia Magazine of History and Biography,* XXIV (April 1916), 131, hereafter *VMHB.*

[16]*Virginia's God be Thanked, or, a Sermon of Thanksgiving for the Happie successe of the
affayres in Virginia this last yeare* . . . (London, 1622), p. 29.

of certain things he had seen, and then concluded by giving his own opinion.

> . . . in a march upp Nansemund river as our men passed by one of their Townes, there yssued out on the shoare a mad crewe dauncinge like Anticks, or our Morris dancers before whom there were Quiockosite (or theire Priest) tossed smoke and flame out of a thinge like a censer. An Indian (by name Memchumps) amongst our men seeing this dance tould us that there would be very much raine presently and indeed there was forthwith exceedinge thunder and lighteninge and much raine within 5. miles and so further of, but not so much there as made their pouder dancke. . . . All which things make me think that there be great witches amongst them and they very familiar with the divill.[17]

A year later Whitaker informed his friend that he was now sure that "Their priests . . . are no other but such as our English Witches are."[18] Whitaker was a Puritan clergyman, and his comments remind us that the theology of the period, especially as interpreted by the Puritans, more than accepted a belief in witchcraft. A recent historian of the colonial Church has pointed out that in the early days the Virginia clergy generally were inclined toward Puritanism, as was the Virginia Company of London, and that the "temper of the government in the colony"[19] was quite Puritan. A few years later under Laud, when Virginia had become a Royal colony, the situation changed. Fundamentally the Virginia Church never returned again to the attitude of these early years, even during the Commonwealth. And here may be the explanation as to why there were no Salem Village witch executions in the Chesapeake region. But that is a consideration of the second part of this paper.

II

Throughout the seventeenth century Devil-worshipping neighbors such as those described by Master Whitaker were for New Englanders "a constant reminder of the possibility of danger from witchcraft."[20] Yet in Virginia, one who follows the record must believe that the trials for witchcraft or dealing in black magic had little connection with any white man's consciousness that the Indians were practicing devilish arts. Witchcraft was a

---

[17]Letter of August 9, 1611. In Alexander Brown, *Genesis of the United States* (Boston, 1897), I, 498-499.

[18]Letter of July 28, 1612, in Alexander Whitaker, *Good Newes from Virginia* (London, 1613), p. 24.

[19]George MacLaren Brydon, *Virginia's Mother Church, and the Political Conditions under Which It Grew* (Richmond, 1947), I, 25.

[20]Kittredge, *Witchcraft*, p. 363.

subject for discussion in the Virginia county and General courts from 1626 through 1706, but in no instance is it ostensibly related by any colonist to the demonism of the aborigines.[21] It is rather the natural outgrowth of folk and theological beliefs about themselves the settlers brought from Britain with them, beliefs some of them might buttress, if they wished, by reading certain of the books which had accompanied or followed them to the New World. That these beliefs had more to do with folklore than theology,[22] that there was no black page of real torture or persecution, seem due to the fact that the Anglican clergy rarely took part in or supported such beliefs, and that the juries of laymen were rational men who shunned hysteria or superstitious credulity.

That there should be investigations of alleged witchcraft was inevitable in any seventeenth-century European society. As legacy from the Middle Ages the belief in the existence of witches was widespread and through the sixteenth century almost universal. In Great Britain it was true that as early as 1584 Reginald Scot's *The Discoverie of Witchcraft* had warned men that they should proceed with caution before they persecuted or prosecuted for alleged black magic, and that so-called witches were really "melancholick doting" old women. But James VI of Scotland, soon to be King of England also, had answered Scot's rational arguments in his *Dæmonologie* in 1597, a treatise which seemed to his contemporaries a powerful reassertion of the necessity for faith in the existence of Satan's arts. And soon after James' accession to the English throne a new "Act against conjuration, witchcraft and dealing with evil spirits" superseded the Act of 5 Elizabeth, the new law being much more severe in its punishment of practitioners of black magic. By 1610 the great Puritan preacher William Perkins had written his "Discourse of the Damned Art of Witchcraft," a sermon-essay included in all later editions of his popular *Works*[23] and more than reinforcing James' *Daemonologie*. During the rest of the century there were dozens of other writers on the subject. A few, like John Cotta in 1616 and John Webster in 1677, warned against prejudiced persecution or suggested that individual cases be examined rationally, like other objects of investigation.[24]

---

[21]Unless one considers the case of the recovered-from-the-dead Indian boy mentioned below such an instance.

[22]Thomas Jefferson Wertenbaker, *The First Americans* (New York, 1927), p. 147.

[23]The "Discourse" first appeared separately at Cambridge in 1610. For the *Works,* see more below.

[24]John Cotta, *The Triall of Witchcraft, Shewing the True and Right Method of Discovery: with a Confutation of Erroneous wayes,* (London, 1616); John Webster, *The Displaying of Supposed Witchcraft . . . ,* (London, 1677). It is significant that both these authors were physicians.

But even in the latter half of the century such men as the pious and prolific Joseph Glanvill more nearly represented majority opinion. In "Against Modern Sadducism in the Matter of Witches and Apparitions"[25] and *Saducismus Triumphatus; or, a Full and Plain Evidence concerning Witches and Apparitions*[26] Glanvill reasserted full belief in witchcraft for a multiplicity of reasons, among them "because it suggests palpable and current evidence of our Immortality."[27]

The unlearned in the colony did not need the King or Glanvill to support a belief in witchcraft. They had brought a deeply grounded conviction of its truth with the rest of their folklore when they came to America. The more literate, before they came to the colony or during visiting periods of education in England, had opportunities to read the treatises which might confirm or controvert their natural skepticism. But there is evidence that many of the most renowned of the polemical books or pamphlets were owned in Virginia itself. By 1621-1622 there had been sent to the colony a set of "Master *Perkins* his works,"[28] a three-volume edition which included in the last the "Discourse" noted above. Later Virginia private libraries well into the eighteenth century included either Perkins' *Works* as a whole or the "Art of Witchcraft."[29] When Ralph Wormeley died in 1701 he owned Webster's *The Displaying of Supposed Witchcraft,* the anti-persecution, reasoned argument.[30] Later William Byrd II had Glanvill "on Witchcraft" as well as Perkins;[31] Thomas Thompson in Westmoreland County in 1716 numbered "Glanceck [*sic*] of Witches Observances"[32] among his possessions. Since our record of these books usually comes from the inventories accompanying probated wills, we may be fairly sure that many or most of these volumes were in the colony long before 1700. Many of Byrd's books, for example, had belonged to his father William Byrd I. That all our early Virginia court records are fragmentary would suggest that many other simi-

---

[25]In *Essays*, pp. 54-56.

[26]Published 1681. This is an enlargement of his 1666 *Philosophical Considerations Concerning Witchcraft.*

[27]*Essays*, p. 60.

[28]Susan M. Kingsbury, ed., *Records of the Virginia Company of London* (Washington, D. C., 1906-1935), III, 576; also W. S. Powell, "Books in the Virginia Colony before 1624," *William and Mary Quarterly*, 3rd ser., V (April 1948), 177-184, hereafter *WMQ.*

[29]Captain Charles Colston in 1724 had "Pirkins Works the last vollume" in his library (*WMQ,* 1st ser., III [October 1894], 132); Colonel William Byrd II owned "Perkins Art of Witchcraft" in 1744 (J. S. Bassett, ed., *The Writings of 'Colonel William Byrd of Westover in Virginia Esqʳ,'* New York, 1901).

[30]*WMQ,* 1st ser., II (Jan. 1894), 171. Inventory of Will. Dr. L. B. Wright points out that Wormeley's friend William Fitzhugh asserted his own personal belief in the damnable sin. Wright, *The First Gentlemen of Virginia* (San Marino, Calif., 1940), pp. 181, 204.

[31]Bassett, ed., *Writings*, pp. 420, 439.

[32]*VMHB*, X (April 1903), 399. This is probably a misspelling of Glanvill.

lar printed materials on the subject were present in the colony. Thus the Virginia gentlemen had almost or equally as much opportunity (as did the New England theocrat) to know the learned arguments on the subject and be influenced by them.

The Massacre of 1622 had set back the infant colony in almost every respect. Virginia's "second start," including a steady and uninterrupted growth in population, came in the years immediately after 1622. It is in these years of increase that the "great witches" ceased to be exclusively Indian.[33] There were enough colonists now to represent all forms of sin. The suspicious and the unfortunate might hope to find black magicians among the whites on whom to blame all sorts of major and minor calamities.

Most or all witchcraft cases originated as hearings before county courts or grand juries and were sent on, if considered serious, to the General Court at Jamestown. In some instances there are actual trials of accused persons; in many more civil suits are brought by individuals defamed as witches against those who spread the scandal. From either situation the modern reader learns a good deal of the temper of plaintiff and defendant and of jury and judges.

The first case of which we have record came up in September 1626.[34] The rather detailed extant evidence is perhaps fragmentary, though the records of this particular period are fairly complete. This evidence consists of a series of depositions attempting to prove Goodwife Joan Wright guilty of practicing witchcraft. Mrs. Wright lived across the river from Jamestown in Surry County and had formerly lived at Kecoughtan in Elizabeth City County. The investigation may have originated in a Surry court. At any rate, the evidence we have came before the General Court, acting perhaps as Grand Jury, of September 11, 1626, at Jamestown, with Sir George Yeardley the Governor presiding. Trivial and even absurd as this evidence may seem today, it was certainly weighed seriously, though there is no existing record of actual trial or presentation for trial. Since the outcome remains in doubt, we see in this case only what certain laymen thought and not what judges decided. The evidence is both first and second hand. The first witness, presumably a county militia lieutenant and therefore possibly

---

[33]Philip A. Bruce, *Institutional History of Virginia in the Seventeenth Century* (New York, 1910), I, 278.

[34]All known Virginia witchcraft records of any apparent significance are noted in the following discussion. It is possible that in some county court records there may be a few other cases entered. Virginia county archives have been so thoroughly examined, however, that this seems unlikely. The present writer would like to know of any others than those here discussed which have come to the attention of readers of this article.

an educated man, appears as credulous and superstitious as the humbler folk who follow him.

Liv^t *Gieles Allingtone* sworne and examined sayeth, That he harde Sargeant *Booth* saye that he was croste by a woman and for twelve months space he havinge very fayre game to shute at, yett he could never kill any thinge but this deponent cannot say that was good wiefe *Wright*. Fourther this deponent sayeth, that he had spoken to good wiefe *Wrighte* for to bring his wiefe to bed, but the saide goodwief beinge left handed, his wiefe desired him to gett Mrs *Graue* to be her midwiefe, which this deponent did, and sayeth that the next daye after his wiefe was delivered, the saide goodwiefe *Wright* went awaye from his house very much discontented, in regarde the other midwiefe had brought his wiefe to bedd, shortlie after this, this deponents wiefes brest grew dangerouslie sore of an Imposture and was a moneth or 5 weeks before she was recovered, Att which tyme This deponent him selfe fell sick and contynued the space of three weeks, And further sayeth that his childe after it was borne fell sick and soe contynued the space of two moneths, and afterwards recovered, And so did Contynue well for the space of a moneth, And afterwards fell into extreeme payne the space of five weeks and so departed.[35]

Rebecca Graye testified that Goodwife Wright prophesied correctly that she, a Mr. Felgate, and Thomas Harris should soon bury their spouses, and that another woman who complained of "a cross man to my husband" was assured that she should bury him shortly, "(wch cam so to pass)."[36] The other witnesses continued in the same vein.

Daniell Watkins sworne and examined sayeth that about *february* last past, this deponent beinge at Mr. *Perryes* Plantatione Ther was *Robert Thresher* who had a cowple of henns pourposinge to send them over to *Elizabeth Arundle* And good wiefe *Wright* beinge there in place, saide to *Robert Thresher, why do you keepe these henns heere tyed upp, The maide you meane to send them to will be dead before the henns come to her.*[37]

Even a plantation owner's wife, Mrs. Isabell Perry, told how Goody Wright threatened to use occult powers to compel a suspected thief to make restitution:

. . . vppon the losinge of a logg of light wood owt of the fforte, good wiefe *Wrighte* rayled vppon a girle of good wiefe *gates* for stealinge of the same, wherevppon good

---

[35]H. R. McIlwaine, ed., *Minutes of the Council and General Court of Colonial Virginia, 1622-1632, 1670-1676* . . . (Richmond, 1924), p. 111. Alexander Brown (*Genesis*, II, 813), discusses a "Giles Allington, gent.," a member of the Virginia Company and grandson of the first Earl of Exeter. He mentions as another person the man who patented lands in Virginia in 1624, though the two were probably close relatives. The ownership of several tracts of land and a military commission indicate the present witness' social position in the colony. For other evidence of Lieutenant Allington as a man of affairs, see McIlwaine, *Minutes*, pp. 53, 147, 157, 197.

[36]McIlwaine, *Minutes*, p. 111.

[37]McIlwaine, *Minutes*, p. 112.

wiefe *gates* Charged the said good wiefe *Wright* with witchcrafte, And said that she had done many bad things at *Kickotan,* wherevppon this Examinate Chid the saide Good wiefe *Wright,* And said vnto her, *yf thow knowest thyselfe Cleare of what she Charged thee, why dost thow not complaine And cleare thyselfe of the same,* To whom good wiefe *Wright* replied, *god forgive them,* and so made light of it, And the said good wiefe *Wright* Threatened good wiefe *Gates* girle and told her, that yf she did nott bringe the light wood againe she would make her daunce starke naked and the next morninge the lightwood was founde in the forte.[38]

Mrs. Perry also quoted Dorethie Behethlem as repeating to her the gossip that Joan Wright was a witch in Kecoughtan before she came to Surry. Mrs. Perry went on to connect the accused's practices with her former life in England, though exactly what purpose this served is not clear.

And fourther this deponent [sayeth] that good wiefe did tell her that when she lived at *hull,* beinge one day Chirninge of butter there cam a woman to the howse who was accompted for a witch, wherevppon she by directions from her dame Clapt the Chirne staffe to the bottom of the Chirne and clapt her handes across vppon the top of it by which means the witch was not able to stire owt of the place where she was for the space of six howers after which time good wiefe *Wright* desired her dame to aske the woman why she did not gett her gone, wherevppon the witche fell downe on her knees and asked her forgivenes and saide her hande was in the Chirne, and could not stire before her maide lifted vpp the staffe of the Chirne, which the saide good wiefe *Wright* did, and the witch went awaye, but to her ℔severance [perception] the witch had both her handes at libertie, and this good wiefe *Wright* affirmeth to be trewe. Fourther Mrs *Pery* sayeth that good wiefe *Wright* told her, that she was at *Hull* her dame beinge sick suspected her selfe to be bewiched, and told good wiefe *Wright* of it, wherevppon by directione from her dame, That at the cominge of a woman, which was suspected, to take a horshwe and flinge it into the oven and when it was red hott, To fflinge it into her dames urine, and so long as the horshwe was hott, the witch was sick at the harte, And when the Irone was colde she was well againe, And this good wiefe *Wright* affirmeth to be trwe alsoe.[39]

A brief testimony from Alice Baylie that Goodwife Wright confessed that she could prophesy death concluded this day's testimony. A week later two people whose testimony had been given second hand appeared in person. Robert Thresher deposed the story of his hens and the prognostication of Elizabeth Arundle's approaching demise.[40] Elizabeth Gates now testified personally regarding Goody Wright's putting spells on chickens in "Kickotan" and further that "goodwiefe *Wright* Threatened her maide she said she would make her dance naked and stand before the Tree"![41]

---

[38]McIlwaine, *Minutes,* p. 112.
[39]*Ibid.*
[40]McIlwaine, *Minutes,* p. 114
[41]*Ibid.*

Poor Goodman Robert Wright, probably in real perplexity, was able amid all this only to swear that "he hath been maried to his wiefe sixteene yeers, but knoweth nothinge by her touching the Crime she is accused of."[42] Since he arrived in the *Swan* in 1608,[43] it is clear that they were married in Virginia.

Evidently the case against Joan Wright was not considered a strong one. As we have noted, there is no record of a presentation for trial. The pattern of evidence, however, is similar to that appearing in the later records of the colony. There are here none of the melodramatic events testified to by children and adults in Salem Village in the 1690's, nor even the accusation of depraved and vicious living on the part of the accused and those associated with her. Here is a series of charges growing out of the griefs and resentments accompanying untimely deaths and perhaps partially from the ill temper of Goody Wright, who may have herself more than half believed that she held the powers her detractors claimed for her. Whenever she lost her temper, it is probable that she at least pretended to possess these powers.

There is no extant known record of another case until 1641, when the period of the Commonwealth had actually begun. Perhaps the several Virginia cases of the next twenty years after this date are more the result of increase in population than of Puritan influence. There is no slightest hint of any ecclesiastical influence save in one of them. And this case is the only one of which the record is extant indicating severe punishment of the accused. In November 1656 in Northumberland County a minister, David Lindsaye, brought accusations against William Harding of "witchcraft sorcery etc."

And an able jury of Twenty-four men were empanelled to try the matter by verdict of which jury they found part of the Articles proved by several deposicons. The Court doth therefore order that the said Wm. Harding shall forthwith receave ten stripes upon his bare back and forever to be Banished this County and that hee depart within the space of two moneths And also to pay all the charges of Court.[44]

One is tempted to suspect Puritan leanings in the Reverend David Lindsaye, a Scot of excellent family.[45] More strongly one may suspect that it was

---

[42]McIlwaine, *Minutes*, p. 112.

[43]J. C. Hotten, ed., *The Original Lists of Persons of Quality . . . Who Went from Great Britain to the American Plantations, 1600-1700 . . .* (New York, 1931), p. 261. The couple had two children who were living in 1624/5.

[44]*WMQ*, 1st ser., I (January 1893), 69.

[45]David Lindsey, Lindsy, Lindsay, or Lindsaye (1603-1667), minister of Yeocomico Parish, was "the first and lawful sonne of the Rt Honorable Sir Hierome Lindsay, K^{nt} of the Mount, Lord-Lyon-King-at-Arms," and a Doctor of Divinity. He left children in Virginia. "Rev. David Lindsy," *WMQ*, 1st ser., XVI (October 1908), 136-138.

the voice of ecclesiastical authority which resulted in the conviction. In Scotland, in New England, and in the Puritan parishes of old England the clergy thundered if any person charged with witchcraft was not prosecuted to the limit.[46] But before we return to 1641 and the more characteristic Virginia investigations, we should perhaps mention the one situation in which an execution for witchcraft is recorded in Virginia.

The reader will observe that we do not say record of execution in Virginia. Conway Robinson summarizes the matter laconically in the only surviving evidence: "Captn Bennett had to appear at the admiralty court to answer the putting to death of *Kath Grady* as a witch at sea."[47] Thus Virginia in 1654 called immediately to account a sea captain who had probably been pressured into executing a poor old woman during a storm or period of sickness in the long voyage. And the court did so despite the fact that witches' malignancy at sea was a common superstition. Ten years and more later the English State Papers were to include an official letter describing solemnly the anticipated loss of a British ship with all on board, because two witches sat in the maintop and could not be dislodged.[48] Virginia can hardly be held responsible for this death, which came within its jurisdiction only because Jamestown was the ship captain's next port of call. But now back to 1641.

In April of that year the wife of George Barker was accused of being a witch by Jane Rookens. The depositions before the General Court, however, are directed against Jane Rookens as a scandalmonger, not against the alleged witch. "The said Rookens" claimed that she did not remember what she had said but was sorry anyway. The court ordered that William Rookens, Jane's husband, pay the Barkers' expenses and the charges of court.[49] It is the first clearcut triumph for sweet reasonableness in the handling of the subject.

On December 1, 1657, Barbara Wingborough was arraigned as a witch before the General Court but acquitted—no further record exists.[50] But we do have a few entries for the period from county court books of other cases and enactments concerning them. Lower Norfolk jurors especially had become incensed at the increase in gossip and accusation of witchcraft. They

---

[46]Wertenbaker, *First Americans*, p. 147.

[47]McIlwaine, *Minutes*, p. 504. The actual records for this period are missing. We have only the summarizing notes of Conway Robinson as evidence.

[48]Captain Silas Taylor to Williamson, November 2, 1662, Harwich. *Calendar of State Papers, Domestic, Charles II, November 1662-September 1668* (London, 1893), p. 4.

[49]McIlwaine, *Minutes*, p. 476.

[50]McIlwaine, *Minutes*, p. 504.

resolved to take severe measures against the principal culprits. On May 23, 1655, at a private court held "at the house of Mr. Edward Hall in Linhaven" they ordered:

> Whereas div[rs] dangerous & scandalous speeches have beene raised by some psons concerning sev[r]all women in this Countie termeing them to be Witches, whereby their reputacons have beene much impaired, and theire lives brought in question (ffor avoydeing the like offence) It is by this Co[rt] ordered that what pson soer shall hereafter raise any such like scandall concerninge any partie whatsoev[r] and shall not be able to pve the same, both upon oath, and by sufficient witnes, such pson soe offending shall in the first place paie A thousand pounds of tob: and likewyse be lyeable to further Censure of the Co[rt].[51]

Four and a half years later, in December 1659, the court showed that it meant business. Ann Godby was arraigned for "Slanders & scandalls Cast upon Women under the notion of Witches," especially for taking and abusing the good name of Mistress Robinson in this respect. After receiving several depositions attesting the scandalmongering, the court decided:

> It is therefore ord[d] that the s[d] Tho: Godby [her husband] shall pay three hundred pounds of tob[o] & Caske fine for her Contempt of the menconed order, (being the first time) & also pay & defray the Cost of sute together with the Witnesses Charges at twenty pounds tob[o] p day als exec.[52]

Perhaps Thomas Godby and other husbands like him touched in that tender part the purse complained to their legislative representatives. Whether instigated by the Burgesses from Lower Norfolk or not, the General Assembly in 1662 passed "An Act for Punishment of Scandalous Persons" which gave the innocent husbands of such persons some protection.

> Whereas many babling women slander and scandalize theire neighbours for which theire poore husbands are often involved in chargeable and vexatious suits, and cast in great damnages. Be it therefore enacted by the authorities aforesaid that in actions of slander occasioned by the wife after judgment passed for the damnages, the woman shall be punished by ducking and if the slander be soe enormous as to be adjudged at greater damnages then five hundred pounds of tob[o] then the woman to suffer a ducking for each five hundred pounds of tob[o] adjudged against the husband if he refuse to pay the tobacco[53]

---

[51]*WMQ*, 1st ser., II (July 1893), 58; also in *Lower Norfolk County Virginia Antiquary*, III (1899-1901), 152.

[52]*WMQ*, 1st ser., II, 59; also in *Lower Norfolk County Virginia Antiquary*, IV (1902), 36.

[53]In Ms. "Acts of Grand Assemblie holden at James Cittie," Jefferson Collection, Library of Congress; also in Hening, *Statutes*, II, 166-167; and G. L. Chumbley, *Colonial Justice in Virginia* (Richmond, 1938), pp. 129-130.

Thus during a period when the greatest English witch hunter, Matthew Hopkins, was at work,[54] Virginia colonists were becoming more and more skeptical regarding allegations of witchcraft — if we are to believe their treatment of such matters. And after the Restoration this skeptical treatment in general continued, as the 1662 enactment indicated that it might.

In November 1668 a judgment was secured before the General Court for calling a woman and her children witches. Pardon was craved, though we do not know what the penalty was.[55] In 1671 in Northumberland County the local court or jury heard depositions accusing a prominent woman, wife of Captain Christopher Neal, of praying that evil befall certain persons. The first deposition is apparently that of a man (Edward Le Breton) who is testifying that he has heard Master Edward Cole defame Mrs. Neal in this way (he has already reported Cole's gossip of her putting death spells on people and cattle):

And further depose that now that his wife was sick he did accuse Mrs. Neal of it alsoe. But a certyne time he sent for Mrs. Neal to come to see his wife, and she did come and after that he saw her come over the threshhold where there is an horshoe nailed and that when she was by his wife shee prayed heartily for her he was then psuaded to the contrary again. And this I heard him relate of all that is above not 10 days since at the house of John Cockrell[56]

Others attest to Cole's defamation of the woman, and then the record concludes with Cole's own acknowledgment of the truth of the depositions "as [to his] tending to defame her with the aspersion of being a witch." He admits that the words "were passionately spoken." He obligated himself to pay all costs of the suit, the whole case affording evidence that all the babblers were not women.[57]

Lower Norfolk County, which had indicated its exasperation with witch-accusers and scandalmongers, was still having trouble after the Stuarts returned to the throne. Certain women continued to act in suspicious ways, and now even people of position in the county were accusing them. On June 15, 1675, the Lower Norfolk jury considered the charges of a justice of the peace and quondam member of the House of Burgesses, Captain William Carver, against Joan or Jane, the wife of Lazarus Jenkins, "concerning

[54]Kittredge, *Witchcraft*, pp. 331-333.
[55]Another Robinson notation in McIlwaine, *Minutes*, p. 513. This may be the same woman mentioned in an entry of October 16, 1668: "Alice Stephens accused as a witch, but not cleared."
[56]*WMQ*, 1st ser., XVII (April 1909), 247-248.
[57]Northumberland County, Record Book, 1666-1672, pp. 179-181, 186-187. A number of depositions not printed in the *WMQ* (cf. note 56) appear in the original records. Only a part of the apology was printed in *WMQ*.

her being familiar with evill spiritts and useing witchcraft &c."[58] Carver was a quarrelsome man, and there was already ill feeling between him and the Jenkinses recorded in a property suit. But the jury ordered a special investigative committee of men and women to "Repayre to the house of the said Lauzarus Jenkings upon the 17th of this Instant June and there to make diligent search concerning the same according to the 118 chapter of doulton."[59] If anything was found, she was to be dealt with after the report was returned to the jury. Presumably the women of this panel made the personal "investigation."

The order was of course that they search the body of the accused for secret witch's marks and probably her house for images. The most prominent of the marks, and the most usual, was the teat by which the Devil was said to suck his victims and collaborators. It might be found in the privy parts or even behind the ear,[60] but it was most commonly discovered beneath the left breast. Evidently the committee found nothing, for Jane Jenkins was not brought to trial.

The Lower Norfolk grand juries were not done with such searching, however. On January 15, 1678/9, John Salmon brought complaint that Mrs. Alice Cartwrite had bewitched his child and thus caused its death. This time the sheriff was ordered to summons for the next day "an able Jury of women" to "Serch the said Alice according to the direction of the Court. Their report was terse:

In the diff betweane Jno Salmon plaintiff agt Alice the wife of Thomas Cartwrite defendt a Jury of women (Mrs. Mary Chichester forewoman) being Impaneled did in open Court upon their oathes declare that they haveing delegently Searched the body of the said Alice & Cann find noe Suspitious marks whereby they Can Judg her to be a witch; butt onely what may and Is usuall on other women. It is therefore the Judgmt of the Court and ordered that Shee bee acquitted & her husbands bond given for her appearance to bee given up.[61]

58*WMQ*, 1st ser., III (January 1895), 163-166. Carver was to end his life as one of the principal followers of Nathaniel Bacon in the rebellion.

59Michael Dalton, *The Country Justice* (first ed. 1618) is the book or authority referred to. This manual prescribes tests for the detection of witches, including a discussion of the location of the teat or teats mentioned below

60See, for example, the testimony of John Bridgeman, Bishop of Chester, May 11, 1635 (*Pryings among Private Papers, Chiefly of the Seventeenth and Eighteenth Centuries. By the Author of "A Life of Sir Kenelm Digby,"* London, 1905). In Exeter in 1682, old women who were convinced that they were witches described "the sucking devils with saucer eyes so naturally that the Jury could not chose but believe them" (Lord Chief Justice North to Secretary of State Jenkins, August 19, 1682, *Calendar of State Papers Domestic, Charles II*, London, 1932, p. 347).

61*WMQ*, 1st ser., I (January 1893), 70; also in *Lower Norfolk County Virginia Antiquary*, I, (1895-1896), 56-57.

On July 8, 1698, John and Ann Byrd sued in the Princess Anne (formerly Lower Norfolk) court in two separate bills Charles Kinsey and John Potts, who "falsely and Scandalously Defamed them," saying among other things that Ann had ridden Kinsey from his house to Elizabeth Russell's and had "rid [Pitts] along the seaside & home to his own house, by which kind of Discourse they were Reported & rendered as if they were witches, or in league with the Devill."[62] Both defendants acknowledged that they had made such accusations, though one admitted that he might have dreamed of the ride. Evidently the jury had some doubts about the whole matter, or at least some prejudice against the plaintiffs as troublemakers, for both verdicts were rendered in favor of the defendants.[63]

The most famous of Lower Norfolk (Princess Anne after 1691) County trials was that of Grace Sherwood in 1705/6, a date lying outside the period covered in other portions of this essay. Since origins of the case lie in the seventeenth century, however, it should be considered briefly. As early as February 4, 1697/8, and September 10, 1698, James and Grace Sherwood had sued Richard Capps, John and Jane Gisburne, and Anthony and Elizabeth Barnes for defamation or slander. The Gisburnes had said that Grace "was a witch and bewitched their piggs to death and bewitched their Cotton." Elizabeth Barnes avowed that "the said Grace came to her one night and rid her and went out of the key hole or crack of the door like a black Catt." As in the case of the Byrds at about the same time, the verdicts were rendered in favor of the defendants.[64]

By 1705/6 Princess Anne County had obviously grown tired of Mrs. Sherwood as a general nuisance. Following a long series of investigations during the spring of 1705/6 inspired by the charges of Luke Hill and his wife, the case went to the General Court (the Governor and Council) and the Attorney General. The latter considered the charges too general and sent them back to the county. He suggested that a jury of women search Grace's house for suspicious images. This jury was summoned but refused to appear. A second female panel was summoned to search her body as well as the house. They likewise refused to appear. On July 5, 1706, a county jury of justices of the peace, despairing of the feminine jury and wishing to settle the long-drawn-out affair, ordered Grace Sherwood "by her own Con-

---

[62]"Riding" their victims was a favorite sport with witches, according to English folklore.
[63]*WMQ*, 1st ser., II (July 1893), 59-60; also in *Lower Norfolk County Virginia Antiquary*, I (1895), 20-21.
[64]"Record of Grace Sherwood's Trial for Witchcraft, in 1705, in Princess Anne County, Virginia," *Collections of the Virginia Historical and Philosophical Society*, I (Richmond, 1833), 69-78; *WMQ*, 1st ser., III (October 1894-April 1895), 99-100, 190-192, 242-245.

sent to be tried in the water by Ducking." Since the weather was rainy, the ordeal was postponed until the following Wednesday. On July 10 the said Grace was taken to John Harper's plantation and put into the water

. . . above mans Debth to try her how She Swims Therein, always having Care of her life to preserve her from Drowning, and as Soon as she Comes Out that [the sheriff] request as many Ansient and Knowing women as possible he Cann to Serch her Carefully For all teats spotts and marks about her body not usual on Others . . . and further it is ord^r that Som women be requested to Shift and Serch her before She goe into the water, that She Carry nothing about her to cause any Further Suspicion.[65]

The poor woman floated even though bound, and moreover was discovered afterwards (evidently the spectacle had attracted some women who were willing to search) to have on her private parts "two things like titts . . . of a Black Coller." According to Dalton and other authorities, this evidence was sufficient to convict her as a witch. She was ordered to be committed to the "Common Gaol" and to be secured in irons. But here the record ends. There is no indication of her appearing later before the General Court. Almost surely she survived further ordeal, for there is record of a Grace Sherwood's will dated August 20, 1733, and probated in 1740,[66] and all details indicate that the ducked woman and the testatrix were one and the same. That the name Witchduck, given the site of the ordeal on an inlet of Lynnhaven Bay, still exists is itself good evidence that such methods of trial were extremely rare in Virginia.

But if we are to believe the detractors, all Satan's alleged minions had not concentrated themselves in Princess Anne in the late seventeenth century. On November 1, 1694, in Westmoreland County, William Earle accused Phyllis Money of casting a spell over Henry Dunkin's horse, of teaching her daughter, Dunkin's wife, to be a witch, and of having taught Dunkin himself to be a wizard. Though Phyllis sued for damages, she received none. A year later Henry Dunkin himself accused John Dunkin and his wife Elizabeth of witchcraft and stated that Elizabeth boasted that she was

---

[65]For the best collection of the records of this case see George Lincoln Burr, ed., *Narratives of the Witchcraft Cases, 1648-1706* (New York, 1914), pp. 435-442. Mr. Burr examined the records personally, though many of them had been published earlier in the *William and Mary Quarterly* and the *Lower Norfolk County Virginia Antiquary*. For a description of a ducking platform and stool, see Susie M. Ames, *Studies of the Virginia Eastern Shore in the Seventeenth Century* (Richmond, 1940), p. 190; or E. M. Earle, *Curious Punishments of Bygone Days* (New York, 1896), pp. 18-20. The reader will recall from the Virginia Act of 1662 that ducking might be a punishment as well as a trial. Grace Sherwood may have accepted it in part as such.

[66]Burr, ed., *Narratives*, p. 442. See also *WMQ*, 1st ser., IV (July 1895), 19-20. The will was presented to the court October 1, 1740.

regularly sucked by the Devil. Had this charge been proved, she was liable to have been burnt at the stake. Instead, she sued for 40,000 pounds of tobacco as damages. She was awarded forty pounds.[67]

In King and Queen County in 1695 William Morris sued a Mrs. Ball for accusing his wife Eleanor of sorcery. Just the year before Mrs. Ball had been sure that Nell Cane had ridden her twice. Now the jury found Mrs. Ball guilty of defamation, five hundred pounds of tobacco being assessed in favor of the plaintiff.[68]

In most of these cases, had there been a strong belief in witchcraft on the part of the jury, the person accused would probably have been arrested and prosecuted on the original criminal charge. Instead, the person or persons originally accused are themselves the plaintiffs in civil suits. That they received small damages or no damages or even dismissal was probably due to the jury's belief that the actual damage to personal reputation was small. In other instances, especially when the originally accused was involved more than once in suits, the jury may have considered that the plaintiff, though wrongfully accused, was actually a nuisance to the community who had brought the scandal upon herself by boasting of supernatural powers, and that it would not encourage such a nuisance by awarding damages.

That his Satanic Majesty continued to exist as the great enemy of mankind was kept continually before later seventeenth-century Virginians by means other than the witchcraft cases. The stock phraseology in court records for many crimes, from petty thievery to child murder, was that the accused or convicted was "lead and instigated by the divell."[69] The Devil's presence was felt too in trial by touch, when the suspected murderer was made to touch or stroke the body of his alleged victim. In Accomack County, for example, when Paul Carter touched the corpse the change in its appearance was proof that he was guilty.[70] Then too it must have been the Devil who in 1676 bewitched the Indian boy, the son of Doegs. The apparently-dead child recovered when he was baptized.[71] This, incidentally, is the only extant end-of-the-century record even suggesting active contemporary Indian connection with witchcraft.

Thus Satan seemed to at least a few to continue to honor Virginia with his presence. That Evil was incarnate, that it employed supernatural means

---

[67]Bruce, *Institutional History*, I, 284.

[68]Essex County, Orders, etc., 1692-1695, pp. 240, 246-247.

[69]E.g., "Ordeal by Touch in Virginia," *VMHB*, IV (October 1896), 189, 192, 194. See also county records of Accomack and Northampton.

[70]Accomack Wills, Deeds, & Orders, 1678-1682, pp. 159-160. See Ames, *Studies*, pp. 175-176; *VMHB*, IV (October 1896), 159-160.

[71]*Virginia Historical Register*, III (April 1850), 66; *VMHB*, XVIII (October 1909), 420.

through chosen human beings to tempt mankind, the average Virginian of 1700 was apparently not at all convinced of. A few individuals, usually simple and superstitious country folk resentful of personal loss in family or property, looked around for a cause or outlet for their emotions. A busybody neighbor who might pretend to occult powers seriously or playfully was a natural candidate for suspicion. But for decades the Virginia justices and juries had weighed critically the charges of intercourse with Satan.[72] There is no evidence that any person was ever driven to confession. Indeed there is no evidence, even in the earlier part of the century, of self confession—springing from personal hallucination—as had happened so often in other places. When charges formal or informal were made, the result in almost every instance, instead of being to bring the accused eventually to rope or fagot,[73] was that the accused brought suit for damages. The one severe punishment—exile and whipping—came only when a Scottish-born clergyman of the Commonwealth period was the plaintiff or prosecutor. Usually the disposition made of the Devil's alleged disciples remained in Virginia a secular and legal matter. That his Satanic Majesty made appearances in human form never got much acknowledgment from any Virginia lawyer or jury.

[72]Perhaps it should be noted that as late as 1736 Virginia justices were warned that witchcraft was still a legal crime though its existence was the subject of controversy among learned men; that weak evidence should never be accepted but that most evidence would be circumstantial; and that conviction of first offense was punishable by one year in prison and quarterly pillory and confession and conviction of second offense was a "Felony, without Clergy." See George Webb, *The Office and Authority of a Justice of Peace* (Williamsburg, 1736), pp. 361-362.

[73]Despite the fact that the New England witches of the 1690's were hanged, there are many records of burnings in British history, especially in Scottish documents.

NOTE.

WITCHCRAFT IN NEW YORK.

THE remarks of the writer of the foregoing *Notes and Observations* in connection with the case of Goodwife Garlick (*ante*, pp. 238, 239), however judicious in general, seem to require some additions by way of correction. Elizabeth Garlick, wife of Joshua Garlick of East Hampton, was brought before the magistrates of that town, on suspicion of witchcraft; and the examination resulted in the order of March 19, 1657–8, to send her for trial to Connecticut, whose jurisdiction was at the same time fully recognized. Her trial took place before a Court of Magistrates, called for the purpose, in Hartford, on the 5th of May, 1658, and resulted in her acquittal. Gov. John Winthrop presided in the Court. An account of the proceedings can be found in the *Historical Magazine*, vol. vi. 53; and a letter printed in the *Colonial Records of Connecticut*, 1636–1665, Appx. v. p. 572, from the copy on file among the archives of that State, in the handwriting of Governor Winthrop, may complete the record of the case.

Another case is said to have occurred in 1660, when Mary Wright, of Oyster Bay, being suspected of witchcraft, was sent to Massachusetts, where, upon trial, she was acquitted of that charge, but convicted of being a Quaker, and banished. Hutchinson's account of this affair (*History of Mass.* : i. 202) furnishes no notice of the alleged witchcraft; and her answers to the Court upon examination, as well as the punishment, indicate that she was in Massachusetts of her own accord, to give her testimony against the rulers there for their cruelty in putting Mary Dyer to death. She was one of those discharged with Wenlock Christopherson in June, 1661, and driven out of that jurisdiction. (Bishop : *N. E. Judged*, 165, part ii. 35.)

In 1665, Ralph Hall and his wife were accused of witchcraft at Brookhaven, and the cause was tried before the Court of Assizes at New York, terminating in their acquittal. The proceedings were printed by Mr. Yates in the appendix to his edition of Smith's *History of New York*, and again in the *Documentary History of New York*, vol. iv. vii. by Dr. O'Callaghan.

18

In 1670, one Katharine Harrison, of Wethersfield in Connecticut, had been indicted, tried by a jury, and found guilty of witchcraft. But the Court refused to sentence her to death or further imprisonment, and discharged her upon payment of her just fees ; at the same time " willing her to minde the fulfilment of removeing from Weathersfield, which is that will tende most to her owne safety and the contentment of the people who are her neighbours." Thus banished from Connecticut, she came to settle in Westchester. She was immediately complained of, and presently ordered to remove, with an admonition to return to her former place of abode. Various proceedings, however, followed, upon which she was bound over to appear at the Assizes upon suspicion of witchcraft ; where she was promptly released from her obligation, with " liberty to remain in the towne of Westchester where she now resides, or anywhere else in the Government during her pleasure." *Colonial Records of Connecticut,* 1665–77 : 132. *Documentary History of New York,* vol. iv. vii.

All these proceedings were taken at common law, or under the English Statute of James I. No law against witchcraft has been found on the statute-book of New York. At the same time, there is no room for doubt that the principal clergymen then in the colony were firm believers in witchcraft, and it may fairly be presumed that far the greater portion of the community shared in their faith. Yet we are informed by Cotton Mather that the opinions of the Dutch and French Ministers of New York, furnished to Sir William Phips while the storm of delusion on the subject was raging in Massachusetts, contributed to destroy the authority of " the spectral testimony," then too much in credit there. Some interesting particulars respecting their intervention were found among the papers of the Rev. JOHN MILLER who was Chaplain to the King's forces at New York in 1692–95. Sir William Phips having become very uneasy upon the convictions and executions which had taken place within his jurisdiction, applied to the New York Ministers through Chief Justice Dudley, for their opinions and advice. Seven questions were presented for consideration, and either directly or through the other ministers, Mr. Miller's opinions also were desired.

" *Question* 1. Is it a fact that there have been witches from the beginning of the world to the present time ?

" 2. What is the true definition of a witch, and in what does his power (*formalis ratio*) consist ?

"3. Does God justly permit the Devil to show and represent to those who are bewitched the images of innocent persons as if they were the authors of the witchcraft?

"4. Is previous malice and cursing to be necessarily proved in order to convict a witch?

"5. Is any one whose figure appears to the person bewitched, and is by him accused as the author of the witchcraft, to be adjudged guilty, and convicted of the witchcraft?

"6. Is the accusation alone of the party supposed to be bewitched, sufficient to prove a man who lives piously, justly, and soberly, guilty?

"7. If the person bewitched, after suffering various and heavy torments, after the paroxysm is over, appears of a strong and firm habit of body, without receiving any other damage, is it not a cause for suspicion of delusion or diabolical possession?

In answer to the First Question, Mr. Miller asserted his belief in the actual existence of Witchcraft from the beginning of the world, taking his authority from Scripture and a variety of heathen authors.

"2. Witchcraft is the art of torturing and destroying men, and it is an art, because it practises certain forms of incantation, uses composition from herbs, &c. : it is performed by the assistance of the Devil, otherwise it is not Witchcraft : the coöperation of the Devil is the *ratio formalis*.

"3. The hearts of men are unknown to us ; we cannot say whether those whom we suppose to be innocent are really so ; and perhaps God permits their representation (in vision to the enchanted) that he may punish their sins, by the subsequent disgrace and punishment which they endure.

"4. If previous malice, &c., can be proved, it will confirm the Witchcraft proved otherwise by all or the principal circumstances mentioned in the *English* statute ; but they are not necessarily to be proved, because legal proof of the circumstances expressed in the statute will suffice for the condemnation of the Witch.

"5, 6. Men, whether they live soberly or impiously, are scarce on that account to be publickly accused, much less found guilty, because the minds of men, especially of the ignorant or depraved, can easily be and frequently are deceived by the Devil.

"7. Since whatever the Devil himself does, or men do by his coöperation, tends to the ruin of those who are tortured, and since I understand some to be in this manner tortured, who, after the paroxysm, are cheerful, healthful and merry, I suppose them not to be maliciously enchanted by any sorcerer, but deluded by the Devil to promote the misery of mankind."

The only account we have of the opinions of the Dutch and French Ministers is that of Mather, who states that " they gave it in under their hands that if we believe no *venefick witchcraft*, we must renounce the Scripture of God, and the consent of almost all the world ; but that yet the *apparition* of a person afflicting another, is a very insufficient proof of a *witch;* nor is it inconsistent with the holy and righteous government of God over men, to permit the affliction of the neighbours, by devils in the *shape* of good men ; and that a good name, obtained by a *good life*, shall not be lost by *meer spectral accusations*."

To the record of this beneficent intervention it may not be improper to add a reference to the fact that several of these victims of persecution in Massachusetts sought and found refuge and protection in New York, until the danger was past.   The historian of the Witchcraft Delusion, the Rev. CHARLES W. UPHAM, D.D., says : " The fact that when Massachusetts was suffering from a fierce and bloody, but brief, persecution by its own Government, New York opened so kind and secure a shelter for those fortunate enough to escape to it, ought to be forever held in grateful remembrance by the people of the old Bay State, and constitutes a part of the history of the Empire State of which she may well be proud." *Historical Magazine*, 2d Series, vi. 215.

Witchcraft in New France
in The Seventeenth Century:
The Social Aspect

Jonathan L. Pearl
Scarborough College, Ontario

Quebec in the seventeenth century is often depicted as a little France in the New World. Populated by first and second generation arrivals, and governed by officials sent over from France, there are many areas in which this picture has some accuracy. But there are others where it does not. There were significant differences in the way in which New and Old France dealt with the problem of witchcraft. These differences were the result of important though perhaps subtle differences in the structure of the two societies.

For the entire seventeenth century, witchcraft was perceived as a significant social, religious and legal problem in France as well as in the whole of Western Europe. In the first quarter of the century, there existed near unanimity on the reality and the danger of witchcraft and on the need to punish convicted witches with death. This unanimity came to an end in the 1630's and 1640's as French intellectuals, in Paris and in provincial capitals, began to lose interest in witchcraft. There was strenuous debate on the danger and authenticity of witches, which deeply affected the members of the Parliament of Paris, who ended their persecution of witches in 1640.[1] The cessation was imposed on the entire kingdom in 1682.[2] The high courts, composed of members of the social and intellectual elites, influenced by ideas of the new scientific rationalism, turned their attentions away from witchcraft.

But the vast majority of Frenchmen continued to believe in magic and witchcraft. They lived in fear of spells cast against themselves, their livestock and their crops. They feared the Devil, and tried to stay alert to avoid his snares. And they continued to accuse others of using

[1]For an excellent discussion of the ending of witchcraft trials in France, see: Robert Mandrou, *Magistrats et Sorciers en France au XVIIe Siècle* (Paris, 1968).
[2]*Ibid.*

diabolical means to harm them. If the high courts paid little heed to these accusations after 1682, the local courts often took these matters very seriously. This world view persisted through the eighteenth century, and has even survived into the mid-twentieth century, among French rural laboring classes.[3]

One could, with justification, expect to find a similar witchcraft problem, with trials and executions, in seventeenth century Quebec. Certainly, in the English colonies of North America trials were conducted, and those found guilty were executed up to the very late seventeenth century, later than in the mother country. Recent studies estimate that there were over three hundred cases tried in New England.[4] The best known of these, in Salem Village, Massachusetts, has been the subject of several probing studies.[5]

Surprisingly, New France was almost untouched by the sort of witchcraft accusations and trials which were endemic in New England and Europe throughout the seventeenth century. There were a few cases in which witchcraft, or spells, seem to have been a factor, but they were not formal witchcraft accusations and trials, and one does not detect the same sense of terror as in the European situation.

After a brief examination of a few well known cases in Quebec, this paper will examine several aspects of the culture and society of New France which related to beliefs and practices of witchcraft. We will, through a comparison of these areas with the society and culture of France, attempt to determine the differences which resulted in an almost total lack of witchcraft persecution in New France.

In his study *"La Sorcellerie au Québec du XVIIe siècle*, Robert-Lionel Seguin, a well known student of the folklore and culture of old Quebec, lists the cases which he has been able to locate in the archives, memoires and documents of the seventeenth century. He presents some twenty-two instances attributable to diabolical or supernatural involvements. However, the majority of these are only passing references in books or letters or in trials for normal criminal offenses.[6] They are not witchcraft cases, in the European sense, at all. Even if Seguin, and the many other historians and folklorists of Quebec have missed some important cases, there can be no doubt that we are dealing with a very low incidence of witchcraft.

---

[3]Constantin Bila, *La Croyance à la Magie au XVIIe Siècle en France* (Paris, 1925), and Marcelle Bouteiller, *Sorciers et Jeteurs de Sort* (Paris, 1958).
[4]Sally Smith Booth, *The Witches of Early America* (New York, 1975), p. 114.
[5]Chadwick Hansen, *Witchcraft at Salem* (New York, 1969), and Paul Boyer and Stephen Nissenbaum, *Salem Possessed* (Cambridge, Mass., 1974).
[6]Robert Lionel Sequin, *La Sorcellerie au Québec du XVIIe Siècle* (Ottawa, 1971) p. 32.

One rare case came beore the seigneurial court of Montreal in 1658. A disappointed suitor, named Besnard, cast a spell on his former sweetheart by the tying of ritual knots in a string. This spell *(nouer l'aiguilette)* was a traditional way of causing impotence in men. It was widely practiced in France and greatly feared. The whole area of human sexuality and fertility was a special target for diabolical spells. Since failure to carry out the sexual act, or to conceive was perceived as very abnormal, and quite mysterious, it was quickly ascribed to supernatural interference.

In this case, the newlyweds, frightened at hearing of the spell, found it impossible to consummate their marriage and accused Besnard of causing "perpetual impotence caused by malefice." The court dissolved the marriage and found Besnard guilty. He was fined seven hundred pounds and banished from Montreal.[7] His accusers quickly remarried other partners. The ex-husband eventually fathered fourteen children and the ex-wife bore eleven,[8] which of course confirmed, in their minds, that their earlier problems had been caused by the Devil and his earthly agent, Besnard.

Seguin states that this verdict demonstrated the mildness of the courts in New France, compared to those of Old France, where, he states, anyone found guilty of witchcraft would have been executed. In fact while thousands of people were executed for witchcraft in Europe, recent research has revealed that many people accused of witchcraft were acquitted, and of the found guilty, a substantial percentage did not suffer capital punishment.[9] Besnard's defense, that he was only joking in order to frighten his rival, might also have saved his life in France. The court's judgment was a severe one, which clearly demonstrates the seriousness with which the casting of spells was regarded by the authorities of New France.

The Jesuit, Paul Ragueneau, in his devotional biography of Mother Catherine of Saint Augustine, reported an execution for witchcraft in Quebec in 1661. A miller was accused of causing the demonic possession of sixteen year old Barbe Hallay, who displayed all the classic symptoms of that affliction. She was taken to the convent in Quebec City and put under the care of Mother Catherine who helped her to recover. The accused witch was tried and found guilty of a number of charges, including blasphemy, profaning the sacraments and false conversion from Protestantism. According to Ragueneau, he was hanged.[10]

[7]*Ibid.*, p. 33.

[8]*Ibid.*, p. 34.

[9]E.W. Monter, "Witchcraft in Geneva, 1537-1662", *Journal of Modern History*, XLIII (June 1971) p. 186.

[10]Paul Ragueneau, *La Vie de la Mère Catherine de Saint Augustine, Religieuse Hospitalière de la Miséricorde de Québec en la Nouvelle France* (Paris, 1671), p. 163.

But there is very little supporting evidence in this case. Seguin states that this miller, not named by Ragueneau, was one Daniel Vuil. But it is not clear why Vuil was executed. The October 1661 entry of the *Jesuit Relations* relates only that, "Daniel Vuil was hanged, − or rather, shot, − and on the 11th another named la violette; and one flogged on Monday the 10th for having traded brandy to the savages."[11]

As mentioned earlier, the high courts of France were in the process of removing witchcraft from the criminal statutes in the second half of the seventeenth century. It would not be surprising for officials in New France, who were of a similar intellectual milieu as the judges of the French courts, and who looked to Paris for guidance and instruction, to tend towards moderation and scepticism in matters relating to witchcraft. They certainly were not witchhunters, interested in encouraging accusations and trials. But this in itself cannot explain the unusual situation in New France. Although the French Parliaments stopped witchcraft persecutions, and ordered the courts below them to conform to their practices, it required a long and difficult fight to end trials and punishment of witches. For most of the people of the kingdom continued to believe, and to accuse others of inflicting evil on them.

These beliefs were especially tenacious in the countryside. Peasant accusations developed from the peasant's own world view, in which a belief in magic and witchcraft played a large role. One finds, in an examination of popular folklore, a profound belief in the supernatural and in the ability of evilly inclined people to manipulate supernatural and natural forces to harm their enemies and society in general. Those Frenchmen, of all social levels, who crossed over to New France took their cultural and religious values with them. Their folkloric and religious outlook was identical to those of their friends and neighbors who stayed at home.

The colonists brought their demons with them. The case of Mother Catherine of Saint Augustine is well known; she was obsessed with demons, who appeared to her disguised as Jesus Christ, the Virgin Mary, and the martyred Father Brebeuf. But such an obsession was not at all the same thing as the notorious diabolical possessions, by witches working in league with the Devil, of entire convents, as had taken place in France. Mother Catherine's biographer, Father Ragueneau, carefully distinguished between her lifelong obsession, which was caused by Satan to tempt her from her Faith, and diabolical possession in which demons acted through human agents to take control of the victim.[12] Mother Catherine resisted her obsession by prayer and service to others,

[11]R. Gold Thwaites, ed., *The Jesuit Relations and Allied Documents*, v. 4, p. 187.
[12]Ragueneau, *op. cit.*

not by being exorcised. No other person was ever accused of causing her problem, and no one was executed as Louis Gaufridi in Aix-en-Province or Urbain Grandier in Loudun had been for causing the possession of nuns.

Traditional French folklore persisted and flourished in New France, which reserved a major place for magical and supernatural occurrences, both good and evil. Paul Sebillot, the great French folklorist, cited an interesting example of the transplanting process. "The emigrants from Saintonge and Poitou," he wrote, "who, to a large extent, contributed to the colonization of New France, brought with them the name of the *Chasse Galérie,* and also probably the legend."[13] The habitants altered the legend a bit by removing the hell-bound hunters from their horses and placing them in canoes.[14] But the doomed souls continued to be heard shouting their ancient cabalistic formula "Acabri! Acabra! as they crossed the sky. The *Chasse Galérie* continued to be regarded as a portent o strange events to come.[15]

It was proverbial that the inhabitants of the Ile d'Orleans, in the St. Lawrence River near Quebec City, were inclined toward witchcraft. People from other places would go there in order to find out about the future, or about events in far-off places.[16] The people of the island were themselves afraid of the power of the Devil. They believed that if someone were dying in the night, and a friend or relative went to fetch a priest, that the Devil, well disguised, would try to delay that person so that he could gain possession of the soul of the poor one who died without a priest's absolution. They would therefore take the precaution of sending two carriages for the priest, so at least one would get through the Devil's trap.[17]

These legends and practices, and many others like them, had a strong hold on the habitants, which lasted for centuries. In the late nineteenth century, a Quebec journalist, one Joseph-Norbert Duguet, thought it necessary to try to discourage the magical beliefs among the province's working people, who "believed in the existence of hidden treasures . . (which) are guarded by an old man . . (or) a Serpent . . or evil spirits and that one cannot get them without the aid of certain formulas or conjurations which are found in various books on witchcraft and malefices."[18]

[13]Paul Sebillot, *Le Folk-Lore de France* (Paris, 1968), v. 1, p. 173.
[14]*Ibid.*
[15]*Bulletin des Recherches Historiques* VI, p. 282.
[16]*Ibid.,* X, p. 22.
[17]Ibid, V, p. 100.
[18]Joseph Norbert Duquet, *Le Véritable Petit Albert ou le Trésor du Peuple* (Quebec, 1881)

Several modern collections of the folklore of Quebec testify to the vivacity of a traditional world view, and to the close relationship of Quebec folklore to that of France. These studies reveal a continuing belief in the powers of the Devil — as a builder of churches, for example — and in the ability of certain people, who make a compact with the Devil to cast spells on people who offend them.[19] Much of this folklore centres around religion, and treats holy objects as magical talismans. In the Gaspèsie, for example, people believe that if one carries a crucifix or a piece of communion wafer in one's wallet, that the wallet will always be full of money.[20] And to recover the body of someone drowned in the sea, one was to throw the Host onto the water in the area in which the person was lost.[21] Traditional sayings and proverbs continue to be a part of everyday life in this region, though occasionally they are updated. Thus there is one saying, "It is bad luck for your car to break down on your wedding day."[22]

The logical centre of opposition to these superstitious beliefs and practices was the Church. But the Church in New France in the seventeenth century was far from the all-powerful monolith which it is often pictured to have been. It suffered from grave problems, many of which were the same as those plaguing the Church in the mother country in that period. Churchmen and civic officials in the colony were constantly begging the French government to dispatch more priests to serve the colonists, but with little success. In 1663, there were only seven secular priests in New France to serve over three thousand habitants. This basic ratio was no worse than in most parts of France, but was of course made very unsatisfactory by the vastness of the colony, by the extended pattern of settlement and by the severe winters. Priests had to travel long distances at all times of year, to bring the Church to the people.

The threat posed by this situation was perceived by the priest who wrote to his superiors in France in 1685, "it is indispensable that we have forty [priests] immediately, so that we might place priests to watch over their parishes . . . many people hear the mass only three or four times a year, and have almost no religion."[23] Another wrote, "It is a pity, Monseigneur, to see the ignorance in which the people, far distant

---

[19]Jean-Claude Dupont, *Le Légendaire de la Beauce* (Quebec, 1974) and Carmen Roy, *La Littérature Orale en Gaspésie* (Ottawa, 1955), also see the works of Marius Barbeau, E.T. Massicotte, and especially the recent works of Jean du Berger of the Archives of Folklore at Laval University, Quebec City.

[20]Roy, *op. cit.*, p. 101.

[21]*Ibid.*, p. 104.

[22]*Ibid.*, p. 99.

[23]*Rapport de l'Archiviste de la Province de Québec, 1939-40*, p. 266. (Hereafter referred to as RAPQ).

from a resident priest, live in this country."[24] A very pointed observation on the state of religious knowledge of the habitants was made by the Jesuit missionary, Father Bruyas. In a document to be read by pious Frenchmen, he discussed the mentality of the Indians, and made this comparison, "I am often asked [by the Indians], if the meat of the moose, bear, etc., is eaten in Paradise. . . they ask impertinent questions, as did one who wanted to know if they went to war in Heaven, if they killed men there; if they took scalps . . . Judge from this the mind of the savages. For my part, I compare them to our French peasants, and I do not think they are more intelligent — except some, who in truth surprise me with their answers."[25]

Both in France and in New France, the rural population suffered from religious ignorance and indifference, partly caused by the insufficient supply of priests.[26] But there are crucial differences in the two situations. In France, many priests, especially in poor rural parishes, were unable to function as moral and religious leaders and educators through their own ignorance of Christian doctrines and practices, or through moral and physical disabilities such as drunkenness or senility.[27] These priests often had to emphasize the magical or supernatural aspects of the religion in order to maintain their place in the community, and could even have stimulated witchcraft beliefs and accusations among their parishioners. In New France, on the other hand, while there were never enough priests to serve effectively the thinly-spread population, those who did make the crossing were highly educated, motivated and dedicated men who diligently worked to improve the standards of religious observance and to reduce the role of magic and superstition.

The population was not very cooperative in this effort. Even where there were churches and priests, it was not easy to get the people to mass. There was competition. The Marquis of Denonville reported, "I know of seigneuries where there are only twenty inhabitants, where there are half that number of cabarets."[28] In Trois-Rivières there were twenty-five houses, and eighteen or twenty sold alcoholic beverages.[29] The early bishops inveighed against the frequenting of cabarets during mass, and against the general lack of modesty and respect for the holy sacraments. Msgr. de Saint Vallier complained that the women dressed immorally, "in the pomps of Satan,"[30] and that the parishioners talked

[24]*Ibid.*, p. 19.
[25]Thwaites, *op. cit.*, 1666-68, "Letter from Bruyas", p. 109.
[26]See Jean Delumeau, *Le Catholicisme entre Luther et Voltaire* (Paris, 1971).
[27]*Ibid.*
[28]RAPQ, p. 268.
[29]*Ibid.*
[30]*Mandements, Lettres Pastorales et Circulaires des Evêques de Québec* (Quebec, 1887), V. 1, p. 107.

during mass. Some would even leave early, missing the sermons. As
the bishop stated, "this custom . . . is an evident mark of undevotion
and irreligion."[31]

The habitants were very skilful and successful at evading the payment
of their church tithes.[32] The Church in New France was not able to
support itself and constantly had to beg money from the King, as its
churches quickly fell into disrepair and decay, and were often not
equipped with the necessary equipment for the proper performance of
the mass and other ceremonies.[33] This situation was not unique to
Quebec, though. It was very similar to that existing in French rural
parishes during this period.[34]

The world view of the habitants was, for all practical purposes, the
world view of the peasants and artisans of France. But as stated earlier,
New France was not a little France transplanted to the new world. There
existed very important social and demographic differences between Old
and New France. In examining these areas, we can perhaps come close
to the reasons for the relative lack of witchcraft proceedings in New
France.

In most of France, agricultural workers lived in small villages, from
which they went out to work their fields. Villages were quite close to
one another. Towns, centres of administration and culture were usually
to be found twenty or so miles apart. The pattern of settlement was very
different in New France. Only Quebec and Montreal, one hundred and
fifty miles apart, even approached the size of small French towns,
having populations of eight hundred and five hundred respectively in
1663.[35] The habitants resisted attempts to settle them in agricultural
villages, where they could effectively defend themselves from the
Indians.[36] Instead they spread for miles along the banks of the St.
Lawrence River in their own family farmsteads. Thus, the basic social
unit of the colony was the large but close-knit farm family rather than a
whole village society. This was bound to make a difference in how
people related to each other, at least in the early stages of the colony's
development. It would tend to reduce the personal and inter-family

[31]Ibid., p. 278. This did not improve over time. See: J.P. Wallot, "Religion and French-
Canadian Mores in the Early Nineteenth Century", Canadian Historical Review, LII
(1971), pp. 51-94.
[32]W.J. Eccles, Canada under Louis XIV (Toronto, 1964), p. 225.
[33]Saint-Vallier, Estat Présent de l'Eglise et de la Colonie Françoise dans la Nouvelle
France par M. l'Evêque de Québec (Paris, 1683), p. 57.
[34]Delumeau, op. cit.
[35]Eccles, op. cit., p. 14.
[36]RAPQ, 1927-7, "Mémoire du Roi Pour Servir d'Instruction Au Sieur Comte de
Frontenac", (7 April 1672), p. 4.

rivalries which flourished in village societies and which could extend over many generations, and which seem to have played an important role in the pattern of witchcraft accusations in Europe.

The villages of France were ancient settlements. As Pierre Goubert points out, "The towns and villages of France stood on or close to sites carved out of forest or steppe many centuries previously, whether in remote Celtic times, or at the height of the Middle Ages. Nineteen and a half out of twenty million people remained bound to the land, plot, hut, cottage or *quartier* where they grew up. Old France is characterized not by unrest, social mobility and popular migration, but by sedentariness."[37]

This sedentary rural village society fashioned for itself, over many centuries, a rich and varied world of supernatural beings and occurrences. Every peculiarity in field and forest was the object of a legend. Mountains, rivers and prairies were all populated by fairies, elves, giants, werewolves, dragons, devils and the souls of the departed, all bent on causing harm to men.[38] The vulnerable villagers tended to be closed and suspicious, nurturing a great fear of strangers. This fear was reflected in their idea of the Devil, who was represented in song, story and popular art as a handsome, well-dressed stranger who could seduce the unwary with his promises.

In New France people of many regions in France lived and worked together, and married and raised families. Newcomers were actively desired, and were welcomed gratefully rather than being feared and distrusted. While the settlers of New France kept their folklore, they had to adapt it to these new conditions. It seems fair to suppose that some of the immediacy of the old legends was lost in the transplanting process.

In other important ways the society of Quebec was an abnormal society. The demographic structures of Old and New France were very different. A study of the distribution of population by sex and age brings to light important insights concerning the place of women in New France, a factor of great importance to this study. Recent studies have shown that, all across Europe, the vast majority — close to eighty per cent — of those accused of witchcraft were women. Furthermore, a substantial percentage were widows. And, though information relating to the age of the accused was not always recorded, the median age of women accused of witchcraft was around sixty years old, which was considered ancient in those times.[39]

[37]Pierre Goubert, *The Ancien Regime: French Society 1600-1750*, tr. Steve Cox (London, 1973) p. 42.
[38]See Sebillot, *op. cit.*, esp. V. 1.
[39]E.W. Monter, *Witchcraft in France and Switzerland: The Borderland during the Reformation* (Ithaca, N.Y. 1976) pp. 120-123.

People of all levels of society believed that women were essentially lustful and deceitful creatures who were naturally inclined toward evil and thus were easily led astray by the devil. Related to this belief was the popular stereotype of the witch as an ugly hag concocting evil spells with the aid of her paramour, the Devil. These attitudes contributed to the very high incidence of females as victims of witchcraft accusations and punishment. But the actual social and economic conditions of women, especially of aged widows, was an important contributing factor as well.

Old widowed women were the least able to support themselves in a difficult rural world. Thus, they tended to be isolated and vulnerable. Often they had to beg for a living, and in this effort, had to rely on threats, to coerce people into giving them food or money. Obviously, they could not threaten physical violence, so they could capitalize on the general belief in the efficacy of spells and witchcraft to frighten people into giving. Of course, if something untoward happened to a person, he could, and often did retaliate by accusing the old woman of bewitching him, his family, livestock or crops.[40]

Thus old women, widowed and poor were very vulnerable to these dangerous accusations. The situation of women was very difficult in traditional European societies, and interlocked with popular stereotypes in such a way as to make life even more difficult. Women always outnumbered men in these societies. Even with the grave dangers of childbirth, women tended to live longer. The burden of heavy physical work and the violence of everyday life cut men's lives short and meant that in France, there were two to three times more widows than widowers.[41] Thus it was extremely difficult for women over forty to remarry. There were few available elderly males, and society strongly disapproved of marriage to younger men.[42]

Deeply engrained social patterns served to limit the birthrate in France. Peasants married fairly late in life, partly because, in a poor agrarian society, people could not marry and start a family. One area which has been studied is the Beauvaisis, north of Paris. In this region, the median age for women to marry for the first time was a bit over twenty-five. Only fifteen percent or less married at twenty or younger.

---

[40]This pattern for witchcraft accusations is discussed in several recent works, including Keith Thomas, *Religion and the Decline of Magic* (London, 1971), Alan Macfarlane, *Witchcraft in Tudor and Stuart England* (New York, 1970), and E.W. Monter, *Witchcraft in France and Switzerland.*

[41]Pierre Goubert, *Cent mille provinciaux au XVIIe Siècle: Beauvais et la Beauvaisis de 1600 à 1730* (Paris, 1968), p. 38.

[42]See: Natalie Z. Davis "The Reasons of Misrule: Youth Groups and Charivaris in Sixteenth Century France", *Past and Present,* L (February 1971), pp. 52-4.

Since a woman was old at forty, ceasing to be fertile, this late age of marriage served as a measure of population control. Furthermore, the peasants must have practiced forms of birth control after marriage, since their babies were spaced, on the average, almost two and one half years apart. The average couple had five children, two or three of whom did not survive into adulthood.[43] These factors led to population stability in seventeenth century France. But these figures, translated to the personal level, meant that women often found themselves in old age, widowed, unable to work for a living, and not having children who were in a position to support them.

In New France, there was a strikingly different situation. Many more men than women made the difficult and dangerous crossing to the colony. Men greatly outnumbered women in Quebec through the whole seventeenth century, with the situation only gradually changing as the population reproduced. This was bound to have profound implications in the realm of the place of women in Quebec society. In 1663 there were twice as many men as women. Furthermore, there were very few unattached women of marriageable age.[44] The habitants were eager to marry.

Royal policy was strongly "populationist" in Canada. The king's council decided that the best way to increase the population was to encourage the habitants to reproduce at a high rate, rather than sending a flood of new immigrants, an expensive and difficult proposition. So the colonists were encouraged to forsake tradition and marry at as young an age as possible. A royal ordinance of 1670 offered young men grants of twenty *livres* if they married at twenty or younger, and young women the same amount for marrying at sixteen or less.[45] The needs of the society, abetted by these grants produced results. In seventeenth century Quebec, girls were married at as young as twelve years old, usually to men much older than themselves.[46] Again, by the early eighteenth century more normal patterns asserted themselves, and the average age for girls to marry rose to 21.9, still substantially below that in France.[47] In addition, and this is of great importance to this study, it seems that most widows were able to remarry in Quebec. Young and old widows remarried fairly quickly. Only widows in their middle years, from thirty

[43]Goubert, *Cent mille provinciaux* pp. 32-39.

[44]Marcel Trudel, *La Population du Canada en 1663* (Montreal, 1973), p. 63.

[45]*Edits, Ordannances Royaux, Déclarations et Arrêts du Conseil d'Etat du Roy Concernant le Canada* (Quebec, 1854-56) V. 1, p. 63.

[46]Marcel Trudel, *The Beginnings of New France*, tr. Patricia Claxton (Toronto, 1973), pp. 258-9.

[47]Jacques Henripin, *La Population Canadienne au Début du XVIIIe Siècle* (Paris, 1954), p. 96.

to forty- five years old, found it difficult to find another husband, undoubtedly because they were likely to have been left with a large number of small children.[48]

The remarriage of widows in itself would serve to increase the birthrate of Quebec. To add to the pressure for large families, a system of royal baby bonuses was established. Couples with ten living legitimate children, of whom none were priests, were given three hundred *livres* a year, while those with twelve children got four hundred. These large families were also to be given special honours in church and in the community.[49]

These efforts were outstandingly successful. Contemporary observers frequently commented on the fecundity of the habitants. The intendant Talon reported that Canadian women bore children almost every year. In 1670 he wrote, "The girls sent last year are married, and almost all are either pregnant or have had children, a sign of the fecundity of this country."[50] If these reports, intended to satisfy his superior in Paris, may have been a bit exaggerated, there is no doubt that the birth-rate in Canada was extraordinarily high, well above fifty per thousand population.[51] Comparable rates are not known for France in the same period, which was a period of unusually rapid population growth in France; the birthrate rose to thirty-nine per thousand, well below that in Quebec in the preceding century.[52]

Thus the French settler in Canada, occupying his own family farmstead, separated from his neighbours, was generally guaranteed a large family to help with the hard work of clearing land, growing crops and helping in defense against Indian attacks. Furthermore, it also meant that, to a great extent, parents who survived into old age had families which were able to care for them when they could no longer work at full capacity. This became a pattern in Quebec and was established by legal contract. Parents would cede their property to their adult children in return for guarantees of support until death. For example, in 1699, one Guillaume Tougard promised, "to feed, lodge and care for his mother (in-law) during her life, in health or illness, whatever her condition."[53] This relationship, which gave a significant degree of security to old people, was made possible only by the extraordinary birthrate of the habitants.

Old women were cared for in Quebec. The chief victims of witchcraft accusations, vulnerable old women who had to beg in order to survive,

[48]*Ibid.*, p. 99.
[49]*Edits.*, V. 1, p. 67.
[50]RAPQ, 1930-31, p. 125.
[51]Henripin, *op. cit.*, p. 40.
[52]*Ibid.*, p. 41.
[53]Seguin, *Civilization*, p. 291.

were, for all practical purposes, non-existent in Quebec in the seventeenth century. The beliefs in magic and witchcraft were still commonly held, but the usual targets for accusations were not there.

A brief comparison between New France and another transplanted society, New England, may help to illustrate this point. While New England cannot be considered a replica of the Mother Country, it was in significant ways, more "normal" in its demographic structure and social behavior than was New France. The several hundred witch trials in Connecticut and Massachusetts are the reflections of this seventeenth-century normality.

New England's population was many times bigger than that of New France. By 1640, there were 16,000 inhabitants of New England. The population had risen to 80,000 by the time of the trials at Salem in 1692. Boston was a thriving mercantile metropolis of 7,000.[54] Salem, a few miles up the coast from Boston, had about 2,000 inhabitants, of whom around 400 lived in Salem Village, the scene of the drama.[55]

The tensions between families and generations in Salem Village have been carefully studied and described.[56] It was the combination of these factors, along with the political and religious situation which caused a witch panic in a society which had known scattered accusations and executions for almost fifty years. Rather than showing the uniqueness of the Salem situation, they confirm Salem's "normal" behavior. In the County of Essex, in England, it was the same interfamilial and intergenerational tensions which seem to have played a large role in the generation of witchcraft accusations.[57]

The great majority of the accused at Salem were women over forty years old. Most of the men and children who were accused were relatives of these women, "a kind of derivative category."[58] The first three accused were "outcasts"; Tituba a West Indian slave, Sarah Good, an ill-tempered old beggar, and "Gammer" Osborne, an aged invalid.[59] As the accusations continued, they involved people from higher on the social scale, and from outside of the Village.[60] This too is a normal pattern in witch panics in European societies.[61]

[54]O.T. Barch, Jr. and H.T. Tefler, *Colonial America* (New York, 1968), p. 251.

[55]Boyer and Nissenbaum, p. 87.

[56]In Boyer and Nissenbaum and John Demos, "Underlying Themes in the Witchcraft of Seventeenth Century New England", *American Historical Review* LXXV (1970), pp. 1311-26.

[57]Macfarlane, p. 168.

[58]Demos, p. 1315

[59]Boyer and Nissenbaum, p. 31.

[60]*Ibid.*, p. 33.

[61]H.C.E. Middlefort, *Witchhunting in Southwest Germany* (1972), p. 175.

The distortion in the demographic structure of New France resulted in an "abnormal" society which because of its imbalanced distribution of population did not perform as a "normal" European society of its time would in reference to witchcraft accusations. In dealing with a problem like witchcraft, where evidence is often so scarce and opinions so strong, it is difficult to present final conclusions. But it does seem that the differences in social structures, occurring in societies which were so similar culturally, are the most important reasons for the extraordinary scarcity of witchcraft proceedings in New France.

————————o————————

La Nouvelle France n'a pas eu à souffrir de l'extrême paranoia pour la magie noire qui était endémique en Nouvelle Angleterre et en Europe au 17ème siècle. Une comparaison des sociétés et cultures de la Vieille et Nouvelle France déterminera les différences qui résultèrent dans la rareté des affaires de sorcellerie en Nouvelle France. Un bref résumé des cas de magie en Nouvelle France a précédé cette comparaison.

Robert Lionel Seguin a relevé 22 cas qui mettent en cause l'influence diabolique ou surnaturelle dans son étude *La Sorcellerie au Québec du XVIIème Siècle*. Les cas qu'il étudie comprennent les sortilèges et les possessions démoniaques: ces deux pratiques étaient traitées sévérement par le tribunal. A la fin du 17ème le parlement français donna l'ordre d'arrêter les persécutions de sorcellerie, mais la plupart des gens continuèrent à y croire et à accuser les autres de la pratiquer. C'étaient surtout les paysans qui s'attachaient aux vieilles croyances et gardaient leurs superstitions. Ces croyances arrivèrent en Nouvelle France avec les colons.

Le folklore de la Nouvelle France révèle la prolongation de la foi dans les pouvoirs du Diable, et dans l'aptitude de certaines personnes à faire des pactes avec lui pour jeter des sorts aux autres. L'insuffisance de prêtres ainsi que l'immensité de la Nouvelle France qu'ils devaient administrer, fit que l'Eglise ne pouvait créer un puissant centre d'opposition aux croyances superstitieuses. Par conséquent, plusiers régions rurales souffrirent de leur ignorance religieuse et en partie aussi de l'indifférence qui venait de la préférence des colons pour les cabarets plutôt que pour les cérémonies religieuses.

L'Unité sociale de base en Nouvelle France était la famille, ce qui évita les rivalités génératives interfamiliales que l'on trouvait dans les communautés villageoises et qui jouaient un rôle vital dans le modèle européen des accusations en sorcellerie. Les villageois français développèrent leur folklore en se basant exclusivement sur les caractéristiques de leurs régions et par ce fait ils devinrent fermés et suspicieux vis à vis des étrangers. Les gens de différentes régions de France vivaient ensemble en Nouvelle France, ce qui évita la continuation de ces superstitions particulières.

Démographiquement, la Nouvelle France n'avait pas ce groupe de vieilles femmes, souvent veuves et économiquement faibles, qui devaient mendier leur nourriture, comme c'était souvent le cas dans les villages français. Ces femmes étaient particulièrement susceptibles d'être accusées de sorcellerie, surtout lorsque l'on sait que le 17ème croyait que toutes les femmes, déjà considérées comme étant en marge de la société, étaient lascives et fourbes. En Nouvelle France les hommes l'emportaient en nombre sur les femmes par deux contre une. Les femmes se mariaient beaucoup plus jeunes et avaient un plus grand nombre d'enfants qui pouvaient s'occuper d'elles pendant leur vieillesse. Les possibilités de remariage étaient également beaucoup plus grandes pour une veuve à cause du surplus d'hommes. Les femmes de Nouvelle France n'étaient donc pas, comme en France, la cible de la plupart des accusations de sorcellerie. La croyance en la sorcellerie existait toujours mais les cibles d'accusation avaient disparu.

Salem, Massachusetts, le centre d'une massive ''chasse à la sorcière'' avait les mêmes vues vis à vis de la magie noire qu'en Europe: une histoire de conflits entre familles et entre générations.

Les conditions démographiques et sociales particulières à la Nouvelle France, lorsqu'on les compare à celles d'Europe et de Nouvelle Angleterre montrent bien qu'elles sont la cause de la rareté des séances de magie noire dans cette colonie.

Acknowledgments

Burr, George Lincoln. "New England's Place in the History of Witchcraft." *Proceedings of the American Antiquarian Society* 21 (1911): 185–217. Courtesy of Yale University Sterling Memorial Library.

Demos, John. "Underlying Themes in the Witchcraft of Seventeenth-Century New England." *American Historical Review* 75 (1970): 1311–26. Courtesy of Yale University Sterling Memorial Library.

Drake, Frederick C. "Witchcraft in the American Colonies, 1647–62." *American Quarterly* 20 (1968): 694–725. Reprinted with permission of the author, and The American Studies Association, publisher. Copyright 1968. Courtesy of Yale University Sterling Memorial Library.

Demos, John. "John Godfrey and His Neighbors: Witchcraft and the Social Web in Colonial Massachuetts." *William and Mary Quarterly* 33 (1976): 242–65. Originally appeared in the *William and Mary Quarterly*. Courtesy of the *William and Mary Quarterly*.

Hall, David D. "Witchcraft and the Limits of Interpretation." *New England Quarterly* 59 (1985): 253–81. Reprinted with the permission of the New England Quarterly Inc. Courtesy of Yale University Sterling Memorial Library.

Hansen, Chadwick. "Andover Witchcraft and the Causes of the Salem Witchcraft Trials." In Howard Kerr and Charles L. Crow, eds., *The Occult in America: New Historical Perspectives* (Urbana: University of Illinois Press, 1983): 38–57. Reprinted with the permission of the University of Illinois Press, publisher. Copyright 1983 by the Board of Trustees of the University of Illinois. Courtesy of Yale University Cross Campus Library.

Kences, James E. "Some Unexplored Relationships of Essex County Witchcraft to the Indian Wars of 1675 and 1689." *Essex Institute Historical Collections* 120 (1984): 179–212. Reprinted with the permission of the Essex Institute, Salem, Massachusetts. Courtesy of the Essex Institute.

Moore, George H. "Notes on the History of Witchcraft in Massachusetts; with Illustrative Documents." *Proceedings of the American Antiquarian Society* 2 (1882): 162–81. Courtesy of Yale University Sterling Memorial Library.

Brown, David C. "The Case of Giles Cory." *Essex Institute Historical Collections* 121 (1985): 282–99. Reprinted with the permission of the Essex Institute, Salem, Massachusetts. Courtesy of the Essex Institute.

Werking, Richard H. "'Reformation is Our Only Preservation': Cotton Mather and Salem Witchcraft." *William and Mary Quarterly* 29 (1972): 281–90. Originally appeared in the *William and Mary Quarterly*. Courtesy of the *William and Mary Quarterly*.

Kibbey, Ann. "Mutations of the Supernatural: Witchcraft, Remarkable Providences, and the Power of Puritan Men." *American Quarterly* 34 (1982): 125–48. Reprinted with the permission of the author, and The American Studies Association, publisher. Copyright 1982. Courtesy of Yale University Sterling Memorial Library.

Wendell, Barrett. "Were the Salem Witches Guiltless?" *Essex Institute Historical Collections* 29 (1892): 129–47. Courtesy of Yale University Sterling Memorial Library.

Caulfield, Ernest. "Pediatric Aspects of the Salem Witchcraft Tragedy: A Lesson in Mental Health." *American Journal of Diseases of Children* 65 (1943): 788–802. Reprinted with the permission of the American Medical Association. Copyright 1943. Courtesy of Yale University Medical Library.

Levermore, Charles H. "Witchcraft in Connecticut." *New Englander* 44 (1885): 788–817. Courtesy of Yale University Sterling Memorial Library.

Parke, Francis Neal. "Witchcraft in Maryland." *Maryland Historical Magazine* 31 (1936): 271–98. Courtesy of Yale University Sterling Memorial Library.

Davis, Richard Beale. "The Devil in Virginia in the Seventeenth Century." *Virginia Magazine of History and Biography* 65 (1957): 131–49. Reprinted with the permission of the Virginia Historical Society. Courtesy of the Virginia Historical Society.

Lyon, John. "Witchcraft in New York." *New York Historical Society Collections* 2 (1869): 273–6. Courtesy of Brian P. Levack.

Pearl, Jonathan L. "Witchcraft in New France in the Seventeenth Century: The Social Aspect." *Historical Reflections* 4 (1977): 191–205. Reprinted with the permission of *Historical Reflections*. Courtesy of Yale University Sterling Memorial Library.